Governance and Public Management

Series Editor
Paul Joyce
INLOGOV
University of Birmingham
Birmingham, UK

IIAS Series: Governance and Public Management
International Institute of Administrative Sciences (IIAS) – *Setting the Governance Agenda Worldwide*

Website: http://www.iias-iisa.org

Edited by Paul Joyce
To cover the diversity of its members, the IIAS has set up four sub-entities:

- The EGPA (European Group for Public Administration)
- The IASIA (International Association of Schools and Institutes of Administration)
- The LAGPA (Latin American Group for Public Administration)
- The AGPA (Asian Group for Public Administration)

Governance and Public Management Series
This IIAS series of books on Governance and Public Management has a focus and breadth that reflects the concerns of the International Institute of Administrative Sciences. The Institute, which was set up in 1930, involves academics and governments from all around the world. The Institute's work involves supporting both practitioners and academics, which it does by encouraging the production of relevant knowledge on public governance and public management and by facilitating its dissemination and utilization.

It is the intention of the series to include books that are forward-looking, have an emphasis on theory and practice, are based on sound understanding of empirical reality, and offer ideas and prescriptions for better public governance and public management. This means the books will include not only facts about causes and effects, but also include ideas for actions and strategies that have positive consequences for the future of public governance and management. The books will offer a point of view about responses to the big challenges facing public governance and management over the next decade, such as sustainable development, the climate crisis, technological change and artificial intelligence (A.I.), poverty, social exclusion, international cooperation, and open government.

All books in the series are subject to Palgrave's rigorous peer review process: https://www.palgrave.com/gb/demystifying-peer-review/792492

More information about this series at
http://www.palgrave.com/gp/series/15021

Sabine Kuhlmann • Isabella Proeller
Dieter Schimanke • Jan Ziekow
Editors

Public Administration in Germany

palgrave
macmillan

Editors
Sabine Kuhlmann
University of Potsdam
Potsdam, Germany

Isabella Proeller
University of Potsdam
Potsdam, Germany

Dieter Schimanke
Ministry of Labour, Women, Health,
Social Affairs of the German Land
Saxony-Anhalt
Magdeburg, Germany

Jan Ziekow
German Research Institute for
Public Administration
Speyer, Germany

ISSN 2524-728X   ISSN 2524-7298 (electronic)
Governance and Public Management
ISBN 978-3-030-53696-1   ISBN 978-3-030-53697-8 (eBook)
https://doi.org/10.1007/978-3-030-53697-8

© The Editor(s) (if applicable) and The Author(s) 2021. This book is an open access publication.

Open Access This book is licensed under the terms of the Creative Commons Attribution 4.0 International License (http://creativecommons.org/licenses/by/4.0/), which permits use, sharing, adaptation, distribution and reproduction in any medium or format, as long as you give appropriate credit to the original author(s) and the source, provide a link to the Creative Commons licence and indicate if changes were made.

The images or other third party material in this book are included in the book's Creative Commons licence, unless indicated otherwise in a credit line to the material. If material is not included in the book's Creative Commons licence and your intended use is not permitted by statutory regulation or exceeds the permitted use, you will need to obtain permission directly from the copyright holder.

The use of general descriptive names, registered names, trademarks, service marks, etc. in this publication does not imply, even in the absence of a specific statement, that such names are exempt from the relevant protective laws and regulations and therefore free for general use.

The publisher, the authors and the editors are safe to assume that the advice and information in this book are believed to be true and accurate at the date of publication. Neither the publisher nor the authors or the editors give a warranty, expressed or implied, with respect to the material contained herein or for any errors or omissions that may have been made. The publisher remains neutral with regard to jurisdictional claims in published maps and institutional affiliations.

This Palgrave Macmillan imprint is published by the registered company Springer Nature Switzerland AG.
The registered company address is: Gewerbestrasse 11, 6330 Cham, Switzerland

FOREWORD

Governments act in an increasingly multilateral and international environment. However, making this cooperation work still depends heavily upon the capacities of national administrations. In many cases, their basic profiles have been shaped by long traditions, while others have undergone a process of transformation. In the context of the European Union, it is vital for member states to realize that European policies work effectively only when public administration is able to meet all new challenges. As an aid to understanding how we act, we decided to offer to the international public administration community an up-to-date edition of articles presenting and analysing the German system, including recent challenges and reforms. We have chosen the context of the European Public Administration Network (EUPAN), a forum for EU intergovernmental cooperation which includes member states and the European Commission, for launching the open access version of the book. The fora and this book consider the basis and standards for an effective and efficient public administration that is citizen-oriented and fosters trust in public institutions. This can support European initiatives for improving the implementation of public programmes and cooperation in the first place between the EU and its member states.

In the international community of public administration scholars and practitioners, there is a growing need for knowledge and information, analyses, reviews and evaluations of present-day Germany's administrative system and recent reforms. German researchers and practitioners are often asked for a publication to meet this need, especially in the arena of the International Institute of Administrative Sciences (IIAS) and its regional

v

institution, the European Group of Public Administration (EGPA), as well as in the world-wide public administration projects of the Deutsche Gesellschaft für Internationale Zusammenarbeit (GIZ) GmbH. The present volume is intended to respond to research and teaching needs and to provide information on the actual practices and reforms.

No English-language publication about the German administrative systems has been on the market since 2001, when the German Section of the IIAS successfully met the demand for such a publication nearly 20 years after the first, published in 1983. However, as these two works were produced before and after German unification, much of their content is now outdated and in need of major revision.[1] I am grateful to all the authors represented in this volume, who are leading academics and practitioners in the field and who cooperated with great enthusiasm to bring forth the new edition within a short period of time. They all take full responsibility for the content they have contributed.

The German Section of the International Institute of Administrative Sciences is deeply grateful to Professor Sabine Kuhlmann (Potsdam), Professor Isabella Proeller (Potsdam), State Secretary Dieter Schimanke (ret., Magdeburg/Hamburg) and Professor Jan Ziekow (Speyer) for developing the idea for this publication and realizing it together with a group of high-level experts in the German public administration.

State Secretary, Hans-Georg Engelke
Federal Ministry of the Interior,
Building and Community
President, German Section of the IIAS

NOTE

1. See König, K., von Oertzen, H.J., Wagener, F. (eds.) (1983). Public Administration in the Federal Republic of Germany. Deventer: Kluwer. König, K., Siedentopf, H. (eds.) (2001). Public Administration in Germany. Baden-Baden: Nomos.

Acknowledgements

We would like to thank the German Section of the International Institute of Administrative Sciences (IIAS) for their confidence in the editors in launching this book project and for their support throughout the process of writing. We very much enjoyed working with the twenty-seven contributing authors and would like to express our appreciation to all of them for their dedication and enthusiasm in bringing this volume together. The fact that we were able to finish this project in less than two years is a testament to their commitment and discipline.

Our gratitude also goes to the German Corporation for International Cooperation (*Deutsche Gesellschaft für Internationale Zusammenarbeit*—GIZ) for their generous support in the publishing of this book. GIZ is a state-owned service provider in the field of international cooperation for sustainable development in all continents. It is specialized, inter alia, in public sector reforms, administrative transformation and civil society participation. This publication is also intended to support the activities of GIZ and serve as a possible reference model for institution building and policy advice in different country contexts.

Furthermore, we owe special thanks to the German Federal Government, specifically the Federal Ministry of the Interior, Building and Community (*Bundesministerium des Innern, für Bau und Heimat*—BMI). Besides co-sponsoring the publication project (Open Access version), some of the contributing authors are also affiliated to the ministry.

The twenty-two chapters of the book, though each taking a specific perspective topic-wise, are based on a common understanding of the main characteristics, attributes and approaches as well as the most relevant

vii

reforms of German public administration. To achieve this understanding and develop a coherent framework for the chapters required intensive communication and interaction between the editors and the authors. In this regard, we would like to extend our thanks to the German County Association (*Deutscher Landkreistag*—DLT) for hosting an authors' workshop, which provided an opportunity for in-depth discussion of the book concept and the individual chapters.

Editing is a hard job and bringing the manuscripts into their final format for publishing is not an easy task. The editors relied very much on the excellent support of Tomás Vellani for overall publication management and Pearl Wallace for language editing. They are deeply indebted to them.

Finally, we would like to express our gratitude to the IIAS, particularly to Fabienne Maron as the IIAS Scientific Director, to our publisher, Palgrave, and above all to Paul Joyce as the IIAS Publication Director, for their interest and unwavering support in publishing this book in the 'Governance and Public Management' series.

Hamburg, Potsdam and Speyer
Sabine Kuhlmann, Isabella Proeller,
Dieter Schimanke, Jan Ziekow

Praise for *Public Administration in Germany*

"Public Administration in the Western sphere, and beyond, wouldn't be what it is without the German legal tradition of the 'Rechtsstaat', or Max Weber's 'bureaucracy'. This book shows not only the foundations of the German system. It also explains, comprehensively and convincingly, how the German 'model' is transforming and adjusting to current and future challenges, while keeping solid principles of rule of law, democracy, and welfare state. Therefore, this book is a lighthouse for all those studying PA and reforming systems."

—Geert Bouckaert, Professor, *Public Governance Institute, KU Leuven, Belgium, and Past-President of the International Institute of Public Administration (IIAS)*

"Everything you always wanted to know about public administration in the country which fathered modern bureaucracy! This book is the indispensable reading for those students, scholars and practitioners who seek to understand the fascinating administrative engine under the hood of the political, social and economic success of contemporary Germany."

—Jean-Michel Eymeri-Douzans, Professor, *University Science Po Toulouse, France. President of the European Group of Public Administration (EGPA)*

"This book is an awesome attempt, covering such significant issues as the historical underpinnings, inter-governmental relationships and other pragmatic policy problems that Germany is currently facing. We ought to congratulate German academics for their successful compilation of this outstanding volume."

—Akira Nakamura, *Distinguished Professor Emeritus, School of Political Science and Economics, Meiji University, Tokyo, Japan, and Past-President of the Asian Association for Public Administration (AAPA)*

"Our global understanding of public administration begins one country at a time. I am therefore pleased to welcome publication of this book. It is an authoritative resource for anyone seeking to understand German systems, particularly 'outsiders' like me. This book will be the standard reference for German administrative systems for decades."

—James L. Perry, *Distinguished Professor Emeritus, Paul H. O'Neill School of Public and Environmental Affairs, Indiana University, Bloomington, USA*

CONTENTS

1 **German Public Administration: Background and Key Issues**   1
Sabine Kuhlmann, Isabella Proeller, Dieter Schimanke, and
Jan Ziekow

Part I   **German Public Administration in the Multilevel
System**   15

2 **Constitutional State and Public Administration**   17
Karl-Peter Sommermann

3 **Administrative Federalism**   35
Nathalie Behnke and Sabine Kropp

4 **Europeanisation and German Public Administration**   53
Hans Hofmann

5 **Federal Administration**   61
Julia Fleischer

6 **The Federal Administration of Interior Affairs**   81
Hans-Heinrich von Knobloch

xii CONTENTS

7 The Peculiarities of the Social Security Systems
(Indirect State Administration) 91
Dieter Schimanke

8 The Administration of the *Länder* 105
Ludger Schrapper

9 Local Self-Government and Administration 123
Kay Ruge and Klaus Ritgen

Part II Politics, Procedures and Resources 143

10 Politics and Administration in Germany 145
Werner Jann and Sylvia Veit

11 Administrative Procedures and Processes 163
Jan Ziekow

12 Control and Accountability: Administrative Courts and
Courts of Audit 185
Veith Mehde

13 Civil Service and Public Employment 205
Christoph Reichard and Eckhard Schröter

14 Public Finance 225
Gisela Färber

Part III Redrawing Structures, Boundaries and Service
Delivery 251

15 Transformation of Public Administration in East
Germany Following Unification 253
Hellmut Wollmann

CONTENTS   xiii

16 Administrative Reforms in the Multilevel System: Reshuffling Tasks and Territories   271
Sabine Kuhlmann and Jörg Bogumil

17 Institutional Differentiation of Public Service Provision in Germany: Corporatisation, Privatisation and Re-Municipalisation   291
Benjamin Friedländer, Manfred Röber, and Christina Schaefer

18 Participatory Administration and Co-production   311
Stephan Grohs

Part IV   Modernizing Processes and Enhancing Management Capacities   329

19 Digital Transformation of the German State   331
Ines Mergel

20 The Federal Ministerial Bureaucracy, the Legislative Process and Better Regulation   357
Sabine Kuhlmann and Sylvia Veit

21 Human Resource Management in German Public Administration   375
John Siegel and Isabella Proeller

22 Public Management Reforms in Germany: New Steering Model and Financial Management Reforms   393
Isabella Proeller and John Siegel

Glossary   411

Notes on Contributors

Nathalie Behnke is professor and head of the working group 'Public Administration, Public Policy' at the Institute of Political Science, Technical University of Darmstadt. Her research is located at the intersection of public administration, comparative federalism and multilevel governance with a focus on coordination within and among governments.

Friederike Bickmann is research associate at the German Research Institute for Public Administration. Her areas of research comprise, inter alia, public participation and regarding open government especially open government data.

Jörg Bogumil is Professor of Public Administration, Local and Regional Politics at the Ruhr University in Bochum and member of the Council of Administration of the International Institute of Administrative Sciences. His areas of research include public administration, local government and regional politics, specially the modernization of the public sector.

Gisela Färber is Professor of Public Finance at the German University of Administrative Sciences and Senior Fellow and Director of the Research Centre for Civil Service at the German Research Institute for Public Administration in Speyer. Her areas of research include all fields of public finance, particularly civil service reforms, fiscal federalism and impact assessment.

Zarina Feller is research associate at the German Research Institute for Public Administration. Her main areas of scientific interest are economic sociology and digital media.

Julia Fleischer is Professor and Chair in German Politics and Government at the University of Potsdam. Her research addresses comparative public administration and governance, particularly organizational behaviour and the digital transformation of public sectors.

Benjamin Friedländer is postdoctoral researcher at the Institute of Public Administration and Management at the Helmut Schmidt University/University of the Armed Forces Hamburg. His areas of research include local government, local public sector reforms and the coordination of public and third sector organizations.

Stephan Grohs is Professor of Political Science at the German University of Administrative Sciences Speyer and Senior Fellow at the German Research Institute for Public Administration. His areas of research include comparative and international public administration, local government and policy implementation in different policy areas (welfare, planning and environment).

Hans Hofmann is Director-General ('Ministerialdirektor') for Public Law, Constitutional Law and Administrative Law at the Federal Ministry of the Interior, Building and Community. He is Honorary Professor at the Law Faculty of the Humboldt-University, Berlin. He is co-editor of commentaries on the German constitution and on the Chancellery and Federal Government.

Werner Jann is Professor Emeritus of Political Science, Administration and Organization at University of Potsdam. His main areas of research and teaching include public sector organization, administration and public policy, governance and better regulation.

Sabine Kropp is Professor of Political Science at the Freie Universität Berlin. Her areas of research include German and comparative federalism, public administration, parliamentarism and regional politics in Eastern Europe, especially in Russia.

Sabine Kuhlmann is Professor of Political Science, Public Administration and Organization at University of Potsdam, Germany, Vice President of the IIAS for Western Europe and Vice-Chair of the National Regulatory Control Council of the German Federal Government. Her areas of research include comparative public administration, public sector reforms, better regulation and local government.

Veith Mehde is Professor of Public Law and Administrative Science at the Law Faculty of Leibniz University Hannover. His research interests include administrative law as well as administrative reforms and their legal aspects.

Ines Mergel is Professor of Public Administration at the University of Konstanz and a fellow of the National Academy of Public Administration (NAPA, Class of 2018). Her research focuses on digital transformation and innovation management in government.

Jan Porth is a research associate at the Institute for Regulatory Impact Analysis and Evaluation within the consultancy branch of the German Research Institute for Public Administration. His areas of research include the digital transformation of the public sector, public finance and local government.

Isabella Proeller is Professor of Public and Nonprofit Management at the University of Potsdam. Her areas of research comprise public management reforms, strategic management and performance-oriented control in public administration.

Christoph Reichard is Professor Emeritus of Public Management at the University of Potsdam. His research covers for instance public personnel management, public financial management and performance management.

Klaus Ritgen is Head of the Division of Constitutional Law at the German County Association.

Manfred Röber is Professor Emeritus of Public Management at the University of Leipzig and Professor of Business Administration at the Andrássy University Budapest. His areas of research include public management, organization theory and administrative reform.

Kay Ruge is Head of the Department of Administrative Organization and Deputy ('Beigeordneter') at the German County Association.

Christina Schaefer is Professor of Public Administration and Management at the Helmut Schmidt University/University of the Armed Forces Hamburg. Her areas of research include public financial management, public decision-making and public corporate governance.

Dieter Schimanke was Professor of Public Administration at the Helmut-Schmidt-University in Hamburg. He became Secretary of State in a state in East Germany after unification (Saxony-Anhalt). Since his retirement, he is Senior Expert in projects of GIZ on reforms of Public Administration (mainly in Eastern Europe and Asia).

Ludger Schrapper is Head of Legal Affairs and Teaching Personnel at the Ministry of School and Education of the German Land Northrhine-Westphalia. His special areas of interest are leadership and civil service law.

Eckhard Schröter is Professor of Public Administration at the German Police University in Münster. His major research interests are in comparative public sector reform, administrative culture, the politics and administration of public security and representative bureaucracy.

Patrick Schweizer is research associate at the Institute for Regulatory Impact Assessment and Evaluation of the German Research Institute for Public Administration in Speyer. His areas of research include impact assessment, especially cost impact assessment and the digitalization of the legislation process.

John Siegel is Professor of Public Administration and Management at the Hamburg University of Applied Sciences. He also teaches public management at the University of Potsdam. His areas of research include strategic and resources management in public sector organizations, particularly organizational capabilities, routines and communication.

Karl-Peter Sommermann is Professor of Public Law, Political Theory and Comparative Law at the German University of Administrative Sciences Speyer and Senior Fellow at the German Research Institute for Public Administration. His areas of research include German and European Constitutional and Administrative Law, Comparative Law and Protection of Human Rights.

Sylvia Veit is Professor of Public Management at the University of Kassel, Germany. Her main areas of research include senior civil servants, bureaucratic politicization, public sector reform and policy advisory systems.

Hans-Heinrich von Knobloch was Director-General ('Ministerialdirektor') for Constitutional and Administrative Law (until 2018) at the Federal Ministry of the Interior, Building and Community (BMI), Berlin.

Hellmut Wollmann is Professor Emeritus of Public Administration at Social Science Institute of Humboldt-University, Berlin. His main fields of research and publication have been comparative public policy and administration, with a focus on subnational levels.

Jan Ziekow is Professor of Public Law and the Director of the German Research Institute for Public Administration. He works on digital modernization of the public sector, reform of local and ministerial administration, citizen participation, sustainable development, better regulation, impact assessment and evaluation, public procurement, regulation of infrastructures, civil service, administrative law.

LIST OF FIGURES

Fig. 3.1	Functional division of labour in the federal hierarchy	40
Fig. 5.1	Organisational chart of the federal chancellery as of April 2018	68
Fig. 7.1	The social budget according to the branches of social security (including the five branches of the social security system: illness, occupational accident, personal care, unemployment, pension)	98
Fig. 14.1	The German tax system	236
Fig. 14.2	Volume of loans and securities at the different levels of government 1970–2018	240
Fig. 14.3	Tax revenue, social contributions and public expenditure in relation to GDP 1970–2018	248

LIST OF TABLES

Table 5.1	Chancellor's organisational decree of 14 March 2018	64
Table 5.2	Federal ministries as of November 2019	67
Table 6.1	Executive agencies of the Ministry of the Interior, Building and Community	85
Table 7.1	Contents of the 12 books of the Social Code	93
Table 7.2	Personnel in administrations on social affairs	94
Table 7.3	Personnel of social security providers ('indirect public administration', 'near governmental units', *Parafisci*)	95
Table 7.4	Social budget 2018—benefits by institutions	96
Table 9.1	Civil service staff	124
Table 9.2	Finances of the communes from 2017 to 2022	126
Table 13.1	Public employment (excluding soldiers) in full-time employment (FTE) by government level and employment category	209
Table 13.2	Public employment (headcount) by career classes or equivalent grades for public employees, excluding soldiers and staff in training	210
Table 14.1	Public expenditure at government level and social insurances in 2018	231
Table 14.2	Public revenue at government level and social insurances in 2018	234
Table 14.3	Distribution of tax revenue between the federal, *Länder* and local governments	238
Table 14.4	Tax revenue of the different government levels and the EU before and after distribution in 2018 (billion euro)	239
Table 14.5	Public debt tax revenue of the different levels of government and the EU before and after distribution as at end of 2018	242

xxiv LIST OF TABLES

Table 14.6	Per capita expenditure of state and local governments and aggregated state-local governments 2018	245
Table 14.7	Changes in the local shares of the compulsory tax sharing revenue of the *Länder* 2000–2019 (percentage of state tax revenue)	246
Table 16.1	Structural and functional reforms in the German *Länder* (sub-ministerial level)	273
Table 16.2	Territorial structures of counties in Germany	279
Table 16.3	Territorial structures of municipalities in Germany	280
Table 16.4	Territorial reforms in the West German *Länder*	282
Table 16.5	Territorial reforms in the East German *Länder*	285
Table 17.1	Public funds, institutions and enterprises by legal form and authority	305
Table 18.1	Types of provider (in %) from 1998 to 2016–17	322
Table 19.1	Overview of laws governing the digital transformation of the German state	337
Table 22.1	Implementation of NSM elements	397
Table 22.2	Implementation of accrual accounting in German *Länder* and local governments	404

CHAPTER 1

German Public Administration: Background and Key Issues

Sabine Kuhlmann, Isabella Proeller, Dieter Schimanke, and Jan Ziekow

1   Introduction: Background and Approach of the Publication

In the international community of Public Administration (PA) of scholars and practitioners, there is a growing need to acquire knowledge and information, analysis, reviews and evaluations about Germany's administrative system and its recent reforms. The German system of public administration, which is embedded in the *Rechtsstaat* culture and deeply

---

S. Kuhlmann • I. Proeller
University of Potsdam, Potsdam, Germany
e-mail: skuhlman@uni-potsdam.de; proeller@uni-potsdam.de

D. Schimanke (✉)
Ministry of Labour, Women, Health, Social Affairs of the German Land Saxony-Anhalt, Magdeburg, Germany
e-mail: Dieterschimanke@aol.com

J. Ziekow
German Research Institute for Public Administration, Speyer, Germany
e-mail: ziekow@foev-speyer.de

© The Author(s) 2021
S. Kuhlmann et al. (eds.), *Public Administration in Germany*,
Governance and Public Management,
https://doi.org/10.1007/978-3-030-53697-8_1

rooted in the legalist tradition, is not simply regarded as a reference model for developing and transition countries. The basic features of the German administrative system have also inspired reform debates and modernisation efforts in OECD countries (Organisation for Economic Co-operation and Development). Due to its federal structure and the pronouncedly decentralised institutional setting, German public administration is regarded as a prime example of multilevel governance and strong local self-government. Furthermore, over the past decades, the traditional profile of the German administrative system has significantly been reshaped and remoulded through reforms, processes of modernisation and the transformation process in East Germany that began with unification. Wide-ranging approaches to reform from territorial amalgamations, privatisation and re-municipalisation, citizen participation, performance and human resource management, to better regulation and digital government, have been pursued at various levels of government and have had varying effects. Within this context, we observe an increasing interest in the academic and practitioner's community to acquire more comprehensive and systematic knowledge about Germany's administrative system, its institutional structures, functional responsibilities, civil service features, multilevel governance and most recent reforms. From a comparative public administration perspective, there is a need for more in-depth institutional knowledge concerning the various administrative systems in order to capture the peculiarities of different models, compare their strengths and weaknesses, and learn from each other while striving for improvement in public administration worldwide.

Against this background, it is a cause for concern and criticism that there has been no English language publication about German administrative systems on the market for about 20 years, when the German Section of the International Institute of Administrative Sciences (IIAS) published the last volume. A number of new topics, for example digital and open government, better regulation, co-production, participatory administration, have since come on the agenda and thus merit analytical attention. This book is about filling this knowledge gap. After two decades, it is time to present a topical, comprehensive yet differentiated analysis of Germany's public administration and its reforms that explicitly targets an international audience of PA practitioners, policy advisors, academics and students. The contributions in this book provide an overview of the key elements of German public administration at the federal, state (*Länder*) and local levels of government and of the current reform processes of the public sector. They focus, inter alia, on the following areas:

- key institutional features of public administration;
- changing relationships between public administration, society and the private sector;
- administrative reforms at different levels of the federal system; and
- new challenges and modernisation approaches, such as digitalisation, open government and better regulation.

The four topics are addressed in this book. Part I outlines the basic features, institutions and legal framework of German public administration at different levels of government and within its multilevel setting. In Part II, the relationship between politics and administration, administrative procedures, controlling and accountability mechanisms as well as key resources of administrative action (staff, finances) is analysed. The subsequent chapters focus on the various fields of administrative reform and modernisation, starting in Part III with reforms intended to reshape the macro-institutional setting of public administration. This includes a historical review of the administrative transformation after unification as well as more recent approaches to reform, such as the redrawing of territorial boundaries and jurisdictions, functional and structural reforms, the redefinition of the relationship between the public and the private sector through privatisation, and the opening up of public administration vis-à-vis citizens and society. Finally, in Part IV, the focus is on changes in the distribution of responsibilities and resources within administrative organisations, the re-engineering of administrative processes, digital innovations and e-administration, the internal reorganisation of decision-making rules designed to enhance management capacities, efficiency in service delivery and the quality of policymaking.

2 Part I: German Public Administration in the Multilevel System

Owing to its legalistic tradition, German public administration is very much rule-driven. *Karl-Peter Sommermann* refers to the concept of *Rechtsstaat*. German public administration is rooted in this tradition, which aims at the protection of human dignity and individual freedom by providing, alongside the principle of legality, the rules, principles and institutions that ensure the prevention of arbitrary state action and the protection of individual rights. A dynamic interpretation of the Basic Law (the German Constitution) of 1949 by the Federal Constitutional Court has constantly specified and extended the normative scope of fundamental rights, which are directly binding upon the legislative, executive and judicial powers. The constitutional principle of the welfare state has not only enhanced the dynamic evolution of the law, but also led to the creation of largely equivalent levels of infrastructure and services in the different territories of the federal state. The continually readjusted cooperation between the federal level and the *Länder* level and among the *Länder* themselves has strengthened the interoperability and coherence of their administrations, and competitive elements have fostered innovation.

The German federal architecture is shaped by a peculiar mix of strong decentralisation and a high degree of autonomy at lower levels of government, combined with an administrative culture of uniformity, solidarity and coordination. *Nathalie Behnke* and *Sabine Kropp* recapitulate the notion of this system as 'administrative federalism' to emphasise the prominent role of executives and administrations in policymaking and policy implementation. The dominant principle of administrative federalism is the territorial principle as opposed to the functional principle, that is governments and administrations at each level are responsible for all the tasks at this level with the exemption of special regulations for sectoral organisations. The federal level relies on the states (*Länder*) for executing its tasks. For their part, the *Länder* executives have rights of co-decision in federal legislation via the *Bundesrat* (Federal Council). While formal jurisdictions are strongly decentralised, a dense web of interlocking powers as well as processes and institutions of coordination induce territorial governments to closely cooperate with each other when implementing (compulsory) joint tasks and coordinating autonomous responsibilities voluntarily. To date, German-style administrative federalism has been successful in curbing conflict caused by dissent among political parties and in implementing policies efficiently. However, trends like the upward shift of tasks from the *Länder* to the federal level and increasing party system fragmentation challenge its continued success and consequently require adaptation.

The three-tier system of German public administration is increasingly being brought in line with the overarching level of the European Union (EU) and in a special form of vertical arrangement. As *Hans Hofmann* calls it, the EU is a union of states *sui generis* (unique). The Member States remain independent states and, in principle, retain their sovereignty. However, the EU's influence on national public administrations is constantly growing due to the increasing number of regulations (laws, bylaws, guidelines) and other EU programmes that require implementation in the Member States. The expanding influence of the EU is not limited to those areas where the Member States have transferred the authority to make laws to the EU, but is also spreading to those areas where the Member States have retained such authority. At the same time, however, there is no systematic codification of the law on administrative procedures at European level and no system of legal remedy for Union citizens equivalent to those at national level.

Germany's federal administration is significantly small in size (around ten per cent of all public employees). This special feature of the country's administrative system—as described by *Julia Fleischer*—is based on the division of responsibilities. The central (federal) level develops and adopts most of the public programmes and laws, and the state level (together with the local level) implements them. The administration at the federal level comprises the ministries, some subordinated agencies for special issues (e.g. the application of drugs, information security and the registration of refugees) and selected operational tasks in single administrative sectors (e.g. foreign affairs, the armed forces, the federal police and the supreme courts). The capacities to prepare and monitor laws are well developed. Moreover, the approaches to innovation and the instruments and tools of internal communication and coordination are exemplary compared to other countries.

According to the Basic Law, the states are, in principle, responsible for public administration, regardless of whether state or federal law is being enforced. The Federation has no authority to enforce state laws. When federal states carry out federal laws, they may do so in their own right or on federal commission. In both cases, the Federation has rights of supervision. *Hans-Heinrich von Knobloch* clearly makes these principles explicit on the relevant case of the portfolio of the Ministry of Interior. The Basic Law has set a narrow framework for the federal administration. The obligations and options of the federal administration are defined in full. However, superior federal authorities responsible for the entire federal territory may be established by law and passed with the consent of the *Bundesrat* for matters on which the Federation has the power to legislate.

The institutions of the social security system are the main providers of services of the welfare state and cover a large share of the public budgets (about 45 per cent of expenditures). On the one hand, the system enjoys a certain degree of autonomy and is therefore called 'indirect state administration', as explained by *Dieter Schimanke*. On the other hand, the steering by federal legislation is quite extensive. However, in implementing this legislation, the institutions are only subject to limited state supervision, which is restricted to legal supervision (*Rechtsaufsicht*). Moreover, the social security institutions can appeal to the 'social courts' against the orders of the supervising state administration.

In Germany's federal system, the administrations of the 16 federal states (*Länder*) have central responsibility for the enforcement of both federal and state law. *Ludger Schrapper* observes that notwithstanding the heterogeneity in terms of their size, administrative tradition and culture, there is relative uniformity in their administrative structures (with the exception of the three city-states). Everywhere, the municipalities, which are part of the state executive under state law, play a significant and, above all, independent role as bodies of public administration. Still, there are some differences which are due to whether the administrations of the *Länder* have a two-tier or a three-tier structure. Within these varying structures, administration seems to be relatively homogeneous, not least because of the very similar staffing structures, career patterns and administrative cultures. Structural reforms of very different scope have been a long-term phenomenon since the 1990s.

The local level, also called the communal level (municipalities, cities and counties), plays a strong administrative and political role in the German system. *Kay Ruge* and *Klaus Ritgen* demonstrate the weight of the communal level in the figures for personnel and budgets. The right to local self-government is guaranteed in the Basic Law and has a long history. Moreover, the communal administration—and especially the county level—serves a second function. It is, in principle, the operational level responsible for implementing the programmes and laws of the federal and state levels. The local authorities mainly differentiate themselves from the federal and regional authorities by the mandates of their elected representative bodies (city council, county council and municipal council). The head of a local administration (mayor or county commissioner) is usually directly elected by the citizens. Finally, the principle of German local self-government and administration is a good example for practising the cornerstones of the European Charter of Local Self-Government.

3 PART II: POLITICS, PROCEDURES AND RESOURCES

The relationship between politics and administration is the key to understand the conditions and interactions between administrations. In their chapter, *Werner Jann* and *Sylvia Veit* examine the relationships between politicians and administrators in Germany, both in institutional and legal terms as well as at all three levels of German executive federalism, that is the federal, state and local level. Using the concept of politicisation, they start with the distinction between politicians and civil servants and the viability of such distinction in practice. The central indicators are party membership and turnover rates after elections. *Jann* and *Veit* examine different dimensions of politicisation both in federal ministries and in the federal states, focusing on typical career patterns as well as the key features of the political-administrative relations at the local level. As a result, the authors identify a high degree of functional politicisation of top positions in public administration.

The dimension of public administration as a 'working state' was introduced into German administrative science as far back as the nineteenth century (von Stein 1870, p. 7). Taking a process-oriented approach, *Jan Ziekow* examines public administration as the interconnection of information, communications, interactions and decisions. As regards German administration, he assumes a distinction between processes and procedures, whereby one feature of these procedures vis-à-vis persons outside the administration is a high degree of juridification by administrative procedure law. He classifies and analyses the administrative processes according to different criteria and empirical and legal categories. Among other things, *Ziekow* deals with service delivery processes, communication, transparency and information, administrative procedure law, management processes, knowledge management, inter-organisational cooperation and administrative oversight.

In order to hold public administration accountable, a differentiated set of instruments is required. *Veith Mehde* emphasises—from a legal point of view—that the concept of accountability is an element of democratic legitimacy. He describes two very different mechanisms. First, the control exercised over the administrative jurisdiction and second, the control exercised by the courts of audit. He particularly emphasises the fact that it is not the role of the administrative courts and courts of audit to hold administration accountable. Rather, their role is to provide other actors—the parliaments, the public, the media, etc.—the opportunity to hold the respective administration accountable. As part of their role in exercising administrative jurisdiction, *Mehde* describes the structure of administrative courts in Germany, the types of their decisions and the depth and extent of their control. He also describes the organisation and scope of review of the courts of audit as well as the effects of their control.

The professionalisation of public service staff is one of the most important aspects of efficient administration. The employment structure and training of these employees is generally characteristic of a national administrative system. Accordingly, *Christoph Reichard* and *Eckhard Schröter* open their chapter on civil service and public employment with the question, 'What kind of an animal is the German civil service?' Their contribution sheds light on the size and structure of public employment in Germany prior to presenting the two different types of employment status in the public service, 'civil servants' on the one hand and 'public employees' on the other. Following an overview of the legal framework and policies relating to the civil service, subsequent sections deal with recruitment and qualifications, compensation schemes and benefits as well as major reform trends.

'Money makes the world go round'—this also applies to public administration. Revenues and expenditures are central to public administration processes. In the chapter on public finance, *Gisela Färber* deals with the principles of budgeting and the budget cycle as well as the generation and distribution of tax revenues in Germany. In the latter context, she addresses, inter alia, the constitutional regulations on the distribution of financial resources and the structure of public expenditure and revenue—providing a general structural analysis as well as a breakdown of tax revenues from a federal perspective. *Färber* goes on to discuss the considerable importance in the German federal financial system of the vertical and horizontal fiscal equalisation between the various administrative units. The chapter closes with an account of public indebtedness and budget deficits in Germany at different government levels.

4   Part III: Redrawing Structures, Boundaries and Service Delivery

In order to understand more recent developments and modernisation efforts in the German administrative system, it is important to consider earlier developments, especially after reunification, which sharply distinguish the German case from other European countries. Against this backdrop, the chapter by *Hellmut Wollmann* reviews the transformation of public administration in East Germany following unification. He focuses on the process and result of the administrative transformation process in East Germany as one of the most comprehensive institutional shifts of the last century. He provides an overview of the peculiarities of the East German mode of transformation (as opposed to other transition countries) and of the 'transfer of institutions' from West to East. In trying to answer the question 'what shapes institutions', he analyses the drivers and triggers of the process as well as the impacts and outcomes of the transformation process achieved so far. *Wollmann* also reviews some remaining problems, legacies and new challenges facing the unified German administration.

Due to the highly decentralised federal structure and the allocation of administrative tasks primarily to sub-national units, reforms in the multi-level system have always played a key role in Germany. *Sabine Kuhlmann* and *Jörg Bogumil* analyse recent territorial, functional and structural reforms in the German *Länder*, which represent three of the most crucial reform trajectories at the sub-national level to date. The chapter sheds light on the variety of reform approaches pursued by the different *Länder* and also highlights some of the factors that account for these differences. *Kuhlmann* and *Bogumil* also address the transfer of state functions to local governments, the restructuring of *Länder* administrations (e.g. the abolishment of the meso level of *Länder* administrations and of single-purpose state agencies), and the redrawing of territorial boundaries at county and municipal levels. In the final section, they give a brief review of the recently failed (territorial) reforms in Eastern Germany.

Administrative reforms not only refer to vertical rescaling of competencies and tasks between levels of government but also to horizontal reorganisations vis-à-vis the private sector on the one hand, and in relation to citizens and society on the other. The chapter by *Benjamin Friedländer, Manfred Röber* and *Christina Schaefer* begins with the observation that in recent decades, the provision of public services in Germany has increasingly been transferred to bodies outside the core administration, which has changed the institutional landscape significantly. The authors examine four dominant institutional trends, namely corporatisation, outsourcing, privatisation and re-municipalisation. They also discuss some of the advantages and disadvantages of public vs. private service provision.

As regards the changing relationship between public administration and citizens/society, two major reform approaches merit attention. First, the co-production of services and the involvement of multiple actors, both in the delivery of services and in decision-making. The trend towards a more participatory administration and co-production with citizens is analysed by *Stephan Grohs* who specifically focuses on the shift from 'traditional' modes of service delivery and decision-making to co-producing features and participatory elements. He also addresses some of the resulting key problems and pitfalls, such as accountability, transparency and legitimacy.

5   PART IV: MODERNISING PROCESSES AND ENHANCING MANAGEMENT CAPACITIES

The fourth part of this book provides an analysis of the reform and modernisation efforts of German public administration, most of which target various internal administrative management capacities. As elsewhere, digitalisation is a ubiquitous and omnipresent organisational challenge for public administrations in Germany. In the chapter on digital transformation, *Ines Mergel* analyses how Germany is managing the transformation of its service delivery structures. She describes how the digital transformation of the public sector is embedded in a large-scale reform to digitalise the service delivery of 575 public services by 2022. *Mergel* also describes the legal basis of digital transformation with its centralised and decentralised organisational embeddedness of administrative responsibilities, and illustrates recent developments with selected cases of implementation.

Second, there has been a significant trend towards 'open government', which *Jan Porth, Friederike Bickmann, Patrick Schweizer* and *Zarina Feller* see as a trend towards greater openness in political and administrative actions. They provide a brief overview of the conceptual understanding of open government, the potential advantages and disadvantages as well as recent developments at the federal level of government in Germany. Three selected sub-fields of open government, namely open government data, open innovation and open budget, are presented in more detail.

The role of public administration is not only limited to service delivery but also extends into the legislative process and its involvement in drawing up and drafting new regulations. *Sylvia Veit* and *Sabine Kuhlmann* explore and describe how 'Better Regulation' has become an influential and established mechanism at the federal level and—in some cases—also at the *Länder* level in Germany. The authors introduce the basic features of the legislative process at the federal level in Germany, address different aspects of Better Regulation and outline the role of the National Regulatory Control Council (*Nationaler Normenkontrollrat*–NKR) as a 'watchdog' for compliance costs, red tape and regulatory impacts.

Public administration—not only in Germany—requires a sufficient number of qualified and motivated staff to produce services and implement policies efficiently, effectively, professionally and reliably. Hence, managing the workforce is one of the most crucial functions in public administration. The chapter by *Isabella Proeller* and *John Siegel* first examines the practices and developments in (core) human resource management (functions). They then turn to a discussion on the importance of leadership, performance-related pay, public service motivation and diversity management. The authors conclude by highlighting some of the major paradoxes of German public human resource management (HRM) in light of current challenges, such as demographic change, digital transformation and capabilities for organisational development.

In the final chapter, *Isabella Proeller* and *John Siegel* analyse two very prominent public management reform trajectories in German public administration over the past three decades since unification. In the 1990s, the New Steering Model emerged as a German variant of the New Public Management (NPM). Since the mid-2000s, local governments in Germany have been subjected to a mandatory reform of their budgeting and accounting system known as the New Municipal Financial Management reforms. These reforms have led to substantial changes, but have really only scratched the surface in terms of changing control mechanisms and the organisational culture.

6 International Context and Lessons to Learn

Each of the chapters highlights and explains selected key features of the German administrative system or relevant approaches to reform, then provides descriptive information about these issues before moving on to problem-oriented analyses of the subject area. At the same time, these analyses are linked to key debates and theories in public administration and policy and are accessible and comprehensible to an international readership not familiar with the German case. Finally, each chapter draws some lessons and conclusions to be considered by international readers when it comes to concept transfer, good practice learning and institutional translations into different national contexts.

The book is designed to serve as a basic reference book for students, academics and practitioners interested in better understanding and contextualising German public administration. It elaborates on the particularities in order to make these understandable to an international readership. To this end, the authors embed their analyses in the international context and refer to formal as well as informal mechanisms and standard operating procedures at work, showing how they differ from other national systems and administrative settings elsewhere. 'Comparing is human' (Raadschelders 2011, p. 831ff.) because it helps to understand one's own (national) administrative system by comparing it with others and recognising its particularities, advantages and disadvantages, strengths and weaknesses (Kuhlmann and Wollmann 2019, p. 2). The aim is thus to stimulate the interest and curiosity of academics and practitioners in the variety of administrative systems beyond national borders and from a trans-European and global perspective.

Furthermore, to encourage international comparisons, each chapter in this book concludes with a 'lessons learned' section. These lessons point out important features and mechanisms that manifest themselves in the German setting and should be considered when referring to the German model in the international debate. For academics, lessons learned might point to the importance/non-importance of certain independent or contextual variables. For practitioners, lessons learned might point to caveats in concept transfer. For both communities, the different chapters may be helpful for a more thorough and informed comparison of the German case.

References

Kuhlmann, S., & Wollmann, H. (2019). *Introduction to Comparative Public Administration. Administrative Systems and Reforms in Europe* (2nd ed.). Cheltenham/Northampton: Edward Elgar.

Raadschelders, J. C. N. (2011). Commentary—Between 'Thick Description' and Large-N Studies. The Fragmentation of Comparative Research. *Public Administration Review, 71*(6), 831–833.

von Stein, L. (1870 [2010]). Handbuch der Verwaltungslehre und des Verwaltungsrechts, Stuttgart: Cotta (reprint U. Schliesky (Ed.)). Tübingen: Mohr.

Open Access This chapter is licensed under the terms of the Creative Commons Attribution 4.0 International License (http://creativecommons.org/licenses/by/4.0/), which permits use, sharing, adaptation, distribution and reproduction in any medium or format, as long as you give appropriate credit to the original author(s) and the source, provide a link to the Creative Commons licence and indicate if changes were made.

The images or other third party material in this chapter are included in the chapter's Creative Commons licence, unless indicated otherwise in a credit line to the material. If material is not included in the chapter's Creative Commons licence and your intended use is not permitted by statutory regulation or exceeds the permitted use, you will need to obtain permission directly from the copyright holder.

PART I

German Public Administration in the Multilevel System

CHAPTER 2

Constitutional State and Public Administration

Karl-Peter Sommermann

1   INTRODUCTION

Among the characteristics of German public administration that are most likely to catch the eye of a foreign observer include the following two phenomena: first, the high density of statutory law (law adopted by the parliament) regulating the organisation, the procedure and the substantive criteria for the activities of public administration; and second, the almost ubiquitous presence of arguments inferred from constitutional law in the legislative process, court rulings and even administrative decisions. The practice to constantly emphasise the interconnection of constitutional and ordinary law can also be seen in legal education, where professors of public law teach administrative law against the background of constitutional law. Unlike in the Romance-speaking countries, most German law faculties do not clearly separate the chairs of constitutional law from those of administrative law, but combine them under the denomination of 'public law', notwithstanding the fact that the holders of the chairs will often specialise more or less in one of the fields.

K.-P. Sommermann (✉)
German Research Institute for Public Administration, Speyer, Germany
e-mail: sommermann@foev-speyer.de

© The Author(s) 2021   17
S. Kuhlmann et al. (eds.), *Public Administration in Germany*,
Governance and Public Management,
https://doi.org/10.1007/978-3-030-53697-8_2

The legalistic orientation of German public administration has not constituted an obstacle to modernisation processes based on managerialist or new governance approaches, but has limited their scope, in particular by pointing out the necessity of constitutional safeguards. This chapter undertakes to elaborate on the guiding constitutional concepts and requirements, which determine the development of German public administration and its capacity to adapt to a changing environment.

2   KEY CONCEPTS OF PUBLIC LAW AND PUBLIC ADMINISTRATION

German public administration has been profoundly shaped by two concepts: by the liberal idea of a *Rechtsstaat* that originated in pre-democratic times and aims at an effective protection of individual freedom, and by the idea of a strictly normative constitution that is binding upon all public powers—the legislator as well as the executive power and the judiciary.

2.1   *The Principle of the Law-Governed State* (Rechtsstaat)

In international and European terminology, the term *Rechtsstaat* has for some time now generally been translated into English as 'rule of law'. This terminological choice and the subsequent exchange of ideas have fostered a conceptual convergence of both principles, even in the national sphere (see Sommermann 2018: 107ff.). Despite their origins in far different contexts and the attachment of the rule of law to the concept of parliamentary sovereignty, they are inspired by similar insights and by the objective to protect individual freedom through reliable laws and prevention of arbitrary state action. The most prominent German author of the first half of the nineteenth century who pushed forward the idea of the *Rechtsstaat* was the liberal Robert von Mohl (1799–1875). His approach even resembles the modern concept of a 'social' *Rechtsstaat*, when he emphasises the obligation of the state to promote the free development of citizens by organising 'the living together of the people in such a manner that each member of it will be supported and fostered, to the highest degree possible, in its free and comprehensive exercise and use of its strengths' (von Mohl 1844: 8). In the further discussion, scholars put more emphasis on the formal requirements of the *Rechtsstaat*, gradually supplementing the core principles of legality and separation of powers (including judicial control by independent courts) by the principles of equal treatment, accountability of those who act on the basis of public powers, legal certainty and proportionality. The *Rechtsstaat*, like the rule of law, relies upon procedural rationality and fairness, although the criteria are not always the same.

2.2 The Constitutional State (Verfassungsstaat)

The modern constitutional state takes up essential elements of the idea of the *Rechtsstaat*. It is characterised by the strict normativity of a constitution, which includes guarantees and enforcement measures for individual freedom, even against parliamentary acts. In the Basic Law, conceived as a counter-concept to overcome the totalitarianism of the Nazi period and, since 1990, the constitution of the reunified Germany, Article 1 (3) already reflects the will of its drafters to establish a strictly normative constitution. It reads: 'The following fundamental rights shall bind the legislature, the executive and the judiciary as directly applicable law.' Furthermore, considering the guarantee of judicial protection in Article 19 (4) and the powers attributed to the Federal Constitutional Court in Article 93, the normative, in no part merely programmatic, character of the Basic Law becomes evident. The normative and formative powers of the Basic Law turned out to be so strong that as early as 1959, the then president of the Federal (Supreme) Administrative Court, Fritz Werner, coined the phrase—nowadays often quoted, not only in Germany—that 'administrative law is constitutional law put into concrete terms' (Werner 1959: 527). This is particularly true for the general principles derived from Article 20 (3) (see Sect. 3.1) and for the normative effect of the fundamental rights (see Sect. 3.3).

2.3 The Integration of the Rechtsstaat and the Verfassungsstaat in the European Union

The German legal system, as any other legal system of the European Union (EU) Member States, is subject to the influence of supranational law. European Union law has not only been triggering legal reforms and the reinterpretation of ordinary law, but also constitutional amendments (cf. Chap. 4). In general, conflicts between European law and domestic constitutional law have largely been avoided by constitutional opening clauses, first, by the general empowerment clause of Article 24 (1) 'to transfer sovereign powers to international organisations', and later since the constitutional reform of December 1992, by a special clause for European integration (Article 23). However, this empowerment finds its limits in other constitutional provisions. The Federal Constitutional Court had already stated with regard to the general clause of Article 24 (1) that it does not authorise the constitutional bodies to give up the constitutional identity of the Federal Republic of Germany through the transfer of powers that will jeopardise the constituent structures of the Basic Law (BVerfGE 73, 339, 375–376). This applies, in particular, to the constitutional elements declared as unchangeable in Article 79 (3) (the so-called eternity clause), that is, 'the division of the Federation into *Länder*, their participation in principle in the legislative process, or the principles laid down in Articles 1 and 20'—Article 1 enshrines the inviolability of human dignity and the direct applicability of fundamental rights; Article 20, basic constitutional principles such as democracy, separation of powers and the rule of law. The 'European Clause' of Article 23, inserted in the Basic Law in 1992, took up the case law of the Federal Constitutional Court. Germany's participation in the development of European integration is admissible as long as the Union 'is committed to democratic, social and federal principles, to the rule of law (principles of a *Rechtsstaat*) and to the principle of subsidiarity and [..] guarantees a level of protection of basic rights essentially comparable to that afforded by this Basic Law', and does not infringe upon the constitutional elements secured by the 'eternity clause'.[1] Since the European Union considers itself to be a *Rechtsunion*, that is, a union governed by the rule of law/*Rechtsstaat* (Article 2 of the Treaty on European Union), there are favourable conditions for a harmonious interaction between the national and the European level in this respect. Despite the fact that 'different national traditions underpin the "rule of law" in the EU' (Nicolaidis and Kleinfeld 2012: 27ff.), the sub-principles of the *Rechtsstaat* mentioned above are, in essence, equally recognised by the European Court of Justice.

This is not always the case regarding the democratic principle. As will be shown (see Sect. 5), the requirement for democratic legitimacy of all state action, laid down in Article 20 (2), bears the potential to generate conflicts with secondary EU law containing organisational prescriptions for the national public administrations.

2.4 Lessons Learned

German history has shown the importance of always maintaining awareness that formal principles, such as the separation of powers, legality, legal security, proportionality and judicial protection by independent courts, are not ends in themselves, but serve the common goal of preventing arbitrary state action and preserving individual rights. When the Nazis came to power, some lawyers tried to reinterpret the *Rechtsstaat*, criticising the mere formal understanding of the notion. They proposed substituting it for a concept focussing on 'national-socialist justice', which would allow sacrificing 'mere formal principles' for the sake of this substantive goal. Such perversion of the *Rechtsstaat* is only conceivable against the background of a former reduction of the *Rechtsstaat* to formal principles. The original idea that led to the establishment of the formal principles mentioned had not been kept alive (cf. Sommermann 1997: 150ff.). Hence, it is indispensable to understand that the fundamental objective of the *Rechtsstaat* is the protection of human dignity and individual freedom, and to centre any discussion on the further development of the concept around this objective. Equally, a mere reference to an unspecified 'justice' (*Rechtsstaat* as state of justice, *Gerechtigkeitsstaat*) bears the risk of opening up the concept to barely controllable contents.

3 THE CONSTITUTIONAL FRAME OF PUBLIC ADMINISTRATION

Notwithstanding the fact that the Basic Law provides only few concrete rules for public administration, numerous organisational, procedural and substantive requirements have been derived from its general principles, its federal architecture and the duty to protect fundamental rights.

3.1 Constitutional Principles

The concept of the *Rechtsstaat* had early on been linked to principles such as proportionality (choice of the less severe appropriate means to attain a legitimate aim that must not be outweighed by the detrimental effects) and legal certainty (prohibition, inter alia, of retroactive regulations or of the revocation of lawful administrative decisions). The administrative courts applied these criteria as general principles, implied in the essence of administrative law as such. With the entering into force of the Basic Law, these principles became, alongside others, part of the positive constitutional law. The Federal Constitutional Court and the legal doctrine considered the principle of the *Rechtsstaat*, which is expressly mentioned in Article 28 (1) of the Basic Law (with regard to the *Länder* constitutions), to be primarily enshrined in Article 20 (3) (BVerfGE 35, 41, 47; 117, 163, 185), which provides that the 'legislature shall be bound by the constitutional order, the executive and the judiciary by law and justice'. From the subjection of the executive power to the law (principle of legality), the jurisprudence furthermore derived, besides the supremacy of the law (*Vorrang des Gesetzes*), the necessity to base administrative action directly or indirectly on a parliamentary act (*Vorbehalt des Gesetzes*). In this sense, Article 80 (1) of the Basic Law determines that the issue of statutory instruments (*Rechtsverordnungen*) requires an explicit parliamentary act of delegation. Consequently, in the German parliamentary system of government, there are no independent statutory orders, as is the case, for example, in the semi-presidential system of France. Furthermore, in the light of the democratic principle, the Federal Constitutional Court has concluded that all 'essential provisions', especially those related to fundamental rights, have to be regulated by the parliament itself and therefore cannot be delegated to the executive power (BVerfGE 49, 89, 126; 139, 148, 174–175). Apart from democratic considerations, this solution ensures that important questions are deliberated in a multistage parliamentary process where the pros and cons are discussed more intensely and more transparently than in a monocratic executive organ. Irrespective of the eminent role played by the parliament, the Federal Constitutional Court recognises a core area of self-responsibility of the executive power, which includes a 'confidential sphere for initiatives, deliberations and actions', in particular in the governmental process of decision-making (BVerfGE 137, 185, 234–235).

The requirement to assign state tasks to the functionally most adequate bodies is attributed to the principle of separation of powers (Article 20 (2)), which, in turn, is considered to be inherent in a *Rechtsstaat* (BVerfGE 68, 1, 86; excerpts in English in Kommers 2012: 139ff.). Further recognised subprinciples of the constitutional principle of the *Rechtsstaat* are a clear attribution of responsibilities, certainty of the law (definiteness, publicity, reliability and consistency of the law as well as protection of legitimate expectations) and proportionality (Heun 2011: 41ff.; Morlok and Michael 2019: 142ff.; Robbers 2019: 49–50; Sommermann 2018: 128ff.). Other more detailed requirements of the *Rechtsstaat* concerning administrative action are the objectivity and impartiality in the exercise of public functions, the duty of administrative authorities to hear the individual before imposing a burden and to give reason for the decision. The federal law and the laws of the sixteen *Länder* on administrative procedure further specify these requirements. The duty to give reason is most important for an effective defence against unlawful acts and has to be seen in the light of the requirement of an effective judicial protection of the rights of individuals. Being part and parcel of the concept of the *Rechtsstaat*, the guarantee of an effective judicial protection against the violation of individual rights by a public authority is explicitly laid down in Article 19 (4) of the Basic Law.

The principle of objectivity and impartiality in the exercise of public functions finds an institutional safeguard in the guarantee of a professional civil service (*Berufsbeamtentum*). Article 33 (4) and (5) of the Basic Law stipulates that the exercise of sovereign authority as a rule should be entrusted to members of the civil service who stand in a relationship of service and loyalty defined by public law, with due regard to the traditional principles of the professional civil service (cf. Chap. 13). The status of this category of civil servants is characterised, inter alia, by employment as lifetime officials, different career tracks (according to qualifications), recruitment and promotion according to the merit principle and loyalty towards the constitution and towards the public employer, the prohibition of strikes and the duty of public employers to grant remuneration and retirement benefits that correspond to the public function exercised by the respective official. Influenced by new concepts in leadership and human resource management, the maintenance of the constitutional guarantee of Article 33 has repeatedly been discussed, but no constitutional reform that would abolish the traditional principles of the *Berufsbeamtentum* has taken place so far.

As far as principles of state policy are concerned, the German constitution enshrines two basic aspirational principles (*Staatszielbestimmungen*): first, the principle of the social state (Article 20 (1)), and second, the principle of environmental protection, also with regard to the responsibility towards future generations (Article 20a). These principles, although they do not convey individual rights, are not merely programmatic proclamations, but have binding character for the legislator, the executive and the judiciary. The legislator must pursue and consider these objectives when making laws, even though the jurisprudence of the Federal Constitutional Court has allowed for a wide margin of discretion and has limited its control to evident violations of the constitutional objectives. However, these principles attain considerable importance when combined with fundamental rights. For the public administration and the courts, the principles of the social state (*Sozialstaat*) and the ecological state (*Umweltstaat*) constitute binding criteria for the interpretation of the law or for the exercise of discretionary powers. The social state, interpreted in the light of the freedom-protecting principle of the *Rechtsstaat*, can rather be qualified as an 'enabling state' that creates and improves the social conditions for a free development of the members of the society than a predominantly transfer-oriented 'welfare state' (Sommermann 2018: 54ff.; Morlok and Michael 2019: 187). The Federal Constitutional Court has derived from the principle of the social state in conjunction with the inviolability and protection of human dignity (Article 1 (1)), a fundamental right to the guarantee of a subsistence minimum, comprising not only a physical but also a sociocultural dimension (BVerfGE 125, 177, 221ff.).

3.2   *The Multilevel Administration of German Federalism*

The federal structure of German public administration entails three main territorial levels of public administration: the federal level, the *Länder* level and the local level (cf. Chaps. 3, 5, and 8). The local administration forms part of the *Länder* administration but enjoys a constitutional right to regulate through bylaws (*Satzungen*), within the limits of the law, all local affairs (Article 28 (2)). Because of their partial legal autonomy, local administration and other self-administrating public bodies created by law are characterised as 'indirect state administration' (*mittelbare Staatsverwaltung*). It should be noted that local authorities partly act as state authorities (*Länder* authorities) of first instance. In this sense, the areas of their own responsibility (*eigener Wirkungskreis*) have to be distinguished from those of delegated responsibility (*übertragener Wirkungskreis*, cf. Chap. 9).

While the Basic Law assigns the majority of legislative competences to the Federation, the overwhelming majority of administrative competences remains with the *Länder*, where the local authorities deliver most of the administrative tasks (Heun 2011: 62). The principle of execution of federal laws by the *Länder* forms part of what is called *Exekutivföderalismus* (executive federalism), characterised by an intertwining of the federal and the *Länder* level (cf. see Chap. 8; for the conceptualisation of the executive federalism in Germany, cf. Dann 2004: 123ff.).

According to Article 87 (3), the federal legislator can establish federal agencies for matters on which the Federation has legislative power and thus create bodies of federal administration. The most important federal agency is the *Bundesnetzagentur* (Federal Network Agency), created in the wake of the privatisation of essential public services in the 1990s and whose regulatory and monitoring tasks lie in the field of telecommunications, postal services, energy and railways. The original administrative competences of the Federation relate to the foreign service, financial administration and federal waterways and shipping. Based on Article 87, a federal border police had been created, which was later transformed into a federal police responsible for border control and security of railways and airports. By and large, the main competence for police matters remains with the *Länder*.

As far as the regulations of the European Union are concerned, their execution conforms to the distribution of administrative competences applicable to national legislation. Likewise, the transposition of Union directives has to be carried out by that legislator or those legislators (federal parliament or *Länder* parliaments) who would be competent in national affairs. According to the principle of federal loyalty, which the Federal Constitutional Court has inferred from the federal principle (Article 20 (1); cf., e.g., the judgements BVerfGE 1, 299, 315, and 133, 241, 262), the *Länder* are obliged vis-à-vis the Federation to take within their sphere of competence responsibility for the implementation of Union law. This is indispensable to prevent Germany breaching obligations under Union law. The same applies to the implementation of international law. In order to prevent unforeseeable obligations for the *Länder*, the Basic Law provides for their participation through the *Bundesrat* in matters concerning the European Union. Participation can even amount to representation of Germany at Union level by a representative of the *Länder* when 'legislative powers exclusive to the *Länder* concerning matters of school education, culture or broadcasting are primarily affected' (Article 23 (6)).

3.3 The Impact of Fundamental Rights on Public Administration

It goes without saying that fundamental rights put limits on the legislative power of the parliament and the rule-making power of public administration. Likewise, they constitute important criteria for the interpretation of the laws and for the exercise of discretionary powers by the administrative authorities. However, the normative scope of the fundamental rights goes far beyond their classical liberal function as defensive rights against intrusions of the public power. According to the German Federal Constitutional Court, the fundamental rights establish

> an objective order of values, and this order strongly reinforces the effect of power of fundamental rights. This value system, which centres upon dignity of the human personality developing freely within the social community, must be looked upon as a fundamental constitutional decision affecting all spheres of law. It serves as a yardstick for measuring and assessing all actions in the areas of legislation, public administration, and adjudication. (BVerfGE 7, 198, 205—leading case)

Subsequently, the Court has inferred duties to protect from the objective dimension of the fundamental rights. The protection must also be ensured by an appropriate administrative organisation and procedural setting (BVerfGE 65, 1, 51; 84, 34, 45–46). The legal doctrine has strengthened this approach by conceptualising administrative organisation and procedure as important steering mechanisms in the realisation of substantive legal rules and principles (Schmidt-Aßmann 2004: 19ff., 244–245; Schuppert 2012: 1073ff.). The jurisprudence to consider fundamental rights as procedural guarantees equally applies to court procedures. In this sense, the Federal Constitutional Court emphasises the duty of the courts 'to make really effective the normative value of the fundamental rights in the respective procedure' (BVerfGE 49, 252, 257).

3.4   Lessons Learned

A constitution can only comply with its task to create a reliable framework for the relations between citizens and the state and for the interaction between state organs if it possesses a strong legal normativity. 'Normative constitutions' (Löwenstein 1957: 147ff.; Grimm 2012: 105ff.) generally are provided with suitable mechanisms of implementation and enforcement. In Germany, the Federal Constitutional Court has particularly enhanced the effectivity of fundamental rights.

In modern societies, the complexity of law is increasing, not least by the necessity to regulate the provision of infrastructure and social services, and to care for the prevention of risks associated with, for instance, new structures of economic power, the evolution of modern technologies, environmental pollution and climate change. The new dimensions given to fundamental rights by the jurisprudence of the German Federal Constitutional Court have to be seen against this background. The promotion of obligations stemming from the principle of the social state backs the derivation of protective duties and procedural guarantees for the state, even from classical liberty rights. The cooperative structures and mechanisms of the federal system, as they have developed over the years, not only contribute to a largely equivalent level of protection and services in the whole German territory, but also reduce dysfunctional conflicts between the federal actors and ensure interoperability and coherence between their administrations. It goes without saying that the optimisation of the cooperation remains a constant task.

4   The Role of Judicial Review

In its efforts to strengthen individual rights, in particular the fundamental rights against state authorities, the drafters provided for the previously mentioned guarantee of an effective judicial protection against the violation of individual rights and for a constitutional control of the legislator. Shortly after the entering into force of the Basic Law in 1951, the functions of the Federal Constitutional Court were supplemented by the competence to adjudicate on individual constitutional complaints.

4.1   The Right to an Effective Judicial Remedy

Under the auspices of the guarantee of judicial protection against the public power in Article 19 (4), the administrative jurisdiction soon developed into a bulwark of citizens against unlawful intrusions or inactivity of administrative authorities (cf. Chap. 12). From the beginning, the Code of Administrative Court Procedure of 1960 took into account that the protective interests of individuals are not limited to the annulment of illegal administrative decisions. They equally comprise claims aiming at the issue of an administrative decision or another performance that has been refused or omitted as well as the declaration of the existence or non-existence of a legal relationship. Hence, the Code provides rules for rescissory actions as well as provisions on actions for performance and on declaratory actions. The same is true for the corresponding specialised codes of the social jurisdiction and the financial jurisdiction. In the codes of all the three branches of administrative jurisdiction, the provisions on the main procedures are accompanied by rules of interim relief that comprise, on the one hand, automatic suspensory effect of rescissory actions or court orders of suspension and the empowerment of the court to issue temporary injunctions on the other. This system meets the requirements which the Federal Constitutional Court has inferred from the guarantee of Article 19 (4), in particular that the protection must be complete (without loopholes) and effective (cf. BVerfGE 35, 263, 274; 115, 81, 92).

Individuals often make use of the protection afforded by the administrative courts. In the general administrative jurisdiction alone (i.e. not including the social and the fiscal jurisdiction), there were about 200,000 new lawsuits and around 80,000 requests lodged for interim relief in 2018.[2] Currently, there are still numerous claims of migrants for recognition as refugees which are pending.

4.2 The Powers of the Constitutional Jurisdiction

The constitutional jurisdiction of the Federation and the *Länder* participates in the protection of individuals against unlawful behaviour on the part of the public administration, especially by adjudicating on constitutional complaints. Since the Federal Constitutional Court has derived a general liberty right from Article 2 (1), which is applicable if none of the special liberty rights is relevant (BVerfGE 6, 32, 36ff.—leading case), all illegal acts that impose a burden have to be seen as affecting a fundamental right. However, before presenting a constitutional complaint, the plaintiff has to exhaust the ordinary remedies before the courts. If the action is dismissed by the last instance, the constitutional complaint that asserts the violation of a fundamental right is generally directed not only against the administrative decision, but also against the last-instance judgement that confirms the administrative act. The constitutional complaint, just as an abstract or a concrete review of statutes, can lead to the annulment of a law if the violation of the fundamental right originates in it. Out of the almost 6000 new cases received by the Federal Constitutional Court in 2018, more than 95 percent were constitutional complaints.

4.3 The Jurisdictionalisation of Administrative and Constitutional Law

If the Federal Constitutional Court finds that a law is unconstitutional, it does not always declare it null and void. It has developed a technique according to which it limits itself to the mere declaration of unconstitutionality in case an annulment would cause disproportionate damage. However, in these cases, the court will generally combine the declaration of unconstitutionality with a time limit within which the legislator has to remedy the situation. In special cases, the court even states that specific transitional rules have to be applied until the new legislation is adopted, thus acting as a *praeceptor legislatoris*, that is, substitute legislator (Sommermann 2018: 98). Furthermore, the jurisprudence of the court has considerably contributed to strengthening judicial control over the exercise of discretionary powers and planning procedures. Therefore, new approaches to regain a broader margin of appreciation for public administration by restricting complete control of the legal application have been discussed (cf. Schmidt-Aßmann 2004: 217ff.), especially by the doctrine of specific empowerments of public administration by the legislator.

With regard to the active role the Federal Constitutional Court plays in the German legal culture, some authors warned that the state of parliamentary legislation would be transformed into a state of constitutional jurisdiction (*verfassungsgerichtlicher Jurisdiktionsstaat*; see in particular Böckenförde 1990: 25). However, it cannot be denied that the predominant role given to the fundamental rights by the constitutional jurisdiction has sensitised public administration for constitutional principles and has ensured over past decades a high degree of protection of the rights of the citizens, who hold the Federal Constitutional Court in high esteem.[3]

4.4 Lessons Learned

In a modern state, which takes responsibility for infrastructure, public services and social benefits, effective judicial control requires more than procedures that are limited to the annulment of illegal administrative decisions. After the Second World War, the drafters of the Basic Law and subsequently the German legislator felt strongly committed to establishing an all-encompassing judicial protection of citizens against unlawful behaviour on the part of the state. Consequently, a system was soon created that provided not only rescissory actions, but also, taking up earlier first approaches, remedies against the inactivity of public administration. In order to allow for timely help, interim relief remedies completed the protective system. In harmony with the main procedures, the administrative courts are empowered to grant interim relief in all conceivable situations where judicial control is needed to protect individual rights. In most

Member States of the European Union, this resynchronisation between the development of the administrative law (which had already expanded into the fields of planning procedures and service delivery much earlier) has taken place only since the 1990s. In the German case, it was the traumatic experience of a dictatorship which gave rise to the early modernisation of the judicial system. The same is true for the remedy of constitutional complaints that considerably strengthened the position of individuals and gave rise to a specification of the constitutional right to effective judicial protection.

5 Constitutional Reform and Constitutional Change

The constitutionalisation of the legal order on the one hand, and its Europeanisation on the other, entails the necessity to constantly adapt the constitution to the changing social and economic situations and supranational context. To date, the Basic Law has been modified sixty-four times, producing a constitutional text more than twice as long as it was in 1949 and, from the aspect of a formal legislative process, in many cases not exemplary for a constitution that should focus on essential points. Most modifications concern the organisational part and the financial constitution. Fundamental rights have undergone only a few modifications to their wording, the most important changes stemming from their dynamic interpretation by the Federal Constitutional Court. Thus, the Court has derived from the right to freely develop one's personality (Article 2 (1)) in conjunction with the protection of human dignity (Article 1 (1)), first a general right to privacy, later (1983) an implicit right to self-determination over personal data (BVerfGE 65, 1, 41ff.) and then (2008) a right to the confidentiality and integrity of information technology systems (BVerfGE 120, 274, 302ff.). Furthermore, the reinterpretation of constitutional rules or principles in the light of European Union law constitute an important factor of constitutional change, that is, a change without a constitutional reform pursuant to Article 79, which would require a two-thirds majority in both chambers, the *Bundestag* and the *Bundesrat*. As far as the principles laid down in Articles 1 and 20 of the Basic Law are concerned, constitutional reforms are not admissible. This has already generated a conflict between obligations arising out of Union law to establish independent agencies, on the one hand, and the principle of democratic legitimation enshrined in Article 20 (1), on the other hand, given that the principle of democratic legitimation and responsibility is deemed to require supervision by the competent minister in order to maintain parliamentary accountability. A solution can only be found in a reinterpretation of Article 20, which means that the understanding of the requirement of an uninterrupted chain of democratic legitimation has to be modified. This appears to be justifiable to the extent that the legislator defines the rules governing the decisions of the agency in a clear and sufficiently precise manner and alternative forms of parliamentary control are established.

6 Conclusion

German public administration has long been influenced by a legalist approach inherent to, and shaped by, the concept of the *Rechtsstaat*. Under the Basic Law of 1949 and the jurisprudence of the Federal Constitutional Court, this approach even became a constitution-centric juridification of public tasks (Frankenberg 2014: 143). Fundamental rights not only are safeguards for individual freedom, but also convey, in the light of the principle of the social state, directives for positive state action. Given the dense normativity of the constitutional obligations inferred from the Basic Law, the law of the European Union poses a major challenge for the adaptability and flexibility of the German legal system.

German federalism is modelled in a way that the infrastructure and the social services are roughly equivalent in the sixteen *Länder.* The intense self-coordination among the *Länder* themselves and between the *Länder* and the Federation strengthens this tendency towards a unitary federal state (*unitarischer Bundesstaat*; Hesse 1962: 13–14). Not least at administrative level, the cooperation between the members of the Federation constitutes an important prerequisite for coping effectively with tasks like internal security, environmental protection, strategies for digitalisation and, as recent developments have shown, migration, climate policy and the fight against pandemic diseases. The latest constitutional reforms have further developed the cooperative federalism to the extent that the Federation can participate in structural tasks at the local level through co-financing educational infrastructure and public housing. The price the *Länder* had to pay was the admission of special controls concerning the use of the funds. The maintenance of a living federalism requires a constant balancing and reconciliation of centripetal and centrifugal forces.

NOTES

1. Cf. the strict interpretation of the eternity clause by the Federal Constitutional Court in its judgement on the Lisbon Treaty, judgement of 30 June 2009, paras. 208, 216ff. (English translation available on the internet at https://www.bundesverfassungsgericht.de/SharedDocs/Entscheidungen/EN/2009/06/es20090630_2bve000208en.html).
2. Statistisches Bundesamt (ed.), Rechtspflege—Verwaltungsgerichte—Fachserie 10 Reihe 2.4–2018, Wiesbaden, 2019, pp. 14 and 40.
3. See Legal Tribune Online of 23 February 2017, available on the internet at https://www.lto.de/recht/hintergruende/h/bverfg-ethik-kodex-vertrauen-bevoelkerung-erhalten-politik-wirtschaft-einfluss/.

REFERENCES

Böckenförde, E. W. (1990). Weichenstellungen der Grundrechtsdogmatik. *In Der Staat, 29*, 1–31.

Dann, P. (2004). *Parlamente im Exekutivföderalismus. Eine Studie zum Verhältnis von föderaler Ordnung und parlamentarischer Demokratie in der Europäischen Union.* Berlin: Springer.

Frankenberg, G. (2014). *Political Technology and the Erosion of the Rule of Law.* Northampton: Edward Elgar.

Grimm, D. (2012). Types of Constitutions. In M. Rosenfeld & A. Sajó (Eds.), *The Oxford Handbook of Comparative Constitutional Law* (pp. 98–132). Oxford University Press.

Hesse, K. (1962). *Der unitarische Bundesstaat.* Karlsruhe: Verlag C.F. Müller.

Heun, W. (2011). *The Constitution of Germany – A Contextual Analysis.* Oxford: Hart Publishers.

Kommers, D. P. (2012). *The Constitutional Jurisprudence of the Federal Republic of Germany* (3rd ed.). Durham: Duke University Press.

Löwenstein, K. (1957). *Political Power and Governmental Process.* Chicago: University of Chicago Press.

Mohl, R. von (1844). *Die Polizei-Wissenschaft nach den Grundsätzen des Rechtsstaates.* 2nd ed. Vol. 1. Tübingen.

Morlok, M., & Michael, L. (2019). *Staatsorganisationsrecht* (4th ed.). Baden-Baden: Nomos.

Nicolaidis, K., & Kleinfeld, R. (2012). *Rethinking Europe's 'Rule of Law' and Enlargement Agenda: The Fundamental Dilemma.* Paper No. 49. Paris.

Robbers, G. (2019). *An Introduction to German Law* (7th ed.). Baden-Baden: Nomos.

Schmidt-Aßmann, E. (2004). *Das Allgemeine Verwaltungsrecht als Ordnungsidee* (2nd ed.). Berlin: Springer.

Schuppert, G. F. (2012). Verwaltungsorganisation und Verwaltungsorganisationsrecht als Steuerungsfaktoren. In W. Hoffmann-Riem, E. Schmidt-Aßmann, & A. Voßkuhle (Eds.), *Grundlagen des Verwaltungsrechts* (Vol. 1, 2nd ed., pp. 1067–1159). Munich: Beck.

Sommermann, K. P. (1997). *Staatsziele und Staatszielbestimmungen*. Tübingen: Mohr Siebeck.

Sommermann, K. P. (2018). Commentary on Art. 20 of the Basic Law. In v. Mangoldt, Klein, Starck *Grundgesetz* (Vol. 2, 7th ed., pp. 1–171). Munich: Beck.

Werner, F. (1959). Verwaltungsrecht als konkretisiertes Verfassungsrecht. In *Deutsches Verwaltungsblatt*, pp. 527–533.

Open Access This chapter is licensed under the terms of the Creative Commons Attribution 4.0 International License (http://creativecommons.org/licenses/by/4.0/), which permits use, sharing, adaptation, distribution and reproduction in any medium or format, as long as you give appropriate credit to the original author(s) and the source, provide a link to the Creative Commons licence and indicate if changes were made.

The images or other third party material in this chapter are included in the chapter's Creative Commons licence, unless indicated otherwise in a credit line to the material. If material is not included in the chapter's Creative Commons licence and your intended use is not permitted by statutory regulation or exceeds the permitted use, you will need to obtain permission directly from the copyright holder.

CHAPTER 3

Administrative Federalism

Nathalie Behnke and Sabine Kropp

1 INTRODUCTION

The German federal state has frequently been analysed through the lens of 'administrative federalism' (see, e.g., Hueglin and Fenna 2015: 54). This denotation builds on two basic dimensions. On the one hand, it emphasises that governments and administrations at all territorial levels are powerful actors in policymaking and implementation processes. On the other hand, compared to other federations, the German model implies that legislation predominantly takes place at the federal level, while the *Länder* (the relevant political sub-federal units) implement federal laws in their own right, through their own administration and at their own cost (Kuhlmann and Wollmann 2019: 93). This specific federal architecture is inherited (as elaborated in Sect. 2) and entails a specific distribution of responsibilities and functions (as elaborated in Sect. 3; see also the chapter

---

N. Behnke (✉)
Technical University of Darmstadt, Darmstadt, Germany
e-mail: nathalie.behnke@tu-darmstadt.de

S. Kropp
Free University Berlin, Berlin, Germany
e-mail: sabine.kropp@fu-berlin.de

© The Author(s) 2021
S. Kuhlmann et al. (eds.), *Public Administration in Germany*,
Governance and Public Management,
https://doi.org/10.1007/978-3-030-53697-8_3

by Schrapper). Accordingly, the strength of the *Länder* is not rooted in exclusive jurisdictions and self-rule, but based on their extensive rights to co-decide on federal bills and their prerogative to implement federal laws. Consequentially, *Länder* administrations are embedded in a dense network of vertical and horizontal relations. Two (types of) organisational bodies are particularly relevant for securing coordination both horizontally among the *Länder* and vertically between the entire *Länder* and the federal level: the *Bundesrat* and the various ministerial councils, among which the prime ministerial council (*Ministerpräsidentenkonferenz*) is the most prominent, as will be elaborated in Sect. 4.

In other federal states providing a more dual federal architecture, such as the United States or Switzerland, horizontal intergovernmental councils primarily fulfil the function of protecting sub-federal policymaking or policy implementation from federal encroachment. Second chambers, where they exist and have some meaningful role in legislation, rarely represent sub-federal interests. By contrast, in Germany, both (types of) bodies represent effective arenas for multilateral coordination, thereby providing various venues for debating and deciding potentially contentious issues. They also serve as arenas where conflicts can be averted at an early stage of the political process. This consensual culture of decision-making in multilevel structures was illustratively described as entangled or interlocking politics (a more or less clumsy translation of *Politikverflechtung* as coined by Fritz W. Scharpf). While critics claim that this cooperative, multilateral decision-making style might lead at best to incremental change, or even to outright decision deadlock, it turned out that these bodies have contributed to a surprisingly high effectiveness of German federalism and a concomitantly low level of litigation between the units of government.

2   Historical Roots of German Administrative Federalism

The peculiar German model of administrative federalism is deeply rooted in German history. Although the German Basic Law was drafted from scratch after the breakdown of the totalitarian regime and the end of the Second World War in 1945, constitutional key institutions were conspicuously taken from federal experiences in the German past and adapted to the requirements of the newly established federal democratic institutional setting. Especially the period from 1867 to 1871 is perceived as a 'critical juncture' in German administrative federalism (Weichlein 2012: 112).

Three basic features have decisively shaped administrative federalism: first, most notably, the executive character of the *Bundesrat*; second, the principle of administrative connectivity (*Verwaltungskonnexität*); and third, the vertical division of powers that runs along functions but not along policies, a principle which entails coordination and cooperation between various governments and bureaucracies across all policy fields. Consequently, bureaucrats are strong players in these intergovernmental settings, because they make coordinative and cooperative activities work (Behnke 2019).

The German empire's constitution adopted in 1871 (*Reichsverfassung*) fostered the administrative character of German federalism. In the nineteenth century, former independent territorial units pooled their sovereignty in order to unite and establish the German nation-state. Most importantly, the *Bundesrat* was designed as an assembly of *Länder* representatives, holding legislative as well as executive powers (Frotscher and Pieroth 2018: 209–212). And the *Bundesrat*, representing *Länder* governments, partially assumed functions of the federal government, which was still weak at that time and had to resort to *Länder* contributions and their administrative resources. Furthermore, as an embodiment of the authoritarian state, the *Bundesrat* enabled the former federal chancellor, Otto von Bismarck, to circumvent parliamentary accountability (Weichlein 2012: 113). Hence, federalism served as a 'fence', protecting the governments and their bureaucracies against parliamentarisation and the upcoming emancipation of the working class. The *Bundesrat* was designed to secure the prerogative of the emperor over the *Reichstag*; for the time being, it also helped regional sovereigns to contain the state parliaments' growing demands for participation.

Since the nineteenth century, the federal government has not been responsible for implementing its own laws, even though residual federal administrative responsibilities do meanwhile exist (Mußgnug 1984: 189). As a rule, the *Länder* executives implemented (and still implement) federal laws and bear the cost involved (*Verwaltungskonnexität*). On the other hand, since the *Länder* take over administrative responsibility for federal matters, they must also be involved in federal legislation, which was (and still is) executed with the requirement that all federal bills pass the *Bundesrat*. The concomitant functional division of labour necessitated intergovernmental coordination and fostered entanglement among the federal units. The developing welfare state and expanding infrastructure (railway construction, trade etc.) pressured governments to find unitary solutions, thereby strengthening cooperation between executive actors across territorial levels. Finally, a legalistic administrative culture developed during the nineteenth century, underpinning since then the German federal culture.

The constitution of the Weimar Republic (1918–1933) did not substantially alter this basic architecture. After the breakdown of the Nazi regime, which had abrogated federalism in 1934, the allies advocated federalisation and decentralisation as a means of containing any potential misuse of governmental power. During the early post-war period (1945–1949), the heads of *Länder* governments (the minister presidents) were leading figures in framing the constitutional debate. Concomitantly, before the Federal Republic was founded in 1949, the ministerial bureaucracies of the *Länder* had already begun to apply horizontal cooperation in various policy fields. After controversial debates in the parliamentary council (*Parlamentarischer Rat*) on drafting the Basic Law in 1948–1949, its representatives ultimately rejected the US-style senate model, which would have stipulated the popular election of senators. Preferring the involvement of *Länder* governments in federal legislation to the principles of immediate legitimation and self-rule, the fathers and mothers of the Basic Law returned to the *Bundesrat* model. In contrast to the 1871 constitution, parliamentary majorities now hold the post-war *Länder* governments accountable; administrations are agents of fully democratised governments. Nevertheless, the administrative character of German federalism is still anchored in the *Bundesrat* and its committee structure, composed of *Länder* bureaucrats rather than elected politicians, and is reflected in a dense web of inter-administrative bodies.

3   Distribution of Responsibilities

In West Germany after the end of the Second World War (1949) and East Germany after reunification (1990) (see the chapter by Wollmann), power was organised in a highly decentralised fashion, granting the *Länder* and their municipalities with a large number of jurisdictions. Power is divided in the 'vertical' dimension between two levels of government—the federal level and the sixteen *Länder*. The local authorities are formally lower administrative units of the *Länder*, but Article 28 of the Basic Law accords them extended rights of autonomy, in particular a functional omnipotence within the territorial boundaries of their jurisdiction (see the chapter by Bogumil/Kuhlmann). Intermediate layers exist 'in between' the local and the *Länder* level. Higher communal associations (*höhere Kommunalverbände*) bundle local authorities' administrative capacities for a larger territory. District organisations (*Regierungspräsidien*) are all-purpose sub-units of the *Land* ministry of the interior exercising direction, control and oversight over the execution of *Länder* tasks in the respective territory. In addition, there are functionally specialised *Länder* offices, for example, environmental offices, health offices and statistical offices, to name but a few.

Division of labour between the federal level and the *Länder* is organised mainly along a functional logic, yet overlapping with a policy-specific logic. Functionally, the federal level holds the majority of legislative powers, while the *Länder* and local authorities fulfil the overwhelming part of executive functions. Policy-wise, a few exceptions exist. For example, the *Länder* have retained legislative competences for culture, education and police and some minor competences. They also have considerable organisational autonomy and decide how they implement policies. This even extends to the regulation of local charters, local fiscal equalisation systems and local responsibility for certain tasks. The division of legislative powers is elaborated mainly in Articles 72 and 74 of the Basic Law. The federal level, on the other hand, relies predominantly on *Länder* administrations to fulfil its tasks. In the case of a few tasks, which are deemed to be of exclusive federal nature, the federal government staffs its own offices at the local level across the territory. These include, for example, the military services, the customs and duty administration, and the intelligence services, as well as the Federal Unemployment Agency and the Federal Office of Migration and Refugees (see Article 87 of the Basic Law).

If the activities of the *Länder* administrations relate to federal laws, the administrations act on behalf of the federal government. If they execute their own laws, they act autonomously. This distinction is laid down in Articles 83–85 of the Basic Law and has implications for the intensity with which the federal government may structure administrative processes and organisations in all *Länder* alike, thereby securing uniform standards of public service delivery. The *Länder*, for their part, can delegate their tasks to the local authorities, where basically the same principle applies: the local authorities, as administrative units that have direct contact with citizens as addressees of norms or as requesting services, act on their own behalf if they perform tasks that fall within the concept of local autonomy. If they take on tasks that have been transferred to them by the *Länder*, they must respect the regulations given by the *Länder* and are subject to legal and functional oversight (*Fachaufsicht*) (see Fig. 3.1).

As a rule, the formal power distribution assigns clearly delineated jurisdictions to each level of government or to single territorial units, thereby establishing political accountability and responsibility for the effective and efficient fulfilment of tasks. However, *joint provision* of tasks across levels of government severely hampers these principles. Nevertheless, with the constitutional reform of 1969, administrative coordination has intensified. The reform defined a considerable number of policy issues such as regional and economic development and the construction of university buildings as joint tasks to be planned, implemented and financed jointly by the federal government and the *Länder* (Articles 91a and 91b of the Basic Law). This instrument of joint tasks has been extended to other policy areas, such as labour administration, digitalisation (see the chapter by Mergel) and comparison of education levels (Articles 91c–91e of the Basic Law). Beyond these constitutionally prescribed joint tasks, voluntary horizontal and vertical cooperation is a pervasive feature of administrative practice in Germany's federal system, as will be discussed further in the next section. The motives for cooperation include, for example, striving for best practices, economies of scale and uniform implementation. In instances of vertical or horizontal cooperation between the *Länder* and the federal level, self-regulatory bodies are often established and jointly staffed by all units

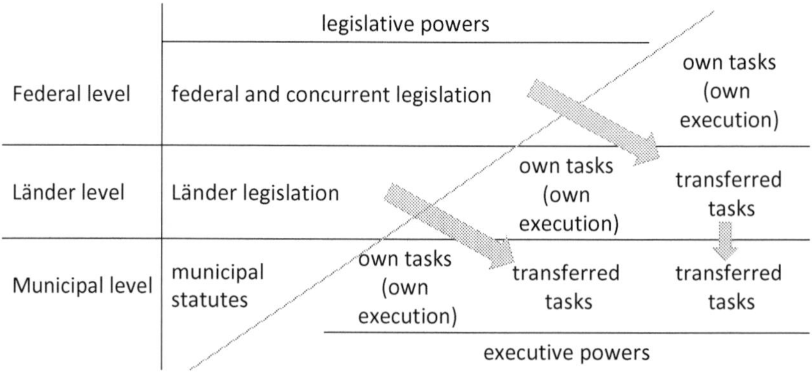

	legislative powers		
Federal level	federal and concurrent legislation		own tasks (own execution)
Länder level	Länder legislation	own tasks (own execution)	transferred tasks
Municipal level	municipal statutes	own tasks (own execution)	transferred tasks	transferred tasks
		executive powers	

Fig. 3.1 Functional division of labour in the federal hierarchy

involved in order to monitor the negotiation process and to govern implementation (e.g. the stability council or the IT planning council).

Financial management largely follows the principle of *administrative connectivity*, meaning that the unit responsible for executing a task or providing a service is obliged to finance it. The rationale behind this principle is to ensure a responsible spending behaviour. As is shown in Fig. 3.1, local authorities shoulder responsibility for the largest share of executive tasks. As they have the smallest allocation of financial resources, the higher levels of government transfer funds by means of tax sharing, fiscal equalisation payments or grant systems to the local level (see the chapter by Färber). Naturally, federal, *Länder* and local governments have diverging opinions about the amount of fiscal transfers necessary to fulfil tasks appropriately. Over the past decades, two trends have become apparent. First, taxes are increasingly being levied collectively. They are distributed in complex nested processes in order to empower each political and administrative unit to finance its own tasks. Second, with increasing amounts being spent by local authorities on welfare state payments, the federal government is willing to adopt larger shares of these payments by transferring money directly to the *Länder* level (e.g. according to Article 104a of the Basic Law). Nonetheless, in spite of this fundamentally cooperative attitude, the level of payments to be made gives rise to much litigation, in particular between local authorities and the *Länder*.

To sum up, the vertical division of power is marked by a predominantly functional allocation of powers, whereas units with territorial jurisdictions and units with functional jurisdictions overlap across the German territory. Control and oversight are exercised mainly by the *Länder* over their local authorities, whereas the relationship between the *Länder* and the federal level is essentially non-hierarchical but marked by mutual rights of co-decision-making, which are exercised in various negotiation arenas (such as joint task committees). This multi-layered and strongly decentralised administration is consistent with Germany's federal tradition and bolstered by a logic of subsidiarity and autonomy. It is balanced, however, by a deeply engrained administrative culture of cooperation and coordination. This specific manifestation of administrative federalism creates—in comparison to other federal architectures—a unique mix of decentralised decision-making, while securing policy homogeneity and a low level of litigation.

4 Coordination and Cooperation: Making Administrative Federalism Work

The allocation of powers to territorial units provides the formal structure for policymaking. Yet, the everyday work of administrations requires constant processes of communication, information and coordination between governments and bureaucracies. These processes of intergovernmental relations are what makes federalism work in everyday politics. Intergovernmental communication and negotiations are institutionalised mainly in two arenas: in *Bundesrat* sessions and in regular meetings of ministerial conferences. Additionally, a multitude of informal meetings, working groups or task forces emerge and disappear on single issues. Undoubtedly, the most prominent institution providing an institutionalised framework for intergovernmental relations is the *Bundesrat*. According to Article 50 of the Basic Law, '(t)he *Länder* shall participate through the *Bundesrat* in the legislation and administration of the Federation and in matters concerning the European Union'. This prescription implies a dual function: while the *Bundesrat* is a second chamber and, as such, involved in federal legislation, due to its composition and working mode, it also serves as a crucial arena for intergovernmental activities (Hegele 2017). The *Bundesrat* co-decides on every federal bill. Around 38–60 percent of all bills in post-war history have been consent bills requiring an absolute majority of votes in the *Länder* assembly. Bills typically require consent if they affect finance and tax issues. Most importantly, however, bills stipulating that the *Länder* administrations execute federal laws in their own right trigger the consent rule. The federalism reform of 2006 relaxed some of these requirements and the percentage of consent bills has since decreased from an average of 55 percent per legislative period to an average of 39 percent (Stecker 2016: 614).

The *Bundesrat* meets roughly every four weeks and in each plenary session votes on about fifty federal bills. In order to shoulder this enormous workload, it is organised in working committees, which are at the top of the administrative coordination pyramid (Hoffmann and Wisser 2012: 601) and are bolstered by numerous more or less formalised administrative bodies and a dense network of informal administrative ties. Most committees are composed of higher-ranking civil servants (*Ständige Sitzungsvertreter*) from the respective *Länder* ministries, but in some committees (i.e. finance), the minister himself or herself takes part. In other 'political committees' (i.e. defence or foreign relations), the minister presidents themselves are involved, since these exclusive federal jurisdictions are naturally not mirrored in the *Länder* cabinets (Sturm and Müller 2013: 147 f.). The discourse in the committees is considerably shaped by the administrative and legal expertise of their members. As participants must often decide on dozens of issues during one meeting, generalists rather than policy specialists participate (Hoffmann and Wisser 2012: 607). Before the meetings, however, the highly specialised civil servants employed in the respective divisions of the *Länder* ministries are required to prepare the issues within a short time period (usually six weeks; see Article 76 (2) of the Basic Law).

In intergovernmental negotiations, territorial, party-based and issue-specific interests interact (Toubeau and Massetti 2013). For example, if distributive programmes, fiscal or tax issues are on the agenda, territorial interests usually prevail over party positions. Notwithstanding, decision-making in the *Bundesrat* plenary sessions depends on political constellations. As the coalition landscape at the *Länder* level—and thus the political composition of the *Bundesrat*—has become increasingly 'multi-coloured' since reunification, majorities nowadays are more often incongruent or even cross-cutting between the *Bundestag* and the *Bundesrat*. As part of the *Länder* governments, coalition parties need to agree on a common voting behaviour because each Land government must cast its votes *en bloc* (Article 51 (3) of the Basic Law). Accordingly, *Länder* coalitions stipulate in their coalition treaties that the government abstain from voting in the *Bundesrat* should the parties in government be unable to come to an agreement. This kind of two-level bargaining, which takes place simultaneously within the federal and *Länder* governments and across the federal units, is, in theory, prone to blockade. Under these conditions, one may find it surprising that the *Bundesrat* has so far voted against a remarkably small fraction of bills; the arbitration committee has only been invoked on rare occasions. From 1994 to 2017, the number of disapproved bills and arbitration committee meetings decreased significantly (from 2.5 percent and 14 percent to 0.1 percent and 0.5 percent, respectively, according to the official statistics on the *Bundesrat* website).

Certainly, party ideology is a relevant factor in shaping Bundesrat negotiations. Compromise and coalition building occur along party lines and across territorial interests, since *Bundesrat* members from the different *Länder* meet in political pre-negotiation circles—so-called A-rounds (Social Democrats), B-rounds (Christian Democrats) and G-rounds (the Greens). Yet, the final vote is shaped by various competing factors. First, even if majorities diverge between the *Bundestag* and the *Bundesrat*, a conflict of interest between the federal and *Länder* governments is managed by the practice that, already at the drafting stage of a bill, the federal legislator usually considers the preferences of *Länder* governments and adapts drafts according to the given majority situation (Burkhart and Manow 2006). Second, party organisations have been decentralised in recent years to a degree that has allowed *Länder* parties to place strong emphasis on territorial interests (Detterbeck 2012: 131ff.), which may cross-cut traditional party lines and open up new options for majority building. Third, civil servants who are involved in everyday legislative work share a similar professional understanding of their job and can moderate party ideological conflicts within bureaucratic networks. Recent research reveals a moderate party politicisation in the *Bundesrat* committees which prepare *Bundesrat* votes (Souris 2018). They share a strong identity as neutral experts in their respective policy fields. At the same time, expertise and party logics are not mutually exclusive; civil servants usually anticipate the will of their political leadership (Mayntz and Scharpf 1975). Depending on the political salience of the issue at stake, civil servants can 'domesticate' party politicisation, and often ministers and the cabinet follow their bureaucrats' expert advice (on civil servant politicisation; see also the chapter by Jann/Veit). Thus, depending on the polarisation of an issue, the administrative model of federalism can be quite effective in containing party conflict in federal coordination (Hoffmann and Wisser 2012).

The second set of relevant intergovernmental arenas besides the *Bundesrat* are so-called ministerial conferences, eighteen sectoral intergovernmental councils composed of ministerial bureaucrats from the *Länder* governments, who are sometimes joined by their counterparts from the federal level (Hegele and Behnke 2017). In addition to the sectoral conferences, the minister presidents' conference is the most prominent coordination arena of the *Länder* governments. Historically, the earliest ministerial conferences were founded in Germany after the Second World War, with the most recent (integration) being added in 2007. While administrative negotiations in the realm of *Bundesrat* sessions serve to provide input from administrative practice to legislative proposals, the meetings and autonomous working groups in and around ministerial conferences serve primarily to coordinate *Länder* interests during other stages of the policy cycle. They can be used to put issues on the political agenda, to influence pre-legislative negotiations or to coordinate policy implementation. Broadly, these meetings serve as a platform to exchange information, form coordinated positions, exert pressure and influence at the federal level, or to harmonise implementation practices. If issues on a ministerial conference's agenda are simultaneously being debated in a legislative bill in the *Bundesrat*, then typically the conference drops the issue to avoid a parallel discussion. Nevertheless, the decision as to which venue to choose if an issue is to be promoted politically—in a ministerial conference or in the *Bundesrat*—is also subject to strategic considerations. In that sense, the two arenas complement each other as fora of intergovernmental relations.

In the conferences, and even more so in the working groups, the logic of bureaucratic decision-making predominates over the logic of political decision-making. This is even more pronounced than in the *Bundesrat* and its committees, although it is in part the same persons who attend both fora. Indeed, the bureaucrats negotiating in ministerial conferences are well aware of the fact that they represent their home department presided by a minister who is, at the same time, member of a coalition party in government. They strive to act as 'honest brokers' for their ministers' political aims within the limits of factual expertise and consensus orientation. However, German civil servants essentially define their role as experts responsible for a policy field and, in accordance with the Weberian legalistic tradition, as advocates securing the rule-bound implementation of law (Hustedt and Salomonsen 2018). Surveys gathering data on the role definitions of political bureaucrats in the higher ministerial ranks suggest that the bureaucrats perceive themselves as representatives of the state but reject the role of party delegates (Mayntz and Derlien 1989; Schwanke and Ebinger 2006: 243). Due to continued coordination, vertical administrative 'brotherhoods' are sustained along policy areas, cutting across the levels of government and even stretching to the EU level.

While federal-*Länder* relations are well institutionalised and partly constitutionally guaranteed, the local authorities have a harder standing in the multilevel game. Without formal involvement in federal legislation and being dependent on the decisions of *Länder* governments, they must rely on lobbying, negotiation and informal representation in federal and *Länder* institutions. As a result, communities have formed associations of interest representation, some dating back more than a hundred years such as the *Deutsche Städtetag* (German Cities Association), the *Städte- und Gemeindebund* (Federation of Cities and Municipalities) and the *Landkreistag* (Counties' Association). Endowed by their members with financial resources and the power to speak in their name, these associations have intensely lobbied federal legislative processes. They have acquired an undisputed position as experts in hearings and an informal chair in federal-*Länder* negotiations. To name just one example, it was due to the persistent intervention on the part of the Counties Association that new provisions were added to Articles 84 and 85 of the Basic Law in the 2006 constitutional reform protecting local authorities from an uncontrolled increase in tasks and concomitant financial burdens.

To sum up, multiple formal and informal, more or less institutionalised, and in part constitutionally guaranteed committees, councils and regular meetings are the backbone of intergovernmental relations. While federal and *Länder* levels are constitutionally on a fairly equal footing with the guaranteed participation of the *Länder* in federal legislation by means of the *Bundesrat*, the local authorities are in a more precarious situation and need to rely on lobbying to secure their influence on multilevel decision-making. In all these institutions and processes, bureaucrats from all levels of government play a crucial role in providing and exchanging information, defending positions, communicating and negotiating policies. Thereby, political ideology and conflict are mediated to a large extent. While they definitely shape position-taking by intergovernmental actors, they rarely develop disruptive power. As a rule, multilevel decision-making proceeds far more smoothly than the complicated formal network of entangled powers, institutions and processes would suggest.

5   TRENDS AND CHALLENGES

In recent decades, the steadily increasing Europeanisation of the German institutional setting has further bolstered administrative federalism, since bureaucratic networks, which are organised along policy fields, connect EU, federal and *Länder* (including local) actors and institutions. In fact, the German model of federalism has proved rather successful in coping with the challenge of creating institutional complementarity across the various territorial levels. It matches the European institutional setting, as it reflects its explicit executive character. In the intertwined European and German multilevel systems, executives of the lower territorial units participate in legislation at the respective higher level, thereby joining executive and legislative functions. This construction clearly empowers administrative actors. In Brussels, national (and sub-federal, if exclusive jurisdictions of the *Länder* are affected) bureaucrats are involved in all stages of policymaking. Similar to the *Bundesrat* model, the national governments and their civil servants negotiate rules and orders in numerous supranational and intergovernmental bodies, which are attached to the European Commission, the council of ministers and other EU institutions.

By applying the expertise of sub-federal ministerial bureaucracies in federal legislation during the early stages of policymaking, administrative federalism has actively contributed to professionalising law-making since 1949. Nonetheless, the German model is under pressure for change and has been the subject of critical debate. First, applying the principal-agent theory, it could be argued that German federalism is prone to agency problems. In this regard, *ministers* as 'principals' are not expected to closely scrutinise their bureaucrats. However, this theory is the subject of controversy; Bogumil et al. suggest that ministers are not always able to enforce their political will, since a growing share of (political) bureaucrats are more inclined to prioritise expertise at the cost of the (politically accountable) minister's political preferences (Bogumil et al. 2012: 166–168). Second, it is beyond question that the administrative (executive) character of cooperative federalism, which also stretches to the EU level, weakens *parliaments* as the primary principals, mainly at the *Länder* level (Kropp 2015), because parliaments face difficulties in scrutinising their governments and administrations and untying package deals in the multilevel intergovernmental game. Administrative federalism has undoubtedly secured legal expertise and may improve the quality of legislation, but, as a flipside, it diminishes transparency and complicates accountability. Even though the *Bundestag* and some resource-strong *Länder* parliaments participate throughout the executive-driven multilevel processes and have thus managed to enlarge their information and scrutiny rights vis-à-vis their governments in EU affairs (Kropp 2013), this does not counterbalance the deficiencies of input legitimacy.

Third, administrative capacity and financial power are not evenly distributed among the German *Länder*. Not surprisingly, some of the smaller *Länder* and city-states face difficulties in drafting their own policy solutions or in implementing laws, even when exclusive jurisdictions, exit options and deviation rights are constitutionally provided. As a result, German federalism is not fully able to exploit its potential to launch competition for best policy solutions and thus fails to serve one of its genuine purposes. Due to weak administrative capacity (which adds to a remarkably unitary federal culture), policymakers do not often tailor regulations and laws to regional needs. Moreover, in intergovernmental bodies, the stronger *Länder* usually dominate the scenery. Overall, the power imbalance among the *Länder* devitalises federalism, a trend that has been enforced by personnel cutbacks across all levels of public administration.

Finally, federal administrative networks are basically able to generate innovative policy solutions transcending the status quo. Although moderate party politicisation is inherent in intergovernmental bodies, which make decisions with broad majorities or even unanimously, blockades rarely emerge from federal negotiations. In the past, even large-scale reforms were adopted, since party positions converged and moved away from the status quo. The German federal system with its strong institutionalised vetoes, however, will come under pressure if party polarisation further increases. Today, three-party *Länder* coalitions are often required to achieve a parliamentary majority. As a result, tensions between cabinet members have increased. This may also affect intergovernmental networks because civil servants are obliged to show loyalty to their respective minister, even if, as experts themselves, they have conflicting views. Under these conditions, consensus building and decision-making in the intergovernmental arenas will become increasingly burdensome.

6 Conclusion and Lessons Learned

As the above considerations have shown, German federalism cannot properly be understood without appreciating the *specific division of functions between the federal and* Länder *levels*, which gives powerful authority to *Länder* executives and administrations in policymaking (by means of the *Bundesrat* negotiations) and in implementation (by means of the *Länder* prerogative). This characteristic and the formation of the *Bundesrat* as second chamber staffed by members of *Länder* governments are historic and deeply ingrained in the German federal tradition. The tight institutional entanglement between executives and administrations at both levels of government requires powerful coordination mechanisms. In everyday policymaking, coordination is achieved across multiple arenas, including committees and working groups of intergovernmental coordination and cooperation in which bureaucrats especially play an important role in curtailing conflicts of interest and harmonising policy implementation. The strong administrative influence has proven to be rather efficient. Implementation runs smoothly, and, while regional variation is being accommodated to some degree by the highly decentralised territorial organisation, living conditions are relatively homogenous across the

German territory (compared to other federal states). However, despite the constitutional requirements to achieve 'equal living conditions' and multiple redistributive programmes, regional disparities have not been eliminated. In an era of policy challenges such as terror prevention, refugee integration, energy transition and digitalisation, the overly complex institutional and procedural architecture of German administrative federalism is constantly being criticised for hindering the development of efficient solutions. According to federal decision-makers, the trend towards even stronger centralisation and unitarisation of policymaking seems to be inherent in new tasks cross-cutting the existing distribution of responsibilities.

In terms of legislation, executive influence on policymaking would, in theory, be prone to causing deadlocks; in practice, however, political conflict is moderated by coordination routines in the intergovernmental arenas. Party affiliation serves to structure coordination procedures, for example, in the A-, B- and G-rounds of pre-plenary coordination in *Bundesrat* and ministerial conference meetings, but it rarely causes outright blockade. Administrative federalism is criticised for its democratic deficit because parliaments, particularly at the *Länder* level, are basically disadvantaged in multilevel games. However, to the extent that recent or ongoing trends such as increasing territorial disparities and the fractionalisation of the political landscape undermine efficient policymaking and implementation, it becomes questionable whether the model of administrative federalism will be robust enough to live up to its promise.

References

Behnke, N. (2019). How Bureaucratic Networks Make Intergovernmental Relations Work—A Mechanism Perspective. In N. Behnke, J. Broschek, & J. Sonnicksen (Eds.), *Configurations, Dynamics and Mechanisms of Multilevel Governance* (pp. 41–59). Basingstoke: Palgrave Macmillan.

Bogumil, J., Ebinger, F., & Jochheim, L. (2012). Spitzenbeamte und ihr Verhalten bei politisch relevanten Entscheidungen. In D. Schimanke, S. Veit, & H. P. Bull (Eds.), *Bürokratie im Irrgarten der Politik* (pp. 151–156), International Institute of Administrative Sciences/Deutsche Sektion: Schriften der Deutschen Sektion des Internationalen Instituts für Verwaltungswissenschaften, Vol. 36. Baden-Baden: Nomos.

Burkhart, S., & Manow, P. (2006). Kompromiss und Konflikt im parteipolitisierten Föderalismus der Bundesrepublik Deutschland. *Zeitschrift für Politikwissenschaft, 16*, 807–824.

Detterbeck, K. (2012). *Multi-level Party Politics in Western Europe* (Comparative Territorial Politics Series). Basingstoke, Hampshire: Palgrave.

Frotscher, W., & Pieroth, B. (2018). *Verfassungsgeschichte.* München: C.H. Beck.

Hegele, Y. (2017). Multidimensional Interests in Horizontal Intergovernmental Coordination: The Case of the German Bundesrat. *Publius: The Journal of Federalism, 48*(2), 244–268.

Hegele, Y., & Behnke, N. (2017). Horizontal Coordination in Cooperative Federalism: The Purpose of Ministerial Conferences in Germany. *Regional & Federal Studies, 27*(5), 529–548. https://doi.org/10.1080/1359756 6.2017.1315716.

Hoffmann, J., & Wisser, M. (2012). Sachverständige Rechsetzung. Die Ausschüsse des Bundesrates in der Gesetzgebung des Bundes. *Zeitschrift für Parlamentsfragen, 43*(3), 598–608.

Hueglin, T., & Fenna, A. (2015). *Comparative Federalism* (2nd ed.). Toronto: University of Toronto Press.

Hustedt, T., & Salomonsen, H. H. (2018). From Neutral Competence to Competent Neutrality? Revisiting Neutral Competence as the Core Normative Foundation of Western Bureaucracy. In H. Byrkjeflot, F. Engelstad, & P. D. Gay (Eds.), *Bureaucracy and Society in Transition: Comparative Perspectives* (pp. 69–88), Comparative Social Research (Yearbook Series), Vol. 33. Bingley: Emerald Publishing Limited.

Kropp, S. (2013). Information und Kontrolle im Deutschen Bundestag. Exekutive und regierungstragende Fraktionen in europäisierten Fachpolitiken. In B. Eberbach-Born, S. Kropp, A. Stuchlik, & W. Zeh (Eds.), *Parlamentarische Kontrolle und Europäische Union* (pp. 179–200). Baden-Baden: Nomos.

Kropp, S. (2015). Federalism and Subnational Parliaments—A Delicate Relationship. In G. Abels & A. Eppler (Eds.), *Subnational Parliaments in an EU Multi-level Parliamentary System: Taking Stock of the Post-Lisbon Era* (pp. 91–126). Innsbruck: Studienverlag.

Kuhlmann, S., & Wollmann, H. (2019). *Introduction to Comparative Public Administration: Administrative Systems and Reforms in Europe* (2nd ed.). Cheltenham: Elgar.

Mayntz, R., & Derlien, H.-U. (1989). Party Patronage and Politicization of the West German Administrative Elite 1970–1987—Towards Hybridization? *Governance, 2*, 384–404.

Mayntz, R., & Scharpf, F. W. (1975). *Policy-Making in the German Federal Bureaucracy.* Amsterdam, Oxford, New York, NY: Elsevier.

Mußgnug, R. (1984). Die Ausführung der Reichsgesetze durch die Länder und die Rechtaufsicht. In K. G. A. Jeserich, H. Pohl, & v. Unruh, G. C. (Eds.), *Deutsche Verwaltungsgeschichte Bd. 3: Das Deutsche Reich bis zum Ende der Monarchie* (pp. 186–206). Stuttgart: Deutsche Verlags-Anstalt.

Schwanke, K., & Ebinger, F. (2006). Politisierung und Rollenverständnis der deutschen administrativen Elite 1970–2005—Wandel trotz Kontinuität. In J. Bogumil, W. Jann, & F. Nullmeier (Eds.), *Politik und Verwaltung. PVS-Sonderheft 37* (pp. 228–249). Wiesbaden: VS-Verlag.

Souris, A. (2018). Europa im Parteienwettstreit in den Ausschüssen des Bundesrates. *Integration, 3,* 210–227.

Stecker, C. (2016). The Effects of Federalism Reform on the Legislative Process in Germany. *Regional & Federal Studies, 26*(5), 603–624. https://doi.org/10.1080/13597566.2016.1236334.

Sturm, R., & Müller, M. M. (2013). Blockadepolitik in den Ausschüssen des Bundesrates—Offene Fragen und erste Antworten. In T. Europäisches Zentrum für Föderalismusforschung (EZFF) (Ed.), *Jahrbuch des Föderalismus* (Vol. 14, pp. 142–154). Baden-Baden: Nomos.

Toubeau, S., & Massetti, E. (2013). The Party Politics of Territorial Reforms in Europe. *West European Politics, 36*(2), 297–316.

Weichlein, S. (2012). Föderalismus und Bundesstaat zwischen dem Alten Reich und der Bundesrepublik Deutschland. In I. Härtel (Ed.), *Handbuch Föderalismus—Föderalismus als demokratische Rechtsordnung und Rechtskultur in Deutschland, Europa und der Welt. Band I: Grundlagen des Föderalismus und der deutsche Bundesstaat* (pp. 101–127). Berlin: Springer.

Open Access This chapter is licensed under the terms of the Creative Commons Attribution 4.0 International License (http://creativecommons.org/licenses/by/4.0/), which permits use, sharing, adaptation, distribution and reproduction in any medium or format, as long as you give appropriate credit to the original author(s) and the source, provide a link to the Creative Commons licence and indicate if changes were made.

The images or other third party material in this chapter are included in the chapter's Creative Commons licence, unless indicated otherwise in a credit line to the material. If material is not included in the chapter's Creative Commons licence and your intended use is not permitted by statutory regulation or exceeds the permitted use, you will need to obtain permission directly from the copyright holder.

CHAPTER 4

Europeanisation and German Public Administration

Hans Hofmann

1 Introduction

The European Union (EU) is not a (federal) state, but rather a union of states *sui generis* created by means of international treaties and having its own legal system. Within the EU, the Member States remain independent states and, in principle, retain their sovereignty. The Member States have defined the EU's competences and areas of activity in various treaties such as the Treaty on European Union (TEU) and the Treaty on the Functioning of the European Union (TFEU), also known as the Treaty of Lisbon. These treaties are called primary law. According to the principle of conferral anchored in these treaties (Article 5 (1) and (2) TEU), the Union may legislate and adopt legally binding acts through its law-making organs only when primary law has conferred on it the competence to do so (Article 2 (1) TFEU). These legal acts constitute secondary law and are adopted above all in the form of regulations, directives and decisions (Article 288 TFEU). The national law of each Member State remains in force alongside.

H. Hofmann (✉)
Federal Ministry of the Interior, Building and Community, Berlin, Germany
e-mail: hans.hofmann@bmi.bund.de

© The Author(s) 2021
S. Kuhlmann et al. (eds.), *Public Administration in Germany*,
Governance and Public Management,
https://doi.org/10.1007/978-3-030-53697-8_4

Primary law governs not only the division of competences between the EU and its Member States, but also the organs of the EU and their procedures, in particular the procedure for adopting legislation. Primary law can therefore be understood as the constitutional law of the EU. However, since its founding as a purely economic partnership of convenience, the EU has developed into a comprehensive union with state-like structures and is characterised by an increasing transfer of sovereign powers from the Member States to the Union.

2   The EU's Striving to Extend Its Jurisdiction

The division of competences between the EU and its Member States sketched out here is not static, nor is the co-existence of national and Union law entirely free of conflict. This relationship has evolved over time through primary law, often in connection with the admission of new EU Member States, but should also be regarded as an ongoing internal struggle over power and influence between the EU and Member States.

Therefore, it would be wrong to describe the division of competences as unquestioned or unchallenged. On the contrary, the Union is constantly striving to become an area of freedom, security and justice, which entails extensive harmonisation of the law. In the EU's multilevel system, harmonisation is brought about by the process known as 'Europeanisation' of the Member States' national legal systems. In this way, over the years, one field of national law after another has been taken into the EU's legal system with the aim of harmonisation (cf. Nemec 2016; Sturm 2017).

This is a comprehensive process encompassing not only individual fields of law, such as law on competition, consumer protection and the environment, but the entire legal system as well: civil law, public and administrative law, criminal law. The Europeanisation of the national legal systems also encompasses all dimensions of the law—law-making, administration and court rulings are all affected.

3   The Principle of Member State Responsibility for Administering and Enforcing EU Law

Although the EU now has extensive power to legislate, it is in principle not responsible for enforcing secondary law (Vincze 2017). For this reason, it does not have its own administrative apparatus comparable to those of the Member States. According to the division of competences set out in primary law, the Member States are responsible for implementing the law (Article 4 (3) TEU).

Enforcement and application of the law has been conferred on the Union (as a rule, the European Commission) as executive in only a few areas, such as oversight of state aid. This is known as the direct implementation of Union law. Then there are other selected areas in which the EU's own agencies take action as legal entities of the Union under public law.

As a result, administration within the EU takes three different forms:

- implementation of national law by the public administrations of the Member States,
- implementation of EU secondary law by the public administrations of the Member States (indirect implementation of Union law) and
- implementation of EU secondary law by organs or agencies of the EU (direct implementation of Union law or EU self-administration) in exceptional cases.

4   To Avoid Discrepancies, Member States Implement EU Law to a Greater Degree than Is Actually Required

The fundamental division of administrative competences means that every Member State enforces Union law with its *own* administrative organisation and its *own* law on administrative procedures (see the chapter 11). The EU is not allowed in principle to intervene in the internal administration of the Member States. However, if the Member States' public administrations carry out the same EU law using different organisational units and under different law on administrative procedures, the problem of different standards arises.

This is why the Court of Justice of the European Union set a limit on the principle of administrative autonomy for the Member States. The administrative autonomy of the Member States 'must be reconciled with the need to apply Community law uniformly so as to avoid unequal treatment of producers and traders' (European Court of Justice, judgement of 21 September 1983, verb. Rs. 205–215/82, Slg 1983, 2633, Tz. 17—*Deutsche Milchkontor GmbH*).

In order to avoid disparities and conflicts in interpretation, national implementation must always obey two principles: the principle of effectiveness (*effet utile*) and the prohibition of discrimination. According to the principle of effectiveness, the application of national procedural law must not interfere with the scope or effectiveness of EU law. In particular, the modalities provided for in national law on administrative procedures must not make it impossible in practice for EU law to take effect.

As a result, national law which is applicable in principle is modified when it is necessary to ensure the uniform application of EU law in accordance with the principle of effectiveness.

The second principle is the prohibition of discrimination, which is also known as the principle of equivalence. This principle means that the procedural rules of national law must be no less favourable when implementing EU law than when ruling on similar but purely domestic legal disputes. The national authorities must proceed with exactly the same degree of care when someone claims a right based on EU law as in similar cases in which they apply national law to a right guaranteed by national law alone. This also means that the authorities must refrain from any differences in treatment which cannot be justified objectively.

In general, EU law now exerts much greater influence in the Member States than can be directly derived from the provisions of primary and secondary law. This is partly due to pressure, not directly from EU or national law, but from administrative logic. If the Member States strictly conformed to the limited scope of EU law when implementing it, doing so would result in two different legal regimes in many areas. One regime would continue to be oriented on the existing national laws, as far as the EU has no legislative competence for the matter, while the second legal regime would be oriented on EU law and would be limited to its scope of application. Having two different legal regimes at the same time would necessarily create much more work for the administration and would be difficult to explain to the public. In order to avoid these difficulties, there is a strong tendency when implementing EU law to make national law conform to it, sometimes well beyond the actual scope of EU law. One example is the implementation of the EU Services Directive (see the chapter 11).

For the EU, this tendency represents a simple way to expand its own influence and is further reinforced by the trend towards greater networking among Member States' public administrations in the European association of public administrations, and by administrative acts having a transnational effect.

5 EU COURT RULINGS

According to Article 19 (1) TEU, the Court of Justice of the European Union makes sure that both the Member States and the EU organs themselves uniformly comply with EU law. As a result of the Member States transferring sovereign powers to the EU, the courts of the Member States are not allowed to rule on the lawfulness of legal acts or administrative actions of the EU. Because the Court of Justice regards both written law (primary and secondary legal acts) and unwritten legal principles (often of its own creation) as EU law, in its rulings, it claims very extensive competences which are not entirely based directly on the Treaties. In this context, the Court argues that the uniform application of Union law is a fundamental principle of the EU, thereby attempting to legitimise a 'Europeanisation' of the Member States' legal systems. This position can lead to conflicts over competence, especially with the constitutional courts of the Member States.

6 LEGAL REMEDY PROVIDED BY THE NATIONAL ADMINISTRATIVE COURTS

In Germany, judicial remedy against measures taken by the public administration is provided in accordance with the individual's right vis-à-vis the public authorities (*subjektives öffentliches Recht*). For this reason, only those persons are entitled to recourse to the courts who can claim that the measure taken by the public authorities has violated their individual rights (see the chapter by Mehde). The legal principle the public authorities are alleged to have violated must therefore at least serve to protect the individual (*Schutznormtheorie*). However, in Germany, unlike other countries, administrative procedures have the nature of a service and usually do not bestow direct individual rights. Simple procedural breaches therefore do not automatically lead to annulment of the decision and can only be challenged together with the substance of the decision. The German system of legal remedy thus does not provide for popular action (*actio popularis*) or collective action against the public administration. However, when there are grounds for recourse to the administrative courts, the court's review is much more thorough than in many other Member States, because the principle of ex officio investigation applies: the court itself must investigate the facts of the case (see the chapter 12). The court thus examines not only the arguments and the evidence provided by the parties themselves; it also conducts its own thorough investigation of the facts of the case and the lawfulness of the administrative measure. This very thorough legal remedy often results in extremely arduous and time-consuming legal proceedings, especially in legal challenges to complex, large-scale projects.

In the field of environmental protection, EU law in particular has expanded recourse to the courts in cases in which the claimant is not directly affected by the alleged violation of rights. A limited right of associations to bring collective action was introduced to implement EU law and intergovernmental agreements (the Aarhus Convention). With this right, recognised environmental protection organisations (associations) can bring legal actions against violations of environmental law that do not violate their own individual rights (see the chapter 12). Such collective actions are extremely important in practical terms for the implementation of EU law. Because the EU does not have an administrative apparatus comparable to those of the Member States, it can monitor the Member States' application of the law in individual cases only to a limited degree. Along with the recourse of individual Union citizens and companies to the Court of Justice and the Member States' extensive reporting obligations vis-à-vis the European Commission, the right of associations to bring collective action is an effective instrument for indirect oversight of the Member States' authorities. Because of the principle of ex officio investigation and the thoroughness of the review in German administrative court proceedings, such collective actions contribute to the much-lamented length of major proceedings in Germany.

7   Lessons Learned

The division of labour between the EU and its Member States actually provides for Union law to be enforced solely by the Member States through their public administrations and in accordance with their administrative law. It has become clear that this principle is not (or no longer) applied consistently. The EU's own agencies enforce Union law in some areas, and Union law is constantly being added to, not only providing for substantive regulation, but also increasingly determining the administrative practices of the Member States. This also has an indirect effect on national administrative procedures outside the immediate scope of Union law, thus reinforcing the latter's impact on public administration in the Member States. At the same time, however, consistent law on administrative procedures is lacking at EU level (see the chapter 11). Although the EU has no general competence to legislate enforcement of such law by the Member States, codification for the area of the EU's own administration would send a strong signal.

The Member States are called on to take a serious and, where necessary, critical look at how Union law is increasingly permeating their national law. Germany has a great interest in supporting to guide future developments and in making a contribution to these developments. Community and national administrative law have a steadily growing influence on each other. Increasing convergence between the two in future could offer an opportunity to address the codification of European law on administrative procedures.

REFERENCES

Nemec, J. (ed.) (2016). *Europeanisation in Public Administration Reforms, Bratislava: NISPAcee*. Selected Revised Papers from the 23rd NISPAcee Annual Conference May 2015.

Sturm, R. (2017). *The Europeanisation of the German System of Government*. German European Policy Series No 03/17. Berlin: Institut für Europäische Politik (IEP).

Vincze, A. (2017). Europäisierung des nationalen Verwaltungsrechts—eine rechtsvergleichende Annäherung. *ZaöRV, 77*, 235–267.

Open Access This chapter is licensed under the terms of the Creative Commons Attribution 4.0 International License (http://creativecommons.org/licenses/by/4.0/), which permits use, sharing, adaptation, distribution and reproduction in any medium or format, as long as you give appropriate credit to the original author(s) and the source, provide a link to the Creative Commons licence and indicate if changes were made.

The images or other third party material in this chapter are included in the chapter's Creative Commons licence, unless indicated otherwise in a credit line to the material. If material is not included in the chapter's Creative Commons licence and your intended use is not permitted by statutory regulation or exceeds the permitted use, you will need to obtain permission directly from the copyright holder.

CHAPTER 5

Federal Administration

Julia Fleischer

1 Introduction

The federal administration in Germany is embedded in the system of executive federalism in its functions and main tasks (see the chapter by Behnke/Kropp) and its structures and procedures follow a Weberian ideal–type bureaucracy. It is strongly shaped by constitutional and codified rules, which guide the structures, competencies and interactions between the different actors. The key features of the German federal ministerial administration are its major focus on policy formulation and its hierarchical organisational structure, whereby duties and responsibilities are assigned to federal ministries and their officials as key actors. Policy formulation follows intra-ministerial and inter-ministerial coordination processes designed to express and arbitrate bureaucratic expertise while acknowledging the political context (see the chapter by Veit/Jann). Against this backdrop, the aim of this chapter is to present the formal framework of federal bureaucracy in Germany, its key organisational features, the patterns and dynamics of policy formulation and coordination as well as discuss previous and current attempts for reform.

J. Fleischer (✉)
University of Potsdam, Potsdam, Germany
e-mail: fleischer@uni-potsdam.de

© The Author(s) 2021
S. Kuhlmann et al. (eds.), *Public Administration in Germany,*
Governance and Public Management,
https://doi.org/10.1007/978-3-030-53697-8_5

2 The Formal Framework for the Federal Administration

The German Basic Law (*Grundgesetz*) acts as the 'legal backbone' for the key principles structuring the federal government and gives the federal government and its administration wide-ranging responsibilities in policy formulation, whereas the state and local levels mostly engage in policy implementation (Article 65 of the Basic Law; see the chapters by Ruge/Ritgen and Schrapper). A single Article of the Basic Law outlines the three key principles structuring the 'constitutional framework of executive action' (Mayntz 1980: 142):

> The Federal Chancellor determines and is responsible for the general policy guidelines. Within these limits federal ministers conduct the affairs of their respective portfolios independently and on their own responsibility. The Federal Government decides as a collegial body on important matters, particularly concerning differences of opinion between federal ministers. (Article 65 of the Basic Law)

Although these three principles distributing the executive power between the leadership of the chancellor (*Kanzlerprinzip*), the cabinet (*Kabinettsprinzip*) and the departmental ministers (*Ressortprinzip*) are perceived to be in permanent imbalance, in practice the third is the most recognised and protected. In addition, two rulebooks further specify the work of the cabinet and the federal administration. For the cabinet, the 'Rules of Procedure of the Federal Government' (*Geschäftsordnung der Bundesregierung*—GOBReg; see GMBl 22.10.2002) are issued by the cabinet and approved by the Federal President in 1951 (Article 65 of the Basic Law), and for the federal ministries, the 'Joint Rules of Procedure of the Federal Ministries' (*Gemeinsame Geschäftsordnung der Bundesministerien*—GGO; see BMI 2011) are formulated in consultation with all other federal ministries, approved by the cabinet and issued by the Ministry of the Interior since 1958.

The constitutional principle of *leadership by the chancellor* is expressed in several chancellorial privileges that contribute to the German 'chancellor democracy' (Hennis 1964). They include the chancellor's right to recommend the appointment and dismissal of federal ministers to the Federal President (Article 64 of the Basic Law). Although the chancellor may also engage in portfolio allocation and therefore determine the number, remit and size of federal ministries, in practice these processes are strongly shaped by coalition governance and the chancellor has limited influence over the political dynamics of portfolio allocation and ministerial (de-) selection, especially for those cabinet positions held by her/his own party. However, chancellors do have the prerogative to issue organisational decrees in order to organise the federal government (*Organisationserlass der Bundeskanzlerin*, Article 65 (1) of the Basic Law; Lehnguth and Vogelgesang 1988). These decrees are often issued after general elections and express the compromise of coalition parties in reallocating portfolios and the corresponding transfer of policy jurisdictions across federal ministries and agencies (see Table 5.1).

Since 1951, German chancellors have issued a total of 45 organisational decrees. The number of decrees issued per legislative period has fluctuated between zero and five, with the highest number after German reunification in 1991. The number of decrees issued by chancellors has slightly increased over time, particularly during the 1990s and early 2000s. That said, since the late 2000s, the chancellor has only issued one organisational decree per legislative period. In addition, the chancellor is responsible for formulating general policy guidelines, which are, inter alia, expressed in government declarations before parliament. In practice, these declarations are often prepared jointly by the chancellery and the affected federal ministries, and either summarise departmental policy initiatives or declare and explain changes to previous departmental policies. In practice, the chancellor's prerogative to draw up general policy guidelines is often used rather as an 'authority reserve' (Holtmann 2008) than a provision of policy goals that cabinet ministers and federal ministries are supposed to follow. Instead, coalition government, party competition, the relevance of the parliamentary parties and the departmental and cabinet principle limit this prerogative. One exception to this overall pattern is foreign and EU policy, where the principle of the chancellor providing general policy guidelines is more regularly applied (Niclauß 1988). However, even with German chancellors becoming increasingly engaged at the international and supranational level, these policies are still most often prepared between the chancellery and affected ministries, most notably the Foreign Office.

The constitutional principle of *leadership by the cabinet* refers to the collective responsibility for government decisions and is further codified in the GOBReg. German cabinet decisions are not prepared and predetermined in cabinet committees, albeit a few of these committees do exist. Instead, the cabinet's agenda is mostly discussed in advance between

Table 5.1 Chancellor's organisational decree of 14 March 2018

In accordance with Section 9 of the Rules of Procedure of the Federal Government, I order with immediate effect:

I.
The Federal Ministry for the Environment, Nature Conservation, Construction and Nuclear Safety receives the denomination Federal Ministry for the Environment, Nature Conservation and Nuclear Safety.

II.
The Federal Ministry of the Interior shall be given the denomination Federal Ministry of of the Interior, for Construction and Community.

III.
The Federal Ministry of the Interior, for Construction and Community receives
1. from the portfolio of the Federal Ministry for the Environment, Nature Conservation and Nuclear Safety the responsibilities for construction, construction industry and federal buildings, for urban development, housing, rural infrastructure and public building law, for the urban development matters of the spatial planning and demographic change;
2. from the portfolio of the Federal Ministry of Transport and Digital Infrastructure the responsibilities for spatial planning, the federal spatial planning plan, flood protection, European spatial development policy, territorial cohesion and demographic change.
The transfers of competences include their related European and international issues as well as general and strategic issues.

IV.
The Federal Chancellery shall receive from the portfolio of the Federal Ministry of the Interior, for Construction and Community the responsibilities for the IT management of the federation, for the IT Council secretariat, and for the joint IT of the federation.

V.
Number I. of the Federal Chancellor's Organizational Decree of 3 May 1989 (BGBl. I p. 901) is worded as follows:
The Federal Intelligence Service is subordinated to the head of the Federal Chancellery. Its representative is a state secretary or a head of department in the Federal Chancellery.

VI.
The details of the transition shall be agreed between the federal government members involved and notified to the head of the Federal Chancellery. The transfer of responsibilities under III.1. corresponds regarding its resources to the agreement of 22 May 2014 between the Federal Ministry for the Environment, Nature Conservation, Construction and Nuclear Safety and the Federal Ministry of Transport and Digital Infrastructure for the implementation of the Organisational Decrees of the Federal Chancellor of 17 December 2013.

Source: Federal Law Gazette (BGBl.) 2018, Part I, No. 10, p. 374

cabinet members, and the cabinet acts rather as a certification body. Hence, informal party bodies oftentimes manage the cabinet's agenda, especially the 'coalition committee', comprising the senior figures from the coalescing parties in government. Controversial issues are solved by the cabinet, although the chancellor may chair a meeting of affected ministers prior to cabinet meetings (Section 17 GOBReg). Hence, the first arbiter for conflicts between cabinet ministers is the cabinet, with the chancellor playing a pivotal role in achieving a compromise. In practice, such conflicts are often solved by either re-defining the subject and thereby changing the number of affected ministries or by scheduling a coalition meeting, if ministers from different parties are involved. Formally the cabinet decides by majority—unless the chancellor rejects the majority decision with reference to the chancellor principle. By convention, German cabinet ministers rarely criticise their cabinet colleagues' proposals if their own jurisdiction is not affected. More generally, the cabinet mostly ratifies decisions already made via inter-ministerial coordination, or compromises moderated by the head of chancellery, and by various bodies of coalition governance.

The constitutional principle of *leadership by departmental ministers* addresses the individual ministerial responsibility of cabinet ministers for their ministry—which they conduct 'independently' and 'on their own responsibility' (Article 65 of the Basic Law). In general, the GOBReg assigns further competencies to cabinet members. The Minister of Finance enjoys a 'qualified veto' that 'can only be overruled by a simple majority in the cabinet supported by the Chancellor' (Section 26 (1) GOBReg). Similarly, the Minister of the Interior and the Minister of Justice may veto cabinet decisions if existing legal or constitutional regulations are violated (Section 26 (2) GOBReg). Furthermore, the GGO allocates responsibilities across ministries and thus shapes the exercise of ministerial responsibility for departmental ministers. The Ministry of the Interior and the Ministry of Justice must be involved in examining all legal norms for compatibility with the Basic Law and in all other cases where doubts arise as to the application of the Basic Law (Sections 45 (1) and 46 GGO). Furthermore, the Ministry of Justice participates in preparing the draft legislation (Section 46 GGO). The Ministry of Finance must give its consent in the case of provisions on taxes and other duties, or if the income or expenditure of the federation, the *Länder* or local governments is affected (Section 51; Annex 6.4 GGO). In addition, many other ministries must be consulted nowadays regarding specific issues affecting its portfolio, ranging from gender mainstreaming to regulatory impact assessment (Annex 6.9 GGO).

German cabinet ministers have no individual responsibility to parliament. Given that cabinet reshuffles are rare events, they are widely

66 J. FLEISCHER

regarded to acquire a departmental perspective in office. At the same time, they enjoy a high level of managerial autonomy and are responsible for policies within their own jurisdiction. However, departmental ministers only rarely undertake policy initiatives personally, and these initiatives are often limited to policies stipulated in the coalition agreement or confined to crises or highly sensitive and publicly debated issues, responses to critics of the ministry or issues suggested by the parliamentary party, the cabinet or influential political personalities (Mayntz and Scharpf 1975: 91). If a policy initiative is launched by the political top level, it receives utmost attention by line officials. The vast majority of the government's policies, however, is initiated and prepared by ministry officials. Following the notion of the departmental principle, they seek to implement and follow their ministry's policy agenda.

3   ORGANISATION OF THE FEDERAL ADMINISTRATION: MINISTRIES AND AGENCIES

More generally, the German federal administration is strongly shaped by the so-called *Rechtsstaat* tradition (Ziller 2008), which emphasises the rule of law and puts legal and formal conditions at the heart of the structure and organisation of government (see the chapter by Sommermann). Accordingly, formal processes, rules and directives apply and provide considerable stability to the administrative apparatus (e.g. König 1991). Moreover, bureaucratic decisions are to be taken in an objective, equitable, impartial and legal-rational manner (Ziller 2008; see the chapters by Ziekow and Mehde). It follows that the federal administration is organised in a quasi-judicial fashion and enjoys at the same time strong continuity, which increases the predictability of bureaucratic behaviour in coordination processes.

As a consequence of the state structure and the corresponding distribution of competencies in executive federalism, the size of the federal administration is relatively small, yet it is a highly specialised and fragmented central government organisation. The current federal government comprises 14 federal ministries and the chancellor's office (see Table 5.2). The number of federal ministries is comparatively stable, ranging from 19 in the 1960s to 13 in the early 2000s. The internal organisation of these federal ministries and its subordinated agencies is often portrayed to resemble a Weberian ideal–type bureaucracy, characterised by a

5 FEDERAL ADMINISTRATION 67

Table 5.2 Federal ministries as of November 2019

Federal Ministry of Finance
Federal Ministry of the Interior, for Building and Community
Federal Foreign Office
Federal Ministry for Economic Affairs and Energy
Federal Ministry of Justice and Consumer Protection
Federal Ministry for Labour and Social Affairs
Federal Ministry of Defence
Federal Ministry for Food and Agriculture
Federal Ministry for Family Affairs, Senior Citizens, Women and Youth
Federal Ministry for Health
Federal Ministry for Transport and Digital Infrastructure
Federal Ministry for the Environment, Nature Conservation and Nuclear Safety
Federal Ministry for Education and Research
Federal Ministry for Economic Cooperation and Development

Source: Federal Cabinet 2018

hierarchical set-up that promotes specialisation and the clear allocation and development of sectoral expertise, while simultaneously contributing to fragmentation and its unintended consequences for coordination.

According to the chancellor principle, the *chancellor's office* (or Federal Chancellery) acts as the main coordination body within the federal administration. Yet, it is less powerful than other government headquarters because of the strong departmental principle and the notion of ministerial responsibility (Fleischer 2011; see Fig. 5.1). The head of the chancellery acts as key coordinator of the federal government, formally he/she also sets the agenda for cabinet meetings and is often involved in arbitrating inter-ministerial conflicts if they reach the cabinet level (see below). However, the chancellery seldom intervenes in the cabinet agenda based on its own policy interests. Instead, cabinet governance and senior party members in government act as crucial agenda-setters for the cabinet.

In accordance with the role of the chancellery as key coordinator and arbiter of potential inter-ministerial conflicts, the chancellery is composed of seven directorates, which incorporate a range of units that 'mirror' the various federal ministries (*Spiegelreferate*; see Fleischer et al. 2018). However, only four directorates truly mirror the rest of the federal administration, while the other three directorates are engaged in EU policy, digitalisation and innovation, and in supervising the intelligence services (as one of the few original tasks of the chancellery and servicing the federal commissioners for the intelligence services located at the chancellery).

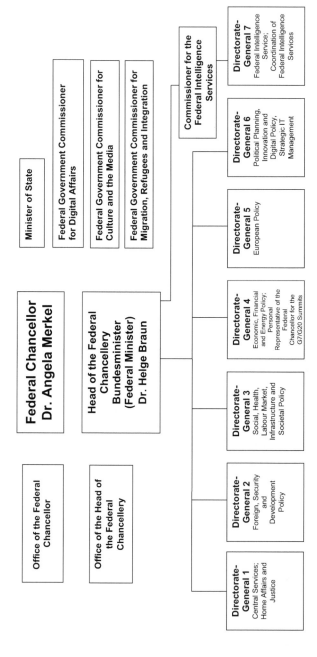

Fig. 5.1 Organisational chart of the federal chancellery as of April 2018

The key task of these mirror units is to proactively engage with the mirroring ministry on its policy proposals prior to cabinet meetings. This includes regular communication and comment, but cannot include a hierarchical request for distinct substantial or other elements of these policy proposals. To facilitate these interactions, officials working in these mirror units are often on secondment from the very ministry that the unit is mirroring. These positions are regarded as springboards for faster promotions in the parent ministry.

The *federal ministries* follow the Weberian ideal–type bureaucratic organisation and are headed by a minister, that is, a political executive who is usually a senior party member. The German ministers are rarely outsiders to the political arena and thus only a few lack a party affiliation and are from the private sector. The federal ministries follow a strong division of labour and a strong hierarchical line organisation.

As a multi-layered branching hierarchy, they are made up of several layers of formal levels with their own types of units, namely the level of *directorates* directly subordinated to the political leadership, the *sub-directorates* and the *divisions*, which can be regarded as the 'backbone' of the federal administration and the core units of policymaking. Besides, each federal ministry incorporates a specific directorate responsible for its internal administration, including human resources, budgeting, legal affairs and so on (coined 'Z Directorate'). Despite the widespread notion of the German federal administration following Weberian ideals, several rather unorthodox types of units can be identified inside the federal ministries as well. These include working groups, staff units tasked with particular responsibilities as well as e.g. federal commissioners and their support units (see Fleischer et al. 2018). More importantly, every German federal ministry hosts a leadership staff unit (*Leitungsbereich*) that is directly subordinated to the minister and engages in various functions and tasks, including policy advice, communication and press relations, and liaison with parliament and the cabinet (see Hustedt 2013). These leadership staff units have grown over the past decades and are mostly occupied by ministry officials rotating into these positions from the line organisation.

The minister is politically supported by one (or more) 'parliamentary state secretaries' who is not part of the internal hierarchical structure, but is a member of parliament and thus often represents the minister in parliament and elsewhere. In contrast, the administrative top officials are called 'administrative state secretaries' and often recruited through internal promotions. Together with their directly subordinated heads of directorates, they represent the class of 'political civil servants', which are the formalised group of political appointees acting as a 'transmission belt' (Hesse and Ellwein 2012) that transmits political signals to the line bureaucrats and bureaucratic expertise to the political executives. A federal law enumerates the ranks in the federal administration allowing for such political recruitments and includes the heads of several federal agencies (Section 30 (1) *Beamtenstatusgesetz*).

Germany has a long tradition of *federal agencies* dating back to Prussian times when these organisations were created as the predecessors of the first government authority that later developed into the ministries. Currently, roughly 90 federal agencies exist, employing more than 90 percent of the federal bureaucratic workforce (Bach 2010). Federal agencies differ in their mandates and tasks: only very few are regulatory agencies with a strong regulatory authority, such as the Federal Competition Authority, the Federal Financial Supervisory Authority and the Federal Network Agency. Given that the federal administration implements very little policy, federal agencies are not usually involved in service delivery. Instead, they often provide policy advice and expertise or may perform administrative tasks and support functions (see the chapter by von Knobloch). However, the federal agencies often enjoy considerable autonomy vis-à-vis their supervising ministry, and, in contrast to other countries, the German federal administration has not set up a specific procedure for monitoring agencies or binding them to particular objectives (in the sense of a contract and contract management; see BMI 2008).

4 Practices of Coordination and Utilisation of Expertise

Despite the various constitutional and codified rules on the organisation of the federal government and administration that follow the German *Rechtsstaat* tradition and its demands for rule-bound behaviour (see the chapter by Sommermann), the German administrative practice at federal level is also strongly oriented towards cooperative administration (Benz 1994) and well prepared and accustomed to negotiating and bargaining, which is very visible at all levels of the inter-ministerial coordination process. At the same time, the federal administration seeks to include expertise from external actors in the inter-ministerial coordination process and has, therefore, established various means to organise this knowledge production.

4.1 Levels and Patterns of Inter-ministerial Coordination

The inter-ministerial coordination in the German federal administration can be distinguished into four ideal-typed dimensions that involve different actors and take place in different arenas. Firstly, in accordance with the departmental principle, line ministries prepare primary and secondary legislation, which is strongly shaped by the provisions of the Joint Rules of Procedure and mostly driven by ministry officials. Secondly, the executive coordination process unfolds within a distinct political context with strong dynamics of party competition. Hence, the leadership staff units within the federal ministries provide a genuine additional coordination loop. Thirdly, and in a similar vein, political appointees perform a crucial role in moderating and arbitrating bureaucratic expertise with political requests; they also prepare cabinet meetings and thus act as crucial gatekeepers for policy proposals to be dealt with in the cabinet. Lastly, the cabinet level itself provides various arenas that are either open to all members or exclusive to some cabinet members.

At the outset, the GGO stipulates the formal requirements for inter-ministerial policymaking by prescribing 'ministry drafts' (*Referentenentwürfe*) as key products (Section 45 (4) GGO). Accordingly, one ministry sponsors each initiative (*Federführung*) and ensures that all the other ministries concerned with the issue are consulted via co-signature (*Mitzeichnung*; Section 15 GGO). In practice, the ministry with the broadest jurisdiction on the issue usually serves as lead ministry; in cases of conflict over leadership, the cabinet decides. Moreover, the rules prescribe the formal inclusion of external stakeholders and organised interests as well as the German *Länder* and municipalities. The majority of policy proposals is prepared by ministry officials following these rules of taking the lead or co-signing a policy proposal initiated by another ministry. It is the prerogative of the lead ministry's unit to decide which external actors to involve and how—yet following the aforementioned rules of always engaging with the *Länder*, municipalities and organised interests.

The typical pattern of inter-ministerial *coordination by ministry officials* can be described as 'negative coordination' (Mayntz and Scharpf 1975), whereby policy drafts presented by the lead ministry's responsible unit to the units in the other ministries as co-signatories are primarily evaluated for their potential (negative) impact on these co-signing units' remit and areas of responsibility. Negative coordination prevails as the most common coordination pattern because it serves both a need for keeping transaction costs at a reasonable level for all units involved and an opportunity for co-signing units to express concerns and request changes if the policy draft violates their turf or contradicts their own existing and future policies. By contrast, 'positive coordination' refers to multilateral policymaking that involves all units potentially affected at the earliest stage possible and allows for discussion and deliberation on alternative actions. However, such processes are rather difficult to set up and conduct, as they require comparatively more resources and levels of trust between the participants—and they are not necessarily prone to result in solutions that can be presented to political superiors and the cabinet.

Moreover, the number of ministerial drafts that federal ministries navigate through the inter-ministerial coordination process differ considerably (see BT 2019). Of the 547 bills issued to parliament by the federal government during the past legislative period (2013–2017), the Ministry of Justice and Consumer Protection issued the highest share (18.1 percent), followed by the Ministry of Finance (17.6 percent) and the Ministry of the Interior (13.3 percent). The smallest number of bills (namely three) was issued by the Ministry for Economic Cooperation and Development (Deutscher Bundestag 2019). It follows that some ministries are more often involved in inter-ministerial coordination than others, not only as lead ministries (as the numbers above illustrate) but also as co-signing ministries. In addition, the timing of cabinet proposals has become more crucial over time. Given the German federal and electoral system, the federal elections are synchronised neither with elections at the state (and local) level nor with the elections to the European Parliament. Under current governing conditions with a coalition government in office that negotiated its legislative programme only after initial coalition talks between different parties failed, political contestations spill down to arenas at the lower levels of inter-ministerial coordination.

The level of *political appointees* performs a crucial transmission function between the bureaucratic expertise embedded in the line hierarchy of ministries, on the one hand, and the political demands and objectives of political executives, on the other. Accordingly, political appointees are the key gatekeepers for policy proposals prepared by ministry officials and also act as negotiators and as 'final resort' in inter-ministerial conflicts before the political level; that is, before ministers under the moderation of the head of chancellery get involved themselves. The key arena for political appointees to clear inter-ministerial conflicts that could not be resolved by departmental officials is their preparatory cabinet meeting under the chairmanship of the head of the chancellery, which is held a day before cabinet meetings.

The meetings are restricted to one administrative state secretary per ministry, although many federal ministries have two or three of these top officials. At the same time, the cabinet agenda can be rather wide-ranging, and it can happen that the representative of the ministry is not the top official heading the branch of the ministry that has been involved in preparing the policy proposal.

Those *arenas at the cabinet level* open to all cabinet members include cabinet committees as well as the cabinet meeting itself. Cabinet committees do not play a strong role in the German federal administration (compared to other European countries). They allow, however, for bringing together a set of federal ministries with responsibilities in a distinct policy issue and for evaluating policy proposals in a more comprehensive manner. Moreover, they are often supported by the distinct group of political appointees (administrative state secretaries and directors-general) that prepares and transmits the cabinet committee's work to the line hierarchy of affected ministries. A few cabinet committees have gained attention, including the current cabinet committee on digitalisation as well as the cabinet committee for climate protection. Hence, cabinet committees may also signal and communicate the cabinet's prioritisation of distinct issues or express the necessity to deal with broader cross-cutting issues in a more comprehensive manner. Moreover, the cabinet meeting itself may serve as a coordination arena.

Besides, the inter-ministerial coordination at the cabinet level also unfolds in arenas that are exclusive and only allow participation of a distinct group of cabinet members. In addition to the aforementioned arbitrations necessary to reach policy compromises, which are moderated by the head of chancellery and, thus, only invite those departmental ministers involved in the conflict, other arenas have been established, especially over the past legislative periods with grand coalitions between the Conservatives (Christian Democratic Union (CDU) and Christian Social Union (CSU)) and the Social Democrats (SPD) in office. For each of the three parties, a genuine arena has been established exclusively for their ministers in office in order to prepare policy coordination among those ministries led by the party. These arenas for party-driven coordination are also present in other areas of the German executive federalism system, most notably to prepare Bundesrat meetings involving *Länder* governments and administrations (see the chapter by Behnke/Kropp). For the federal government and administration, however, they are rather novel, as they separate all three parties in the cabinet rather than offering a combined arena for at least

那 J. FLEISCHER

those ministers from the CDU/CSU acting in parliament as a joint parliamentary group (*Fraktionsgemeinschaft*). Each of the three arenas is supported by an administrative state secretary who serves as a gatekeeper and involves subordinated ministry officials for monitoring and drafting policy ideas.

4.2 External Expertise in Inter-ministerial Coordination

Next to the highly specialised and well-equipped bureaucratic workforce inside the federal ministries and federal agencies, the federal ministries also generate and incorporate external expertise into their inter-ministerial coordination activities in various ways. Firstly, ministries establish and maintain *permanent advisory bodies and councils*. These advisory bodies may take different forms (see Fleischer 2015). Over the past decades, several cabinets have been particularly active in creating novel advisory bodies, especially the first Brandt cabinet in the late 1960s, but also the aftermath of the German reunification witnessed an increase in such advisory arrangements. A closer sectoral examination shows that a disproportionately large number of advisory bodies was set up in the areas of the interior, environment, health, food and consumer protection, while significantly fewer advisory bodies were established in the areas of economic cooperation, post and telecommunications, and justice (ibid.). The most prominent permanent advisory bodies include the German Council of Economic Experts (*Sachverständigenrat zur Begutachtung der gesamtwirtschaftlichen Entwicklung*) and the German Advisory Council on the Environment (*Sachverständigenrat für Umweltfragen*), which advise the corresponding ministry, generate data and produce reports on a regular basis.

The cabinet or individual ministers will occasionally establish ad hoc or *temporary expert commissions* to provide policy advice, often on major policy reforms or complex and cross-cutting issues that benefit from the generation and inclusion of external knowledge and advice. However, a crucial function of both permanent and temporary commissions is also the creation of legitimacy for distinct policy compromises or the utilisation of these bodies as a magnet for blame. The current coalition agreement has announced almost 20 new temporary commissions to address various policy issues and topics in its coalition agreement. In rare instances, these expert commissions are set up as an executive inquiry into policy scandals (see Fleischer 2016). Yet, the impact of these experts in permanent and temporary arrangements is often unclear. Nevertheless, even though many of these bodies produce reports that may lack an immediate impact, they are often incorporated into political debates within the government and between government and parliament, or are made available to the general public.

Lastly, the German federal administration had already introduced tools of evidence-based policymaking in the 1970s. Since 2000, a *regulatory impact assessment* (*Gesetzesfolgenabschätzung*, GFA) has been required for every draft bill presented to parliament (via revision of the GGO; see the chapter by Kuhlmann/Veit). The GFA process assesses the intended and unintended effects of policy drafts and potential policy and instrumental alternatives. In 2009, the GFA was extended by incorporating the sustainability impact assessment into the GGO, thus stipulating the evaluation of potential environmental, economic and social consequences of all policy drafts submitted to parliament. As part of this sustainability impact assessment, all policy proposals must be assessed for their long-term consequences for Germany's National Sustainable Development Strategy and the UN Sustainable Development Goals.

5 The German Federal Administration as a Reluctant Yet Mostly Unconcerned Reformer

The formal responsibilities for reforming the federal administration are scattered across the federal ministries. Despite some central tasks allocated to the Ministry of the Interior, especially in regulating the civil service, each ministry has its own directorate responsible for its internal administration—and thus also for its potential internal reforms. In other words, federal ministers are expected to exercise responsibility for their own ministry by managing its human resources, internal organisation and budget as well as its analogue and digital resources largely autonomously. Consequently, government-wide reforms are not put forward by a single key actor or by the chancellery. More importantly, given the federal state structure and corresponding assignments of tasks and functions, the federal administration is not as involved in service delivery as its counterparts in other countries and thus does not benefit directly or as much from potential reforms of its inner structures and procedures as other administrations. Nevertheless, two dynamics can be identified as recent reform trends at the federal level: on the one hand, the current scheme of regulatory impact assessment and sustainability impact assessment, which is wide-ranging and well-equipped, also in comparison with other countries (see above), and, on the other hand, the digital transformation of society and administration, which is also putting pressure on the federal administration to introduce reform measures.

More generally, the recently advanced debate on the digitalisation of federal bureaucracy has indicated some reluctance to change existing structures and procedures (see the chapter by Mergel). A team explicitly coined 'the agile team' (Tech4Germany) that was originally set up as a temporary unit has very recently been extended and affiliated to the head of chancellery. Its task is to support and identify suitable digitalisation initiatives across the federal administration. Similarly, the federal ministries are now involved in so-called digitalisation labs bringing together federal, state and municipal actors as well as external actors and end-users in order to increase the acceptance of jointly developed solutions for the digitalisation of distinct public services, which the federal government committed itself to, namely to offer these services by the end of 2022 (Online Access Act 2017). In addition, other rather unorthodox organisational arrangements can be observed, mostly on a temporary basis. These include teams and working groups on digitalisation and digital topics; for example, the Ministry for Labour Affairs has an internal 'think tank' (*Denkfabrik*) experimenting with novel ways to organise its bureaucratic work. They also include policy labs for piloting novel ideas in the realm of digital transformation, for example, in the Ministry of Transport and Digital Infrastructure to discuss the future of mobility. Besides these more structural innovations, some procedural innovations can also be observed, for example, the piloting of artificial intelligence (AI)-supported crises prediction simulations in the Foreign Office and the Ministry of Defence, or the numerous online platforms to invite and incorporate external actors more strongly into policy design. Yet, as mentioned above, these initiatives are rather piecemeal and rely heavily on the support of the ministry's political leadership as well as the initiative of line officials to foster innovative ways for executive decision-making and coordination. At the same time, the German federal government is not as advanced as other European governments in utilising and providing open data.

6   Lessons Learned

The German federal administration is governed by various formal frameworks that result in a firm and hierarchical organisational structure supporting the principles of leadership by the chancellor and the cabinet, but especially the principle of leadership by individual cabinet ministers. This crucial departmental principle also strongly influences the practices of coordination and puts the key policy work inside the highly specialised federal ministries. These ministries rely not only on their highly skilled workforce but also on delegated agencies and their generation of expertise and information as well as external expertise. Following the distribution of competencies and the resulting lack of pressure for reform (as the federal level does not deliver very many services directly to the citizens), the federal administration has widely maintained its organisational and procedural patterns of federal policymaking over time. The more recent digital transformation, however, increases the need for adaptation in the rather fragmented patterns of policymaking in and by the federal administration.

References

Bach, T. (2010). Policy and Management Autonomy of Federal Agencies in Germany. In P. Lægreid & K. Verhoest (Eds.), *Governance of Public Sector Organizations: Proliferation, Autonomy and Performance* (pp. 89–110). London: Palgrave Macmillan.

Benz, A. (1994). *Kooperative Verwaltung: Funktionen, Voraussetzungen und Folgen.* Baden-Baden: Nomos Verlagsgesellschaft.

Bundesministerium des Innern (BMI). (2008). *Grundsätze zur Ausübung der Fachaufsicht der Bundesministerien über den Geschäftsbereich.* Berlin.

Bundesministerium des Innern (BMI). (2011). Joint Rules of Procedure of the Federal Ministries (GGO). Retrieved from https://www.bmi.bund.de/SharedDocs/downloads/EN/themen/moderne-verwaltung/ggo_en.pdf?__blob=publicationFile&v=1.

Deutscher Bundestag (BT). (2019). Datenhandbuch zur Geschichte des Deutschen Bundestages seit 1990. Retrieved from https://www.bundestag.de/datenhandbuch.

Federal Cabinet. (2018). Official Order of Precedence for the Federal Ministers and Rules for Reciprocal Representation by Members of the Government, 14 March 2018.

78   J. FLEISCHER

Fleischer, J. (2011). Steering from the German Centre: More Policy Coordination and Fewer Policy Initiatives. In B. G. Peters, J. Pierre, & C. Dahlström (Eds.), *Steering from the Centre: Strengthening Political Control in Western Democracies* (pp. 54–79). Toronto, ON: University of Toronto Press.

Fleischer, J. (2015). Organisierte Expertise und die Legitimation der Verwaltung: Sektorale und strukturpolitische Dynamiken der Gremienlandschaft auf Bundesebene. *der moderne staat, 8*(2), 315–335.

Fleischer, J. (2016). Accountability under Inquiry: Inquiry Committees after Internal Security Crises. In T. Christensen & P. Lægreid (Eds.), *The Ashgate Research Companion to Accountability and Welfare State Reforms in Europe* (pp. 180–193). Surrey: Ashgate.

Fleischer, J., Bertels, J., & Schulze-Gabrechten, L. (2018). *Stabilität und Flexibilität. Wie und warum ändern sich Ministerien?* Baden-Baden: Nomos-Verlagsgesellschaft.

Hennis, W. (1964). *Richtlinienkompetenz und Regierungstechnik.* Tübingen: Mohr.

Hesse, J. J., & Ellwein, T. (2012). *Das Regierungssystem der Bundesrepublik Deutschland* (12th ed.). Opladen: Westdeutscher Verlag.

Holtmann, E. (2008). Die Richtlinienkompetenz des Bundeskanzlers—kein Phantom? In E. Holtmann & W. J. Patzelt (Eds.), *Führen Regierungen tatsächlich? Zur Praxis gouvernementalen Handelns* (pp. 73–84). Wiesbaden: VS Verlag für Sozialwissenschaften.

Hustedt, T. (2013). *Ministerialverwaltung im Wandel: Stuktur und Rolle der Leitungsbereiche im deutsch-dänischen Vergleich.* Baden-Baden: Nomos-Verlagsgesellschaft.

König, K. (1991). Formalisierung und Informalisierung im Regierungszentrum. In H.-H. Hartwich & G. Wewer (Eds.), *Regieren in der Bundesrepublik— Formale und informale Komponenten des Regierens* (pp. 203–220). Opladen: Leske + Budrich.

Lehnguth, G., & Vogelgesang, K. (1988). Die Organisationserlasse der Bundeskanzler seit Bestehen der Bundesrepublik Deutschland im Lichte der politischen Entwicklung. *Archiv des öffentlichen Rechts, 113*(4), 531–582.

Mayntz, R. (Ed.). (1980). *Implementation politischer Programme I.* Königstein, Ts: Verlagsgruppe Athenäum.

Mayntz, R., & Scharpf, F. W. (1975). *Policy-Making in the German Federal Bureaucracy.* Amsterdam; New York: Elsevier.

Niclauß, K. (1988). *Kanzlerdemokratie. Bonner Regierungspraxis von Konrad Adenauer bis Helmut Kohl.* Stuttgart: Kohlhammer.

Ziller, J. (2008). The Continental System of Administrative Legality. In B. G. Peters & J. Pierre (Eds.), *Handbook of Public Administration* (pp. 167–175). London: Sage.

Open Access This chapter is licensed under the terms of the Creative Commons Attribution 4.0 International License (http://creativecommons.org/licenses/by/4.0/), which permits use, sharing, adaptation, distribution and reproduction in any medium or format, as long as you give appropriate credit to the original author(s) and the source, provide a link to the Creative Commons licence and indicate if changes were made.

The images or other third party material in this chapter are included in the chapter's Creative Commons licence, unless indicated otherwise in a credit line to the material. If material is not included in the chapter's Creative Commons licence and your intended use is not permitted by statutory regulation or exceeds the permitted use, you will need to obtain permission directly from the copyright holder.

CHAPTER 6

The Federal Administration of Interior Affairs

Hans-Heinrich von Knobloch

1 Introduction: Federal Administration/ State Administration

As enshrined in the Basic Law, federalism is based on the principle that all the powers not specifically assigned to the Federation as central state are reserved to the *Länder*. According to Article 30 of the Basic Law, the exercise of state powers and the discharge of state functions is a matter for the German states (*Länder*) unless otherwise provided for or permitted by the Basic Law. The same applies to public administration. According to Article 83 of the Basic Law, the *Länder* execute federal laws in their own right unless the Basic Law otherwise provides or permits. The Basic Law contains special provisions on the content and limits of the federal administration (Articles 83 to 91).

If the *Länder* carry out federal laws in their own right, as is usually the case, there are three ways in which the Federal Government may exert influence: firstly, by issuing general administrative rules with the consent of the *Bundesrat*; secondly, by exercising oversight to ensure that the *Länder* execute federal laws in accordance with the law (Article 84); and thirdly, the Federal Government may take the necessary steps to compel

---

H.-H. von Knobloch (✉)
Federal Ministry of the Interior, Building and Community (until 2018),
Berlin, Germany

© The Author(s) 2021
S. Kuhlmann et al. (eds.), *Public Administration in Germany*,
Governance and Public Management,
https://doi.org/10.1007/978-3-030-53697-8_6

81

the *Länder* to carry out their duties (Article 37). Such steps would be taken only as a last resort and require the consent of the *Bundesrat*. This instrument has never been used since the Basic Law entered into force and is only a theoretical option in the state practice of relations between the Federation and the *Länder*.

If the *Länder* execute federal laws as a delegated matter, such laws require the consent of the *Bundesrat*, that is, the chamber representing the *Länder*, which must also consent to general administrative regulations of the Federation. The Federation has a comprehensive right to issue instructions, which is related to the lawfulness and expediency of the execution (Article 85 of the Basic Law).

In the exercise of oversight and the administration by delegated authority, the authority to act lies with the *Länder* (external action and accountability); that is, they are accountable in court and out of court for executive actions.

2   EXCEPTION: FEDERAL ADMINISTRATION

Further, the Basic Law contains provisions on the execution of federal laws by the Federation itself (federal administration [*bundeseigene Verwaltung*] in accordance with Articles 86 and 87). A distinction is drawn here between obligatory and optional federal administration. According to Article 87 (1), first sentence of the Basic Law, obligatory federal administration comprises the foreign service, the federal financial administration, the administration of federal waterways and shipping as well as the federal defence administration according to Article 87b of the Basic Law. According to Article 87 (1), second sentence of the Basic Law, the federal administration may comprise the Federal Police, the Federal Criminal Police Office and the Federal Office for the Protection of the Constitution. A federal law is required to establish each of these authorities.

In addition, according to Article 87 (3), first sentence of the Basic Law, autonomous superior federal authorities and new federal corporations and institutions under public law may be established by a federal law for matters for which the Federation has the power to legislate. A federal law is required for these central authorities active throughout the federal territory because they perform tasks which are, in principle, the responsibility of the *Länder*. Federal authorities at intermediate and lower levels may be established with the consent of the *Bundesrat* and an absolute majority of the *Bundestag* in cases of urgent need.

Taken together, these provisions express the central message for Germany's administrative federalism: the framework for the federal administration is more narrowly defined than that of the *Länder*. As the state authority with a concentration on legislation (including the Federal Government's right to introduce legislation), the Federation is supposed to be able to claim key areas of administration only under certain conditions. The prohibition on mixed and joint administration between the Federation and the *Länder* is an additional instrument to contain federal administrative activity. Nor is the evolution of legal form a way to intervene in the powers of the *Länder*. The Federation is prohibited from departing from the form of public law in order to assume responsibilities of the *Länder*, for example, through foundations by means of private law. This applies in particular to the totality of services (see Wolff 2018).

3 STRUCTURE OF THE FEDERAL ADMINISTRATION

The internal structure of the federal administration follows the same principles found in the administrations of the *Länder*. As in the *Länder* (see Chap. 8 and Kloepfer 2011 and Kloepfer and Greve 2018), a distinction is drawn between direct federal administration by federal authorities without legal personality and indirect federal administration by independent legal entities having legal personality, namely corporations, institutions or foundations under public law.

The direct federal administration, that is, that which is bound by instructions, is divided into three levels: central, intermediate and lower. Examples are as follows:

- The central level includes the federal ministries as supreme federal authorities, the superior federal authorities immediately subordinate to them and responsible for the entire federal territory, and the federal institutions without legal personality.
- The intermediate level includes the regional finance offices and the waterways and shipping directorates.
- The lower level includes the main customs offices, the Bundeswehr careers centre and the waterway and shipping offices.

Within this structure, a comprehensive right to issue legal and expert instructions applies. Its functioning in compliance with the rule of law depends on the integrity and expertise of the public service (in particular

84 H.-H. VON KNOBLOCH

the civil service) and its adherence to law and justice (Article 20 (3) of the Basic Law). At the top of the instruction-giving hierarchy is the federal minister as head of the supreme federal authority; he or she also belongs to the government sphere and holds office by virtue of the federal chancellor's authority to organise. As the federal chancellor is elected by the *Bundestag*, this chain of authority ensures the necessary democratic legitimation of every administrative act at the federal level.

The activity of all authorities is subject to the law on their area of responsibility and the obligations of constitutional law, in particular regarding fundamental rights, and to the general and specific federal law on administrative procedures (see the chapter by Ziekow). This activity is subject to comprehensive supervision by the Federal Administrative Court and the Federal Constitutional Court (see Chap. 12). The Federation alone has the authority to carry out federal administrative tasks (responsibility and external representation).

In terms of organisation, the reason for establishing superior federal authorities is the need for an effective structure for carrying out non-ministerial, subject-related tasks. Delegating additional authority to the administration is intended to enable the ministerial level to devote itself to its policy-related tasks. This often happens as the result of an increased workload, which the ministry is not able to handle or new developments, in particular concerning administrative processes, such as the shift to digital technologies and the security of data and information. Decisions on overall policy remain the responsibility of the relevant ministry.

4   The BMI and Its Executive Agencies

The Federal Ministry of the Interior, Building and Community (BMI) is the ministry responsible for the classic interior affairs of the Federation (see Fröhlich et al. 1997). The principle of ministerial autonomy notwithstanding, the supreme federal authorities are guided by the general internal administration at the federal level, which is based at the BMI. Although its areas of responsibility have changed numerous times since it was established 70 years ago, the federal ministry has always kept BMI in its German abbreviation. Within the Federal Government, the BMI is the ministry responsible for issues related to the Constitution (together with the Ministry of Justice), organisation, public service law and security. Police matters and public security, including protection of the Constitution, migration and emergency management as well as the public service are key tasks. The BMI's executive agencies reflect the ministry's broad range of tasks and make up its administrative substructure (Table 6.1):

The BMI has the most executive agencies of any federal ministry (20). The Federal Ministry for Economic Affairs and Energy (BMWi) has six executive agencies, including the Federal Cartel Office; the Federal Ministry of Health (BMG) has five, including the Federal Institute for Drugs and Medical Devices; and the Federal Ministry for the Environment, Nature Conservation and Nuclear Safety (BMU) has four, including the Federal Environment Agency.

Including the Federal Police, which employs roughly 46,300 staff (the state police forces employ approximately 270,000), the BMI is responsible for around 60,000 federal civil servants and other federal staff. Only about 1100 of them work within the federal ministry itself.

Table 6.1 Executive agencies of the Ministry of the Interior, Building and Community

- Federal Equalisation of Burdens Office (BAA)
- Federal Office for Central Services and Unresolved Property Issues (BADV)
- Federal Office for Migration and Refugees (BAMF)
- Federal Office of Civil Protection and Disaster Response (BBK)
- Federal Office for Building and Regional Planning (BBR)
- Federal Agency for Public Safety Digital Radio (BDBOS)
- Procurement Office of the Federal Ministry of the Interior (BeschA)
- Federal Office for the Protection of the Constitution (BfV)
- Federal Institute for Population Research (BIB)
- Federal Institute of Sport Science (BISp)
- Federal Criminal Police Office (BKA)
- Federal Agency for Cartography and Geodesy (BKG)
- Federal Agency for Civic Education (BpB)
- Federal Police (BPoL)
- Federal Office for Information Security (BSI)
- Federal Office of Administration (BVA)
- Federal Statistical Office (Destatis)
- Federal University of Administrative Sciences (HS Bund)
- Federal Agency for Technical Relief (THW)
- Central Office for Information Technology in the Security Sector (ZITiS)

See the website of the BMI: https://www.bmi.bund.de/EN/ministry/ministry-node.html

5 SUPERVISION

Expert supervision is usually performed at the order of the minister by the organisational unit responsible for the matter in question (*Fachreferat*); administrative supervision is performed by the relevant divisions of the directorate-general responsible for central tasks (see Pieper 2006). Daily practice is characterised by close and trusting interaction between ministries and their executive agencies. The division requests reports on specific matters as needed and, as a rule, responds by issuing instructions, either in agreement with the action proposed by the superior federal authority or rejecting the proposed action and suggesting an alternative. It is also standard for the executive agency to report to the ministry on its own initiative and ask for instructions. If there are very many similar cases, for example, with regard to nationality law (responsibility of the Federal Office of Administration), a single standard procedure is often agreed below the level of administrative regulations. After new legislation enters into force, the ministry usually consults the relevant executive agency concerning the practical application. Ministries regularly schedule meetings with all their executive agencies on matters of mutual concern (budget, staffing, organisation, supervisory practice). These meetings are usually led by the minister or an administrative state secretary depending on the priority of tasks carried out by the executive agency.

Supervision of the ministry's remit (so-called subordinated sector) is generally considered a key task of the relevant ministry. This is based on the principle of relieving supreme federal authorities of the task of processing individual cases and on the executive agencies' need for guidelines whose policy orientation can only be formulated by the ministry. Supervisory tasks are therefore diverse, requiring knowledge of the subject and policy expertise as well as a culture of leadership. The supreme federal authorities conducting supervision need to provide their executive agencies with understandable, clear and practicable instructions where needed, along with the specific description of the space for discretionary decisions wherever possible. In addition to respect for the hierarchy, an understanding for the productivity of the executive agencies is also needed. Looking after their personnel and material resources and representing their concerns to the parliament are priorities of supervision.

In some cases, the outlines of supervision have become less clear in recent years, partly due to the assertiveness and importance of the executive agencies and partly due to a misunderstanding of the requirement to follow instructions, which is felt to interfere with the nature and content of the tasks to be carried out. However, it should be noted that there are, in principle, no areas in which instructions do not apply. Executive agencies are not autonomous even if they are privatised or assigned the legal form of institutions. In every case, a minister will be politically accountable to the *Bundestag* for his actions or failure to act. The minister will be able to fulfil this responsibility only if he or she has the authority to give instructions, at least concerning the lawfulness of the activity. If functions belonging to expert supervision are delegated to bodies such as management boards of institutions under public law, organisational responsibility remains with the supreme federal authority. Nor can target agreements concluded between the ministries and individual executive agencies take the place of the ministries' right to issue instructions in a specific case (see also Chap. 22). Therefore, they do not reinforce the instrument of classic supervision and are allowed by law only within a narrowly defined framework.

6   EXCURSUS: 'MINISTER-FREE ZONES'

Within the hierarchical structure of government administration, the principle of being bound by instructions (*Weisungsgebundenheit*) applies in all but a few exceptional cases. So-called minister-free zones always require a legal basis and important objective reasons (see Schmidt-Bleibtreu et al. 2017). These reasons might be a greater need for neutrality in performing duties or for independent decision-makers having special expertise. For example, a minister has, at most, limited possibilities to provide technical supervision and instructions when it comes to decisions made by the audit offices and audit committees. Within the remit of the BMI, the compilation of statistics by the Federal Statistical Office is largely governed by community law, which takes precedence over national law. Community law requires the independence of the European Union's statistical office Eurostat, of the EU Member States' statistical offices and their directors, and gives this independence priority over the principle of democratic legitimation.

Distinct from 'minister-free zones' is the complete independence of supervision in the case of institutions which, according to the Constitution or Union law, are not part of the administrative hierarchy. For example, the Basic Law guarantees the independence of the *Bundesbank* (Federal Central Bank) and the *Bundesrechnungshof* (Federal Court of Audit). The

European Court of Justice ruled that the federal and state data protection officers in Germany, as in the other EU member states, must become independent bodies and no longer fall within the remit of a ministry (see below). The administrations of the German *Bundestag*, the *Bundesrat* and the Federal Constitutional Court are also independent of supervision in a broader sense. However, they too are subject to oversight by independent courts.

7 CENTRAL SERVICE PROVIDER: FEDERAL OFFICE OF ADMINISTRATION

The Federal Office of Administration (BVA) is a superior federal authority within the remit of the BMI that provides services for all the federal ministries. The law establishing the BVA dates from 1959 and is based on Article 87 (3), first sentence of the Basic Law. The BVA performs special tasks of the federal administration with which it has been entrusted by law or based on a law (e.g. matters related to nationality, resettlement, emigration, German schools abroad and civil servants). It also performs tasks assigned to it by other federal ministries in agreement with the BMI. In these cases, the relevant federal ministries perform expert supervision, while the BMI remains responsible for administrative supervision and organisation. Thanks to its diverse tasks, for years the BVA has viewed itself as the engine of digital transformation in the federal administration (see Ritgen 2019).

8 FROM SUPERIOR FEDERAL AUTHORITY TO SUPREME FEDERAL AUTHORITY: FEDERAL COMMISSIONER FOR DATA PROTECTION AND FREEDOM OF INFORMATION

Outside the remit of the BMI, the Federal Commissioner for Data Protection and Freedom of Information (BfDI) monitors federal bodies' compliance with data protection law. Following its creation in 1978, the federal commissioner's office was located within the BMI until a decision of the European Court of Justice in 2016 called for its independence. Since then, the BfDI answers only to the *Bundestag* and is no longer under the supervision of the Federal Government. In this regard, the BfDI's status is very similar to that of the *Bundesrechnungshof* (see Chap. 12), and it has the task of monitoring and advising the government and parliament. The BfDI must be consulted on proposed legislation relevant to data protection, but he or she has no right of veto even if he or she identifies violations of data protection law. But the entry into force of the EU's General Data Protection Regulation has strengthened the BfDI's position. In practical terms, the BfDI and the data protection commissioners of the *Länder* act as the defenders of citizens' fundamental right to privacy. The European Court of Justice also regards compliance with the General Data Protection Regulation in all the EU Member States as an important task (see Thomé 2018).

9 Lessons Learned

For the federal administration to be effective, it must also be lean. Good relations between supreme and superior federal authorities must be maintained with the help of supervision based on trust and the rule of law. This also applies to functions carried out by bodies under private law, in which case legal supervision and the responsibility of organisation must remain entirely with the Federation. Target instruments do not make appropriate instruments of supervision.

Key future projects of the federal administration are the digital transformation of the administration, IT security and modernisation of the administrative registers (see Chap. 19). With regard to IT security, the Federal Office for Information Security (BSI) was established by law already in 1991 and has steadily expanded since then.

References

Basic Law. Retrieved from https://www.gesetze-im-internet.de/englisch_gg/.

BMI Website. Retrieved from https://www.bmi.bund.de/EN/ministry/ministry-node.html.

Fröhlich, S., Haverkamp, R., & v. der Heide, H.·J., v. Köckritz, S., & Schiffer, E (Eds.). (1997). *Das Bonner Innenministerium*. Bonn: Osang.

Kloepfer, M. (2011). *Verfassungsrecht* (Vol. 1). München: Beck.

Kloepfer, M., & Greve, H. (2018). *Staatsrecht kompakt* (3rd ed.). Baden-Baden: Nomos.

Pieper, S. U. (2006). *Aufsicht: Verfassungs- und verwaltungsrechtliche Strukturanalyse (Völkerrecht, Europarecht, Staatsrecht)*. München: Heymanns.

Ritgen, K. (Ed.). (2019). *Digitalisierung und Arbeit 4.0*. Münster: Freiherr vom Stein Gesellschaft.

Schmidt-Bleibtreu, B., Hofmann, H., & Henneke, H.-G. (2017). *GG— Kommentar zum Grundgesetz* (17th ed.). München: Heymanns.

Thomé, S. (2018). *Reform der Datenschutzaufsicht*. Wiesbaden: Springer Vieweg.
Wolff, H. A. (Ed.). (2018). *Grundgesetz für die Bundesrepublik Deutschland. Handkommentar* (12th ed.). Baden-Baden: Nomos.

Open Access This chapter is licensed under the terms of the Creative Commons Attribution 4.0 International License (http://creativecommons.org/licenses/by/4.0/), which permits use, sharing, adaptation, distribution and reproduction in any medium or format, as long as you give appropriate credit to the original author(s) and the source, provide a link to the Creative Commons licence and indicate if changes were made.

The images or other third party material in this chapter are included in the chapter's Creative Commons licence, unless indicated otherwise in a credit line to the material. If material is not included in the chapter's Creative Commons licence and your intended use is not permitted by statutory regulation or exceeds the permitted use, you will need to obtain permission directly from the copyright holder.

CHAPTER 7

The Peculiarities of the Social Security Systems (Indirect State Administration)

Dieter Schimanke

1 The Welfare State, Its Programmes (Laws) and Entrenchment in Administrative Federalism

Germany is a welfare state. Over the years, it has been shaped by different directions and waves of development. The welfare system is a highly differentiated social system in terms of benefits and therefore target groups, institutions and financing. The welfare state has constitutional status (Article 20 (1) of the Basic Law).

Social policy is characterised by three principles: the public welfare principle, the compensation principle and the insurance principle. Social assistance is the expression of the first principle that entails benefits in situations of personal need, where the individual is not able to care for his or her personal needs without assistance. These are financed through tax revenue. The compensation principle is an expression of the solidarity of the public community as a whole. The benefits are also financed through tax

---

D. Schimanke (✉)
Ministry of Labour, Women, Health, Social Affairs of the German Land
Saxony-Anhalt, Magdeburg, Germany

© The Author(s) 2021　　　　　　　　　　　　　　　　　　91
S. Kuhlmann et al. (eds.), *Public Administration in Germany*,
Governance and Public Management,
https://doi.org/10.1007/978-3-030-53697-8_7

revenue. These include, for example, a benefit to the community with respect to the upbringing of children (child benefit—*Kindergeld*) or sacrifices for the community (e.g. victims of war, violent crimes and vaccination injuries). The third principle, the insurance principle, has the biggest influence over the German welfare state. It finds expression in the five branches of the social insurance system. These have their roots in the early labour movement and in the legislation introduced during the time of Chancellor Bismarck, namely health insurance (1883), occupational accident insurance (1884) and pension insurance (1889). The structure of the organisation and administration as well as the financing were already contained in this legislation. Financing is effected through contributions to the social insurance, which are calculated based on the wages by applying a nonconstant percentage over time (either with contributions from both the employee and employer or, in the case of occupational accident insurance, from the employer[1]). With regard to pension insurance, a considerable part of the financing comes from tax revenue or is subsidized by the federal budget (over the years this has increased to approximately €100 billion or 30% of pension insurance expenditure in 2019; one reason for financing from tax revenues is that services not related to employment but to social policy are included, for example pension benefits for child-rearing periods). In respect of unemployment insurance, the federal government provides liquidity assistance in the form of loans.

The Federal Republic of Germany, as established under the Basic Law of 1949, has continued to build on the historical bases of social policy of the later years of the nineteenth century and the early years of the twentieth century (e.g. unemployment insurance was added in 1927). In recent decades, the state has further developed the substance of the social security systems (e.g. by introducing far-reaching pension reforms, expanding the unemployment insurance system to an active labour market policy and introducing in 1995 long-term care insurance, the so-called fifth pillar of the social insurance system). The various areas of social policy and associated functions are allocated to the three levels of the German administrative system (federal, state and local government level). Alongside there are also independent institutions dealing with social insurance covering the risks of illness, long-term care, old-age (pensions), unemployment and occupational accidents.

All three levels of the administrative system, therefore, have a responsibility in relation to the welfare state and its various programmes (laws). The central level is dominant in the area of legislation, especially on

7 THE PECULIARITIES OF THE SOCIAL SECURITY SYSTEMS... 93

Table 7.1 Contents of the 12 books of the Social Code

Book number	Title and content
Book I	Universal principles and fundamental principles
Book II	Basic income support for job seekers
Book III	Promotion of employment
Book IV	Common regulations for the social insurance systems
Book V	Statutory health insurance
Book VI	Statutory pension insurance
Book VII	Statutory occupational accident insurance
Book VIII	Child and youth welfare
Book IX	Rehabilitation and participation of disabled persons
Book X	Administrative procedures and protection of social data
Book XI	Social long-term care insurance
Book XII	Social assistance and services

account of its role in the codification of social law in the form of Social Codes (*Sozialgesetzbücher*) and in the legal supervision of most of the social insurance institutions. To date, there are 12 Books of the Social Code (*Sozialgesetzbuch*—SGB) covering the aspects shown in Table 7.1.

Book X of the Social Code sets out the basic principles of the administrative procedures. It not only follows the principles of the Administrative Procedures Act (*Verwaltungsverfahrensgesetz*) (cf. Chap. 11), but also contains special rules applicable to the social administrations.

In addition, there is further federal legislation pertaining to benefits, inter alia, for the target groups of trainees, children, victims of war and other so-called sacrificial victims (*Aufopferungen*, e.g. people injured by compulsory vaccination), and recipients of housing benefits. The recently introduced basic income support is codified in two of the social codes mentioned above. The benefits for job seekers are contained in SGB II, and for pensioners and persons unable to work in SGB XII. Basic income support is, at the same time, however, a prime example of administrative federalism: the municipalities execute federal law in respect of pensioners as delegated matters (*übertragene Angelegenheiten*) and in respect of persons with diminished earning capacity as mandated matters (*Auftragsangelegenheiten*) (with the result that the federal government has a direct right of control over the latter). In respect of job seekers, a form of mixed administration between the federal administration (Federal Employment Agency) and the municipalities has been created, which is

94   D. SCHIMANKE

problematic from a constitutional point of view. This situation has been 'healed' by an amendment to the constitution (Article 91e of the Basic Law), but remains an exception in administrative federalism, which is shaped by the principle of having a clear assignment of responsibilities.

Within the administrative system of Germany, the implementation of social policy is broadly in accordance with the above-mentioned three principles in light of the following attributes: the public welfare principle has its main focus on local government; the compensation principle is a distinctive feature of the state administration; and the insurance principle is located mainly at the federal level.

2   AREAS OF SOCIAL BENEFITS AND THEIR ALLOCATION WITHIN THE ADMINISTRATIVE SYSTEM OF GERMANY

The individual areas of social policy and their related expenses are outlined in the social budget (cf. BMAS 2019b). These relate to non-cash benefits (e.g. medicine, vehicle, guide dog) and cash benefits (e.g. child benefit) as well as personal support benefits (e.g. care at home).[2]

Personnel expenditure pertaining to social policy is spread across all public budgets based on the division of responsibilities. The charts pertaining to activities in social administration show a total of 705,600 full-time equivalent (FTE) jobs (including social security providers). This represents 16.7% of all FTE in public administration. As can be gleaned from the summary table of the distribution between the three levels of federal administrative system and the social insurances (Table 7.2), the focus of executory social administration lies with the municipalities and counties (local administration) on the one hand and the social security institutions and agencies on the other.

Table 7.2 Personnel in administrations on social affairs

	FTE (full-time equivalent)
Federal	7225
States	29,180
Local level	342,455
Social insurance systems	326,740
Total	**705,600**

Source: Statistisches Bundesamt (2019) Finanzen und Steuern. Personal des öffentlichen Dienstes 2018. Fachserie 14, Reihe 6, p. 53

Table 7.3 Personnel of social security providers ('indirect public administration', 'near governmental units', *Parafisci*)

Function	FTE (full-time equivalent)
Health insurance	126,680
Occupational accident insurance	22,705
Pension insurance	53,445
Other organisations	7950 (with rounding differences)
Union of miners' insurance and social insurance for the agricultural sector	14,740
Federal Employment Agency	101,225
Total	326,740

Note: The numbers are taken from this publication of the Federal Agency of Statistics. For the category 'Other organisations' the following explanation is given: sums might not fit due to rounding differences caused by security reasons

Source: Statistisches Bundesamt (2019) Finanzen und Steuern. Personal des öffentlichen Dienstes 2018. Fachserie 14, Reihe 6, p. 74

The social security providers are independent public institutions and agencies alongside the administrations at the federal, state and local levels. They employ their own personnel, which is shown separately in the statistics (Tables 7.2 and 7.3). The budgets are separate and are also different to the budgets of the three territorial authorities (*Gebietskörperschaften*). Consequently, the social security providers are also labelled 'indirect public administration' (*mittelbare Staatsverwaltung*) or 'near governmental units' (*Parafisci*). Their independence is evidenced by their special legal status (corporate body subject to public law (*Körperschaft des öffentlichen Rechts*), Section 29 (1) SGB IV). Corporate body means that they have members (the insured individuals and the employers) and legal capacity, which means that they can enforce their rights through the courts (e.g. against measures of government supervision) and can be sued themselves (e.g. by the insured in respect of benefits). The limits to state supervision and control (see part 3 below) are also interconnected with this semi-autonomous status.

Compared to an expenditure budget of €634.5 billion (Table 7.4: total of sections 1 and 2), the number of contingent personnel in the social insurance systems amounting to 326,740 FTE, or 7.9% of all persons employed in the public service, is relatively small. This is because the different institutions of the social security systems mainly provide financial transfers as routine cases of mass administration. The share of the expenditure budgets of the social insurance systems in relation to the

Table 7.4 Social budget 2018—benefits by institutions

Social budget 2018	1991	2000	2010	2015	2016	2017p	2018s
	million Euro						
Social budget total	**395,601**	**608,516**	**771,452**	**889,688**	**929,824**	**965,332**	**995,986**
1. Social security systems	**252,674**	**396,711**	**471,227**	**534,066**	**554,325**	**579,547**	**598,811**
1.1 Pension insurance	133,180	217,429	253,742	282,524	293,326	304,112	313,078
1.2 Health insurance	92,682	132,079	173,879	211,874	220,553	228,321	237,384
1.3 Long-term care insurance	–	16,668	21,483	27,941	29,576	37,436	39,782
1.4 Accident insurance	7640	10,834	12,060	12,871	13,339	13,605	13,861
1.5 Unemployment insurance	35,640	49,695	36,171	27,368	26,732	26,670	26,392
2. Special schemes	**3568**	**5735**	**27,885**	**33,024**	**34,026**	**35,176**	**35,654**
2.1 Old age insurance for farmers	2457	3270	2945	2767	2711	2808	2703
2.2 Pension funds for certain professions	1111	1958	4323	5647	5974	6398	6521
2.3 Private old age insurance	–	–	160	390	450	510	570
2.4 Private health insurance	–	–	19,654	23,108	23,684	24,051	24,363
2.5 Private long-term care insurance	–	507	804	1113	1207	1409	1497
3. Public administration schemes	**35,636**	**51,667**	**60,006**	**71,492**	**74,355**	**77,494**	**80,802**
3.1 Pensions	23,309	34,937	43,839	52,862	55,177	57,679	60,271
3.2 Family allowance	5866	7084	3254	3828	3928	4041	4168
3.3 Financial assistance	6461	9646	12,914	14,802	15,250	15,775	16,363
4. Employer schemes	**41,912**	**53,132**	**68,001**	**86,487**	**91,202**	**93,665**	**97,109**
4.1 Continued remuneration	23,441	27,246	32,494	46,246	49,806	51,521	53,981
4.2 Company pension scheme	11,213	16,609	23,600	27,090	27,826	28,208	28,328
4.3 Supplementary benefits	5960	8193	10,691	11,894	12,313	12,677	13,541
4.4 Other benefits by employers	1299	1084	1216	1256	1257	1258	1260
5. Compensation schemes	**8736**	**6441**	**3188**	**2625**	**2555**	**2466**	**2398**
5.1 Social compensation	6496	4471	1929	1085	965	866	788
5.2 Equalisation of burdens	477	133	31	14	12	11	9

5.3 Reparations	973	1204	893	1075	1136	1117	1092
5.4 Other compensations	790	633	330	451	442	472	510
6. Support and welfare schemes	**55,566**	**100,252**	**149,007**	**168,765**	**180,059**	**184,312**	**188,357**
6.1 Child benefits and family allowance system	10,435	33,143	41,955	43,130	44,166	45,288	46,227
6.2 Child benefit / Parental allowance	3232	3732	4778	6817	6740	6841	7272
6.3 Subsistence income for job seekers	–	–	46,375	42,151	42,684	45,020	44,025
6.4 Unemployment benefit other employment promotion	9042	15,094	552	677	728	841	1020
6.5 Vocational training and upgrading training assistance	1326	875	2186	2369	2237	2378	2215
6.6 Social welfare	18,103	25,763	25,606	36,587	42,036	39,199	39,934
6.7 Child and youth welfare	10,900	17,328	25,648	36,296	40,227	43,517	46,532
6.8 Housing benefit.	2527	4315	1908	737	1242	1228	1132
For information:							
Tax benefits without family allowance system	*27,180*	*38,064*	*30,141*	*28,878*	*29,297*	*29,609*	*30,368*

Institutions without set off. Social budget total and social insurance systems consolidated with contributions by the state Data as at May 2019

p provisional, *s* estimated

Source: Sozialbudget (BMAS 2019b: 9)

expenditure of all public budgets is rather high with 43.3% (see Chap. 14, Table 12.1: €648 billion out of €1429 billion).

If one takes the extent of the individual benefits and the budgets as a basis, the social insurances are dominant in the policy and administrative areas of social benefits. The expenditure of the social insurances amounts to approximately two-thirds of the entire social budget (cf. Table 7.4).

The social budget share of gross domestic product (GDP) is 29.4% (of which the social insurance systems, with a share of 17.7% of GDP, cover approximately two-thirds; cf. Sozialbudget 2018: 12). The social budget covers about 45% of the expenditure of all public budgets. The funding comprises of 34.5% social security contributions by the employers, 30.9% social security contributions by the insured and 33% subsidies by the state (Fig. 7.1).

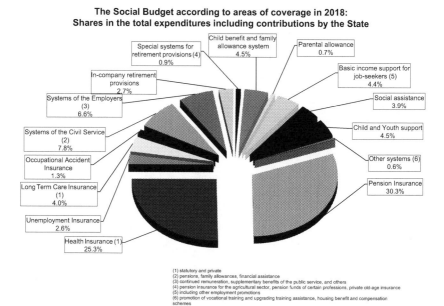

Fig. 7.1 The social budget according to the branches of social security (including the five branches of the social security system: illness, occupational accident, personal care, unemployment, pension). Pension insurance: 30.3%, health insurance: 25.3%, long-term care insurance: 4.0%, systems of civil service: 7.8%,

3 The Special Status of the Social Security Systems and Their Relationship to the General Administrative System

3.1 The Legal Bases of the Public Institutions in the Social Security Systems

The social security institutions and agencies have been established as independent bodies alongside general public administration. They are granted by law the status of public corporate body with legal capacity and the right to self-administration (*rechtsfähige öffentliche Körperschaft mit Selbstverwaltungscharakter*) (Section 29 SGB IV). The regulatory framework for organisation, finances, human resource management, decision-taking, etc. is based on federal laws, on the one hand, (mainly on SGB IV) and ordinances, which are passed by the committees of the social security institutions and agencies, on the other. The supervisory authority (*Aufsichtsbehörde*) has to either approve these ordinances (cf. Section 195 SGB V) or raise objections if they are inconsistent with the applicable laws. The representative committee (governing board—*Vertreterversammlung*) is elected every six years by the members (i.e. usually the insured individuals and the employers). An exception is the unemployment insurance. In this regard, the Federal Ministry for Labour and Social Affairs appoints the members of the governing board pursuant to nominations from the employers' associations and trade unions as well as from the federal government, states and municipalities. The representative committee

---

Fig. 7.1 in-company retirement provisions: 2.7%, child benefit and family allowance system: 4.5%, basic income support for job seekers: 4.4%, child and youth support: 4.5%, unemployment insurance: 2.6%, occupational accident insurance: 1.3%, systems of the employers: 6.6%, special systems for retirement provisions: 0.9%, parental allowance: 0.7%, social assistance: 3.9%, other systems: 0.6%. (1) Statutory and private, (2) pensions, family allowances, financial assistance, (3) continued remuneration, supplementary benefits of the public service and others, (4) pension insurance for the agricultural sector, pension funds of certain professions, private old-age insurance, (5) including other employment promotions, (6) promotion of vocational training and upgrading training assistance, housing benefit and compensation schemes. (Source: Sozialbudget 2018 (BMAS 2019b): 6) (governing board) elects the executive board. The executive board does not need to be confirmed by a public authority (with the exception that the executive board of the Federal Employment Agency (*Verwaltungsrat*) is appointed by the federal government, based on the recommendation of the governing board).

The bodies of the social security systems draw up yearly budgets. In this regard, the budget principles are similar to those set out in the federal budget code (budget code; see Chap. 14) and in the social code (Section 67ff. SGB IV). The supervisory authority may request the budget and can object to it if it is in contravention of legal requirements. The unemployment insurance and the miners' pension insurance budgets require the approval of the responsible federal ministry since the federal government is liable as guarantor. In respect of the general pension insurance at the federal level, the liquidity assistance provided by the federal government only leads to an obligation to advise on the budget. An approval by the federal government is not required.

The way elections are structured, the creation of programmes (by way of ordinances) and the restrictive rules in respect of the budgets differ greatly from the scope of autonomy characteristic of local self-government with direct elections by the citizens and broad areas of autonomous decision-making (see Chap. 9). This is because almost all the benefits provided by the social insurances are regulated by federal laws and manifest as legal rights of the insured (Section 38 SGB I)—with only very limited discretion on the part of self-government (cf. Reit 2015). The institutions are formed by representatives elected by employers and insured individuals. In this regard, this form of self-government can also be characterised as a special type of self-government with autonomous legitimation and restricted scope for decision-making (cf. Schimanke 2001). Their origin lies in the pre-democratic time of the Bismarck era and aimed at promoting social stability by involving employees and employers directly in the internal decision-making structures. The social security systems are now incorporated into the fundamental principles and the constitutional framework of the Basic Law (Article 74 (1), number 12; Article 87 [2]).

3.2   Oversight of the Social Security Systems

The social security institutions and agencies are independent bodies yet part of public administration ('indirect public administration', 'near governmental units'). They are bound by the laws and are required to

7 THE PECULIARITIES OF THE SOCIAL SECURITY SYSTEMS... 101

implement them. The federal and state governments have to ensure that the social security systems implement legislation and work within the legal framework. Government oversight extends to ensuring that legislation and other laws are observed (Section 87 (1) SGB IV and Section 393 (1) SGB III) and, thus, is limited to legal supervision (cf. Chap. 6). However, in exceptional cases related to the so-called delegated tasks (*übertragene Aufgaben*), the oversight extends beyond examining the legality of measures to expert supervision (*Fachaufsicht*), which means that in these cases administrative expediency can also be evaluated. Examples in this regard are prevention tasks for occupational accident insurance or the family benefits offices (*Familienkassen*) of the Federal Employment Agency (execution of the Law on Child Benefits).

The structure and responsibilities of the supervisory authorities reflect the features of administrative federalism (cf. Section 90 SGB IV). As a rule, the states have supervisory authority over the social security systems, which is limited to the area of one state (up to 3 states when they agree on supervision, cf. Article 87 (2), sentence 2 of the Basic Law). This mainly applies to regional health insurers, occupational accident insurers and the regional authorities of pension insurance. Usually, the state ministries of social affairs carry out the supervision; some states have tasked their own government agencies with this. In the vast majority of cases, the oversight function is vested in the Federal Government and is carried out either by the ministry responsible (usually the Federal Ministry for Labour and Social Affairs) or its subordinate, the Federal Office for Social Security. The supervisory authorities meet regularly to exchange experiences (Section 90 paragraph 4 SGB IV). This practical approach has brought about the expansion of administrative federalism to very intensive networks.

The legal supervision by government agencies is the expression of a legitimate interest of the state and its responsibility to ensure that institutions and social security benefits comply with legal requirements (cf. Beschorner 2015; Kahl 2013: 514). In this regard, the independent status as a corporate body subject to public law with right to self-government (*Körperschaft des öffentlichen Rechts mit Selbstverwaltung*) has to be taken into account. It follows that legal supervision, when choosing supervisory means, has to be mindful of the leeway afforded by legislation (especially in form of the so-called scope for appreciation (*unbestimmter Rechtsbegriff*) and discretion (see Chap. 12); internal organisation and budgets). The principle of the least invasive interference applies—as codified in Section

89 SGB IV—ultimately an expression of the rule of law principle (*Ausdruck des Rechtsstaatsprinzips*) (see Chap. 2). The Federal Social Court upholds that a decision, which is justifiable, should not be objected to. Oversight can be pre-emptive or repressive. Consultation applies in the first place. Once a violation of law becomes evident, an objection will be raised with the requirement to remedy such violation within a certain period of time. It is only then that an administrative decision obligating compliance (*Verpflichtungsbescheid*) is issued against the social security system in question. This administrative decision constitutes an exercise of discretion by the oversight authority. The latter can uphold the decision (e.g. declare invalid an election or budget) as soon as it becomes legally binding. Since the social security systems are corporate bodies with legal capacity, they can take legal action before the social courts against the administrative decisions of the legal supervision.

4   Lessons Learned

It may be advisable to develop a policy field with broader scope in the structured (federative) administrative system that is independent or semi-autonomous of the constitutional point of view and thus unburdens the state and the general administration. General public administration will be unburdened by operational functions. The social security institutions and agencies have a vested right to decide for themselves on ordinances, personnel and budgets (so-called functional self-government). The state, via legal supervision, has the task and opportunity to monitor compliance with legal requirements. The system of semi-independent authorities responsible for social security benefits does not insignificantly contribute to the fact that the institutions of the public sector are accepted and legitimised.

Notes

1. Employers have the significant advantage that occupational accident insurances (mainly named 'Berufsgenossenschaft'/employers mutual insurance association) assume the liability of the employers in cases of occupational accidents. Moreover, for several decades now the occupational accident insurances also cover the claims of voluntary services.
2. A detailed survey is published by the Federal Ministry of Labour and Social Affairs: BMAS 2019a. https://www.bmas.de/SharedDocs/Downloads/DE/PDF-Publikationen/a998-social-security-at-a-glance-total-summary.pdf?__blob=publicationFile&v=9.

References

Beschorner, J. (2015). Staatsaufsicht über Sozialversicherungsträger. In L. Mülheims, K. Hummel, S. Peters-Lange, E. Toepler, & I. Schumann (Eds.), *Handbuch Sozialversicherungswissenschaft* (pp. 777–798). Wiesbaden: Springer.

Federal Ministry of Labour and Social Affairs (BMAS) (Ed.). (2019a). Devision KS 3. *Social Security at a Glance 2019.* Bonn.

Federal Ministry of Labour and Social Affairs (BMAS) (Ed.). (2019b). *Sozialbudget 2018.* Bonn. Retrieved from https://www.bmas.de/SharedDocs/Downloads/DE/PDF-Publikationen/a230-18-sozialbudget-2018.pdf?__blob=publicationFile&v=2.

Kahl, W. (2013). Begriff, Funktionen und Konzepte von Kontrolle. In W. Hoffmann-Riem, E. Schmidt-Aßmann, & A. Voßkuhle (Eds.), *Grundlagen des Verwaltungsrechts* (Vol. III, 2nd ed., pp. 459–591). München: Beck.

Reit, N.-A. (2015). Rechtliche Determinanten der Selbstverwaltung in der Sozialversicherung. In L. Mülheims, K. Hummel, S. Peters-Lange, E. Toepler, & I. Schumann (Eds.), *Handbuch Sozialversicherungswissenschaft* (pp. 763–776). Wiesbaden: Springer.

Schimanke, D. (2001). Self-Administration Outside Local Government—With Special Reference to Self-Administration in the Field of Social Insurance. In K. König & H. Siedentopf (Eds.), *Public Administration in Germany* (pp. 215–226). Baden-Baden: Nomos.

Open Access This chapter is licensed under the terms of the Creative Commons Attribution 4.0 International License (http://creativecommons.org/licenses/by/4.0/), which permits use, sharing, adaptation, distribution and reproduction in any medium or format, as long as you give appropriate credit to the original author(s) and the source, provide a link to the Creative Commons licence and indicate if changes were made.

The images or other third party material in this chapter are included in the chapter's Creative Commons licence, unless indicated otherwise in a credit line to the material. If material is not included in the chapter's Creative Commons licence and your intended use is not permitted by statutory regulation or exceeds the permitted use, you will need to obtain permission directly from the copyright holder.

CHAPTER 8

The Administration of the *Länder*

Ludger Schrapper

1   Administrations of the *Länder* (Federal States) in the System of German Federalism

The German federal constitution or Basic Law (*Grundgesetz*) shapes the relationship between state and federal government in the exercise of state functions in the sense of a rule-exception relationship. Article 30 of the Basic Law reads: 'The exercise of state powers and the fulfilment of state responsibilities is a matter for the *Länder*, unless this *Grundgesetz* does not provide or permit otherwise'. Historically, this rule-exception relationship is based on the fact that the *Länder* legally created the federal power in 1949, not the other way around. In apparent contrast to this, the Basic Law, especially in the area of law enforcement (execution of the law), constitutes a strong interdependence of the federal levels. According to Article 83 of the Basic Law, federal laws are, in principle, not executed by the federal administration but by the state administrations. As a rule,

---

Rule in everyday life is administration. (Max Weber)

L. Schrapper (✉)
Ministry of School and Education of the Land North Rhine-Westphalia,
Düsseldorf, Germany
e-mail: ludger.schrapper@msb.nrw.de

© The Author(s) 2021   105
S. Kuhlmann et al. (eds.), *Public Administration in Germany*,
Governance and Public Management,
https://doi.org/10.1007/978-3-030-53697-8_8

execution is carried out by the *Länder* 'on their own behalf', that is, in principle, free from tight controls and regulating administrative supervision by the federal government. However, the level of control needs to be distinguished. In the execution of federal laws according to Article 84 of the Basic Law, the federal government—with a few exceptions—is only entitled to ensure laws executed by the *Länder* are in accordance with the law. Where the execution is 'by order' of the federal government according to Article 85 of the Basic Law, the federal government is only entitled to ensure the appropriateness of execution per Article 85 (4) and—with certain restrictions—issue individual instructions. As an exception to the provisions of Articles 83, 86 and 87 of the Basic Law, the federal administration assigns enforcement powers to the Federation and thus it has the power to establish its own law enforcement agencies, notably the foreign service and authorities for the waterways and shipping, border police and intelligence service. The main agencies at the federal level are the Federal Employment Agency and the social insurance institutions.

The enforcement of the federal laws thus described is carried out at the *Länder* level by administrative bodies (direct state administration) and, above all, by the municipal administrations. It is estimated that around 80 percent of all public tasks are carried out at the municipal level (Grunow 2003). From the federal point of view, however, the direct administrations of the *Länder* and the municipalities are a unit. This is also made clear in Article 84 (1), seventh sentence of the Basic Law: 'By federal law tasks may not be transferred to municipalities and municipal associations'.

Taking the special form of German federalism, the strong position of the *Länder* executive is justified in relation to both the federal administration and the internal relationship with the local legislature. In contrast to the so-called senate model with more political representation by the federal states, such as in the United States or Switzerland, according to the Basic Law, the *Bundesrat* (Federal Council) is the representative body of the *Länder* governments. Thus, participation in federal legislation becomes a task of their executive, depending solely on their decision-making. The classification of this system, known as 'executive federalism' (Münch 2002) or 'administrative federalism' (Grunow 2003), is correct (cf. also Kuhlmann and Wollmann 2019), although the political dimension of participation in the *Bundesrat* against the background of the different (party) political majorities and, thus, political-ideological orientations of the *Länder* governments plays a major role.

Another important field of *Länder* cooperation induced by federalism is the permanent structure of so-called minister conferences, the oldest of which, the *Kultusminister Konferenz* (the Standing Conference of the Ministers of Education and Cultural Affairs), was established in 1948. The heads of the different ministries hold their coordination meetings twice a year, and the chair changes annually. Below the top level, a substructure of permanent working parties prepares the issues together with a close network of *Länder* officials.

A comparison of the staffing levels of federal and *Länder* administrations reflects the above-described central role of *Länder* administrations and their municipalities in law enforcement in the federal system. Around 656,000 federal civil servants work in the public sector (excluding military personnel) compared to more than 3.4 million employees (as of 2017) in both *Länder* and local government. On the other hand, at the federal level, the proportion of employees in the areas of political management and central administration is disproportionately high at 21,000. In addition, 15.7 percent (3300 employees) of the functions are top functions in the so-called grade B (salary range from €95,000 to €180,000). At the level of the *Länder* administrations, this compares with only about 60,000 employees in these areas, including top jobs of 7.1 percent (4300 excluding municipalities). By far the largest proportion of employees in the *Länder* civil service is in education (schools and universities) with around 1,168,800 staff (56 percent), followed by 234,000 officers (11 percent) in the 16 *Länder* police forces (compared to 40,600 federal police).

2 Basic Conditions for the Administrative Organisation

In attempting to depict a comparison of the administrations of the German *Länder*, the following conclusion can be drawn: the considerable heterogeneity of the baseline conditions, such as size of the area, the number of inhabitants, the economic or the topographical structure—despite all the differences in terminology and details—is the opposite of a relative homogeneity of administrative structures. This was—and still is—based on the influencing power of the Prussian administrative traditions, which live on in particular through the nationwide, almost standardised, training of civil servants and comparable career patterns. Nevertheless, it cannot be denied that a *Land* like North Rhine-Westphalia with a population of 17.9 million needs, at least partially, different administrative structures to Mecklenburg-Western Pomerania with only 1.6 million inhabitants or

Saarland with 0.99 million. Therefore, almost all of the large territorial states of the Federal Republic have a three-tier system compared with the states of Brandenburg, Mecklenburg-Western Pomerania, Schleswig-Holstein and Saarland, whose administrative structure is organised in two tiers. Niedersachsen (Lower Saxony) is a special case, having abolished its regional middle level, contrary to a long tradition, in 2005. Significant deviations in the administrative structure also result from the distinction between the German so-called territorial states and city-states, which—for Hamburg and Bremen—can only be explained by a long-standing tradition rooted in the Middle Ages. In the case of Berlin, its special status after the end of the Second World War as a territory under the responsibility of all four occupying powers has not changed. In the city-states, state and municipal affairs are carried out by a single administration. In Berlin and Hamburg, due to the size of the cities, with the so-called district administrations in Berlin and the urban district office (*Ortsamt*) in Bremen, there is an additional inner-city administrative level. The city of Bremerhaven is also part of the city-state of Bremen. In addition, in city-states, public authorities are set up as independent bodies of public administration, which can be described as indirect *Länder* administration.

3 Basic Structures of the Administrations of the *Länder*

The State Organisation Acts of the Länder (*Landesorganisationsgesetze—LOG*) classify their subjects as legal persons (legal entities). Like natural persons, they have a fundamental legal capacity in the sense of a broad legal capacity to act in all areas of law. In the field of public law, there are three basic types: corporation (*Körperschaft*), institution (*Anstalt*) and foundation (*Stiftung*). The federal and *Länder* governments are categorised as territorial communities (*Gebietskörperschaft*), that is, associations of all people residing in a demarcated area. Legal persons act through their bodies (*Organe*), which are legally constituted units with defined powers. At the top level of the state organisation, these are for the *Länder* the parliament, the *Länder* government as the head of the executive branch and the bodies of the judiciary. Within the executive branch, the authority (*Behörde*) is the standard type of body.

The *Länder* can have their executive tasks performed by their own bodies (authorities). One speaks then of direct *Land* administration. However, they can also transfer certain tasks to independent legal entities, most of which are municipalities. These bodies of the indirect *Land* administration set up their own budgets and have their own staff.

3.1 Direct Land Administration

Where the *Länder* directly execute law and carry out other executive tasks, they act through the authorities and other forms of organisation of the direct state administration. The regulation of the administrative structure is usually reserved for the legislator (cf. Article 77, fourth sentence, *Land* constitution of North Rhine-Westphalia). The establishment of individual organisational units (e.g. authorities) is again a matter of self-organisation of the executive.

3.1.1 Upper Administrative Level

Beyond the question of whether the direct administration of the *Länder* is structured in two or three tiers (see below), the highest executive level, as in the federal administration, is formed by different ministries, such as the Ministry of Finance and the Ministry of Education and Research. Organisationally, they fall into the category of the highest *Länder* authorities. The appointment of ministers and, thus, the determination of the number of ministries as well as the technical competencies are the responsibility of the minister president of the respective *Land*, who, as head of government, has been given this power. Instead of a federal chancellery, he has a so-called state chancellery (in some *Länder* a ministry of state), which handles the administrative coordination of the other ministries. In the city-states, the heads of state have the title of 'mayor' following the urban tradition, and the *Land* governments are referred to as the 'senate'. In work and function, there are far-reaching parallels between the ministerial administrations of the federation and those of the *Länder*. Central tasks include the drafting of legislation and the political-technical control (supervision) of the subordinate administration. The organisational structure is based predominantly on a so-called line organisation and, according to the German administration tradition, with few personnel in staff functions. In the direction of their ministries, the ministers are supported as political representatives by one—rarely several—state secretary with civil servant status (permanent secretaries). They are so-called political officials and—as an exception to the civil service guarantee of permanent employment status—can be relieved of their duties at any time and put into temporary retirement if compliance with the political principles of the respective *Land* government is no longer guaranteed. The basic organisational units of the state ministries—again parallel to the federal administration—are the units, which are bundled into departments and, in larger state administrations such as North Rhine-Westphalia, additionally subdivided into sub-departments (groups). Unlike the federal government, the department heads are generally not political officials in the legal sense just described.

With regard to the size relation of ministries as the uppermost administrative level to the respective overall administration, the ministerial administration of the *Länder* is rather disproportionate in comparison to the Federation. An indicator may be the number of top officials in grades B2–B11. The functions from the first management level (head of unit) up to the head of department are assigned these grades throughout. Here, there are approximately 3300 top civil servants in the federal service with an approximate total of 328,000 employees (excluding military personnel) compared with only around 4300 top officials in the *Länder* services with a total of approximately 2,378,000 non-municipal employees. This is due, on the one hand, to the lack of 'big' ministries, such as defence and foreign affairs, in the area of the *Länder*. Above all, however, the much stronger orientation of the administrations of the *Länder* towards actual administration is evident here. This is particularly noticeable in the area of school education. For example, in North Rhine-Westphalia, the ratio of supervisory ministerial administration to the total body of staff in the area of school education is 1:500.

In addition to the ministries as the highest state authorities, under the state organisation acts, each *Land* has a higher state authority (*Obere Landesbehörde*). These bodies are directly subordinate to the ministries and do not assume any political leadership tasks, but instead sector-specific tasks that require special expertise. They belong to the upper level of the administrative structure because their territorial jurisdiction covers the entire state territory. As a rule—at least in three-tiered state administrations—they do not have their own administrative base, but in certain cases have supervisory powers over the middle- or lower-level authorities. A typical upper state authority is the state criminal police office with coordination functions as regards combatting crime and special forensic expertise. The same applies to the state environmental agencies with special advisory skills and laboratory capacities. Also worthy of mention are the personnel and pension offices which manage the salaries and pensions of active and former state employees.

The so-called *Landesbetriebe* (state enterprises) have a similar function to the upper *Land* authorities. As an organisational type, they are a consequence of the theories of New Public Management (NPM) and have had an impact on the administrative organisation since the beginning of the 2000s. They are responsible for providing the administration with marketable services. With regard to their product range they are therefore competing with private enterprises, but in some cases are nevertheless entitled to establish for other public authorities of the state administration an obligation to 'buy' their services. The obligation to draw up a business plan, and also to account according to commercial law, is designed to create cost transparency. In state-owned enterprises, for example, the *Länder* are responsible for organising the administration of their real estate or for all tasks relating to road construction and maintenance. More recently, the necessary IT services have been provided by state-owned enterprises.

Finally, as administrative organisations with *Land*-wide competence, the *Einrichtungen* (institutions) should be mentioned. In contrast to state authorities, they perform public tasks in the internal relationship of the administration. These may be tasks in the field of staff training as provided by the administrative colleges of the *Länder*. Typical state institutions also include public archives or institutes charged with development of school-specific programmes or with scientific-technical specialised tasks.

3.1.2 Regional Meso Level

Below the level of the ministerial administration, it is possible to differentiate between two structural models according to whether there is a regionally located central authority between the state level and the municipal level. With the exception of the state of Lower Saxony, all large and populous German states have a meso-level administrative district. It coordinates the various actors at the local level in their district and, moreover, directly performs those administrative tasks which require a certain concentration of technical or legal expertise. The traditional rule type of a regional mid-authority is the administrative district authority, which is also called the *Bezirksregierung* (regional government) or *Regierungspräsidium* (Regional Commissioner's Office). It draws on the Prussian administrative tradition of the early nineteenth century and is characterised by a bundling—and thus coordination—of numerous administrative tasks in one authority. In terms of supervision, a 'general representation of the state government' is established for the various regions of the *Land* (cf. Article 8 (1) of the State Organisation Act (*Landesorganisationsgesetz*—LOG) of North Rhine-Westphalia, NRW). The bundling authority avoids the establishment of special administrations ranging from the highest department (ministry) down to the local level, which bring with them the dangers of a technical-mental 'pillarisation', a hampered reconciliation of interests by deficient communication structures and a lack of regional networking (Schrapper 1994; Bogumil and Ebinger 2008). Because of the bundling effects described above, the organisational model is also described as the concentrated three-stage principle (Bogumil 2007; Reiners 2010). Despite their mature organisational development, the administrative district authorities have been the subject of structural reforms like almost no other area of state administration (cf. Chap. 16).

The structuring in administrative districts with the *Bezirksregierung* as administrative body can be found in North Rhine-Westphalia, Bavaria, Baden-Württemberg and Hesse. The population in these districts varies from over 1 million in the more rural areas of Bavaria (Upper Palatinate, Upper Franconia and Lower Bavaria) to 5.3 million in the conurbation Rhine/Ruhr in North Rhine-Westphalia (Düsseldorf and Cologne). The tasks are defined by the categories of 'order' (e.g. traffic and air supervision, disaster control, building supervision and food supervision), 'allowance' (e.g. support programmes for economic policy, urban planning, culture and sport), 'approval' (environmental and occupational safety, goods and passenger transport) and 'regional planning' (Bogumil 2007). In addition, the administrative district authorities are usually responsible for the legal and financial supervision of local authorities. Worth mentioning is the subsidiary competence of the district governments for all state administration tasks that are not explicitly assigned to other authorities (cf. Section 8 (3) LOG NRW). In view of new short-term enforcement tasks emerging (e.g. in the field of genetic engineering), this subsidiary role has repeatedly proven its necessity.

In addition to the traditional concept of the concentrated three-stage principle described above, hybrids of the model of the regional bundling authority can be found in the states of Rhineland-Palatinate and in the three (East) German ('new') *Länder* of Saxony, Saxony-Anhalt and Thuringia. In 2000, Rhineland-Palatinate bundled together its three intermediate authorities (the administrative districts of Koblenz, Neustadt and Trier) not only regionally, but also functionally. This was done due to their small size, which is slightly below average in comparison with the

Federation (e.g. the Trier district has 500,000 inhabitants). The authorities were reorganised and replaced by the Supervision and Services Directorate and two Structural and Approval Directorates. In fact, the directorates act in part as bundling authorities because they are anchored in the structure of the state administration, that is, only sectorally. After German unification in 1990, the (East) German *Land* of Thuringia decided directly for a state-wide concentrated intermediate level with a so-called State Administration Office as 'functional equivalent' (Bogumil and Ebinger 2008), whereas Saxony and Saxony-Anhalt have since gone through dissolving their earlier established administrative districts (cf. Chap. 16).

The *Länder* of Brandenburg, Mecklenburg-Western Pomerania, Saarland and Schleswig-Holstein completely dispense with a middle level of the state administration. At least in terms of number of inhabitants, they belong to the smallest territorial states. The typical functions of a regional administrative level are not required against the background of a municipal area structure with a clearly below average number of rural and urban districts (districts and independent cities). This is particularly evident in the state of Mecklenburg-Western Pomerania, which has taken several reform steps to divide its territory into only six large so-called *Kreise* (counties) and two county-free cities (Rostock and Schwerin). The representation of municipal administration in the area is expected to reach its limits here. In contrast to this, despite its considerable size, the state of Brandenburg also has a two-tier administrative structure with as many as 14 counties and 4 county-free cities. Here, the need for a coordinating intermediate or regional administrative level cannot be completely ruled out.

3.1.3 Lower State Authorities

The fulfilment of public tasks by the administration at the local or regional-local level takes place within a dual administrative structure. A distinction needs to be made between state-owned 'lower' authorities, which are subordinate to the service and technical supervision of a state intermediate authority, or, more rarely, to an upper or even to the highest state authority. The vast majority of public duties, on the other hand, are performed by the municipal authorities as indirect state administration (see above). This is due to their constitutional special status described above, according to which—from a federal law perspective—they are part of the state administration, but also have a right guaranteed by the federal constitution to self-govern their own affairs, that is, those of the local community. In this area, the municipal authorities are only subject to legal supervision of the *Land*. As a third category of public tasks, in addition to the original state tasks (e.g. police or financial administration) and 'own affairs', those tasks are to be mentioned where the *Länder* reserve a broader supervisory right, which includes the expediency of task fulfilment.

In this case, a distinction is made between the different municipal traditions of the *Länder* according to whether these 'transferred' tasks (dualistic model), insofar as legally dogmatic, are comparable to the so-called Order Management laid down in Article 85 of the Basic Law or whether a monistic model is used, according to which municipal authorities basically only perform municipal tasks, which in certain cases, especially in the area of security, are legally defined as so-called 'compulsory tasks to be performed according to instructions' and thus subject to greater control.

The difference described above will result in direct consequences for the organisation of the authorities. In the dualistic model with the legal concept of the so-called delegated *Wirkungskreis* (realm of influence), the tasks performed by certain local authorities (*Landräte*—county administrators, and *Oberbürgermeister*—lord mayors) retain their state character; they remain *Land* tasks. As a result, the bodies of the counties and city districts act as 'lower land administrative authorities' (cf. Section 8 (1) LOG Brandenburg: 'General lower *Land* authorities are the county administrators and lord mayors'). Here they are subject to unrestricted specialist supervision by the upper and intermediate *Land* authorities and not only to legal supervision, as in their 'own affairs'. In addition, there are some requirements of the *Land* for the authorities.

The concept of the delegated realm of influence can be found mainly in the southern and eastern German states, whereas for north-western Germany, especially North Rhine-Westphalia, the monistic task concept is relevant. This, in turn, requires an organisational differentiation according to whether public tasks can be performed as municipal mandatory tasks (according to instructions) or whether they are originally federal tasks that require comprehensive control powers of intermediate or upper *Land* authorities (usually in the field of internal security and disaster control). In these cases, the superior authorities can access the administrative head of a county (*Landrat*—county administrator) or, in some cases that of a county-free city (*Oberbürgermeister*—lord mayor), who is then fully subject to the authority of the higher authorities, in this sense 'borrowed administration'. Legally, the district administrator (or the lord mayor) acts as the 'lower state administrative authority'.

The state-owned lower authorities are part of the direct state administration. In the majority of *Länder* these are typically the tax offices; in *Länder* with delegated realm of influence, these are the police service agencies or the school inspectorate. The tasks performed have a clear, definable territorial reference and therefore justify the establishment of locally based units.

3.2 *Indirect* Land *Government*

As a matter of principle, according to their own degree of state autonomy, the *Länder* decide to what extent they delegate the execution of public tasks to independent agencies. However, there is a significant exception here. In the case of local or municipal authorities (counties and cities), Article 28 (2) of the Basic Law as federal constitution already guarantees their right to 'regulate all matters of the local community on their own responsibility within the limits prescribed by the law'. However, the qualification of a public task as a 'local matter' is neither selectively changeable nor unchangeable for *Länder* legislation over time because the local references of a matter can change with its social, economic or technical framework (Federal Constitutional Court 2014). But the legislator has to observe a vital core area of self-government and even a 'priority of jurisdiction' of the local authorities (cf. Ruge, Chap. 5).

Other important representatives of the indirect state administration are the universities, which employ 22 percent of the *Länder* personnel. This applies regardless of their affiliation to a territorial state or city-state. Their status, unlike that of a local authority, is not constitutionally anchored. The provisions of freedom of scholarship under Article 5 (3) of the Basic Law define this as such. Also worth mentioning are the self-governing institutions of professional bodies such as the chambers of industry and commerce as well as the chambers of crafts and chambers of the 'liberal professions', such as lawyers, auditors, doctors and so on. In addition to the management of their own affairs, individual state tasks for execution are also delegated to them.

4   PERSONNEL STRUCTURE
AND ADMINISTRATIVE CULTURE

As mentioned at the outset, the central role of the *Länder* in executing law in the federal system is reflected in the size of their administrative staff. As already stated, a distinction must be made between the bodies of direct and indirect state administration, in particular local authorities (counties and cities).

Of the already mentioned more than 3.4 million employees (as of 2017) in these areas, 2,387,000 employees and thus 50.1 percent of the total civil service in Germany (4,179,000, including social security and military personnel) account for the direct state administration. This mainly reflects the responsibility of the *Länder* for school and university education. Consequently, there are approximately 1,170,000 employees working in these areas, that is, 28 percent of the total civil service in Germany. Another consequence of this responsibility is the significantly disproportionate share of women in the administrations of the *Länder* compared with the federal administration, namely 57 percent compared to the federal administration with 29 percent. This, in turn, results in a noticeably higher proportion of part-time employees of around 32 percent (of which 45 percent are female), compared to 11 percent in the federal administration.

Differences in the range of tasks carried out by the federal administration and the administrations of the *Länder* are also reflected in the remuneration structure, which, in turn, allows conclusions to be drawn about the qualifications of the staff and the hierarchy of functions. As already mentioned in this context, there is a disproportionate share of top functions in the federal area in relation to the total number of employees (excluding military personnel) of 10.1 percent compared with 0.18 percent in the administrations of the *Länder*. By contrast, the percentage of staff in the middle segment of the *Länder* (civil service grades A11–A13 and salary levels EG11–EG13 for non-civil servants) is clearly disproportionate—40 percent of the total number of employees compared to 15.6 percent in the federal administration (including military personnel and social insurance). The main reason for this, as already mentioned, is the importance of the education sector for the *Länder*; the vast majority of teachers are assigned grades A12 and A13. In addition, the employees in these categories of general administration form the functional group of the administrative work and thus the backbone of a management that tends to be oriented towards enforcement rather than management and control.

With regard to age of staff, there is a relative over-proportional ageing of the civil service compared to the private sector (Schrapper 2013). When comparing the administrations of federal and *Länder* governments, there are no significant differences. The proportion of the age group '60 plus' (the statutory pension age will be raised in intermediate steps to 67 years by 2031) is 8.8 percent of the total staff in the federal administration and 11.5 percent in the state administrations. For staff below the age of 30 (Federation 24.4 percent; *Länder* 13 percent), the difference is explained by the high proportion of regular soldiers serving for a fixed period with ratings, identifiable by the relatively low remuneration levels. In the area of this functional level, 9.2 percent of the employees work in the federal government and only 0.2 percent in the *Länder*.

In addition to the professional self-image, the personnel structure of the administrations gives rise to the distinct character of the administrative culture prevailing there. In a differentiated administration such as the *Land* administration, however, subdivided subcultures obviously exist, for example, in the areas of school, police, justice and general services. To identify a definable 'culture of state administration' is virtually impossible. Drawing a comparison between the *Länder* administrations and with the federal government, there are hardly any significant differences to be found in the various sectors. The professional self-conception of the general administration in federal and *Länder* governments in the upper-intermediate service is characterised by a high proportion of civil servants with similar educational backgrounds from specific administrative colleges (Wiegand-Hoffmeister 2011). Accordingly, career changes between administrations are in legal and practical terms not a problem. In spite of the distribution of more legislative competences in the field of remuneration to the *Länder* by the constitutional reform in 2006, this is still helped by a (still) fairly uniform remuneration structure nationwide. However, the tendency here is clearly towards increasing spreading, which could prove to be an obstacle to mobility in the future and could, therefore, also be the cause of increasing partitioning (Battis 2009). Salaries already differ by up to 10 percent in the various salary levels between the federal government and the *Länder*, and also between the *Länder* themselves, where there is a north-south divide.

For the group of university-trained civil servants (higher service) in the general administration, a factual monopoly of jurists is still a characteristic feature of the German administrative culture and tradition (Bull 2018; Hebeler 2008). Whether this results in consequences for the habitus of the administration or even its willingness to reform is a controversial subject of administrative research (Hammerschmidt et al. 2010; Kroll et al. 2012).

5 Lessons Learned

5.1 Structural Reforms: More than a Political Playground?

The history of administrative reforms in the administrations of the Länder is, above all, a history of administrative structural reforms (for the process of 'communalisation' cf. Kuhlmann and Wollmann 2019). From a critical perspective, this is primarily due to the fact that the intervention in structures serves politically plausible expectations (cost reduction and de-bureaucratisation or 'slim state') and avoids more conflict-laden mission-critical decisions (Grotz et al. 2017). For example, the abolition of public authorities—reduced by 66 percent in the period from 1992 to 2014—did not lead to a proportional reduction in staff numbers. An additional factor is that interference in the structure and staffing levels in the central policy fields of education and homeland security with their large bodies of personnel would not be conveyable in political terms.

The main object of interventions in the structure were the administrative district authorities as central or regional bundling authorities. Again, one could assume a superior motive. Thus, the structure of the highest level of administration of the ministries follows immediately obvious political premises and, of course, changes in the cycle of electoral periods and the resulting change of government; the interventions are shallow and involve less structures than responsibilities. Regional bundling authorities are sufficiently complex entities with purely administrative functions. In the large and populous West German *Länder*, the district governments are firmly anchored as the regional authority of the meso level; only Lower Saxony forms a counter model, but one beset with virulent problems (see Chap. 16).

5.2 Prepared for the Future? Digitalisation as a Major Challenge

In comparison to the more endogenous reform drivers described above, such as the situation of public budgets, the current and future dominant driver for reforms in the process of organisation, and possibly also for the organisational structure of the state administration, is digitalisation. Systemically anchored obstacles such as the 'friction losses of federalism' (Martini 2017) or a traditional, overly complex administrative culture designed for decentralised and clearly defined responsibilities as well as administrative secrecy (Hagen and Lühr 2019) are considered as causes of incompatibilities. In this difficult reform environment, the federal government has already laid down the foundations for further development with the passing of the eGovernment Act (EGovG) in 2013 and the Online Access Act (OZG) in 2017, which in part required an amendment to Article 91c (5) of the Basic Law due to the cross-level portal network. The federal, state and local authorities are committed to making all their administrative services available via a nationwide access platform by the end of 2022. As a result, not only will business processes have to be IT-capable, but the professionalism as well as the attitude of employees and executives will have to be further developed (Winners 2019).

References

Battis, U. (2009). Stand und Weiterentwicklung des deutschen Öffentlichen Dienstes. *Der Moderne Staat, 2*, 93.

Bogumil, J. (2007). Verwaltungsstrukturreformen in den Bundesländern-Abschaffung oder Reorganisation der Bezirksregierungen? *Zeitschrift für Gesetzgebung, 22*(3), 246–259.

Bogumil, J., & Ebinger, F. (2008). *Gutachterliche Stellungnahme zum Thema "Vor- und Nachteile des zwei- und dreistufigen Verwaltungsaufbaus vor dem Hintergrund der Struktur der Thüringer Landesverwaltung".* Bochum: Ruhr-Universität Bochum.

Bull, H. (2018). Bessere Juristen für die Verwaltung. *Verwaltung und Management, 24*(6), 273–286.

Bundesverfassungsgericht (Federal Constitutional Court). (2014). Decision of 19.11.2014, Az. 2 BvL 2/13.

Grotz, F., Götz, A., Lewandowsky, M., & Wehrkamp, H. (2017). *Verwaltungsstrukturreformen in den deutschen Ländern.* Wiesbaden: Springer.

120 L. SCHRAPPER

Grunow, D. (2003). Die öffentliche Verwaltung in der modernen Gesellschaft. In D. Grunow (Ed.), *Verwaltung in Nordrhein-Westfalen*. Münster: Aschendorf.

Hagen, M., & Lühr, H. (2019). Wie kommt der Amtsschimmel auf die Datenautobahn—Der lange Weg von der Verwaltung 1.0 bis zur Digitalisierung. In H. Lühr, R. Jablowski, & S. Smentek (Eds.), *Handbuch Digitale Verwaltung*. Kommunal-und Schul-Verlag: Wiesbaden.

Hammerschmidt, G., Proeller, I., Reichard, C., Röber, M., & Geißler, R. (2010). *Verwaltungsführung Heute*. Berlin: Institut für den öffentlichen Sektor.

Hebeler, T. (2008). *Verwaltungspersonal*. Baden-Baden: Nomos.

Kroll, A., Krause, T., Vogel, D., & Proeller, I. (2012). Was bestimmt die Reformbereitschaft von Führungskräften in der Verwaltung? *Verwaltung und Management, 18*(2), 75–80.

Kuhlmann, S., & Wollmann, H. (2019). *Introduction to Comparative Public Administration*. Northampton, MA: Edward Elgar Publishing.

Martini, M. (2017). Transformation der Verwaltung durch Digitalisierung. *Die Öffentliche Verwaltung, 63*(11), 443–454.

Münch, U. (2002). Vom Gestaltungsföderalismus zum Beteiligungsföderalismus. In H. Wehling (Ed.), *Die deutschen Länder*. Opladen.

Reiners, M. (2010). Regierungsbezirke im Vergleich–Voraussetzungen umfassenden organisatorischen Wandels. *Zeitschrift für vergleichende Politikwissenschaft, 4*(1), 105–129.

Schrapper, L. (1994). Bezirksregierungen in Deutschland–die Bündelungsbehörde der Mittelinstanz im Vergleich. *Die Öffentliche Verwaltung, 57*(4), 157–162.

Schrapper, L. (2013). Der öffentliche Dienst im demografischen Wandel– Herausforderungen für das Personalmanagement. *Die Verwaltung, 46*, 441.

Wiegand-Hoffmeister, B. (2011). Bologna und die Zukunft der internen Verwaltungsfachhochschulen. In L. Schrapper (Ed.), *Ausbildung für die öffentliche Verwaltung*. Nomos: Baden-Baden.

Winners, C. (2019). Führungskräfte für die digitale Zukunft fit machen. *Innovative Verwaltung, 15*, 37–39.

Open Access This chapter is licensed under the terms of the Creative Commons Attribution 4.0 International License (http://creativecommons.org/licenses/by/4.0/), which permits use, sharing, adaptation, distribution and reproduction in any medium or format, as long as you give appropriate credit to the original author(s) and the source, provide a link to the Creative Commons licence and indicate if changes were made.

The images or other third party material in this chapter are included in the chapter's Creative Commons licence, unless indicated otherwise in a credit line to the material. If material is not included in the chapter's Creative Commons licence and your intended use is not permitted by statutory regulation or exceeds the permitted use, you will need to obtain permission directly from the copyright holder.

CHAPTER 9

Local Self-Government and Administration

Kay Ruge and Klaus Ritgen

1 Introduction

Germany has a long tradition in local self-government. The modern approach goes back to the beginning of the nineteenth century at the time of significant reform in the different states, especially in Prussia (reforms developed and implemented by Stein). The principles of local self-government have been strengthened over the past two centuries in the different states with ups and downs. The federal and state constitutions of 1948 and 1949 follow these principles and guarantee strong local self-government. In fact, the cornerstone of the institution of local self-government in Germany is mirrored in the European Charter of Local Self-Government of October 1985.[1] Germany was among one of the first states to sign this charter because its principles reflect and underline the existing system of local self-government in Germany. Therefore, the approaches and practices in the different German states offer a broad basis for studying the functioning of a well-established local self-government and its relationship to state authorities. Moreover, local self-government is

---

K. Ruge • K. Ritgen (✉)
German County Association, Berlin, Germany
e-mail: Kay.Ruge@landkreistag.de; klaus.ritgen@landkreistag.de

© The Author(s) 2021   123
S. Kuhlmann et al. (eds.), *Public Administration in Germany*,
Governance and Public Management,
https://doi.org/10.1007/978-3-030-53697-8_9

not uniform across all the 16 states. This opens up the opportunity for comparative research and argumentation on 'best practice'.

In 2017, there were 11,455 local authorities in Germany, including 107 county-free cities, 294 counties and 11,054 municipalities belonging to a county. These municipalities, cities and counties are responsible for a variety of original tasks as well as for the performance of large parts of federal and *Land* laws. Local authorities are usually entrusted by the *Länder* with the performance of federal or *Land* laws. There are two models to be distinguished here: either the states (*Länder*) transfer tasks to the local authorities so that after the transfer they are, as it were, their own municipal tasks, or the local authorities perform them as external tasks and thus act on behalf of the state. The result of both models leads to a largely decentralised administration in Germany. There are, however, federal administrative authorities as well as numerous regional administrative authorities of the states (see Chaps. 6 and 8). The majority of civil service staff, which includes teachers, professors and police officers, are employed in the state administrative authorities.

The administrations of the local authorities are embedded in the politico-administrative system of Germany and cover significant functions. Two central indicators that underline the weight of the local authorities are the number of personnel and the finances. The local authorities account for 30 per cent of public service personnel (Table 9.1).

This high number of personnel reflects the functions of local authorities to deliver most of the public services in direct contact with the citizens (the number of personnel in the states is only higher due to large numbers of public servants working in the three areas of education, that is schools and universities, police and courts). The first and most important point of

Table 9.1 Civil service staff

Sector	FTE[2]	%
Federation	474,100	11.3
Federal states	2,105,200	50.4
Local authorities	1,271,300	30.4
Social security	328,500	7.9
Total	4,179,100	100

Source: German Federal Statistical Office (2019) Finances and taxes. Civil service staff 2018. Special series 14, Series 6, p. 25

contact for citizens and companies regarding most administrative matters is either the town hall of their town or municipality, or the county administration of their county. These services are often organised in centres of administrative services called *Bürgerämter* (one-stop shops).

Insofar as the weight of the local authorities in public finances is concerned, the central budgets of the local authorities cover roughly one-third of public expenditure (excluding social security). However, the expenditure is not only assessed in the central budgets of the local authorities, but also in special budgets established for the different local goods (local public transportation, water provision and sewage, waste collection, institutions of culture, etc.; see Chap. 14). In addition, the local authorities implement a major share of the public investments (often co-financed by the states or out of the federal programmes). (cf. Deutscher Landkreistag 2019; Deutscher Städtetag 2017; Zimmermann and Döring 2019). Table 9.2 summarises the main items of revenue and expenditure of the communes (excluding the three city-states).

The following provides an overview of the very different structures of cities, counties and municipalities (Sect. 2). The special position of municipalities in the German administrative system would remain incomprehensible without looking at the constitutional entrenchment of the local self-government rules, which also result in guidelines for local territorial reforms (Sect. 3). Section 4 proceeds with a description of the main features of the rules governing the organisational aspects of local authorities—the local constitutional law. A brief description of the role of local government associations in Sect. 5 concludes this chapter.

2 Cities, Counties and Municipalities

The distinction between counties and municipalities is fundamental for understanding the structure of local self-government bodies in Germany (Kuhlmann and Wollmann 2019: 92ff.).

2.1 The Various Bodies of Local Self-Government

A distinction is laid down in Article 28 of the Basic Law. Article 28 (2), first sentence of the Basic Law grants municipalities the right to take responsibility for all matters of the local community. The Basic Law thus ties in with historically developed forms of settlement to which it grants a special status of the 'right to self-government', a special constitutional

Table 9.2 Finances of the communes from 2017 to 2022

Revenue/Expenditure	2017	2018	2019	2020	2021	2022
	Billion euro					
Revenue	**243.80**	**253.94**	**264.6**	**274.8**	**283.5**	**290.6**
Taxes	95.90	101.21	103.4	107.7	111.8	115.7
Including:						
Property taxes	12.50	12.69	12.8	13.0	13.1	13.2
Trade tax revenues	40.06	42.21	42.2	44.7	46.4	47.7
Share of income tax	36.30	37.92	39.2	40.7	42.8	45.0
Share of VAT	5.51	6.79	7.5	7.7	7.9	8.0
For information only:						
Gross trade tax revenue	48.17	50.72	49.9	50.1	52.0	53.5
Fees	19.41	19.96	20.5	20.9	21.1	21.3
Current allocations from state/federal government	88.43	91.42	97.1	100.0	104.3	107.4
Investment allocations from state/federal government	7.42	8.44	10.6	13.,0	13.0	12.5
Other revenue	32.63	32.91	32. 95	33.2	33.4	33.7
Expenditure	**234.07**	**245.26**	**259.0**	**270.7**	**281.3**	**291.2**
Personnel	59.13	62.12	65.3	67.9	70.3	72.4
Material expenses	49.53	51.14	53.1	54.8	56.4	57.8
Social benefits	58.77	59.07	61.7	64.2	66.4	68.7
Interest	2.71	2.47	2.5	2.5	2.6	2.6
Investments in real assets						
Including:	24.42	27.60	31.7	34.9	37.3	39.5
Construction measures	18.22	20.82	23.9	26.5	28.6	30.4
Acquisition of property, plant and equipment	6.20	6.78	7.7	8.4	8.7	9.0
Other expenses	39.52	42.85	44.8	46.4	48.4	50.2
Financial balance	**9.73**	**8.68**	**5.6**	**4.1**	**2.2**	**-0.6**

Source: Local Government Associations, Deutscher Landkreistag, October 2019: 499. The figures for the years from 2019 to 2022 are based on surveys, statistics and projections

position, also vis-à-vis the *Länder* and the Federation (Engels 2014: 227ff.).

In addition to the municipalities there are the associations thereof (Article 28 (2), second sentence of the Basic Law), which essentially refers to the counties. The counties are not a creation of the Basic Law either, but rather entities whose origins can be found in the early history of German administration. They have a dual nature. On the one hand, a county is an association of municipalities, which are therefore also referred to as 'municipalities belonging to a county'. On the other hand, counties—like the municipalities—are also considered local authorities with the constitutional right of self-government.

This general dualism is important for the allocation of municipal tasks (for more on common tasks, see Sect. 2.3 below). Obviously, the counties are predestined to perform tasks, which by their nature have a supra-local reference that goes beyond the boundaries of the municipalities belonging to them. This applies, for example, to ensuring local public transportation in rural areas. Due to their size and administrative power, counties are also more efficient than municipalities.

The general dualism at the local level is suspended when it comes to the structure of county-free cities. County-free cities are considered municipalities that do not belong to an overarching municipal association. The local level in county-free cities is, therefore, not of a dual nature but (in principle) of a singular one.

2.2 Population and Size of County-Free Cities, Counties and Municipalities Belonging to a County

While counties have a comparatively higher degree of homogeneity regarding population (and size of their territory), the population of (county-free) cities and municipalities (belonging to a county) differ vastly.

The largest county-free city is Munich with approximately 1.5 million inhabitants, followed by Cologne with around 1.1 million inhabitants and Frankfurt/Main with roughly 740,000 inhabitants.[3] At the lower end of the scale are the county-free cities of Zweibrücken (34,500), Suhl (35,600) and Pirmasens (40,400). The most populated county is the county of Recklinghausen with 620,000 inhabitants, while the least populated is the county of Lüchow-Dannenberg with just under 49,000 inhabitants. In this respect, however, these are exceptions. The vast majority of the 294 counties in Germany have between 150,000 and 250,000 inhabitants and cover an area from 1100 km² to 1500 km². On a national average, 37 municipalities belong to a county. By contrast, the situation is completely heterogeneous among municipalities belonging to a county. There are, for example, some municipalities with less than 100 inhabitants, while others have 100,000 inhabitants.

In some states, attempts have been made to address this disparity by merging the small and very small communes into more powerful municipalities. Especially in Hesse, North Rhine-Westphalia and Saarland, regional reforms in the 1970s led to the creation of larger, more powerful municipalities (see Chap. 16). In Hesse, for example, the number of municipalities decreased from a total of 2691 in 1960 to only 416 in 1978. In particular, the number of municipalities with less than 5000 inhabitants decreased from 2589 to 141. A similar pattern can be seen in North Rhine-Westphalia, where the number of municipalities dropped from 2277 in 1968 to 396 after the implementation of the reform in 1978. In Saarland, which had 345 municipalities before the reform, only 50 existed afterwards.

In the new states of Saxony and Saxony-Anhalt, too, there was a significant reduction in the number of municipalities at the municipal level after German reunification. However, unlike in Hesse, North Rhine-Westphalia and Saarland, the model of the united municipalities was not consistently applied in these states. Here, and also in particular in Baden-Württemberg, Bavaria, Brandenburg, Mecklenburg-Western Pomerania, Lower Saxony, Rhineland-Palatinate, Schleswig-Holstein and Thuringia, together with a few united municipalities, a considerably high number of small and very small municipalities continue to exist, which have been combined into municipal associations acting below the county level to compensate for their lack of capacity. These associations, described as administrative partnerships (*Verwaltungsgemeinschaften*), municipal associations (*Ämter*), or 'double-decker' municipalities (*Verbandsgemeinde*), are essentially distinguished by the fact that they perform most of the administrative tasks of their member municipalities in a quasi-managing capacity and are thus able to provide the necessary administrative structures. The member municipalities of such associations also have their own mayor and a municipal representative body (municipal council). Consequently, self-governing local politics also takes place in these often very small communes.

2.3   Common Tasks of County-Free Cities, Counties and Municipalities Belonging to a County

As mentioned in the introduction, there are two groups of tasks that are performed by the local authorities. In addition to their original tasks, there are the tasks that have been assigned to them by the state (Federation, *Länder*). The heterogeneity of the municipalities just described presents a challenge for a legislator who wants to transfer tasks to the local authorities. It is necessary to ensure that only tasks are entrusted to those local authorities where the performance required for enforcement can be expected.

Where the municipalities perform the tasks of the states, the situation is very heterogeneous when compared to the rest of the country (cf. Lange 2019). In the following, an overview of the tasks typically performed either by the counties or the municipalities belonging to a county is given. The tasks of the county-free cities result from an overview of both bundles of tasks.

2.3.1 *The Common Tasks at the* County Level *Are Primarily*

- financial support for job seekers according to Social Code Book (SGB) II, including integration/re-integration in the labour market. This task is either performed by local job centres or joint institutions together with the Federal Employment Agency (see Chap. 7);
- authority for secondary schools or vocational schools, adult education centres;
- fire and disaster protection as responsible body over the lower disaster control authorities. The counties each have their own laws on disaster control in an emergency. Although the municipalities are responsible for equipment, facilities and maintenance of the fire departments, the counties set up control centres through which fire departments and emergency services are alerted;
- public health and veterinary inspection;
- county hospitals;
- organisation of the emergency and ambulance services in the rural area;
- public child and youth welfare (SGB VIII);
- 'classic' social welfare (e.g. financial support for those of retirement age receiving too little pension, or for those who are unable to earn their living (completely) on their own due to illness (SGB XII);
- waste disposal, including maintenance of landfills and waste consulting; environment protection and nature conservation;
- guarantee of public transportation in rural areas and maintenance of county roads;
- integration of refugees and other migrants (besides communes, social welfare organisations and others);
- economic development (e.g. guaranteeing an extensive broadband supply; own companies for development of commercial zones); and

130 K. RUGE AND K. RITGEN

- miscellaneous administrative tasks, such as motor vehicle registration, weapons law enforcement, issue of building permits, and other matters of regulatory state law ('transferred tasks').

2.3.2 The Municipalities Belonging to a County Are Responsible for the Following

- authorities of schools and adult education centres where a county is not responsible;
- nurseries (can also be provided by welfare organisations or private companies);
- kindergartens, nursery schools, after-school clubs;
- fire departments and brigades;
- cultural institutions such as libraries and museums, and other public facilities, namely sports facilities and parks, swimming pools, city halls and communication centres;
- funeral services and cemeteries;
- maintenance of public road network (municipal roads);
- planning sovereignty grants municipalities the power to organise and shape their territory by creating land-use and development plans, whereas the counties issue building permits;
- the municipalities also perform state administrative tasks, for example ID and civil status registration; these services are typically provided in special centres of administrative services (one-stop shops).

2.4 State Authority and Local Supervision

The question of whether local authorities perform original or delegated tasks plays a role, particularly in the state powers of instruction and state supervision of the local authorities (Knemeyer 2007).

The state has no authority to issue directives on the original tasks of the local authorities. Its control is limited to legal supervision only. Therefore, the state can only monitor and check that the local authority is complying with the law in the performance of its tasks (*Rechtsaufsicht*—legal supervision; see von Knobloch and Schimanke).

The state can make it compulsory for local authorities to perform an original task ('compulsory tasks'). In this case, the local authority can only decide on the method used for performing the task, but not on whether it should fulfil the task since it is obligated to do so. A legal supervision remains.

With regard to the tasks delegated, a distinction should be made. If the transferred tasks become the local authorities' own tasks ('monistic system'), the state can not only oblige the local authorities to perform the tasks, but also grant itself a right to issue instructions regarding the method of task fulfilment ('duty to fulfil according to instructions'). In those states where tasks do not lose their state character even after they have been transferred to the local authorities ('dual system'), that is external tasks for local authorities ('matters of mandate'), this right to issue instructions already follows from the remaining public character of the task.

3 LOCAL SELF-GOVERNMENT AND ITS CONSTITUTIONAL FOUNDATIONS

The role of local authorities in the German administrative system is largely shaped by the fact that they enjoy a special status, which is the guaranteed right to local self-government provided by the constitution. Furthermore, the constitution requires that representative bodies (municipal, city or county council) are directly elected by the people in the local authorities. This special form of the right to self-government of the local authorities has a long tradition in Germany and is closely linked to the principle of subsidiarity (Norton 1994: 237ff.; Hendler 1984), which the Basic Law was able to take up in 1949. The involvement or participation of municipal or county citizens primarily takes place through elections, but increasingly also through plebiscitary instruments (Chap. 18). This not only serves to legitimise the administration, but also aims particularly at the quality of the decisions to be taken. The point is to create effective rights of participation for those affected and to involve external expertise, or rather to activate those involved in their own affairs, thus literally meaning 'self'-administration (Decisions of the Federal Constitutional Court: BVerfGE 79, 127; BVerfGE, 138, 1, 18).

3.1 The Constitutional Guarantee of Local Self-Government Right

The federal constitution guarantees local self-government in Article 28 (2) of the Basic Law. Furthermore, the constitutions of the states guarantee the right to self-administration. As they largely correspond to the Basic Law in this respect, they are not specifically mentioned in the following.

3.1.1 Article 28 (2) of the Basic Law as Institutional Guarantee of the Local Self-Government of the Municipalities and Associations of Municipalities (Counties)[4]

When 'associations of municipalities' are mentioned in the Basic Law, they primarily refer to the counties. On the one hand, according to Article 28 (2) of the Basic Law, municipalities and the associations thereof are subject to the legal regulations of the federal and regional governments. The right of self-government exists within the limits of the laws. Therefore, for example, tasks can be assigned to the local authorities by law, or the territorial borders of municipalities and associations of municipalities can be changed (see Chap. 16). On the other hand, legislators must respect the self-government right of the municipalities and the associations thereof in all these actions. In addition, municipalities and the municipal associations can sue for violations of their rights by a federal or state legislator before the state constitutional courts or the Federal Constitutional Court.

In detail, the constitutional guarantee for municipalities and associations of municipalities results in the following legal positions (Dreier 2015: 719ff.).

a) Population and territorial surface

First, according to Article 28 (2) of the Basic Law, municipalities and associations of municipalities in Germany must be guaranteed the right to self-administration. The federal states, therefore, have no authority to eliminate municipalities and the associations thereof on their territory and replace them with other random administrative bodies. However, this does not mean that every municipality or association of municipalities has a guarantee of existence. Instead, state legislators may legally dissolve individual municipalities or association of municipalities or merge them with others.

b) Tasks

The Basic Law empowers the municipalities to take care of all matters of the *local* community. This is their sphere of competence. As far as a local community matters are concerned, the municipalities may act without any further legal mandate. Local matters are those tasks which concern the living conditions and the coexistence of local people or have a specific reference to it.

There is no such regulation for the counties in the Basic Law. However, according to a general clause, some state constitutions as well as county codes of the *Länder* transfer the right to perform all supra-local public tasks to the counties.

c) Autonomy

Article 28 (2) of the Basic Law guarantees the municipalities and the associations thereof the right to regulate their affairs 'on their own responsibility' within the boundaries of the legal framework. This principle of autonomy forms the core of the right to self-government. In this context, autonomy means freedom from state regulation regarding the methods, that is regarding if, when and how tasks are to be performed (BVerfGE 119, 331, 362); comprehensive state control is thus excluded (BVerfGE 138, 1, 17). This autonomy refers first and foremost to the original tasks of the local authorities and, thus, to the affairs for which they are already responsible.

d) Right to cooperate

The principle of autonomy includes the power of local authorities to decide for themselves whether a certain task can be performed autonomously or together with other administrative bodies (the so-called right to cooperation, BVerfGE 138, 1, 17ff.). This right of intermunicipal cooperation is further developed by the federal states in their own laws (Oebbecke 2007). Intermunicipal cooperation can take place institutionally, for example through an administration association jointly supported by several local authorities (especially in the legal form of a *Zweckverband*), or it can be regulated by contract.

3.1.2 Principles of Financial Autonomy (Article 28 (2), Third Sentence of the Basic Law)

Article 28 (2), third sentence of the Basic Law is also a part of the constitutional recognition of the municipal self-government guarantee that applies equally to both the municipalities and associations of municipalities. It determines that principles of financial autonomy are included in the self-government guarantee. This rule, which was only integrated into the Basic Law in 1994, stipulates that an entitlement to minimum funding is part of the municipal self-government guarantee. This complies with the jurisdiction of the constitutional courts in some states and the Federal Administrative Court (Henneke 2018: 1142ff.). The Federal Constitutional Court has repeatedly emphasised that under Article 28 (2), third sentence of the Basic Law 'the state' is bound to provide the municipalities with the funds necessary to fulfil their tasks. The term 'state' stands primarily for the federal states (BVerfGE 138,1, 19). There is no scope in this chapter to further elaborate on the financing details of the local authorities (see Werner 2006; Schweisfurth and Wallmann 2019).

4 Fundamentals of Local Constitutional Law

4.1 Introduction

In every state there are municipal and county codes which primarily contain regulations on the organisational rights of municipalities and counties ('local constitutional law'). These municipal and county codes, which in some federal states have also been incorporated into a single law, are supplemented by laws that regulate the local right to vote ('local electoral law'), the right to levy local taxes ('local taxation law') and the cooperation between local authorities.

4.1.1 Elections and Forms of Direct Democracy at the Local Level
a) Elections

The voting right is granted to German citizens who have reached the age of 18. However, the voting age in some states is 16, depending on the local electoral law. Article 28 (1), third sentence of the Basic Law extends the voting right to citizens of other Member States of the European Union, while third-country nationals are not entitled to vote at local level. These guidelines apply equally to the right to stand as a candidate ('eligibility of candidates'). But in this respect, the right to vote in the local government elections of the states occasionally requires a voting age of 18 (instead of 16), or a longer residency in the local authority (six months instead of three), than for the exercise of the voting right. Members of the local representative bodies are directly elected by the citizen (city, municipal or county councillor) as well as mayors and, in most states, county commissioners too. In addition, the municipal law also foresees the establishment of various advisory boards, particularly advisory boards for foreigners and integration. However, the advisory boards have no rights of decision, though in many cases they have rights of proposal or rights of consultation.

The duration of the electoral period for the local representative bodies is now five years in almost every state, with the exception of Bavaria, which is six years. In addition, some differences exist in the rules that determine the design of each respective electoral system, especially as Article 28 (1), second sentence of the Basic Law allows for considerable flexibility. For this reason, the right to vote in local government elections differs substantially from federal and state electoral law.

b) Local consultations and other direct democratic instruments

In addition to the right to vote, there is also the right of consultation (Neumann 2007). Through 'referendums' citizens have the opportunity to take binding decisions in place of the local representative bodies. In fact, since the 1990s, the respective regulations have been incorporated into all the municipal charters at both municipal and county level. Obviously, due to their complex procedures, such instruments cannot replace the continuing resolution of the local representative body, but only supplement it on a case-by-case basis. Hence, under Article 28 (2), second sentence of the Basic Law, the local level has a clear precedence over representative democracy.

The procedure for direct democratic decision-making at the local level is two-tiered. At the first tier, a so-called citizens' initiative takes place. If it is declared admissible and receives the necessary support from the citizens, the local representative body must then decide if it wants to allow the initiative. If the application is rejected, a referendum follows. The objective and contextual applicability of direct democracy at the local level is limited; certain matters cannot be made subject of citizens' initiatives and referendums. The list of matters for which such instruments are not allowed varies from state to state. Referendums typically exclude personnel matters and the internal organisation of the local administration. The budget statutes are also regularly excluded.

4.2   *The Local Bodies*

As local authorities, the municipalities are only capable of acting through their bodies. The core of local constitutional law is based on the regulations defining the bodies of a local authority, how they are created, the relationship between them, and what specific tasks they must perform. Despite a harmonisation of local constitutional systems, there are still differences between the states in these matters. Most states have now at least reduced the number of their local bodies to two. Thus, the local representative body only has to face one executive body. This dualism has been implemented in the states of Bavaria (at municipal level), Baden-Württemberg, Hesse, Mecklenburg-Western Pomerania, Rhineland-Palatinate, Saarland (at municipal level), Saxony, Saxony-Anhalt, Thuringia and Schleswig-Holstein. In most of these states, the executive body is organised monocratically and is represented by a mayor or a commissioner of the county. It is only in Hesse where its implementation is still in the hands of a college, namely the municipal board (Section 65ff. of the

Municipal Code of Hesse, HGO) or the county committee (Section 36ff. of the County Code of Hesse, HKO), which consists of the respective mayor or commissioner of a county and the deputies.

By contrast, the local authorities in the states of Brandenburg, Lower Saxony and North Rhine-Westphalia have three bodies. In Bavaria and Saarland (only) the counties have a third body. In these states, besides the representative body and the mayor or commissioner of the county, there is another body to which a certain number of deputies or members of the representative body belong, in addition to the respective chief administrative officer.

The following description is limited to the role of the local representative bodies and the respective chief administrative officer.

4.2.1 The Local Representative Bodies

The main body of every local authority is the local representative body, that is the municipal and city council as well as the county council (Ehlers 2007). The council is the central leading body of the local authority (BVerfGE 47, 253, 275). Article 28 (1), second sentence of the Basic Law, stipulates the representation of the people in the municipalities and counties. This body takes precedence over all others at the local level.

a) Internal organisation

The size of the local representative bodies varies in the federal states and depends on the number of inhabitants.

There is also a diverse range of regulations determining whether the respective chief administrative officer belongs to the representative body and which function he holds. According to the local public law in a number of states, the respective chief administrative officer (mayor or commissioner of a county) is by virtue of office a member and chairman of the local representative body. In other states, however, the chief administrative officer is part of the representative body, but not its chairman. Lastly, there are states where the chief administrative officer is not a member of any representative body.

Political groups are usually formed in the municipal and county councils as in the case of parliaments (Suerbaum 2007). Similarities to parliamentary law exist insofar as, according to the local law of all states, the formation of committees is stipulated. With regard to committees, a distinction should be made between mandatory and optional. In some states, it is foreseen that committees not only consult but also make decisions on behalf of the representative body.

b) Competences

The formation of a representative body at municipal and county level is stipulated by constitutional law as mandatory (Article 28 (1), second sentence of the Basic Law). Consequently, the most important management and control tasks for each local authority must be reserved for the representative bodies.

Beyond the area of the constitutionally mandatory statutory tasks, the state legislators are free to decide on which body they wish to assign the tasks and the range of tasks, which entails a wide variety of regulations. In principle, however, the representative bodies are responsible for all matters unless they are explicitly assigned to another local body, particularly to the chief administrative officer or the above-mentioned 'third' body (municipal board or county committee).

4.2.2 *The Chief Administrative Officer*

All local authorities in Germany have a chief administrative officer. In the counties, the officer is called the commissioner of the county (*Landrat*). In the municipalities, the chief administrative officer is referred to as the mayor (*Bürgermeister*) in the cities, and, in accordance with the relevant state law, in larger municipalities he/she is referred to as the lord mayor (*Oberbürgermeister*). Except for smaller municipalities, the chief administrative officials are employed full-time and are salaried.

a) Direct election of the chief administrative officials

Mayors employed full-time are directly elected by the people. It is only in the case of voluntary mayors of smaller municipalities that an election by the representative body is foreseen according to the local constitutional law of some states (e.g. in Brandenburg). The commissioners of the counties are also directly elected in the majority of states, but not all.

b) Responsibilities

As already indicated, the local government codes of the states also exhibit considerable variations in the assignment of responsibilities to the bodies. The basic premise is that chief administrative officials are responsible if no competence of the representative body exists. The chief administrative officials are usually responsible for executing the council's decisions and for managing all the ongoing administrative matters. They are also responsible for the external representation of the local authority.

c) The commissioner of the county as lower state administrative authority

One feature deserves special mention regarding the commissioner of the county. In some federal states, the commissioner of a county is not only the chief administrative officer, he also acts as the lowest tier of the regional authority (Meyer 2007: 702).

5 The Local Government Associations

The interests of local authorities in the federal state and at European level are represented by the three local government associations at the federal level: the German Association of Cities (*Deutscher Städtetag*—DST) as the leading representative of the county-free cities; the German County Association (*Deutscher Landkreistag*—DLT) as representative of the 294 counties; and the German Association of Towns and Municipalities (*Deutscher Städte- und Gemeindebund*—DStGB) as representative of all municipalities belonging to a county. There are also corresponding regional associations at state level. In addition to their respective headquarters, the three local government associations at federal level each maintains a European office in Brussels.

Unlike many state constitutions, the Basic Law does not provide for any participation or consultation rights of local government associations. As regards draft legislation by the federal government, the procedure on participation and consultation is set out in the Joint Rules of Procedure of the Federal Ministries (GGO).[5] According to Section 41 GGO, the opinions of local government associations at federal level are to be obtained before drafting a legislative proposal that affects the concerns of local authorities. The impacts on the budgets of the local authorities must be listed separately in accordance with Section 44 (3) GGO. In compliance with Section 47 (1) GGO, the ministry responsible forwards the draft legislation prepared on this basis to the local government associations as early as possible if local issues are involved.

In the Rules of Procedure of the German Federal Parliament, Sections 66 (2), 69 (5) and 70 (4) contain provisions on the participation of the local government associations.[6] Essentially, in any matter of crucial interest that affects the municipalities and associations of municipalities, the local government associations at federal level should be given the opportunity to issue a statement before decision-making. Substantial interests are adopted if the relevant legislation is fully or partially implemented by the municipalities (or associations of municipalities), their public finances are directly affected or their administrative organisation is influenced.

6 Lessons Learned

Germany observes the principles laid down in the European Charter of Local Self-Government. Moreover, the municipalities and especially the counties are the main operational level for implementing the state laws. This weight at the communal level is underlined by the number of personnel and size of the communal budget: the communal level covers around one-third of the public service personnel and public budgets (excluding social security). Based on their traditional roots of the early nineteenth century, the modern communal administration and local self-government contribute significantly to the quality of public service delivery and to legitimation acceptance of public administration in general. The decentralised system with a wide range of responsibilities and decision-making authority has provided the basis that facilitates initiatives and approaches to modernising public administration and reforms in various fields.

Notes

1. Council of Europe. European Treaties Series No. 122. Strasbourg October 15, 1985. https://www.coe.int/en/web/conventions/full-list/-/conventions/rms/090000168007a088.
2. FTE = full-time equivalent.
3. The two largest cities in Germany are Berlin with roughly 3.6 million inhabitants and Hamburg with around 1.8 million inhabitants. However, these two cities and Bremen are, at the same time, state-constituted federal states ('city-states', see Sect. 2.4).
4. The fundamental text of Article 28 (2) of the Basic Law: 'Municipalities must be guaranteed the right to regulate all local affairs on their own responsibility, within the limits prescribed by the laws. Within the limits of their functions designated by a law, associations of municipalities shall also have the right of self-government in accordance with the laws. The guarantee of self-government shall extend to the bases of financial autonomy; these bases shall include the right of municipalities to a source of tax revenues based upon economic ability and the right to establish the rates at which these sources shall be taxed'.
5. GGO in German: https://www.bmi.bund.de/SharedDocs/downloads/DE/veroeffentlichungen/themen/ministerium/ggo.pdf;jsessionid=59DED0A808AAB54FE2E6A222EF25B74B.2_cid364?__blob=publicationFile&v=2.
6. Rules of Procedure (German Federal Parliament) in English: https://www.btg-bestellservice.de/pdf/80060000.pdf.

REFERENCES

Deutscher Landkreistag (Ed.). (2019, October). *Kommunalfinanzbericht 2018/2019*. Der Landkreis. Stuttgart: Kohlhammer.

Deutscher Städtetag (Ed.). (2017). *Gemeindefinanzbericht 2017*. Köln: Deutscher Städtetag. Retrieved from http://www.staedtetag.de/imperia/md/content/dst/veroeffentlichungen/gemeindefinanzbericht/gemeindefinanzbericht_2017_langfassung.pdf.

Dreier, H. (2015). Commentary on Article 28 of the Basic Law (in German). In H. Dreier (Ed.), *Grundgesetz, Kommentar, Band II* (pp. 657–762). Tübingen: Mohr Siebeck.

Ehlers, D. (2007). Die Gemeindevertretung. In T. Mann & G. Püttner (Eds.), *Handbuch der kommunalen Wissenschaft und Praxis* (Vol. 1, pp. 459–534). Berlin: Springer.

Engels, A. (2014). *Die Verfassungsgarantie kommunaler Selbstverwaltung*. Tübingen: Mohr Siebeck.

Hendler, R. (1984). *Selbstverwaltung als Ordnungsprinzip*. Köln: Carl Heymanns.

Henneke, H.-G. (2018). Commentary of Article 28 of the Basic Law (in German). In B. Schmidt-Bleibtreu, H. Hofmann, H.-G. Henneke, & G. G. Grundgesetz (Eds.), *14th Edition and Loose-Leaf-System*. Köln: Carl Heymanns.

Knemeyer, F.-L. (2007). Die Staatsaufsicht über die Gemeinden und Kreise. In T. Mann & G. Püttner (Eds.), *Handbuch der kommunalen Wissenschaft und Praxis* (Vol. 1, pp. 217–245). Berlin: Springer.

Kuhlmann, S., & Wollmann, H. (2019). *Introduction to Comparative Public Administration*. Cheltenham and Northampton: Edward Elgar Publishing.

Lange, K. (2019). *Kommunalrecht* (2nd ed.). Tübingen: Mohr Siebeck.

Meyer, H. (2007). Die Entwicklung der Kreisverfassungssysteme. In T. Mann & G. Püttner (Eds.), *Handbuch der kommunalen Wissenschaft und Praxis* (Vol. 1, pp. 661–715). Berlin: Springer.

Neumann, P. (2007). Bürgerbegehren und Bürgerentscheid. In T. Mann & G. Püttner (Eds.), *Handbuch der kommunalen Wissenschaft und Praxis* (Vol. 1, pp. 353–377). Berlin: Springer.

Norton, A. (1994). *International Handbook of Local and Regional Government*. Aldershot and Brookfield: Edward Elgar Publishing Company.

Oebbecke, J. (2007). Kommunale Gemeinschaftsarbeit. In T. Mann & G. Püttner (Eds.), *Handbuch der kommunalen Wissenschaft und Praxis* (Vol. 1, pp. 843–872). Berlin: Springer.

Schweisfurth, T., & Wallmann, W. (2019). *Haushalts- und Finanzwirtschaft der Kommunen*. Berlin: Berliner Wissenschafts-Verlag.

Suerbaum, J. (2007). Die Fraktionen in den kommunalen Vertretungskörperschaften. In T. Mann & G. Püttner (Eds.), *Handbuch der kommunalen Wissenschaft und Praxis* (Vol. 1, pp. 535–550). Berlin: Springer.

Werner, J. (2006). Local Government Organization and Finance: Germany. In A. Shah (Ed.), *Local Governance in Industrial Countries* (pp. 117–148). Washington, DC: World Bank.

Zimmermann, H., & Döring, T. (2019). *Kommunalfinanzen* (4th ed.). Berlin: Berliner Wissenschafts-Verlag.

Open Access This chapter is licensed under the terms of the Creative Commons Attribution 4.0 International License (http://creativecommons.org/licenses/by/4.0/), which permits use, sharing, adaptation, distribution and reproduction in any medium or format, as long as you give appropriate credit to the original author(s) and the source, provide a link to the Creative Commons licence and indicate if changes were made.

The images or other third party material in this chapter are included in the chapter's Creative Commons licence, unless indicated otherwise in a credit line to the material. If material is not included in the chapter's Creative Commons licence and your intended use is not permitted by statutory regulation or exceeds the permitted use, you will need to obtain permission directly from the copyright holder.

PART II

Politics, Procedures and Resources

CHAPTER 10

Politics and Administration in Germany

Werner Jann and Sylvia Veit

1 Introduction

The relationship between 'politics' and 'administration' in both practical and theoretical terms is one of the most controversial and, at the same time, often not well understood features of modern states. Especially the close institutional links between politics and administration in Germany, which have a long history, are internationally not well known.

In public administration literature, two ideal types of political-administrative relations are distinguished. On the one hand, there is the assumption of a basic 'dichotomy' between politics and administration, going back to the ground-breaking work of Woodrow Wilson (1887) and Max Weber ([2019] 1922) in the late nineteenth century and early twentieth century. They described politics and administration as two different spheres of public life, both governed by their own rationalities: while politics is concerned with power, legitimacy and the formulation of

W. Jann (✉)
University of Potsdam, Potsdam, Germany
e-mail: jann@uni-potsdam.de

S. Veit
University of Kassel, Kassel, Germany
e-mail: sveit@uni-kassel.de

© The Author(s) 2021
S. Kuhlmann et al. (eds.), *Public Administration in Germany*,
Governance and Public Management,
https://doi.org/10.1007/978-3-030-53697-8_10

145

policies, administration stands for professionalism, legality and the implementation of policies. Although Wilson and Weber saw the bureaucracy as an 'instrument' of political power, both had severe doubts that professional bureaucracies could be controlled by amateur politicians. In this context, Weber stressed the dependency of politicians on bureaucrats because of two types of knowledge: *Fachwissen* (which is a bureaucrat's superior professional expertise) and *Dienstwissen* (which is their procedural and institutional knowledge of the functioning of public administration). From this perspective, administrations become powerful for their own sake, eventually creating the 'iron cage' of modern bureaucracies. This understanding has been taken up by modern economic principal–agency theories. Here, too, the principals—the politicians—have great problems controlling what their agents—the bureaucracies—are doing, so the relationship becomes one of permanent distrust and power and blame games.

On the other hand, there is a less theoretical, more empirical understanding of the relationship, which argues that there is and can be no clear distinction between politics and administration, fundamentally questioning the 'instrumentalist' concept. This argument has been at the core of social science-oriented public administration and policy studies, first in the United States, but also after the Second World War in Western Europe (for Germany, e.g. Mayntz and Scharpf 1975). A seminal international study of ministerial bureaucracies—the Comparative Elite Study (CES) (Aberbach et al. (1981)—showed that in all Western countries the image of the 'classical bureaucrat' as an apolitical instrument in the hands of his masters does not reflect the real relationship between politics and administrations and that most modern civil servants in the ministerial bureaucracy see themselves as 'political administrators' instead. They acknowledge, and most of them generally appreciate, the political aspects of their profession. Public administration scholars call this phenomenon 'functional politicisation' (Mayntz and Derlien 1989).

In practical and normative terms, the first ideal type—the 'instrumentalist' concept with its emphasis on a neutral and apolitical civil service—resembles the so-called Westminster model known from the (former) Commonwealth or the Scandinavian countries (where principal–agent problems play an important role in political and theoretical discussions). Simple, and many would argue naïve, models of New Public Management (NPM) tried to establish this concept as a baseline for public sector reforms in the 1980s and 1990s, arguing that politics should only be concerned with the 'what' of public policies, while the 'how' should be left to administration.

The second ideal type, which assumes that there is no clear and simple distinction between politics and administration, is usually represented by the US system with its large number of political appointees (Lewis 2012), but also, in a much less open way, by many South and East-European countries (Meyer Sahling 2008). In these countries, governments may often pay lip service to the neutral and apolitical civil servant, while replacing large numbers of them after elections or for other political reasons.

Germany falls somewhere between these two ideal types. The traditional view holds that the civil service is above politics and in the old Hegelian-inspired state theories, which were prominent and dominant at least until the first half of the twentieth century, only the civil service could guarantee the common good, if necessary, even against politicians, interest groups and parties merely representing special interests. This ideology of the apolitical, neutral civil servant only interested in the common good was brutally discredited in the Nazi period (1933–1945). Already in the late Weimar republic, many top civil servants were decisively anti-democratic, supported right-wing parties and ideas, and later played an important role in the rise and crimes of the National Socialist German Worker's Party (NSDAP) (Jann 2003). Many indeed joined the NSDAP after Germany became a one-party state in 1933.[1] In 1930, a famous liberal constitutional lawyer, Gustav Radbruch, had already characterised the apolitical civil servant as the 'living lie of the authoritarian state' (*Lebenslüge des Obrigkeitsstaates*). But even before these devastating experiences, a simple distinction between politics and administration has never been a defining feature of the German political and administrative system. The German system had early on developed some quite unique institutional features to create linkages between the two spheres, for example the concepts of the 'political civil servant' (*politischer Beamter*) at the ministerial level and the 'elected civil servant' (*Wahlbeamter*) at the local level.

Our aim in this chapter is to look at the relationships between politicians and administrators in Germany in institutional and legal terms, but especially also in its empirical manifestations at the federal, state and local level. We start with a simple, actor-oriented distinction between politicians and civil servants. The first are elected for a limited period of time (and may be removed if they lose support), while the second are appointed, usually for a (lifelong) career. Politicians are dependent on political support, while civil servants are not, at least in theory. But how true are these distinctions in practice? In order to discuss these questions, we use the concept of politicisation as an analytical lens. Two core dimensions of politicisation are distinguished. The first dimension is functional politicisation (whether and how both politicians and bureaucrats are engaged in different kinds of policymaking tasks). The second dimension is party politicisation (whether and how does party political attachment play a role for administrative careers). Empirically, we will look at party membership (the most straightforward measure of party politicisation) and turnover rates after elections as well as the relevance of 'political craft' for administrative careers.

The following sections are structured as follows. We start with a description of political-administrative relations at federal level, thereby focussing on both dimensions of politicisation and on typical career patterns in federal ministries. Subsequently, a similar overview is given for the *Länder* level. Afterwards, the main characteristics of political-administrative relations at local level are examined. The chapter ends with concluding remarks and lessons for transfer.

2   POLITICS AND ADMINISTRATION IN FEDERAL MINISTRIES

In the German federal system, the *Länder* and their local governments are responsible for the implementation of most laws, while the federal level dominates the law-making process and policymaking (see chapters Fleischer; Schrapper; Kuhlmann/Veit). This deep involvement of federal ministerial officials in policymaking is reflected in a special legal construct, the so-called political civil servant *(politische Beamte)*. According to Section 54 of the Federal Civil Service Act *(Bundesbeamtengesetz)*, civil servants in the two highest ranks in the federal ministerial hierarchy—administrative state secretaries *(beamtete Staatssekretäre,* who are the official administrative heads of ministries) and directors-general *(Ministerialdirektoren,* who are the heads of directorates)—are political civil servants. They traditionally have a background in the career civil service, but serve at the request of their ministers and can be sent into retirement at any time and without any given reason, while they keep their earned pension rights and can be recalled at any time. The basic idea is that ministers should be able to choose their most important officials and advisors from civil servants they trust and if this trust—for whatever reason—no longer holds, replace them.

The institution of 'political civil servant' and the 'political retirement' tradition in Germany date back to the middle of the nineteenth century. During this period, the 'lifetime principle' for civil servants was introduced in Prussia. This meant that civil servants could no longer be dismissed unless they committed a civil offence. This raised the question of how to constrain the power of civil servants and especially how to secure a distinct degree of harmony between the monarch and top civil servants. Therefore, in 1849 in Prussia (when quite a few civil servants had shown sympathies with the failed 1848 revolution), a new ordinance was introduced that, for the first time, enumerated the leading positions within state administration. It stated that civil servants in these positions could be temporarily retired by the king at any time. In the following decades, the position of a 'political civil servant' was introduced in many German *Länder* and from 1871 onwards at national level.

Administrative state secretaries are not to be confused with parliamentary state secretaries who are elected members of the *Bundestag* and support the minister in maintaining good relations between the ministry and the parliament. When the institution of parliamentary state secretaries was first introduced in 1967, the minister was given a great deal of leeway over which tasks to delegate to the parliamentary state secretary. The influence parliamentary state secretaries exert on the internal affairs of the ministry is considered not very strong compared to that of the administrative state secretary.

Besides the federal chancellor, there are currently 15 federal ministers and 35 parliamentary state secretaries, so all in all 50 executive politicians in the federal government, and about 125 political civil servants (25 administrative state secretaries and about 100 directors-general, all in all far less than one per cent of all higher civil servants at the federal level). All other civil servants in federal ministries, that is heads of sub-directorates, heads of divisions *(Referatsleiter)* and all lower ranks are career civil servants in tenure positions. This does not mean, however, that they do not fulfil politicised functions or have no party affiliation.

Germany was one of the country cases explored in the CES study by Aberbach et al. (1981). This study revealed that senior officials in federal ministries—not only political civil servants but also civil servants in lower ranks—are, even more so than in other Western democracies, deeply involved in the process of policymaking. They not only develop draft laws and draft policies but also play a prominent role in intra-governmental coordination as well as negotiation and coordination with other levels of government and external actors, such as interest groups (see also Mayntz and Scharpf 1975). A replication of CES in the second half of the 1980s (Mayntz and Derlien 1989) as well as more recent studies (Ebinger et al. 2018; Ebinger et al. 2019) confirm these findings and underline that most senior officials in federal ministries not only appreciate the political side of their job but also anticipate political considerations when fulfilling their tasks. Thus, the main focus of the federal level on policymaking is reflected in a high degree of functional politicisation among civil servants in federal ministries. Functional politicisation is higher in ministries than in federal agencies, and higher for top positions than for lower hierarchical ranks (Ebinger et al. 2018).

The concept of functional politicisation is closely related to the concept of 'political craft', which was developed by Klaus Goetz (1997) based on empirical work on the federal ministerial bureaucracy in Germany. He defines political craft as 'the ability to assess the likely political implications and ramifications of policy proposals; to consider a specific issue within the broader context of the government's programme; to anticipate and, where necessary, influence or even manipulate the reactions of other actors in the policymaking process (...); and to design processes that maximise the chances for the realisation of ministers' substantive objectives. To do all this, senior officials need to be able to draw on personal networks of information and communication that extend beyond their own ministry (...)' (Goetz 1997: 754). Thus, political craft means not only having the ability to act in a functional politicised manner, but also having the willingness and ability to play an active part in the political process by drawing on political networks.

Empirical studies examining the career background of political civil servants in federal ministries have repeatedly shown that many of them gain professional experience in civil service positions close to politics, such as personal assistant to a minister or head of the ministers' office, in the federal chancellery or as party staff in parliament while being on leave from their position in the ministry (Schröter 2004; Veit and Scholz 2016) earlier in their career. All these positions are not only suitable for acquiring 'political craft' during a career in the civil service, they can also reflect a civil servant's political attachment. Thus, it does not come as a surprise that many higher-ranking civil servants in Germany are party members.

One important and defining feature of the German system is that all civil servants, from the lowest to the highest level, can be members of political parties, and very often are. Allowing party membership (even for soldiers) is one of the many lessons the 'founding fathers' of the Federal Republic drew from the experiences of the downfall of the Weimar Republic and the rise and success of Nazi Germany. As a result, Germans prefer their civil servants to declare their political standing and not hide behind a false veil of political disinterest. This does not mean that all civil servants are members of a political party, but that being a member is a legitimate and respectable expression of one's political views (Jann and Veit 2015). In practice, the political activities of civil servants are far less restrained than in many other countries. Highly visible activities for left or right-wing radical parties are, however, forbidden.

Promotion to the top positions in federal ministries depends both on professional competence and on party political attachment and loyalty (Bach and Veit 2018). Political civil servants are mostly, but not necessarily, members of the same political party as the minister (Fleischer 2016) and most of them are replaced after a change in government (Ebinger et al. 2018). The share of party members and civil servants with clear party-political loyalties among top civil servants is high, even among 'non-political' heads of sub-directorates and divisions (Bach and Veit 2018; Ebinger et al. 2018). All this points to the relevance of political patronage and there can be no doubt that party membership is relevant for top administrative careers in the German civil service. But while top civil servants may depend on political support for their careers, this relationship cuts both ways. Ministers are just as much, or perhaps even more, dependent on the support, the loyalty and especially the professionalism and expertise of top civil servants.

Despite the particular relevance of 'political craft', the careers of executive politicians and 'political civil servants' in federal ministries have traditionally been clearly separated: top civil servants do not usually come from a career in parliament or as a minister and ministers do not usually come from the top civil service (Derlien 2003), even though there have recently been some well-known exceptions. Civil service careers in federal ministries—similar to other parts of public administration in Germany—are characterised by a low inter-sectoral and intra-sectoral mobility, that is in most cases, ministerial civil servants spend their whole career within the jurisdiction of one ministry—the only exception being the secondments to the chancellery or the federal parliament mentioned earlier. Despite the high degree of continuity in civil service careers in federal ministries, some changes have been observed over the decades. First, the typical 'pure civil service career' where an individual enters the civil service directly after graduation and remains there until retirement is no longer the norm. The latest figures show that less than one-fifth of the administrative state secretaries belong to this group. All others have work experience outside public administration, often in academia, in the judiciary, or in some kind of political function (Veit and Scholz 2016). Among the directors-general, 'pure civil service careers' are more common, but here mixed careers have also been growing in importance in recent years. Second, the former 'monopoly of jurists' in the federal senior civil service has converted into a mere dominance: over the years, the proportion of jurists among senior civil servants has gradually declined. While in 1954 more than three-quarters of the administrative top positions in Bonn were held by jurists, this decreased to about 50 per cent in the 2000s (Veit and Scholz 2016).

In sum, political-administrative relations in federal ministries in Germany are characterised by close collaboration in policymaking and a high degree of functional and party politicisation of top bureaucrats on the one hand, and clearly differentiated career patterns of politicians and bureaucrats on the other. However, the growing importance of ministerial officials having professional experience in the political sector indicate some changes. Surprisingly, these changes are more rapid at the *Länder* level as will be shown in the next section.

3   POLITICS AND ADMINISTRATION IN *LÄNDER* MINISTRIES

More than half of all public employees in Germany work in one of the 16 *Länder*, but only a very small number of them in ministries. *Länder* ministries resemble federal ministries in many respects (similar institutional framework, similar structure, etc.) but differ with regard to their task portfolio as the law-making competency of the *Länder* is restricted to a limited number of policy fields, most importantly education and police (see chapter Schrapper). The involvement of *Länder* ministerial officials in policymaking varies considerably across ministries and implementation and oversight responsibilities are usually more important than policymaking.

The number of 'political civil servants' in the *Länder* is therefore smaller than at federal level. The number of *Länder* ministries (besides the state chancellery) varies between 7 and 12. Each *Land* ministry is headed by a minister. In most *Länder*, there are no parliamentary state secretaries. In all *Länder* except Bavaria, the highest-ranking civil servant in each ministry (the administrative state secretary) is a 'political civil servant' who—like his counterpart at federal level—can be sent into temporary retirement on the minister's behalf. Heads of directorates in *Länder* ministries and all lower-ranking officials are career officials in tenure positions, even though heads of the police force (*Polizeipräsident*) and regional administrations (*Regierungspräsident*) are also often political civil servants. All in all, the number of political civil servants does not exceed 20, even in the largest *Länder*.

As at federal level, administrative state secretaries in *Länder* ministries are usually recruited from the civil service: out of all the administrative state secretaries appointed between 2000 and 2018, 85 per cent had at least one year's work experience in the civil service and roughly half of them had more than ten years of civil service experience at the time of their appointment.[2] However, mixed careers, that is careers in different sectors, especially between administration and politics (members of parliament becoming permanent secretaries, civil servants becoming ministers), are more common than at the federal level. Similar to the federal level, there is a high proportion of jurists and women are under-represented in top administrative and political positions in the German *Länder*. The under-representation of women in administrative offices is, however, much more pronounced as discussions on issues relating to representativeness are less intense when it comes to public administration.

Thirty years after the demise of the German Democratic Republic and reunification in 1990, considerable differences still remain between East and West Germany. After German unification, the implementation of democratic political institutions and, in particular, the establishment of a functioning public administration after the West German model, was supported by a wide-ranging recruitment of West German civil servants to leadership positions in the East German *Länder* (and local) administrations (see chapter Wollmann). Our data analysis reveals that in the East German *Länder* of Brandenburg, Mecklenburg-Western Pomerania, Saxony-Anhalt, Saxony and Thuringia, the proportion of administrative state secretaries who were born in East Germany is still rather low, ranging from under 20 per cent (Saxony) to more than 30 per cent (e.g. Brandenburg). Thus, most administrative state secretaries still come from the western part of Germany. This differs greatly from the *Länder* ministers, where the proportion of East Germans is much higher.

With regard to politicisation in *Länder* ministries, five empirical findings are particularly striking. First, the proportion of party members is high (similar to the federal level). Second, administrative state secretaries have very often acquired professional experience in the world of politics (be it as an elected politician, party professional or civil servant with experience in offices close to politics, such as personal assistant to a minister) at earlier stages in their careers. More than two-thirds of all administrative state secretaries have this kind of experience. On the other hand, many ministers (about one-third) have professional experience in the public sector. This indicates that political and administrative careers in the German *Länder* are not as strictly separated as at federal level. Third, and again different from the federal level, almost every fifth political civil servant (18 per cent) was a full-time professional politician (member of parliament) before being appointed as a political civil servant. This, again, reflects the higher hybridisation of administrative and political careers at *Länder* level. Fourth, political experience at local level (as elected mayor or council) is widespread but decreasing over time. Whereas at the beginning of the 2000s, 38 per cent of the administrative state secretaries in the German *Länder* had such a background, this percentage decreased to less than 25 per cent between 2015 and 2018. Fifth, the importance of having relevant experience as a party professional or in civil service offices close to politics has increased considerably over time. This resembles developments at the federal level and presumably reflects the increasing importance of 'political craft' for administrative top positions at both levels of government.

4   Politics and Administration at the Local Level

At the local level, there are two competing understandings about the relationship between politics and administration. Traditionally, local government in Germany is not legally defined as politics, but ever since the famous Stein-Hardenberg reforms at the beginning of the nineteenth century, as local self-administration *(lokale Selbstverwaltung)*. Taking this view, local government is essentially apolitical. Politics does not and should not play an important role ('there are no conservative street lights or social-democratic public conveniences') and the elected councils at local level, by legal definition, are not local parliaments but part of the administration. The same holds true for elected mayors, heads of counties *(Landräte)* and other local politicians. Mayors and heads of counties as 'elected civil servants' (*Wahlbeamte*) are both part and head of the local administration.

Local government is in the German constitutional tradition and doctrine part of the *Länder* administration (Kuhlmann and Wollmann 2019: 92ff.) and due to the autonomy of the *Länder* in determining their organisational structure, there is a large and sometimes confusing organisational variance between them. This overall variance has been somewhat reduced since the 1990s in all of the *Länder* when the direct election of mayors (and in most of them county heads too) became the norm. Even though they are 'elected civil servants', as directly elected politicians they have a strong direct legitimacy, actually much stronger than other executive politicians in Germany. They are elected for a term of five to ten years,[3] but they can be removed by different forms of recall, usually through a combination of direct democratic and representative procedures. As Kuhlmann and Wollmann (2019: 95) point out, 'it is worth noting that the local executive is acting as a politically accountable local politician rather than as 'agent of the state', even in the conduct of delegated business', that is in those areas where they act as direct representatives of state and federal government and can be instructed by higher levels.

Those who hold the second view have therefore argued for quite some time that local self-administration is in reality highly politicised, that party politics plays an ever more important role, both for elected mayors and especially for councils at all levels, which for all practical concerns act just like local parliaments. This goes along with the normative argument that local government should align itself to competitive party democracy in order to ensure transparency and control of hitherto opaque administrative decision-making and to enable political participation. Again, the basic assumption is that there is no apolitical administration.

At the local level, the empirical reality is more complex, but it shows many interconnections and networks between politics and administration, probably even more so than at the state or federal level. The new reality has been described as self-government instead of self-administration (for more details see Bogumil and Holtkamp 2013).

While there is a wide consensus that local administrations in Germany have become much more politicised in recent years, there are, at the same time, a number of important distinctions between the different forms of politicisation, which have to do with, among others, size, institutional settings and the traditions of local government in different parts of Germany. In larger municipalities, especially in the more industrialised parts of Germany (like North Rhine-Westphalia) party politicisation of councils and of mayoral elections have become the norm. Careers in politics are made, first of all, through political parties, councils are organised between opposition and governing factions, and many decisions are made along party lines. In more rural, smaller municipalities, especially in the southern part of Germany (like Baden-Württemberg), local careers are usually much less determined by parties; there are more members of councils, mayors and heads of counties who do not belong to a party, and decision-making at local level is more consensual. If you compare all the German *Länder*, more are on the consensus side, especially in East Germany. All in all, the relevance of political parties thus may decrease, while executive leadership (by elected civil servants) and consensual decision-making are gaining ground. At the same time, elements of direct democracy and citizen participation at the local level have been strengthened in all German *Länder* and, moreover, are much more widely used (even in the form of more recalls of mayors) than before.

Furthermore, there is a second, quite often overlooked, element that creates a close relationship between elections, political parties, councils and administrations, which is the institution of the so-called *Beigeordnete* (adjunct mayors or adjunct head of counties). Here, too, these vary confusingly from *Land* to *Land* but, in general, these positions are obligatory in all larger municipalities and counties. *Beigeordnete* are elected by the local council for a fixed term of up to eight years and are the responsible heads of larger sections of local administrations like ministers in state and federal governments (one of them is usually the *Kämmerer*, the chief financial officer in local government). They are usually full-time employees (unless they work in small municipalities) and, like mayors and heads of counties, 'elected civil servants'. An interesting feature is that they are not elected on the lines of 'government and opposition' but mostly by proportional representation. Thus, all major parties and other groups in local councils are represented in proportion to their strength in the political leadership of local administrations. In some *Länder*, this proportional electoral system is even mandated in the legal rules for local government (i.e. in Baden-Württemberg and Saxony), but even if not required, it is widely used nearly everywhere.

When looking at these close interactions between politics and administration in Germany, it is not surprising that the simple New Public Management mantra of a clear division between politics and administration never really caught on in German local governments. It was not only the legal definition that local councils are part of local administrations which prevented this simple division of labour, but also the traditional understanding of all elected local 'politicians' that they are, of course, responsible for all elements of local administration, especially for the implementation of policies, not only for 'strategic goals and objectives', and that, at the same time, administrators obviously fulfil political functions. Therefore, in all empirical evaluations of NPM reforms in Germany, the 'clear division of politics and administration' is the element which, by far, is implemented the least (Kuhlmann et al. 2008: 855).

5   Lessons Learned

A clear distinction or even dichotomy between politics and administration has never been and is not a defining characteristic of the German political-administrative system. Instead, at the federal, state and local level we observe many close interrelations and interactions between elected politicians and appointed civil servants. Civil servants in Germany are used to and generally appreciate the functional politicisation of their jobs, that is their close involvement in all stages of the policy process, from policy formation, goal definition, negotiation within and outside government, and the interaction with citizens and interest groups in the implementation of policies. Obtaining 'political craft' has therefore become an important part of the learning and job experience of top civil servants. At the same time, political parties play an important role in German public administrations because all civil servants have the right to join a political party and many of them actually practice this right. For many civil servants—but certainly not for all—their political affiliation is well known within their administration. This political orientation does not impede their role as civil servants, indeed their loyalty to serve all democratically elected leaders is taken for granted and civil servants are expected to exercise some restraint when engaging in their political activities.

While at the federal level the careers of politicians and civil servants are still quite separate, that is very few top administrators become politicians and even fewer politicians end up as civil servants, this is gradually changing at the *Länder* level. Here we observe a growing number of 'hybrid' careers, that is people originally working outside the civil service, for example for political parties or in parliament, are appointed to higher civil servant positions and may even end up later in their careers as ministers. At the local level, there is historically an even closer relationship between politics and administration. By legal definition, even local councils are part of the administration, but the close interaction is especially guaranteed by 'elected civil servants' (*Wahlbeamte*), that is mayors and adjunct mayors, who belong both to the sphere of politics and administration.

Both at the federal and *Länder* level, the institution of 'political civil servants' plays an important role. While Prussian public administration has been the empirical inspiration for the Weberian ideal-type of merit bureaucracy, the political importance of top civil servants has, nevertheless, been acknowledged since the middle of the nineteenth century. When the position of civil servants was strengthened by the introduction of lifelong tenure, the understanding grew that trust between rulers and their top administrators is necessary for government and that rulers, therefore, should be able to choose their top civil servants and, if necessary, retire them. Thus, the institution of the 'political civil servant' was invented.

For German ministers at federal and *Länder* level, this means that they are free to choose the top officials in the ministry they lead and can send them into retirement at any time if, for any reason, they no longer enjoy their unlimited trust. Political civil servants, therefore, act as linkages between the professional bureaucracy and the political leadership, helping to create mutual understanding and trust as well as helping to soften misunderstandings and suspicion between both spheres. The typical blame games between politicians and civil servants, or even 'a government of strangers', are therefore rather unusual in Germany. The relationship between politics and administration and between elected politicians and appointed civil servants is also in Germany never without its tensions and conflicts, but all in all the politicised civil service, both in functional and political terms, seems to have led to fewer conflicts, misunderstandings and blame games than in other democratic countries. Top civil servants in Germany need both professional expertise and political craft, they do not pretend to be apolitical and neutral, and the German public usually knows where their top officials come from and what they stand for.

The German institutions and experiences cannot be easily transferred to other political systems. The institutional setting in Germany depends not only on a highly regulated legal system but even more so on a large number of informal rules, which define appropriate behaviour and have been developed and adapted over a long time. Nevertheless, the main idea is relevant for other countries and cultures: a neutral and apolitical civil service should not be taken as given and the political role of civil servants should be accepted, made transparent and not be hidden behind unrealistic assumptions and false pretentions.

NOTES

1. By 1934, two-thirds of all top civil servants in German ministries were members of the NSDAP; the share increased to more than 90 per cent in 1939 and later, own data.
2. All numbers presented in this section stem from an analysis of all administrative state secretary appointments in the German *Länder* (except Bavaria) between 2000 and 2018 (N = 1119) that was conducted with a research grant by the Thyssen Foundation as part of the research project 'Government Constellations and the Politicisation of Bureaucracy'. Data collection is based on biographical data derived from different public sources such as ministry and personal websites, media coverage and parliamentary documents.
3. Term of office differs across the *Länder*.

REFERENCES

Aberbach, J., Putnam, R., & Rockman, B. (1981). *Bureaucrats and Politicians in Western Democracies*. Cambridge, MA/London: Routledge.

Bach, T., & Veit, S. (2018). The Determinants of Promotion to High Public Office in Germany: Partisan Loyalty, Political Craft, or Managerial Competencies? *Journal of Administrative Research and Theory, 28*(2), 254–269.

Bogumil, J., & Holtkamp, L. (2013). *Kommunalpolitik und Kommunalverwaltung—Eine praxisorientierte Einführung*. Bonn: Bundeszentrale für politische Bildung.

Derlien, H.-U. (2003). Mandarins or Managers? The Bureaucratic Elite in Bonn, 1970 to 1987 and Beyond. *Governance, 16*, 401–428.

Ebinger, F., Lux, N., Kintzinger, C., & Garske, B. (2018). Die Deutsche Verwaltungselite der Regierungen Brandt bis Merkel II. Herkunft, Zusammensetzung und Politisierung der Führungskräfte in den Bundesministerien. *der moderne staat—Zeitschrift für Public Policy, Recht und Management, 11*(2), 389–411. https://doi.org/10.3224/dms.v11i2.01.

Ebinger, F., Veit, S., & Fromm, N. (2019). The Partisan-Professional Dichotomy Revisited: Politicization and Decision-Making of Senior Civil Servants. *Public Administration, 97*(4), 861–876.

Fleischer, J. (2016). Partisan and Professional Control: Predictors of Bureaucratic Tenure in Germany. *Acta Politica, 51*(4), 433–450.

Goetz, K. H. (1997). Acquiring Political Craft: Training Grounds for Top Officials in the German Core Executive. *Public Administration, 75*(4), 753–775.

Jann, W. (2003). State, Administration and Governance in Germany—Competing Traditions and Dominant Narratives. *Public Administration, 81*(1), 95–118.

Jann, W., & Veit, S. (2015). Germany. In M. Van Wart, A. Hondeghem, E. Schwella, & P. Suino (Eds.), *IIAS series Governance and Public Management. Leadership and Culture: Comparative Models of Top Civil Servant Training* (pp. 183–198). Basingstoke: Palgrave Macmillan.

Kuhlmann, S., & Wollmann, H. (2019). *Introduction to Comparative Public Administration* (2nd ed.). Cheltenham/Northampton: Edward Elgar.

Kuhlmann, S., Bogumil, J., & Grohs, S. (2008). Evaluating Administrative Modernization in German Local Governments: Success or Failure of the 'New Steering Model'? *Public Administration Review, 68*(5), 851–863.

Lewis, D. E. (2012). Presidential Politicization of the Executive Branch in the United States. In M. Lodge & K. Wegrich (Eds.), *Executive Politics in Times of Crisis* (pp. 41–62). London: Palgrave Macmillan UK. https://doi.org/10.1057/9781137010261_3.

Mayntz, R., & Derlien, H.-U. (1989). Party Patronage and Politicization of the West German Administrative Elite 1970–1987—Toward Hybridization? *Governance: An International Journal of Policy and Administration, 2*(4), 384–404.

Mayntz, R., & Scharpf, F. W. (1975). *Policy-Making in the German Federal Bureaucracy*. Amsterdam: Elsevier.

Meyer Sahling, J. H. (2008). The Changing Colours of the Post-Communist State. *European Journal of Political Research, 47*, 1–33.

Schröter, E. (2004). The Politicization of the German Civil Service: A Three-Dimensional Portrait of the Ministerial Bureaucracy. In B. G. Peters & J. Pierre (Eds.), *Politicization of the Civil Service in Comparative Perspective: A Quest for Control* (1st ed.). London and New York: Routledge.

Veit, S., & Scholz, S. (2016). Linking Administrative Career Patterns and Politicisation: Signalling Effects in the Careers of Top Civil Servants in Germany. *International Review of Administrative Sciences, 82*(3), 516–535.

Weber, M. (2019). *Economy and Society: A New Translation by Keith Tribe*. Cambridge, MA: Harvard University Press.

Wilson, W. (1887). The Study of Administration. *Political Science Quarterly, 2*(2), 197–222.

Open Access This chapter is licensed under the terms of the Creative Commons Attribution 4.0 International License (http://creativecommons.org/licenses/by/4.0/), which permits use, sharing, adaptation, distribution and reproduction in any medium or format, as long as you give appropriate credit to the original author(s) and the source, provide a link to the Creative Commons licence and indicate if changes were made.

The images or other third party material in this chapter are included in the chapter's Creative Commons licence, unless indicated otherwise in a credit line to the material. If material is not included in the chapter's Creative Commons licence and your intended use is not permitted by statutory regulation or exceeds the permitted use, you will need to obtain permission directly from the copyright holder.

CHAPTER 11

Administrative Procedures and Processes

Jan Ziekow

1 Introduction

The title of this chapter, which distinguishes between administrative procedures and processes, already indicates that the view of the procedural 'working' side of the administration is of central importance for the respective administrative cultural understanding. The German understanding of administration is strongly determined by organisation. In this sense, the administration is an organisation subdivided hierarchically and structured by the normative assignment of functions and responsibilities into units of expertise, the 'organisational structure', the framework for the interactions and actions of the administration. Because of this organisational reference, the entirety of the procedures and processes of the administration is called the 'process organisation'. This differs from an understanding that summarises the processes of the administration as 'business processes' and is more process-oriented. However, in the course of New Public Management a much stronger process orientation of the German administrations has taken place (cf. Lenk 2012).

J. Ziekow (✉)
German Research Institute for Public Administration, Speyer, Germany
e-mail: ziekow@foev-speyer.de

© The Author(s) 2021
S. Kuhlmann et al. (eds.), *Public Administration in Germany*,
Governance and Public Management,
https://doi.org/10.1007/978-3-030-53697-8_11

163

164   J. ZIEKOW

While the term procedure has functional connotations and includes aspects such as ensuring transparency, accountability and participation, provision of legitimacy, and ensuring rights and the correctness of the result (Ponce 2005: 552–553), process refers to the totality of administrative workflows for preparing and delivering a service.

2   CLASSIFICATION OF PROCESSES

The literature on the processes of public administration makes a distinction between different forms of process, based predominantly on the process map known from process management with the three stages of core, management and support processes (cf. Bundesministerium des Innern Bundesverwaltungsamt 2018: 4.2; KGSt 2011: 16):

- The core processes of companies are the value-added processes directly related to the customer's wishes that 'give the company its face'. In public administration, this means the service provision processes directly serving the realisation of the unit's strategic goals, usually delivering services to persons outside the organisation.
- Support processes are usually intra-organisational processes that provide the resources or services needed to perform the core processes.
- Management processes—also referred to as leadership or control processes—are processes that are not directly related to actual service provision, but serve to formulate the strategic goals of the organisation and set and enforce standards for performance and a framework for the other types of process.

Not completely identical to the above categorisation is the classification of processes in relation to the boundaries of the respective administrative organisation:

- Processes that are exclusively within the respective administrative organisation, for example those that take place in a ministry, are intra-organisational. These are support and management processes.
- Inter-organisational processes are processes between two or more administrative organisational units. These can be structured at the same level in the form of cooperation and support, or hierarchically. As a rule, these are support and management processes, but

inter-organisational core processes in cooperative service provision are also possible.

- Extra-organisational processes are performed by an organisational unit of the administration to persons or companies outside the administration. These are, almost without exception, core processes to the clients of the administration. The procedures in which these extra-organisational core processes run are usually summarised under the term administrative procedures (see Sect. 1 above).

The presentation of the administrative procedures and processes in this chapter follows the above distinction according to the organisational reference point. Since the German administration is to be classified as a legalistic type of administrative culture, the process of administration in Germany is largely regulated by laws and subordinate acts.

3 Extra-Organisational Procedures

Extra-organisational procedures relate to the administration's 'external' actions, that is those oriented towards citizens and businesses. These actions are to be classified as core processes, as these interventions towards citizens and companies are usually among the core tasks of the respective administrative unit. The conduct of extra-organisational procedures is strongly determined by the interaction with the point of reference of the process, that is the citizen or company. Therefore, for a comprehensive understanding of the extra-organisational procedures in addition to the actual processes of 'outward' service delivery (see Sect. 3.1 below), the communication between the administration and the recipients of the services (see Sect. 3.2 below) is also of importance. The prerequisite for successful communication is information. Therefore, transparency and information are conditions of success for the provision of services by the administration (see Sect. 3.3 below).

3.1 Service Delivery Processes

The discussion about the introduction of New Public Management to the German administration has led to a shift towards a broader understanding of the notion of administrative performance, brought about by product orientation as part of New Public Management. This has established an understanding that defines 'service' as the administration's output created to accomplish each task.

Accordingly, the circle of what is regarded as a 'service' of the administration is large. The spectrum includes financial support and consultations, but also rules and prohibitions, their enforced execution and much more. All services at all levels of the German administration are recorded in a central service catalogue (LeiKa).

The understanding of services as output generated by the administration and the great heterogeneity of services have focussed attention on the need for a differentiated view of this process of output generation. In order to reduce the complexity associated with it for the individual administrations and enable role-model learning, the project of a National Process Library was initially pursued. As an online tool, the aim of this National Process Library was to successively compile and retrieve as many process models as possible at all administrative levels and according to certain order patterns. Since no agreement could be reached on the financing modes, the further development of the National Process Library was discontinued in 2015. Notwithstanding, process libraries are still operated by individual federal states and—for the municipal administrations—by the Local Governments' Joint Agency for Administrative Management (KGSt).

An awareness that providing high quality administrative services and customer satisfaction requires the ability of administrations to develop and establish business processes tailored to their needs has evolved. This has not been ignored but, on the contrary, has been supported by the standardisation and modularisation of processes. This makes it possible, at least for comparable services or process elements, to reduce complexity and make use of proven standard process elements. The digitalisation of the administration makes it possible to call up standard descriptions and modules with regard to the respective service and modify them to measure. In order to enable administrations either to fully model business processes or to modify standardised elements for the individual service, business process management with the goal of optimising business processes has been established at all administrative levels. In addition, business process management is understood as a means of procedurally implementing the digitalisation of administration.

At the level of the federal administration, this increased 'thinking and acting in processes' has been triggered by a project for joint and integrated process optimisation. The Federal Ministry of the Interior (BMI) has initiated the formation of a process management network consisting of process experts from various federal administrations who discuss problems of process management and successful solutions. Among other things, this network has developed a guide to strategic process management for senior managers in public administration (Netzwerk Prozessmanagement 2018). Corresponding process management instructions are available in various federal states. For the municipal level, the KGSt had already presented guidance on process management in 2011 (KGSt 2011).

In addition to establishing and consistently implementing business process management, recent efforts with regard to public service delivery processes have focussed on increasing efficiency in the interests of citizens and businesses and on the digital architecture of business processes. The requirements of the European Union Services Directive on 'single contact' have reinforced a trend towards the introduction of front office/back office structures. This trend already existed at the local level in the form of local 'one-stop shops' for administrative services that were designed to facilitate access for citizens. The function of a local one-stop shop for administrative services is to bundle communication with citizens when using municipal services, such as the renewal of ID cards and the application for social benefits. The fact that only one point of contact for all citizens' matters, which is close to their residences and which will promptly take care of their requests, makes the administration more citizen-oriented. In the course of the digitalisation of the administration, electronic service portals have supplemented the local one-stop shops for administrative services, through which many processes between the citizens and the municipal administration can be handled web-based.

For the digitalisation of the processes, see Sect. 3.2 below.

3.2 Communication

Efforts in Germany to make communication between the administrations and their customers more citizen-friendly and faster by digitalisation initially focussed on asynchronous communication. In this respect, the goal has been to improve the low communication security of a simple email through the establishment of so-called trust services. A central measure has been the establishment of De-Mail services, which may only be offered by accredited companies. However, the use of De-Mail services has remained low in practice. EU-wide safety standards are set by European Regulation (EU) No. 910/2014 on electronic identification and trust services for electronic transactions in the internal market.

A fundamental new approach has been taken with the 2017 Online Access Act (OZG). It stipulates that all administrative services must be offered via electronic administrative portals. However, this does not have to be done exclusively. In addition, the administrations can continue to provide their services in other forms of communication using the multi-channel concept. To facilitate communication for the users, the portals of the individual administrations remain in place but are linked to form an integrated portal network. All administrative services accessible in the portal network are identified uniformly via an individual user account. An electronic mailbox is connected to the user account for secure communication between the authority and the user (cf. Martini and Wiesner 2018; for the digitalisation of public administration cf. Chap. 19, Appendix).

3.3 Transparency and Information

Both within and outside a specific administrative procedure, public authorities are obliged to provide information to citizens. This aims to ensure both the general transparency of the administration and the citizens' confidence in it as well as the protection of the subjective rights of those involved in an administrative procedure.

Within a specific administrative procedure, which should end with a decision by the authority:

- There is the right of the affected party to a hearing by the authority. This right serves to ensure a fair procedure. The person concerned must be given the opportunity to speak before a decision concerning his or her rights is taken, so as to be able to influence the proceeding and its outcome (Section 28 of the Administrative Procedures Act—APA).
- The parties have the right of access to files. This serves to ensure the realisation of the legal hearing and observance of the 'equality of arms principle' by the participants (Section 29 APA).
- In certain proceedings, an applicant may determine the status of the application processed by the authority via the Internet at any time.

Even outside concrete administrative procedures, various information is provided by the authorities to improve transparency and the information situation (cf. Müller et al. 2019):

- Under the Freedom of Information Act (IFG), every citizen has a subjective right of access to official information from any authority. In certain cases, this right does not exist if it is necessary for the protection of particular public interests, the protection of the regulatory decision-making process, the protection of personal data or the protection of business or trade secrets. The right of access to information can be enforced in court.
- In addition to the right of access to information, there are more recent transparency regulations in the federal states *(Länder)* of Hamburg and the Rhineland-Palatinate. In these states, public authorities are required to make certain information that is relevant to the public accessible to everyone via a transparency platform on the Internet.

In addition, there is the nationwide metadata portal GovData where the open data provided by federal, state and local governments can be accessed. Various federal states and municipalities also operate their own open data portals.

3.4 Law

The administrative processes that transcend the intra-organisational and inter-organisational area and address citizens or businesses are almost completely regulated. The reason lies directly in the German understanding of the constitutional state.

3.4.1 Functions of Administrative Procedure Law

Because the state is more powerful than all other actors, mere private law is not an effective means of protecting the freedom of the citizen against the state. This requires a special law for the containment of state power in the form of public law. In Germany, special importance is assigned to general administrative procedure law. Located between the Basic Law and sector-specific special administrative law, the Administrative Procedures Act (APA) functions as a transmission belt, which forwards the standards of constitutional law to daily administrative practice. The APA represents the stabilising backbone of administrative law as a whole. It systematises the central legal institutions, so that regardless of which specific administrative law applies in a given individual case, the same basic patterns are accessed. This establishes transparency and predictability.

In the German federal system, the individual federal states and the federal government respectively regulate the administrative procedures with an individual administrative procedures act for their own administrations. Except for minor deviations, however, these laws contain the same procedural rules.

3.4.2 Structures and Principles of Administrative Procedure Law

In accordance with its aim to contain the power of the state, the APA applies only to sovereign acts of the state, that is acts in which the state relies on public law. If the state acts as a private citizen under private law, the APA is not applicable. Even when the state does act under public law, the APA only applies if the action intended by the administration takes the form of an administrative act or a public law contract *vis-à-vis* the citizen. These are the two most important forms of action by the administration, which are connected with special impacts. The principle of freedom of form should enable the administration to carry out administrative procedures in a simple, expedient and expeditious manner in the interests of citizens and businesses. Only specific decisions are governed by specific procedural rules.

Despite the principle of freedom of the administrative procedure, the APA contains various provisions that the administration must adhere to in order to respect the requirement of a fair trial and protect the interests of the parties (cf. Rowe and Winterhoff 2001). These provisions are mainly:

- The investigative or ex officio investigation principle. On the one hand, this central procedural principle results from the rule of law, in particular the principle of the legality of the administration because it is about clarifying the facts in the public interest. On the other hand, what is behind the principle of ex officio investigation is the legal protection of those involved, in particular the citizen. For this reason, Section 24 APA expressly states that the authority must also take into account all circumstances that are favourable to the participants.
- The duty of support and care of the authority to the participants of the proceedings. The civil servant should not only be a servant of the state but also act as a helper for the citizen to create 'equality of arms' for the parties and prevent the realisation of rights from failure due to ignorance, inexperience or awkwardness in dealing with authorities.
- The right to be heard by the authorities (cf. Sect. 3.3 above).

- The right of access to the files (cf. Sect. 3.3 above).
- The legal bounds of discretion of the authorities. At its discretion, the administration may only decide if a law has allowed this for the specific decision in question. Even if this is the case, the discretion of the authority is not unlimited, but may only be exercised within the framework laid down in the APA.
- The confidence protection principle. This principle protects the person concerned by ensuring that unilateral revocations of decisions already taken by the authorities are not revoked without taking account of the person's trust (legitimate expectation) in the existence of the decision.

3.4.3 Reform Discussions and Recent Developments

More recent discussions and developments with regard to administrative procedure law can be grouped together into three blocks: firstly, changes directly related to the APA; secondly, procedural regulations in the field of digitalisation; and thirdly, considerations at the level of the European Union.

Discussions concerning the amendment of the APA have related, among other things, to the participation of citizens and the acceleration of approval procedures:

- The result of the discussion to strengthen citizen participation was the inclusion of a provision in Section 25 (3) APA, according to which the public is to be involved in major industrial and transport projects before the permit application is submitted to the authority. This provision is significant because, according to earlier German understandings, the general public was not involved in an authorisation procedure, only those whose own rights were actually affected. The public also includes associations which represent the interests of environmental issues and are officially recognised for that purpose (Section 73 (4) APA, Section 2 of the Environmental Appeals Act [UmwRG]).
- For several decades now, Germany has been debating whether the granting of permits for the construction of economic or infrastructure projects takes too long, thus impairing economic development. The most recent law of this kind is the 'Law on the Acceleration of Planning and Approval Procedures in the Transport Sector', which came into force at the end of 2018.

The second big block of recent developments is the discussion about the legal regulation of digital administrative procedures. In the legalistic German administrative culture, there is a high degree of consensus that at least the basic rules of digital administrative procedures should be regulated by law. These regulations have been partly laid down in the APA, and partly in special procedural laws. In particular, basic rules were added to the APA relating to the conditions under which electronic communications can achieve legally binding effects in administrative proceedings (Section 3a APA), the duty to take account of important information from participants in automatic electronic procedures (Section 24 (1) APA), the legal equality of an automatically issued administrative act with a man-made administrative act (Section 35a APA) and the possibility of notification of an administrative act via retrieval from an Internet portal (Section 41 (2a) APA).

Added to this are the e-government laws, that is the acts to promote electronic government for electronic administration issues. These special procedural laws have been adopted for both the federal administration and the administrations of most *Länder*. Among other things, they include provisions on the electronic submission of documents in the administrative procedure, electronic record keeping and access to files, and open data (on the Online Access Act (OZG) cf. Sect. 3.2. above).

A third major thread of discussion is the relationship between German administrative procedure law and the law of the European Union. A new impetus for the importance of the European idea for national administrative procedure law has been provided by a Europe-wide research network, the Research Network on EU Administrative Law (ReNEUAL). After several years of work, this network has developed the 'ReNEUAL Model Rules on EU Administrative Procedure' from an analysis of EU law and the administrative law of the Member States. The approach of the ReNMR corresponds to a great extent to the development of German administrative procedure law. The principle of analysing the different legal subsystems and, through comparative analysis, identifying congruent components and extracting the best elements in order to establish an optimal system at a higher level, one which subsequently establishes a set of propositions to guide the further development of the different legal subsystems, is deeply rooted in the tradition of German federalism. The model rules have initiated reflection on the revision of German law in various regulatory areas of administrative procedure law.

4 Intra-Organisational Processes

Intra-organisational processes designate support and management processes within the respective administrative unit. They serve to set the strategic goals and framework for the organisation and its task fulfilment as well as support the execution of the core processes.

4.1 Management and Support Processes

In the course of the discussion about gearing German administrations more strongly to the principles of New Public Management, the instruments associated with management and support processes have now been further incorporated into the administration. This concerns, for example, the instrument of controlling, which has been implemented in municipal financial reporting at local authority level with the change from cash-based accounting budgetary management to a product-based budget. Since these questions are dealt with in more detail in the Chap. 16, this will not be discussed in detail here. The same applies to performance management, which is also the subject of the Chap. 16.

Quality management is understood as a comprehensive procedural approach, for which German public administrations rely on two basic models (Löffler 2018: 6–10):

- The series of standards ISO 9000 et seq. of the International Organisation for Standardisation (ISO), implemented in Germany in the corresponding standards of the German Institute for Standardisation (DIN), with the core elements being customer orientation, leadership, inclusion of persons, process-oriented approach, improvement, evidence-based decision-making and relationship management, formulates the requirement for an external certification of quality management.
- The Common Assessment Framework (CAF), on the other hand, is a quality assessment instrument in the form of a self-assessment tool, agreed for the civil service of the EU Member States in 2000. It aims to develop and strengthen the administrations' ability for self-assessment in a comprehensive internal communication process and to develop improvements.

Quality management is now carried out in many German authorities, both at the level of the local governments and the administrations of the federal states as well as the federal government. The main challenge is to implement the improvement requirements identified by quality management (Löffler 2018: 10).

It is, therefore, essential that change management should also be part of the quality management process right from the start and that the change process be developed out of the quality management implemented. However, change management also has significance beyond quality management. In view of the intense pressure for change to which the administrations are being subjected, not only through digitalisation but certainly also because of it, methods of change management are, at any rate, widely used in major change processes in German administrations (Die Bundesregierung, Change Management 2019). Recent approaches emphasise above all the necessary change in the thinking of administration employees.

The greater involvement of project-related thinking with the associated project management in German administrations is reflected by a situation-related relativisation of the line organisation structure with a fixed assignment of tasks. This is especially the case for temporary tasks with a high degree of complexity. As a rule, the Joint Rules of Procedure of the Federal Ministries (GGO) provide for the establishment of project-related management by specially established project teams in such tasks (Section 10 (2) GGO). In 2013, the federal government introduced the 'Practical Guide to Project Management for Public Administration'.

4.2 Knowledge Management

The traditional knowledge management of the administration has consisted mainly in archiving and file systems and the individual knowledge of the employees. For almost every German administration there are filing orders or similar administrative instructions that specify in which system the information available to the administrations must be stored in file form so that they can be retrieved as simply as possible.

Due to digitalisation, knowledge management has also undergone a major transformation. First, the knowledge available and the quantity of information and data to be processed by the administrations have grown exponentially. Second, the requirements related to the speed of access and retrieval of knowledge have increased significantly. Third, IT solutions provide the ability to integrate and prepare large pools of knowledge tailored to the needs of each administrative unit.

An empirical study compiled in 2013 showed considerable deficits in the knowledge management of the authorities at that time and room for improvement in the introduction of knowledge management systems (Materna GmbH and Hochschule Harz 2013: 65–67). Since then, a great deal of effort has been made to provide knowledge management solutions tailored to the needs of each agency, thereby anchoring knowledge management broadly in the administration. For example, the Federal Administration Office, a superior federal authority with service functions for the federal administration, offers an intranet solution (OfficeNet) for federal authorities with the option of agency-specific configuration. The authorities using OfficeNet work together in a specialist network and exchange their experiences and perspectives on possible further developments both in workshops and via an online platform. For municipal administrations, the KGSt has a knowledge management best practices database.

From 2020 onwards, the federal authorities are subject to the obligation under Section 6 of the E-Government Act (EGovG) to keep their files electronically. For the period ending 2019, a software solution was initially introduced in several federal agencies as part of a pilot project. In the second phase of the project, the e-file solution provided by the Federal Information Technology Centre, the IT service provider of the federal government, will be introduced for all federal authorities deemed suitable for this purpose based on a capability maturity model.

4.3 Law

The processes within a single administrative unit are generally not governed by legislation in the strict sense (laws enacted by parliament or legal authorisation). The normative control of the internal administrative procedure is governed by administrative rules adopted by the executive itself.

In certain cases, however, rules related to questions on administrative internal processes are established through formal law. These questions concern important preconditions for proximity to the citizen and speed of administration. An example of this is the legal obligation to keep all files electronically (cf. Sect. 4.2 above).

5 Inter-Organisational Processes

Inter-organisational processes take place between different administrative organisational units, regardless of whether they are in a horizontal or vertical (hierarchical) relationship. These processes serve to ensure and improve the effectiveness and efficiency of task performance and the lawfulness of administrative action. To this extent, processes between administrative units can be divided into three categories: communication and cooperation, the support of one administrative unit by another outside cooperative relations and the supervision of one administrative unit by another.

5.1 Inter-Organisational Communication and Cooperation

Communication and cooperation between different administrative units take place in daily work to meet many different kinds of requirements and in various forms. It is an essential element of an active authority culture that authorities inform one another and, if necessary, cooperate to fulfil their tasks more effectively and efficiently. In this respect, two groups of communication and cooperation can be distinguished:

- The communication or cooperation is related to the processes of service provision by at least one of the communicating or cooperating authorities. In this regard, we speak of performance-related cooperation.
- The cooperation is generally for mutual information between authorities. This communication also serves to improve service provision, but only indirectly. Examples are joint meetings or inter-ministerial informal permanent working groups, as set up in Germany both between the federal ministries for the coordination of government work at the working level and in committees on which the relevant ministries of all federal states are represented. These forms of cooperation are not directly related to the process.

As far as performance is concerned, a distinction can be made between communication and cooperation:

- Communication should be understood as the interaction between several administrative units in the context of a specific process of service provision.

11 ADMINISTRATIVE PROCEDURES AND PROCESSES 177

- Cooperation, by contrast, means that formal or informal arrangements are established, independent of a concrete service delivery process, and that after their establishment they are then process owners, or at least contribute to the process.

5.1.1 Performance-Related Communication

In the context of a concrete service provision process, authorities communicate to ensure that all the aspects that are important in that process are incorporated into it and taken into account in the provision of services. This is usually about technical aspects, for example where environmental authorities are involved in approval procedures for industrial plants, or about the impact of the outcome of proceedings on the activities of the administrative unit concerned. The latter, for example, is when the municipality has to be involved in the approval of construction projects by state authorities as this limits the ability of the municipality in terms of future development planning.

On the one hand, this communication can be informal. In this case, the competent authority asks another authority for information which the requesting authority does not have, for example information to assess the impact of certain environmental emissions. On the other hand, the communication is formal if different authorities are required by law to be involved in the service delivery process. The significance of the part contributions provided for by law may differ:

- Involvement is a contribution by an authority to a procedure for which another authority is responsible if the intention is to introduce a specific technical aspect into the procedure. The responsible authority is not bound by the view of the other authority.
- This is different to co-decision. Here, the partial contribution of the other authority is binding for the responsible authority.

5.1.2 Performance-Related Cooperation

For cooperation between different administrative units aimed at improving the fulfilment of the tasks of the participating units with regard to specific service provision processes, two basic cases can be distinguished:

- The cooperation provides *internal* services to the administrative units involved in the cooperation so that they can deliver their services more effectively and efficiently.

178 J. ZIEKOW

- The cooperation concerns not only internal support processes but also—directly—the service provision processes *towards citizens* and companies.

For the first case group, the provision of performance-related support through cooperation, the term shared service (centre) is generally used. Such shared services exist in Germany both horizontally and vertically (Schuppan 2018). In horizontal cooperation, administrative organisations cooperate at the same level with mostly identical tasks. Especially at municipal level, there are numerous examples in the back-office area. They concern, for example, the operation of a common building yard or joint legal department by several municipalities. By far the most important example, however, is shared services in the area of IT. Here a common IT service centre for several municipalities is set up. Vertical cooperation across multiple levels of administration is also found, especially in the IT sector, in the form of a common IT service centre of municipalities with one or more federal states. An example of such a cooperation is the information service provider Dataport. Knowledge sharing, or cross-organisational knowledge management, has been discussed many times (cf. Schulz 2012), but is still in its infancy in terms of practical implementation in Germany. New impetus has come from the discussion under the heading of Data Driven Government (cf. Fadavian et al. 2019).

The cooperation processes directly affecting the provision of services to citizens and businesses are numerous, especially at municipal level. For this, the term 'intercommunal cooperation' is common. The legal forms of intercommunal cooperation are governed by laws on municipal cooperation. There are two basic forms:

- Several municipalities set up a new organisation with its own legal capacity. The organisation performs specific tasks for all municipalities participating in it and performs the service delivery processes to citizens and businesses.
- Several municipalities sign an agreement mandating one of the participating municipalities to perform a specific task for all the other municipalities involved. The process responsibility then lies with the mandated municipality.

5.2 Inter-Organisational Support

According to the German understanding of the functional definition of administration, it is assumed that every authority is able to fulfil its assigned tasks with its own personnel and material resources. If, however, difficulties arise in individual cases, this should not lead to the task in question not being fulfilled. Due to the public interest in effectively fulfilling administrative tasks, in such a situation the authority must request another authority to provide so-called administrative assistance instead. The authority requested to provide the assistance is obliged to do so. In this case the costs it incurs are reimbursed.

The obligation to give assistance has two limitations: firstly, assistance must be complementary and the actual task must be performed by the authority responsible for the task. Secondly, the assistance may only be provided on a case-by-case basis and not constantly. If an agency constantly needs the help of other agencies to fulfil its tasks, its resources need to be improved.

5.3 Inter-Organisational Control

The responsibility of the government to the parliament under German constitutional law presupposes that the government can fulfil this responsibility and have sufficient opportunities to control and influence the performance of the tasks by the administration. This presupposes the right to give orders to the subordinate authorities and civil servants and control of the way in which the assigned tasks are performed. For this purpose, inter-organisational procedures for the control of the authorities by the superordinate authority are established. (For control and accountability by administrative courts and courts of audit see Chap. 12.)

In this respect, a distinction must be made between administrative and technical supervision. Administrative supervision is usually understood as the supervision of the structure, internal order, use and distribution of personnel and other resources, as well as general management and personnel matters of the supervised body. Technical supervision refers to the legitimate and appropriate exercise of the technical tasks of the supervised body. The means of technical supervision typically includes the power of the technical supervisory authority to demand information, request submission of files, carry out examinations, issue instructions and, if these are

180   J. ZIEKOW

not obeyed, take control of the matter by asserting the right of action beyond defined competence.

A third form of supervision besides service and technical supervision is legal supervision. This is limited to reviewing the lawfulness of the decisions of the subordinate authority and does not extend to whether the content of the decision is appropriate. A control restricted to legal supervision usually exists when the subordinate authority has the right of self-government. The most important example is the municipalities.

5.4   Law

Processes in the relationship of several administrative units to one another can only be governed by an administrative regulation if there is a joint upper authority or joint body that issues the regulation. An example of a decree by a joint higher authority is the instruction of a ministry to all lower authorities as to how they are to cooperate in certain cases, which deadlines have to be met between the authorities, etc. An example of procedural rules issued by a joint body of several authorities is the Joint Rules of Procedure of the Federal Ministries (GGO), which is adopted by the federal government as a collegiate body. Among other things, it regulates the cooperation and procedure of the federal ministries in the preparation of cabinet bills.

Inter-organisational procedural rules, adopted in the form of an act of parliament concern, for example:

- the regulation of performance-related communication between public authorities (cf. Sect. 5.1.1 above);
- supervision of one authority over the other (cf. Sect. 5.2 above); and
- administrative assistance (cf. Sect. 5.3 above).

6   LESSONS LEARNED

As for the question to what extent can the experiences of the German administration be regarded as a reference point for development in other countries, the first thing that applies is the same for all transfers of institutions from the administrative culture of one state into another: the structures and administrative processes are embedded in complex environmental systems of a political, legal, social, economic and cultural nature. This usually excludes a transfer in the sense of a simple takeover. Rather, it requires a careful examination of the conditions under which the experiences and institutions of a foreign administrative culture can be made fruitful for one's own structures and administrative processes.

Within this framework, three possible factors from the German experience, which go beyond the general principles of business process and procedure management and are essential for each administration, can be summarised as follows:

- A defining structural attribute of the highly diversified administrative landscape in Germany is its strong involvement in networks and cooperation with other authorities. The examples mentioned above are the creation of learning networks, the joint further development of knowledge management solutions, shared services, in particular in the form of strong intercommunal cooperation, and the obligation to provide mutual assistance to the authorities to fulfil their tasks. This serves to optimise the fulfilment of tasks through mutual learning processes and assistance and the enhancement of synergies.
- Also characteristic of the German understanding of administrative procedures is the legal regulation that puts citizens in a strong position *vis-à-vis* the administration. The APA can certainly be described as an 'export hit'. It is the more or less modified basis for the adoption of administrative procedural law codifications in different countries. The reasons for APA's success lie mainly in its systematic clarity and concentration on the key principles and legal institutions. The high degree of abstraction associated with it makes the provisions of administrative procedure law appear flexible and adaptable to different legal systems.
- Especially for administrative systems that are as highly diversified as Germany's, that is in countries where administration is highly decentralised, the German solution, which preserves the autonomy of administrations and their IT systems and provides nevertheless all administrative services via electronic portals with a uniform user account regardless of which authority is competent, can be a helpful reference.

References

Bundesministerium des Innern, Bundesverwaltungsamt. (2018). *Handbuch für Organisationsuntersuchungen und Personalbedarfsermittlung.*

Die Bundesregierung. (2019). *Change Management—Anwendungshilfe zu Veränderungsprozessen in der öffentlichen Verwaltung.* Berlin.

Fadavian, B., Franzen-Paustenbach, D., Rehfeld, D. et al. (2019). *Data Driven Government.* Berlin.

KGSt. (2011). *Von der Prozessoptimierung zum Prozessmanagement (Teil 1) KGSt-Bericht 3/2011.* Köln.

Lenk, K. (2012). Die Bedeutung von Prozessen und von Prozessdenken für die Modernisierung der öffentlichen Verwaltung. In U. Schliesky & S. Schulz (Eds.), *Die Erneuerung des arbeitenden Staates* (pp. 9–30). Baden-Baden: Nomos.

Löffler, E. (2018). Qualitätsmanagement. In S. Veit, C. Reichard, & G. Wewer (Eds.), *Handbuch zur Verwaltungsreform.* Wiesbaden: Springer VS.

Martini, M., & Wiesner, C. (2018). Bürgerkonto, Portalverbund. In S. Veit, C. Reichard, & G. Wewer (Eds.), *Handbuch zur Verwaltungsreform.* Wiesbaden: Springer VS.

Materna GmbH, Hochschule Harz. (2013). *Wissensmanagement in öffentlichen Verwaltungen.*

Müller, C. E., Engewald, B., & Herr, M. (2019). Freedom of Information in Germany. In D. Dragos, P. Kovač, & A. Marseille (Eds.), *The Laws of Transparency in Action. A European Perspective* (pp. 205–254). Basingstoke: Palgrave Macmillan.

Netzwerk Prozessmanagement. (2018). *Einführung in das strategische Prozessmanagement der öffentlichen Verwaltung.*

Ponce, J. (2005). Good Administration and Administrative Procedures. *Indiana Journal of Global Legal Studies, 12*(2, Art. 10), 551–588.

Rowe, N., & Winterhoff, C. (2001). Participants' Rights and Duties in German Administrative Law. *European Review of Public Law, 13*, 1117–1143.

Schulz, S. (2012). Vernetztes Wissen—Shared Services im Wissensmanagement. In U. Schliesky & S. Schulz (Eds.), *Die Erneuerung des arbeitenden Staates* (pp. 113–140). Baden-Baden: Nomos.

Schuppan, T. (2018). Shared Service Center. In S. Veit, C. Reichard, & G. Wewer (Eds.), *Handbuch zur Verwaltungsreform.* Wiesbaden: Springer VS.

Open Access This chapter is licensed under the terms of the Creative Commons Attribution 4.0 International License (http://creativecommons.org/licenses/by/4.0/), which permits use, sharing, adaptation, distribution and reproduction in any medium or format, as long as you give appropriate credit to the original author(s) and the source, provide a link to the Creative Commons licence and indicate if changes were made.

The images or other third party material in this chapter are included in the chapter's Creative Commons licence, unless indicated otherwise in a credit line to the material. If material is not included in the chapter's Creative Commons licence and your intended use is not permitted by statutory regulation or exceeds the permitted use, you will need to obtain permission directly from the copyright holder.

CHAPTER 12

Control and Accountability: Administrative Courts and Courts of Audit

Veith Mehde

1 Introduction

In this chapter, two very different mechanisms are described. Both of them play a central role in the system, guaranteeing an adequate level of control of the administration in Germany (for a broad picture of both means of control see Kempny 2017). At all levels—the federal (Bund), the state (*Länder*) and the local level—the respective administration is a potential object of control by administrative courts and by audit offices. The administrative courts form—by and large—a joint system. As one of the characteristics of this joint system, cases are generally decided by courts established by the *Länder*, even when they invoke questions regulated by federal law, while the highest court of appeal in all matters regarding the application of federal law is a federal court. In contrast to this, there are no formal links between the different courts of audits in Germany. Rather, the federal level and each of the *Länder* have instituted them in their respective constitutions and have fulfilled their constitutional obligation to establish them as independent bodies. At the local level, similar

V. Mehde (✉)
Leibniz University Hannover, Hannover, Germany
e-mail: mehde@jura.uni-hannover.de

© The Author(s) 2021
S. Kuhlmann et al. (eds.), *Public Administration in Germany*,
Governance and Public Management,
https://doi.org/10.1007/978-3-030-53697-8_12

185

186   V. MEHDE

instruments are in place under the supervision of the respective *Land* that controls the financial propriety and efficiency of actions by the local governments in their territory.

In both scientific and general public debate, control is regarded as 'a necessary evil' (Püttner 2001: 560). As will be shown, the mechanisms of control described in this chapter are well-established (for a typology see Püttner 2001: 561). The same could be said about the concept of accountability, which, from a legal point of view, is an element of the more complex concept of democratic legitimacy. In this sense, it is not the role of administrative courts and courts of audit to hold the administration accountable. Rather, their efforts to control the administration give other actors—parliaments, the public, the media and so on—the possibility to hold the respective administration accountable.

2   Administrative Courts

The control of administrative actions by specialised courts has a long history in Germany (see von Oertzen and Hauschild 2001: 569–570; Ramsauer 2019: 24–25). The fact that administrative courts are not the 'ordinary' courts does not imply any privileges on the part of the administration. Part of the judicial system as set out by Article 95 of the Basic Law—the *Grundgesetz* (GG)—comprises 'ordinary courts' on the one hand, and specialised courts on the other. The latter are set up in the fields of administrative law, tax law, employment law and social security law. This set of different types of courts shows that their creation is a question of professional specialisation, not of institutional privileges.

The relevant rules regarding the system of control as exercised by the administrative courts can be found in the *Grundgesetz*—Basic Law,[1] the *Verwaltungsverfahrensgesetz*—Administrative Procedure Act (APA),[2] and the *Verwaltungsgerichtsordnung*—Code of Administrative Court Procedure (CACP).[3]

2.1   The Structure of Administrative Courts in Germany

As previously mentioned, the German judiciary is divided into five different branches. Three of these five branches are courts with a certain control function regarding some part of the administration. Apart from the administrative courts in the strict sense, there are the so-called finance courts for all matters regarding the application of tax law. A similar level of specialisation can be observed with regard to the social courts in matters regarding social security, which include legal questions regarding pensions and public healthcare and other matters that involve a public insurance system or social benefits provided by public administration. In these cases, due to the explicit responsibility of these specialised entities—that is, specialised administrative courts—the administrative courts as such do not get involved. In contrast to this, claims of damages against the public administration have to be pursued in the ordinary courts just as in cases of civil litigation. Other laws give the administrative courts exclusive jurisdiction to review certain administrative decisions. Probably the most prominent cases involve matters regarding the individual employment of civil servants (while public employees have to pursue their claims in the so-called labour courts).

If neither of the two preceding constellations—exclusive jurisdiction of the administrative courts or of any other specialised court—is given, the so-called administrative court's universal clause is applicable (see von Oertzen and Hauschild 2001: 570). According to Section 40 (1), first sentence of CACP: 'Recourse to the administrative courts shall be available in all public-law disputes of a non-constitutional nature, insofar as the disputes are not explicitly allocated to another court by a federal statute.' The *Länder* have the same power to allocate disputes to other courts in all matters of '(p)ublic-law disputes in the field of *Land* law' (Section 40 (1), sentence 2 CACP). The application of the clause therefore requires a definition of the term 'public-law dispute' (see Singh 2001: 197ff.). In most cases, though, the interpretation is not a problem because in practice the application of the norm is quite well-established and normally does not give rise to any relevant legal problem.

There are three levels of administrative courts in Germany (Singh 2001: 187ff.). Most cases have to be filed in the administrative courts (*Verwaltungsgericht*), which are courts of first instance with a regional configuration (see Mehde 2017: 119ff.). Appeal can be granted to or by the higher administrative court (*Oberverwaltungsgericht* or *Verwaltungsgerichtshof*), of which there can only be one in each *Land* (Section 2 CACP). The *Länder* Berlin and Brandenburg have established a joint *Oberverwaltungsgericht* so that there is a total of fifteen among the sixteen German *Länder*. Both the administrative courts and the higher administrative courts are established by the *Länder*. In contrast to the compulsory establishment of only one higher administrative court, the *Länder* are free to decide how many administrative courts they want to have and how large their judicial districts should be. Especially the more populous states have a number of administrative courts—and therefore judicial districts—while smaller states (the city-states Berlin, Bremen and Hamburg as well as Saarland and Schleswig-Holstein) have established only one (Mehde 2017: 128; von Oertzen and Hauschild 2001: 572; Singh 2001: 187–188). These courts apply law enacted by the *Länder* or the local governments as well as federal law, so that the federal government and its administrative bodies can be sued before the administrative court in the respective judicial district.

The Federal Administrative Court (*Bundesverwaltungsgericht*) is the highest court of appeal in the field of administrative law. While the administrative courts and the higher administrative courts apply law passed by the parliaments at the federal level or in the respective *Land* as well as by rule-making bodies at the local level, the jurisdiction of the Federal Administrative Court is restricted to questions of federal law. As a consequence, the interpretation of the law of the *Länder* falls within the exclusive jurisdiction of the administrative courts in the respective *Land*, with the court of last instance in these cases being the respective *Oberverwaltungsgericht*. It should be noted, though, that many questions of administrative law have to be seen in the context of the constitutional and European framework, which can provide an angle to assume a federal jurisdiction (see Mehde 2017: 136).

2.2 Empirical Facts

Cases that have to be decided by the administrative courts often mirror practical developments, namely special challenges the executive is faced with. Especially the number of cases pending with the courts of first instance can give an impression which topics are most controversial in the relationship between the various parts of the state and citizens. In the ten years between 2007 and 2016, pending before the administrative courts were—on average—between 100,000 and 150,000 cases (all figures regarding administrative courts are according to Statistisches Bundesamt 2019b: 12–13). The year 2017 saw an increase to almost 190,000, followed by a massive peak with more than 338,000 in 2018. An explanation for this increase can be found in the number of cases pending before the chambers with special jurisdiction for asylum cases. They saw a decrease from just over 67,000 in 2004 to just under 10,000 in 2010. From then on, the number increased, slowly at first and then very significantly towards the end of the decade (2017: 104,060; 2018: 242,077). Here, of course, the effects of the so-called refugee crisis of late 2015 can be seen as in 2016 and the following years, many of those who came to Germany received the decision regarding their right to stay in Germany from the Federal Office for Migration and Refugees. The figures for the chambers that have no jurisdiction for asylum cases have developed quite differently: these parts of the administrative courts of first instance have seen a constant decrease in the number of cases pending, from 175,048 (2004) to 86,275 (2013). The figures stayed at approximately the same level in the years following (2017: 85,113; 2018: 95,998). As the number of new cases also remains more or less stable (2014: 104,408; 2015: 94,206; 2016: 89,755; 2017: 92,171; 2018: 90,253), the—relatively modest—increase since 2017 probably cannot be explained by the number of new cases, but is far more likely a consequence of a massive shift of resources in the direction of the chambers dealing with asylum cases. That this was also regarded as a political challenge in need of decisive actions is proved by the fact that the number of positions for judges in the administrative courts of first instance saw a considerable increase from just under 1400 in 2013 to just over 1900 in 2018 (Bundesamt für Justiz 2019).

By and large, the social courts of first instance have an even higher number of cases to decide (the following figures are all according to Statistisches Bundesamt 2019a: 14–15). The figures for cases pending have remained stable at a very high level: from 355,379 in 2005 to 445,559 in 2018, reaching a peak in 2012 (497,697). Of the cases concluded in 2018, around a third dealt with questions regarding the second book of the social code (Statistisches Bundesamt 2019a: 28), which provides the legal basis for the rights of people searching for employment and which was the subject of major reforms in the first decade of the century. As a consequence of the high number of cases, it could well be said—at least quantitatively—that the social courts are the more relevant type of administrative courts. Nevertheless, the following remarks will focus on courts officially called 'administrative courts', as they can be regarded as the most important point of reference in the development of administrative law and have, thereby, also contributed to the perception of the law in other areas, such as social security law.

190   V. MEHDE

2.3   Types of Decisions

Three types of applications can be filed with the administrative courts (see von Oertzen and Hauschild 2001: 575; Singh 2001: 210ff.): first, motions to quash an administrative act; second, motions to force the administration to do something or refrain from doing something; and third, motions to declare that a certain legal relationship exists or does not exist or that an administrative act is void. Conceptually, the motion to quash an administrative act can be regarded as the basic structure. In this case, the administration made a formal decision that was issued and that is still in place. Following the motion, the court then decides the matter directly. Section 113 (1), first sentence of CACP, determines: 'Insofar as the administrative act is unlawful and the plaintiff's rights have been violated, the court shall rescind the administrative act and any ruling on an objection.' When the judgement of the court enters into effect, the administrative act becomes invalid. In cases where the administrative act has ceased to have any effect before the judgement of the court could be delivered, the plaintiff can file a motion to declare the administrative act illegal and an infringement of his or her rights. A declaration of illegality is, in effect, also possible if the action of the administration does not qualify as a formal administrative act.[4] This declaration can also be made with regard to the different types of executive legislation. While only the respective (federal or *Länder*) constitutional court can rule statutes passed by parliament at the federal or *Länder* level to be unconstitutional—and thereby void—all administrative courts can regard 'other legal provisions ranking below the statutes of a *Land*' (see Section 47 (1), no. 2 CACP) or of the federation (the Bund) as illegal and therefore not applicable. If the administration refuses to grant an administrative act, the courts can order the administration to do so or, if the administration has scope for decision-making (see previous Sect. 2.2), force the administration to decide again, 'taking the legal view of the court into consideration' (Section 113 (5), sentence 2 CACP). If the matter the plaintiff applies for is not an administrative act, similar rules apply.

In all cases where the plaintiff—for whatever reason—does not have the time to wait for a judgement following the regular procedure, the court can grant interim injunctions (see von Oertzen and Hauschild 2001: 581–582; Singh 2001: 237ff.). As a general rule, interim injunctions cannot replace decisions taken in the ordinary procedures. Nevertheless, the protection of the plaintiff's rights is the priority that can be a justification for taking decisions that are, in effect, final if this is the only possibility to protect the respective rights.

Altogether, this brief description shows that the various possible constellations are covered in a system that tries to make available effective legal remedies in all cases where infringements of rights can be avoided or amended, or at least to provide a retroactive control mechanism when the infringement of rights has already ended. The differences in the applications lead to equivalent procedural differences, but they are no reason to raise doubts about the universal protection of rights by the administrative courts.

2.4   Depth of Control

The administrative courts use the same methodology as the administration to decide a particular case in its decision-making process. This also implies that the German system of judicial review, in principle, does not accept the notion that there should be scope for administrative actions not fully reviewable by the courts. That is to say, even very vague words in any given law—be it 'public interest', 'proportionality', 'trust' or similar terms open to interpretation—will be interpreted by the courts independently. Any difference between the interpretation found by the administration, on the one hand, and the finding by the court on the other, will lead to the conclusion that the original administrative decision violated the law (Ramsauer 2019: 33–34). This rule is backed by a constitutional right, enforceable in all courts, including the Federal Constitutional Court (*Bundesverfassungsgericht*). The respective norm, Article 19 (4), sentence 1 of the Basic Law, reads as follows: 'Should any person's rights be violated by public authority, he may have recourse to the courts.' This is understood by the *Bundesverfassungsgericht* and the various administrative courts as prescribing a full judicial review of undetermined legal norms in all cases where the claimant's rights would be violated if the administrative actions were illegal. Consequently, the vast scope of the judicial review regarding the application of the law is not only a legal rule but also a basic right.

Two exceptions to the rule regarding the full control of the application of norms are accepted (see Ramsauer 2019: 30ff.). The courts distinguish between the provisions of the norm itself and the legal consequences, that is, the actions the administration can take because the norm is applicable in the respective case. The latter concerns situations where the

192   V. MEHDE

administration can act without authorisation in the law because its actions do not involve any interference with rights and are not regulated by any applicable norm. More often, the administration is granted discretion whenever the law explicitly says so. The norm indicates this fact by stating that certain actions 'may' or 'can' be taken.

2.4.1   Exception No. 1: Discretion

The legal concept of administrative discretion concerns the legal consequences whenever the conditions of an application of a certain norm are met. Section 40 of APA reads as follows: 'Where an authority is empowered to act at its discretion, it shall do so in accordance with the purpose of such empowerment and shall respect the legal limits to such discretionary powers.' The rule shows that discretion is regarded as an exception—and that this exception is granted by the law itself. It is not stated explicitly, but undoubtedly implies that the administrative courts have to accept that, only in this case, the administration has the final say on which decision should be taken in a specific context and that the administrative courts then have no authority to give the final decision in the case under consideration. This is confirmed by Section 114, first sentence of CACP, which reads as follows: 'Insofar as the administrative authority is empowered to act in its discretion, the court shall also examine whether the administrative act or the refusal or omission of the administrative act is unlawful because the statutory limits of discretion have been overstepped or discretion has been used in a manner not corresponding to the purpose of the empowerment.' This description shows the difference. In the case of 'regular' control, the courts provide the authoritative interpretation of a given norm, which is binding for the administration in the case under review. In the case of discretion, the role of the courts is restricted to the question of whether the administration made mistakes in the application of the norm. In other words, the norms mentioned demonstrate the shift from the question 'What is the right interpretation of the law?' to 'Was the administration right in its application of the law?'

The exercise of discretionary powers does not imply an authorisation to 'free' decision-making. The courts apply the above-mentioned Section 114 (1) of CACP in a way that allows them to cover a broad spectrum of aspects relevant in all administrative decision-making. The starting point are four clearly defined types of 'discretion mistakes' that can be made by the administration (Singh 2001: 156ff.). The first two of these types—the first dichotomy of possible mistakes—could be regarded as mere formalities: the courts ask if the deciding administration was aware of the scope of its discretionary power and if it saw the boundaries of the law established. The former aspects include cases in which the administration did not see at all that it had been granted discretionary power. Of course, this is a rather theoretical idea which—in times of highly professionalised administrations—does not play a noticeable role. In contrast to this, the precise definition of boundaries is very relevant in practice, as it includes the question of whether the respective decision was proportionate. Proportionality is probably the single most important topic in all matters involving administrative discretion. The concept gives the court broad power to determine whether the decision is necessary—that is, is there an equally effective alternative that would infringe rights to a lesser degree? More importantly, it also implies the question of whether there was an adequate balance between the aim of the decision and the impairment of the addressee's rights. Considering that this requires a weighing of legal positions that tend to be virtually impossible to compare, it seems fair to say that there are no clear-cut rules that can guide this balancing act.

The second dichotomy of possible mistakes refers to the merits of the decision under consideration. The joint headline for this kind of mistake is 'wrongful exercise of discretion'. The starting point of this concept is the above-mentioned provision that ties the administrative decision to the purpose of the norm providing the administration with discretionary powers (Section 40 APA; Section 114 (1) CACP). In relation to this purpose, the court can establish which aspects of the case should be considered when taking the decision and vice versa. In other words, the courts scrutinise the reasons the administration gives for the respective decision. They will then decide if the arguments are legitimate in the application of the legal norm or if a certain aspect of the cases should have been considered or should have played a larger role in determining the decision. In both variances, the courts regard any mistake as a reason to declare the exercise of discretion as wrongful and, therefore, the respective decision as unlawful.

2.4.2 Exception No. 2: Scope for Appreciation

In the other case where courts do not control the interpretation of legal norms to its full extent—administrative scope for the application of the legal terms—the primary interpretative role of the administration is typically not stated explicitly in the respective law. It should also be noted that in the German system, the courts generally have to investigate all relevant facts irrespective of the evidence provided by the parties (von Oertzen and Hauschild 2001: 576), so that the role of the courts is always a very relevant one. Nevertheless, there is no doubt that, in certain instances, there are factual problems regarding a full-scale review of administrative actions (see Ramsauer 2019: 35ff.). A typical example in this respect is the appraisal civil servants receive after a certain period of time. The grade any given person has to receive for a given achievement is defined by legal norms. Obviously, from a merely practical point of view, it is impossible for an administrative court to reconstruct the personal behaviour and the achievements of the respective civil servant over such a long period of time, thereby finding the 'right' grade. Very similar problems arise with regard to exams (see Bundesverfassungsgericht 1991a, 1991b). Other constellations in this regard concern specific decision-making processes. In all these cases, the restricted role of the courts could be described as an exercise in legal realism. The courts do realise that a tighter form of control would be nothing less than hubris.

As with discretion, the courts in these cases do not abstain from all forms of control but rather change the method they apply, asking if the administration made a mistake in taking the specific decision. The types of mistakes that lead to quashing the respective decision are very similar to the ones described with regard to administrative discretion. The *Bundesverfassungsgericht* points out that the control by the administrative court has to meet certain substantial standards. In particular, it rules that it is not within the scope of the decision-making by the administration to grade a position that is arguable or has foundation in the relevant scientific literature as being wrong (Bundesverfassungsgericht 1991a: 55; see also Bundesverfassungsgericht 1991b: 79).

2.5   *Extent of Control*

The description has shown that the different types of motions, in addition to the wide-ranging interpretation of the law, seem to lead to a near-complete control of the administrative action under review by the courts. Obviously, this is not the full picture. There are safeguards in place that prevent a complete dominance of administrative decision-making by the courts. The most important instrument in this respect is the restriction the German system provides for the question of *locus standi* (the *Klagebefugnis*) (see Singh 2001: 214ff.). Control of administrative actions by administrative courts is an intended element of the German *Rechtsstaat* and therefore, of course, no accident. Nevertheless, it would be wrong to assume that the law established the courts as institutions of general control or even as a means to dominate executive decision-making. Rather, the protection of rights is the focus of judicial review, with the question of legality being one part of this. In fact, it could well be argued that the role of the administrative courts is not to control the administration, but rather to provide a remedy when rights are violated by the administration. The vast possibilities the courts have to exercise control in every case they have to decide is only acceptable because access to the court is clearly defined and restricted. The previously mentioned Article 19 (4), first sentence of the Basic Law, while guaranteeing access to the court in the case of violations of rights, has, in practice, been turned into a provision that reduces the court's role to one of protector of these rights, thereby effectively barring them from all other forms of control.

Section 42 (2) of CACP plays the role of a kind of gatekeeper. It states, 'Unless otherwise provided by law, the action shall only be admissible if the plaintiff claims that his/her rights have been violated by the administrative act or its refusal or omission.' This rule, directly applicable only to rescissory actions and enforcement actions (see Section 42 (2) CACP), is applied in all cases brought before the administrative courts. The courts will only decide on the merits of the case if a violation of the claimant's rights seems plausible. The previously mentioned Section 113 (1), first sentence of CACP, stresses this point even further, stating that the court will rescind the administrative act only if two conditions are met: illegality of the act and violation of the plaintiff's rights. The same rule—court action only in the case of violations of the plaintiff's rights—applies with regard to enforcement actions as is clearly stated in Section 113 (5), first sentence of CACP. In some constellations, the question of whether a certain rule is not only 'objective' law but also grants a 'subjective' right might prove to be more problematic than the legality of the administrative action itself, and it might thereby determine the outcome of the case. This is particularly relevant in 'triangular legal relationships', that is, whenever a third party tries to get an administrative act rescinded that was addressed to someone else, such as in the case of someone trying to invalidate his or her neighbour's building permission.

These restrictions give rise to a number of questions relating to the obligations stemming from EU law (see, e.g., Mehde 2010: 400 f.; Ramsauer 2019: 29; Siegel 2012: 456). Unlike the approach described under Section 42 (2) of CACP, the European legislature seems to regard the courts in the EU member states much more as instruments to safeguard the implementation of European law (Schlacke 2014: 11; see also Mehde 2010: 401). At the very least, it can be said that the European Court of Justice (ECJ) tends to rule much more generously when the question arises as to whether the plaintiff has a legal right with the consequence of *locus standi* (Steinbeiß-Winkelmann 2010: 1233, 1234). The German legislature as well as the courts have tended to widen the rules on *locus standi* in the respective areas of the law without challenging the concept as such. To the above-mentioned rules a general reservation, 'unless EU law requires otherwise', must be added.

It should also be noted that as another development introduced by European as well as by international law, in a number of fields, the law now grants *locus standi* to certain, formally accredited associations (NGOs) that are engaged in the respective fields. This privilege is restricted to legal provisions for which there is typically no claimant under the traditional system, as the negative effects concern aspects of the environment, that is, no person or legal entity. The respective rights are not laid down in the CACP but in the special legislation. The most relevant of these can be found in environmental law, namely the Aarhus Convention and Directive 2003/35/EC of the European Parliament and of the Council (see Siegel 2012: 145–146). It should also be mentioned that there are certain areas in which the *Länder* can decide to allow associations to bring claims in restricted areas, such as matters concerning animal protection.

2.6 Remaining Aspects Concerning Judicial Control

It is one of the features of the German system that judgements tend to have greater effect than the law requires (see Mehde 2010: 382; Ramsauer 2019: 42ff.). In most cases, the formal binding effect is restricted to the plaintiff and the defendant—normally the administration acting or failing to act—and possible third parties subpoenaed to the concrete proceedings. In fact, though, the administration tends to apply the merits of the judgements in the same way as they would apply legal norms. The administration and the individuals acting on behalf of the administration can avoid criticism or at least deflect possible blame away from themselves when they are able to depict their decision as a necessary consequence of court rulings, even if these rulings are—in a strictly legal sense—not binding for them with regard to the case under consideration (Mehde 2010: 384). This can be described as a matter of precise interpretation of the law and as an element of the German *Rechtsstaat* or the legalistic tradition respectively. From a different point of view and equally arguable, the same phenomenon can be regarded as an overly cautious approach that undermines the primary role of the executive in the application of the law.

3 Courts of Audit

Unlike the courts of justice, the courts of audit can decide themselves if and when to look into a certain matter. In general, the scope of their control is restricted to questions of financial propriety and efficiency. In federal law, the legal base can be found in Article 114 (2), first and second sentences of the Basic Law: 'The Federal Court of Audit, whose members shall enjoy judicial independence, shall audit the account and determine whether public finances have been properly and efficiently administered. It shall submit an annual report directly to the Bundestag and the Bundesrat as well as to the Federal Government.' The provisions determine the basic organisational structure as well as the scope of review and the manner in which its work can gain effect. It should be noted that this is only a minimal requirement. Article 114 (2), sentence 3, determines that further powers can be transferred to the court by federal law. In fact, the role of the federal court and its president has been extended and organisational features further developed in statutes, namely the *Bundesrechnungshof* Act (BA).[5]

In accordance with a long-standing tradition, the president of the federal court is also appointed to the position of 'Federal Performance Commissioner'.[6] In this position, he or she has a broad spectrum of possibilities to advise both the legislature and the executive and can also be asked to provide expert opinions.[7] Nevertheless, the role does not feature as prominently in practice as its description or the possibilities implied by it might suggest.

In the *Länder*, the respective constitutions contain equivalent provisions. Therefore, there is a total of seventeen courts of audit in Germany, one at the federal level and one in each one of the sixteen *Länder*—all with 'similar institutional design' (Seyfried 2016: 494). At the local level, similar institutional arrangements have been established in the local government laws of the *Länder*.

3.1 Organisational Features

As '(i)ndependence is one of the most important preconditions for the effectiveness of' supreme audit institutions (Seyfried 2016: 494), the aspect of the organisational design that seems most relevant is the fact that the courts of audit are independent institutions bound only by the law that cannot be ordered to perform their functions in any specific way (Seyfried 2016: 494 f.; von Wedel 2001: 586 f.). As the above-mentioned constitutional requirement points out, the members enjoy the most independent status possible in the public sector: judicial independence. Pursuant to Section 3 (1) of BA, the members of the *Bundesrechnungshof* are the president, the vice-president, the senior audit directors and audit directors. These members—but only three audit directors—serve on the *Senate* of the *Bundesrechnungshof*. Its independent character is further guaranteed by the fact that both the president and the vice-president are not appointed by the government of the day—as would be the case with 'ordinary' high-ranking positions in the administration—but elected by the Bundestag and the Bundesrat, respectively, and appointed by the federal president (Section 3 (2), sentence 1, and Section 5 (2), sentences 1–3 BA; for a description of the procedure in the federal states see Seyfried 2016: 495ff.). The appointees chosen are elected for a term of twelve years, cannot be re-elected and have to retire after their time in office (Section 3 (2), sentence 2, and Section 5 (1), sentence 4 BA). According to Section 7 of BA, the duties are assigned to the different entities within the *Bundesrechnungshof* by the president, the vice-president and the *Senate*.

3.2 Scope of Review

In accordance with the provisions of Article 114 (2), sentence 1 of the Basic Law, the court of audit controls the respective administration, which includes all transactions of any financial relevance (von Wedel 2001: 587). There are different kinds of audits, with the courts being able to freely determine the different aspects (von Wedel 2001: 589). The measures applied are propriety, on the one hand, and efficiency, on the other. Propriety includes the question of whether budgetary means were spent in the way prescribed by the budget. This can be controlled quite effectively when the officials from the courts of audit establishing the facts have access to the invoices and other documents relating to particular spending processes. The question of efficient expenditure gives rise to more complex deliberations (see Engels 2015: 116ff.). Obviously, various definitions can be applied. There are basically two variables: the costs and the effects. Both have to be put in relation to each other (von Wedel 2001: 588). Efficiency requires an optimal relation between the two. It is part of the responsible assessment by the court of audit if this standard has been met in a particular case. It is part of the role of these institutions that their impact largely depends on the soundness of their assessments. This is probably the most effective instrument to ensure that the evaluations have a firm basis.

While the original role described in Article 114 (2) of the Basic Law is a retroactive one, the courts of audit have subsequently been given an advisory role that they can exercise before a final decision is made by the government or the parliament (von Wedel 2001: 591). It can also be described as a change in the 'audit philosophy' that the courts try to get involved in planning processes at an early stage (Engels 2015: 118).

3.3 Effects

The courts of audit have no executive powers and perform no judicial functions (von Wedel 2001: 593). The above-mentioned Article 114 of the Basic Law mentions the audit and the annual publication of findings as the only activity by the *Bundesrechnungshof*. In fact, courts of audit act by informing the relevant administrative entities as well as the respective parliaments and/or the relevant parliamentary committees. In particular, relevant findings have to be published (see Kempny 2017: 241ff.). Before the publication, the findings are normally discussed with the respective administrations and, if relevant, existing supervisory bodies (von Wedel 2001: 590). In reality, reports by the courts of audit only become part of the political debate when 'wasteful' spending is denounced—typically in the annual reports, less frequently when the courts of audit are commissioned to file special reports. Over the course of a year, with budgets and bureaucracies as big as those of the German *Länder* and at the federal level, it is literally unthinkable that the courts of audit do not find some kind of spending that can be described as unnecessary or otherwise wasteful. From a point of acceptance of the system as a part of democratic legitimacy, this effect bears a certain ambivalence, as this kind of critique might not be regarded as a normal form of control that is part of a well-functioning system but, on the contrary, might be misunderstood as evidence of systemic failure on the side of the administration and possibly of the government of the day.

4 Lessons Learned

The control mechanisms described in this chapter enable the public as well as the electorate to hold the executive accountable. Both types of control have almost nothing in common but, at the same time, and in many respects, complement one another. They are important parts of a system that, overall, leads to an acceptable level of control and which plays an important role in guaranteeing an adequate level of democratic legitimacy of the administration.

In the case of the courts, it should be noted that the essential idea behind the mechanism is not to control the executive in a general way. Their role is designed to help people as well as other entities that can bear subjective rights to enforce their rights effectively. In order to fulfil this task, courts have to control the legality of administrative actions. In addition, the law as well as the courts have developed a number of mechanisms that give them the possibility to rule on cases even when there is no question of a present violation of rights involved, mainly because the administrative action has already occurred and cannot be revoked retroactively. Mainly as a consequence of the adaption of EU requirements, in some areas, the courts get involved at the request of organisations that do not invoke their own legal rights. Rather, their claims involve interests in the topic that do not fulfil the necessary requirements for the establishment of a legal right. Altogether, this leads to a mechanism which has effects far beyond the particular case. Administrative courts, in this sense, are the authoritative source of the interpretation of the law. In many instances, when an administrative court has ruled on a certain matter involving an interpretation of a certain legal rule, the administration will consider the relevant legal question as settled. Administrations often apply the essential findings of the courts as if they were the law itself even when they deal with cases on which the court's decision has no direct effect.

In the case of courts of audit, the control is exercised in a clearly defined but certainly broad fashion without the need for initiation by external actors. Administrations have to fear that a control may be exercised, which could lead to an embarrassing—published—claim of wasteful spending. This possibility should already have a restricting effect on administrations so that the lack of formally binding executive powers is likely not missed.

NOTES

1. All translations of this law in accordance with https://www.gesetze-im-internet.de/englisch_gg/englisch_gg.html#p0108 (all websites quoted in this chapter were last visited on 10 January 2020).
2. All translations of this law in accordance with https://www.bmi.bund.de/SharedDocs/downloads/EN/gesetztestexte/VwVfg_en.pdf?__blob=publicationFile&;v=1.
3. All translations of this law in accordance with http://www.gesetze-im-internet.de/englisch_vwgo/englisch_vwgo.html#p0545.
4. The administrative act is defined in Section 35, first sentence of APA: 'An administrative act shall be any order, decision or other sovereign measure taken by an authority to regulate an individual case in the sphere of public law and intended to have a direct, external legal effect.'
5. All translations of this law in accordance with https://www.bundesrechnungshof.de/en/bundesrechnungshof/rechtsgrundlagen/bundesrechnungshof-act.
6. https://www.bundesrechnungshof.de/en/bundesrechnungshof/bundesbeauftragter-bwv?set_language=en.
7. https://www.bundesrechnungshof.de/en/bundesrechnungshof/bundesbeauftragter-bwv/status-and-tasks?set_language=en.

REFERENCES

Bundesamt für Justiz, Personalbestand der Verwaltungsgerichtsbarkeit, Stand: 16.10.2019, Retrieved January 10, 2020, from https://www.bundesjustizamt.de/DE/SharedDocs/Publikationen/Justizstatistik/Personalbestand_VG.pdf?__blob=publicationFile&v=13.

Bundesverfassungsgericht. (1991a). BVerfGE 84, 34–58.

Bundesverfassungsgericht. (1991b). BVerfGE 84, 59–82.

Engels, D. (2015). Der haushaltsrechtliche Grundsatz der Wirtschaftlichkeit. *Verwaltung & Management, 21*(3), 115–124.

Kempny, S. (2017). *Verwaltungskontrolle—Zur Systematisierung der Mittel zur Sicherung administrativer Rationalität unter besonderer Berücksichtigung der Gerichte und der Rechnungshöfe.* Tübingen: Mohr Siebeck.

Mehde, V. (2010). Verwaltungskontrolle als Daueraufgabe der Verwaltungsgerichtsbarkeit. *Die Verwaltung, 43*(3), 379–404.

Mehde, V. (2017). Regionale Verwaltungsgerichtsbarkeit in Deutschland. In P. Bußjäger & A. Gamper (Eds.), *Landesverwaltungsgerichtsbarkeit— Funktionsbedingungen und internationaler Vergleich* (pp. 119–137). Wien: New academic press.

von Oertzen, H. J., & Hauschild, C. (2001). The Control of Public Administration by Administrative Courts. In K. König & H. Siedentopf (Eds.), *Public Administration in Germany* (pp. 559–568). Baden-Baden: Nomos Verlagsgesellschaft.

Püttner, G. (2001). The Web of Controls on Public Administration. In K. König & H. Siedentopf (Eds.), *Public Administration in Germany* (pp. 569–584). Baden-Baden: Nomos Verlagsgesellschaft.

Ramsauer, U. (2019). Funktionen der Verwaltungsgerichtsbarkeit. In R. Rubel & J. Ziekow (Eds.), *Die Verwaltung und ihr Recht* (pp. 21–46). Baden-Baden: Nomos Verlagsgesellschaft.

Schlacke, S. (2014). Zur fortschreitenden Europäisierung des (Umwelt-) Rechtsschutzes—Schutznormdoktrin und Verfahrensfehlerlehre erneut unter Anpassungsdruck. *Neue Zeitschrift für Verwaltungsrecht, 33*(1), 11–18.

Seyfried, M. (2016). Setting a Fox to Guard the Henhouse? Determinants in Elections for Presidents of Supreme Audit Institutions—Evidence from the German Federal States (1991–2011). *Managerial Auditing Journal, 31*(4/5), 492–511.

Siegel, T. (2012). *Europäisierung des Öffentlichen Rechts.* Tübingen: Mohr Siebeck.

Singh, M. P. (2001). *German Administrative Law in Common Law Perspective.* Berlin et al.: Springer.

Statistisches Bundesamt (Destatis) (2019a). Rechtspflege—Sozialgerichte. Fachserie 10. Reihe 2.7. Retrieved January 10, 2020, from https://www.destatis.de/DE/Themen/Staat/Justiz-Rechtspflege/_inhalt.html;jsessionid=910 5B2C509AA6550634F1CE91C14EF8F.internet742.

Statistisches Bundesamt (Destatis) (2019b). Rechtspflege—Verwaltungsgerichte. Fachserie 10. Reihe 2.4. Retrieved January 10, 2020, from https://www.destatis.de/DE/Themen/Staat/Justiz-Rechtspflege/_inhalt.html;jsessionid=910 5B2C509AA6550634F1CE91C14EF8F.internet742.

Steinbeiß-Winkelmann, C. (2010). Europäisierung des Verwaltungsrechtsschutzes—Anmerkungen zu einer 'unendlichen Geschichte'. *Neue Juristische Wochenschrift, 63*(18), 1233–1238.

von Wedel, H. (2001). Government Audit in Germany. In K. König & H. Siedentopf (Eds.), *Public Administration in Germany* (pp. 585–594). Baden-Baden: Nomos Verlagsgesellschaft.

Open Access This chapter is licensed under the terms of the Creative Commons Attribution 4.0 International License (http://creativecommons.org/licenses/by/4.0/), which permits use, sharing, adaptation, distribution and reproduction in any medium or format, as long as you give appropriate credit to the original author(s) and the source, provide a link to the Creative Commons licence and indicate if changes were made.

The images or other third party material in this chapter are included in the chapter's Creative Commons licence, unless indicated otherwise in a credit line to the material. If material is not included in the chapter's Creative Commons licence and your intended use is not permitted by statutory regulation or exceeds the permitted use, you will need to obtain permission directly from the copyright holder.

CHAPTER 13

Civil Service and Public Employment

Christoph Reichard and Eckhard Schröter

1 Introduction

The term 'civil service' denotes more than the body of personnel in the employ of government. It also refers to a set of rules and institutional arrangements embedded in political and administrative traditions and cultures. It is this wider concept of the German civil service and public employment system that we refer to in this chapter. Our chapter addresses the total public sector workforce regardless of the level of government (federal, state or local) or employment status (governed by public or private law). In doing so, we are in part being untrue to the German usage of the term 'civil service' (*Beamtentum*), which is reserved for holders of a 'civil servant' status (*Beamte*) governed by public law (see below for further details). Rather, in the following we refer to paid public sector personnel generally, including civil servants and public employees at the federal, state and local levels. To be sure, the body of public personnel is

---

C. Reichard (✉)
University of Potsdam, Potsdam, Germany
e-mail: Reichard@uni-potsdam.de

E. Schröter
German Police University, Münster, Germany
e-mail: Eckhard.Schroeter@dhpol.de

© The Author(s) 2021
S. Kuhlmann et al. (eds.), *Public Administration in Germany*,
Governance and Public Management,
https://doi.org/10.1007/978-3-030-53697-8_13

no monolith. It brings together a diverse group of professions and occupations in a variety of sectoral policies and administrative tasks. For the sake of clarity and consistency, we confine ourselves in what follows, unless otherwise stated, to the administrative core of the civil service, which is trusted with non-technical tasks in the executive apparatus of government.

2   CIVIL SERVICE SYSTEMS COMPARED: WHAT KIND OF AN ANIMAL IS THE GERMAN CIVIL SERVICE?

When looking at foreign civil service systems from the outside, we tend to search for commonalities and differences that we can relate to systems that are more familiar (van der Meer et al. 2015). For a more systematic review, a number of dimensions suggest themselves against which national civil service systems can be compared. A first and simple question to answer is to what extent the civil service has evolved as a distinct set of employment regulations and as a body of personnel separate from the private labour market. In this respect, the prevailing notion of statehood plays a decisive role. State traditions that place a higher emphasis on the role of 'the state' *vis-à-vis* society and the economy, and in which public administration is trusted with a more comprehensive set of responsibilities to contribute to the development of society at large (often typified by the French or German variants of the continental European tradition)—as opposed to the Anglo-Saxon state tradition with a more instrumental role of the state (as function of the political, societal and economic forces)—tend to produce civil service systems, which carry a greater social prestige, are more distinct from private sector employment, and form a greater identity as 'servants of the state'. This argument is underpinned by legal and religious traditions in Europe, in which the Roman Catholic tradition of codified law is pitted against the case-based common law tradition. Finally, the sequence of historical developments seems to make an important difference in this respect. As a rule, the bureaucratisation and professionalisation of the civil service (and public administration as a whole) in German states preceded the advent of mass democracy. As a consequence, judicial control of the legality of administrative acts had been well in place long before (party-)political control of the executive apparatus was established. Pulling these threads together, we can conclude from this section that the German civil service—based on a strong public law and *Rechtsstaat* tradition—differs from many Anglo-Saxon public employment systems in that it is a well-established body of personnel systematically governed distinct from private-sector employment.

The question of open and closed civil service systems is another litmus test for international comparison. When compared to public employment in the US (at one end of the spectrum), the German approach is classified as particularly closed. One of the underlying reasons for this classification lies in the dominant career-based system of the German civil service, which differs systematically from job-based or position-based approaches in other systems (primarily those of Anglo-Saxon or Scandinavian provenience). It follows from the career system that entry into the civil service typically takes place in an early part of the work biography—with an expectation that the individual completes his or her work life in the employ of government. For this reason, a high level of job security is coupled with disincentives to leave government service early. In addition, loyalty to the public employer is rewarded, for example, by extra pension benefits and, of course, opportunities to move up the career ladder. In line with this thinking, seniority is a significant factor for promotion and remuneration. In return for government's loyalty, public employers impose specific duties on their employees (particularly on 'civil servants' as a distinguished status group), which requires them to show political moderation while in office and may even restrict—in the case of civil servants—their civil liberties (e.g. the right to go on strike). What is more, government employment and access to specific grades in the career ladder is, as a rule, dependent on certain levels of qualification and types of exams—qualifications and exams that are often (and sometimes exclusively) offered by government-run training institutions. Compare this system to the position-based system, the significant number of lateral entrants and rather frequent intersectoral changes, for example, in the US civil service (in-and-outers), and the relatively closed nature of the German civil service system is easily discernible. In relation to its French neighbour, however, the German system of public employment shows strong elements of openness. The key reason for this change in perspective can be found in the decentralised structure of Germany's politico-administrative system, which by definition provides more access points to public sector employment. Even at the same level of government, individual public organisations tend to pursue—though governed by the same set of regulations—their own recruitment, selection and hiring processes independent of one another. Due to the lack of a central personnel or civil service agency, public personnel policies tend to be—within the boundaries of the law—more decentralised and pluralist than in France. This trend is further reinforced by the relative plurality of institutions of higher learning that provide talent pools for admission to the higher civil service.

3   How Does the German Civil Service Measure Up? Size and Structure of Public Employment

The size and structure of public employment not only mirrors the relevance and resources of the public sector in any given nation; it is also indicative of the relative power of levels of government, the significance of particular government functions as well as current and future challenges for human resource management in government organisations. Regarding our earlier discussion on statistical problems, the data presented below cover general government employment only and exclude, for example, employees of state-owned enterprises and other legally independent entities or organisations that provide public goods or services on a for-profit or not-for-profit basis.

Compared to other industrialised countries, the size of the German public sector in terms of employment is relatively moderate. General government employment relative to total employment amounts to no more than 12 per cent, which ranges significantly below the Organisation of Economic Co-operation and Development (OECD) average of 18.1 per cent. In fact, only a few nations fall below this level (notably Japan and South Korea), while Anglo-Saxon countries show employment levels closer to the OECD average and Nordic countries top the list with levels hovering around the 30 per cent mark (OECD 2019, 85). However, one should be quick to make mention of the fact that the vast majority of social services in Germany tend to be provided by welfare associations that operate—by definition—outside the public sector for statistical purposes. Interestingly, the relative size of the public sector—after years of contraction—has now reached the levels of the late 1960s and early 1970s, which ushered in a phase of massive increases in public employment (in Germany and much of the OECD world). In Germany, this development reached its peak shortly after German unification, when about 15 per cent of all employees were on the government's payroll (1991). In absolute numbers, there were at that time some 6.7 million people in the employ of the public sector—a number that is now down to 4.8 million employees. Given the much higher levels of public employment in what used to be the German Democratic Republic, the integration of the public workforce in

13 CIVIL SERVICE AND PUBLIC EMPLOYMENT 209

the eastern German states resulted in a significant increase in public personnel numbers. However, public employment cut backs (in the whole of the country) began as early as the mid-1990s and were primarily driven by fiscal concerns, but also by reform measures such as contracting-out, privatisation and corporatisation.

For a more differentiated picture, Table 13.1 shows the distribution of the total public workforce across levels of government and between the two major employment categories (civil servants and public employees; see below for more details).

As for levels of government, the figures in Table 13.1 reflect the division of labour in Germany's variant of federalism, which shifts administrative responsibilities *per se* to the states or *Länder* as well as to local government as major service providers. It flows from this that more than half of total government staff is employed by the *Länder* where the bulk of executive and personnel-intensive tasks are carried out. In particular, *Länder* governments employ teachers, police officers and members of law enforcement agencies and the judiciary. In comparison, the size of federal government in terms of employment figures is conspicuously small with less than eight per cent of the total (when military personnel are included, this percentage goes up slightly to roughly ten per cent).[1]

As for employment categories, civil servants only account for a little more than one-third (38.4 per cent) of the entire public workforce in Germany, while nearly two-thirds qualify as 'public employees' (for the specifics of these status differences see below). However, the relative (numerical) strength of these status groups varies significantly across levels

Table 13.1 Public employment (excluding soldiers) in full-time employment (FTE) by government level and employment category (as of 30 June 2017; rounding differences possible)

Government level	Civil servants	Public employees	Total FTEs	Total %
Federal government	173,200	135,500	308,700	7.7
Länder government	1,169,900	935,100	2,105,000	52.4
Local government	172,000	1,099,300	1,271,300	31.7
Social insurance administration (incl. employment offices)	26,800	301,700	328,500	8.2
Total	1,541,900	2,471,600	4,013,500	100.0

Source: Destatis (2018, 86)

of government. While the federal and *Länder* levels employ more civil servants than public employees (56.1 per cent and 55.6 per cent respectively), the opposite holds true at the local level, where civil servants are a small minority representing only 13.5 per cent of the total local workforce.

In Table 13.2, we continue our analysis by breaking down personnel numbers according to their position in the administrative hierarchy. In doing so, we employ a well-established, but very broadly defined measure and refer to the legal classification of 'career classes' in the German civil service as well as their equivalents with regard to the grading of the jobs of public employees. As shown below, Germany's public sector workforce is structured into different career classes, following the traditional civil service system.

As the data reveal, the vast majority of civil servants are employed in the 'middle management' and 'senior management' categories, while the lion's share of public employees is grouped under the lower category of 'clerical services'. It should be noted that career structures have considerably changed over time, particularly with regard to civil servants. Over the past thirty years, for example, the proportion of civil servants qualifying for senior management has more than doubled.

In addition to the data provided in Tables 13.1 and 13.2, we can distil from available statistics a number of important developments and potential challenges to which we will return in our concluding section. To begin with, the German public sector is no exception from the more general trend in many OECD countries that shows, in quantitative terms, an increasing 'feminisation' of public employment. In fact, no less than 57 per cent of public sector staff are women (DBB 2019). However, this

Table 13.2 Public employment (headcount) by career classes or equivalent grades for public employees, excluding soldiers and staff in training (as of 30 June 2017)

Career class/grade	Civil servants		Public employees	
	Number	%	Number	%
Senior management	596,500	38.1	378,400	14.1
Middle management	783,500	50.1	838,900	31.3
Clerical services	182,700	11.7	1,463,700	54.6
Total	1,562,700	100	2,681,000	100.0

Source: Authors' own compilation based on Destatis (2018, 29, 57, 82)

percentage also raises serious questions about gender-specific employment patterns since women are more likely to work in the 'public employees' category or in specific sectors of government employment (such as social services, healthcare or teaching) and tend to occupy positions in lower and middle management.

A related feature to female employment is the increase in part-time work in the German public sector. In fact, German public employers seem to offer attractive opportunities to work part-time as roughly one-third of the total workforce (32 per cent, the majority of whom are women) has made part-time arrangements. Again, this trend provides more of a mixed bag. On the one hand, part-time arrangements signal a greater openness and flexibility on the part of public employers to make the workplace more inclusive through rearranging work schedules to establish a better work-life balance or new work models. On the other hand, this trend may also reflect the government's austerity measures and still shows a significant imbalance between men and women working part-time.

Finally, the data reveal the urgency of demographic challenges in the public sector. While Germany's society as a whole is ageing, Germany's public sector workforce is even more so: in 2017, no less than 27 per cent of the total staff employed by government authorities were aged fifty-five and over. This tidal wave of retirees raises complex questions about future talent pools, the attractiveness of the public sector as an employer and the management of an increasingly diverse government workforce.

4 How Does the German Civil Service Work? Major Characteristics and Features

4.1 The Weberian Bureaucrat as a 'Leitmotif': 'Civil Servant' and 'Public Employee' as Competing but Also Converging Status Models

Given its historical and cultural legacy, the process of bureaucratisation of the modern (European) nation state is the foundation on which the German professional civil service still rests.[2] The reference to bureaucratisation suggests that core elements of that newly institutionalised civil service aspire to the ideal-typical characteristics of the Weberian bureaucratic staff organisation. In line with Weber's ideas, the appointment of a civil servant is a unilateral administrative act—as opposed to a bilateral contractual agreement. It also flows from this that employment conditions (including compensation and benefits) are exclusively governed by public law. This model of a government bureaucrat has served as a leitmotif for public employment in Germany to this day—despite the variations and changes to which we will turn below.

The institution of the 'public employee'—introduced in 1920, marking the advent of an expanding public sector with extended welfare services—deviates from the traditional role model. Designed as a private-law employment status, the labor conditions of public employees are the result of collective bargaining between government and labour representatives. In keeping with this principle, the social insurance regulations (i.e. health benefits and pension plans) for private-sector employment will generally apply—and so do the rules for industrial action, which, of course, safeguard the right to go on strike.

However, it is also fair to say that the status of 'public employee' emulates the traditional role model of a 'civil servant'—notwithstanding its roots in private labour law. Most importantly, public employees also enjoy high levels of job security and—under certain conditions—even job tenure equivalent to that of a civil servant. Also, compensation schemes have significantly converged, extra benefits have been added and, in practice, a career system is also in place for public employees (who are, in principle, hired for a specific job)—provided they bring equivalent levels of formal education and job experience. While differences in the nature of these employment categories still exist, the role model of public employment—to all intents and purposes—is more unified than the duality of the German employment system suggests.

In administrative practice, the growing similarity between the status groups is also reflected in the relatively indiscriminate use of the different personnel categories when it comes to filling public sector positions. Constitutional law stipulates that 'the exercise of sovereign authority on a regular basis' shall be reserved for civil servants (Article 33 (4) of the Basic Law), which in particular applies, for example, to police officers, tax inspectors, law enforcement officers, court administrators and members of the prison service. In general government employment, however, the practice of assigning certain functions to civil servants or public employees varies significantly across the nation. Rather than applying a systematic yardstick for making these decisions, the allocation of civil servants or public employees to specific public sector posts primarily reflects historical path-dependencies or political policy preferences at the relevant government level.

Still, the formal bifurcation of the employment categories in public sector employment remains a constant bone of contention. For one, each employment status creates its own group of people (constituency)—which provides a base for organised interests—who fight to protect their privileges or to even out any remaining differences. On top of that, there also appears to be a more fundamental, if not ideological, debate as to what status proves to be more efficient and/or legitimate. The real divide, however, is rather the distinction between employment inside and outside the public sector.

4.2 Steering and Coordination in the German Civil Service: Legal Frames, Collective Bargaining and Civil Service Politics

As for the steering and coordination of public sector employment, there are two major coordination and guidance mechanisms in public sector employment primarily at work: legal frames and collective bargaining agreements. One should be quick to add that both mechanisms are deeply entrenched in political and professional cultures. In addition, organised interests in the form of public sector unions play a significant role in the governance of the German civil service.

The remarkable stability and continuity of the German civil service is owed largely to the constitutionally enshrined 'fundamental principles', which govern the status of civil servants nationwide. This set of rules, upheld and interpreted by authoritative rulings of the Federal Constitutional Court, provides a powerful legal frame for any civil service policy in the country. In a similar vein, federal government serves as a rule-maker, not only for its own jurisdiction of federal civil servants, but also for civil servants of state or *Länder* government. However, this role has been drastically curtailed in the wake of the devolution of federal government prerogatives to the *Länder* as part of a constitutional reform package (the so-called Reform of Federalism I of 2006). As a result, the detailed rules governing the recruitment, employment conditions, benefits, pay scales and pension schemes of civil servants in the *Länder* have been decentralised, while a broader nationwide frame of basic principles is still in place, allowing, among other things, for the transfer of civil servants across states as well as between federal and state governments, and vice versa.

The system, however, is not only vertically decentralised but also horizontally fragmented. From an organisational point of view, Germany does not utilise a nationwide civil service commission or agency, which tends to centralise recruitment, selection or hiring processes with uniform standards. At the level of federal and state governments, the competencies for personnel affairs are widely dispersed with individual government departments being in charge of their own hiring decisions. The relevant ministries of the interior have primarily procedural competencies and coordinative functions, and oversee civil service training institutions in their jurisdictions. At the local government level, personnel functions tend to be more concentrated in single human resource management (HRM) departments, although various operative functions have been decentralised to line departments in the wake of the New Public Management (NPM) reforms of the 1990s (e.g. Demmke and Moilanen 2010, 143).

In addition to legal frames, collective bargaining—designed for determining the rules of engagement for public employees—provides another major instrument of coordination and steering. Remarkable by any international standard, the level of collective bargaining is rather centralised and comprehensive. Negotiations are organised in a corporatist setting of interest mediation with peak organisations of public sector unions facing representatives of public sector employers. These talks are held in different rounds: one bargaining agreement covers all *Länder* governments and their employees, whereas another round of negotiations covers federal government as well as local government employees.

While public employees rely on the bargaining powers of strongly organised public sector unions (vested with the power of taking industrial action), civil servants are stripped of the right to go on strike and are dependent on legislative acts taken by federal parliament or state assemblies to determine their working conditions. What appears at first sight to be a disadvantageous situation for the 'servants of the state' may not be such a bad deal after all. To begin with, political conventions seem to soften the blow rather comfortably because federal and state governments and legislatures tend to follow suit (albeit with some delay or minor changes) once an agreement has been reached for public employees. What is more, civil servants as a collective status group tend to find many advocates sympathetic to their cause in German legislatures. After all, roughly one-third of the members of the national parliament (*Bundestag*) and almost half of the delegates of state assemblies hold a civil service status.

In addition, the interests of civil servants and public employees alike are represented at the organisational level by so-called personnel councils, which are an integral part of Germany's system of co-determination that applies to both the private and public sectors of employment. As a result, each administrative entity has such a personnel council as part of its own governance structure. This council has specific rights and responsibilities whenever employees' interests are at stake—a wide jurisdiction, which gives representatives of public personnel at the organisational level far-reaching co-decision rights in matters of organisational changes, recruitment and promotion decisions or the allocation of performance-based payments to the workforce.

4.3 Recruitment and Qualification

Given its strong emphasis on professionalism and formal qualifications as entry requirements, education and training play a central role in civil service regulations and policies. The German public sector is a large and multifaceted employer and major provider of numerous education and training programmes. Although government institutions recruit various categories of already well-educated and trained staff, for example in areas such as engineering, healthcare and teaching, the government is also very active in providing its own separate training programmes in a wide range of occupational fields for about 200,000 trainees. Apart from general administration, these specialised training programmes are offered, for example, to future police officers, tax inspectors, court administrators, social insurance officials and social workers.

Germany belongs to a group of countries that require comprehensive pre-service education and training as an essential qualification for future members of the public sector workforce. Accordingly, applicants for a civil service position usually have at first to pass an intensive educational programme, either in the form of an apprenticeship or as a study programme at a public or government-specific university (Reichard and Schröter 2018).

Access points to the administrative career ladder are, in principle, organised according to distinct levels of education. In the 'clerical class' category, skilled (manual and non-manual) workers and service personnel who have successfully completed a two- or three-year apprenticeship on the job coupled with training in a vocational school (dual system) provide basic administrative or technical services. One level up, entry into the middle management range of the civil service, often referred to as the 'backbone of the civil service', requires a three-year bachelor's degree. As a rule, this degree has to be completed at a university of applied sciences, which caters specifically to prospective civil servants and offers courses of study approved by the relevant interior ministry as an entry qualification. Senior management levels of government employment are filled by university graduates (bringing with them a master's degree or equivalent) recruited from the university system at large—most frequently from programmes in law, but also from the social and political sciences, public management and administration, and economics. In addition, successful candidates have to complete a two-year traineeship programme (or 'preparatory service') before they qualify for tenure as a civil servant.

4.4 Compensation Schemes and Benefits

Salaries of civil servants depend on the assigned post or rank (i.e. the pay grade in the respective career class).[3] Compensation for the majority of civil servants is based on pay scale A, covering fifteen grades from A2 (simple manual tasks) to A16 (section head of a ministry). For more senior grades, there is a specific pay scale B with eleven grades. While the latter scale is not subdivided, each grade of scale A is split up into eight different steps. A civil servant gradually passes the different steps of a grade before he or she may be promoted to the next grade. Advancement to the next step is based on individual performance and seniority. Additionally, civil servants receive various kinds of allowances, for example family allowance. For the past twenty years, civil servants have had the opportunity to receive additional one-off bonus payments for outstanding performance. At the federal level, the number of performance-based bonuses are, however, generally limited to 15 per cent of that status group in an organisation. Also, these payments are not supposed to exceed seven per cent of the basic salary level.

The compensation of public employees is based on the collective agreements drawn up between the public employers and the trade unions and is determined by the actual task requirements. Actually, the pay scale for public employees largely follows the pay scale A for civil servants: it consists of fifteen grades (groups) and each grade is subdivided into six steps. Although, in theory, public employees are assigned to certain positions, in practice they enjoy similar promotion opportunities as civil servants. In addition to other kinds of allowances, public employees may also receive performance-based pay, although with currently usually only one per cent of salaries in a rather marginal form (Kuhlmann and Wollmann 2019). The practice of performance-based pay for public employees is quite diverse in the various government institutions (for more details see Chap. 21).

Civil servants in Germany are entitled to comparatively high pension levels. In fact, the replacement rate can be as high as 71.75 per cent, depending on the number of years served. These pension payments are largely financed out of the general budget (as opposed to special pension provisions or any kind of insurance system). Civil servants do not make any significant contributions themselves to their pension plans during their active period of service.[4] Understandably, the current pension system for civil servants is causing growing fiscal concerns, particularly in view of the 'tidal wave' of prospective retirees in the years to come. How to cope with this huge fiscal challenge is part of a controversial and soul-searching debate in German politics. Public employees, in contrast, receive their retirement payments from the national statutory pension insurance system. Additionally, they receive payments from a supplementary occupational pension scheme as agreed between government representatives and the unions. Like any other private sector employee, public employees make mandatory monthly contributions to public insurance funds (covering the risks of unemployment, sickness, long-term care as well as old age). According to the principle of parity, contributions to public insurance funds in Germany are equally divided between employers and employees.

Civil servants also enjoy privileges with regard to their healthcare. In contrast to public employees, they opt out of the statutory public health insurance system and subscribe to a private health plan. In addition, they are entitled to government allowances to cover health-related expenses. As a rule, about half of these costs are covered by the government allowance, while the other half is taken care of by the insurance plan.

In the past—and particularly with regard to certain professions like engineering, computer science or information technology and management—compensation in the German public sector was often perceived as being uncompetitive compared to the private sector. More recently, public sector pay, at least in some professions and career classes, appears to have become more attractive. Although the 'service to the public' may indeed be seen as advantageous by many applicants (compared to for-profit employers), and while the afore-mentioned social benefits and relative job security may also count for 'going public', the increasing competition for young talent in a period of demographic change will still most probably be a major challenge for public employers.

4.5 The German Civil Service at the Interface Between Politics and Administration

Despite its legitimate claim to Weberian and bureaucratic heritage, the German civil service is at the same time an institution that operates in a highly politicised environment of an open society and a liberal mass democracy (see also Chap. 10). In fact, a lot of civil service rules and practices are—beyond the image of the law-clad nature of regulations—the result of political bargaining and negotiations. In addition, many civil servants and public employees take an active role in interest mediation and party politics.

The German administrative system does not treat civil servants (let alone public employees)—in stark contrast, for example, to the British case—as political eunuchs. Irrespective of their rank, they are free to be openly affiliated with political parties and stand for elections at any level of government without jeopardising their civil service privileges. (Once elected to legislative office, for example, they are entitled to take leave of absence, a period of time that will, nonetheless, count towards the promotion clock.) Indeed, a significant percentage of civil servants, particularly in the higher ranks of the administrative hierarchy, carry party books[5]—a fact that prompted a British observer to nickname the then West German civil service a 'party-book administration' (Dyson 1977). While discussions about party-political patronage of civil service posts flare up recurrently at the margins of the political discourse, it is widely recognised that this political affiliation signifies a healthy relationship between political parties and civil service members in a liberal democracy (for this discussion see also Schröter 2004).

5 How the German Civil Service Has Changed or Is Supposed to Change: Major Challenges and Reform Trends

The German civil service system has shown a remarkable degree of stability and continuity over a long period of time. In a country known for its drastic regime changes during the past century—all of which have had severe repercussions for European and world politics too—the established orthodoxy of a civil service model based on the tenets of a Weberian professional staff organisation stands out for its hyperstability. Rather than documenting and analysing processes of administrative change, it appears even more rewarding to discuss and explain the degree of continuity.

A major source of stability are the constitutionally enshrined traditional principles of the civil service. As a consequence, the bar for 'game-changing' innovative projects has been raised too high for most reform coalitions. Moreover, the decentralised and fragmented nature of the administrative system does not allow for one single, resourceful political actor. What is more, the current institutional arrangements serve the organised interests of their constituencies. Seen from this angle, it is not the persistent legal frames, but the balance of political power and interest representation that keep the current set of regulations in place. What also stabilises the existing system is the fact that public sector employment still carries an element of social prestige and the established principles of the civil service are generally respected by the public (rather than challenged by high levels of public disgruntlement and discontent). It is indicative that the most ambitious reform of civil service law during the early 1970s—following a political sea change from a right-of-centre to a left-of-centre government led by Social Democrats—was eventually aborted. While the reform proposals aiming at a unified employee status and less opaque approaches to personnel management still provide a rich source for intellectual stimulation and academic analysis, they have failed miserably in politics.

This is not to say, however, that change has never come to the established system of public sector employment. Rather, most developments in the civil service have been immanent to this existing paradigm of public bureaucracies. In other words, we have seen changes leading to 'more or less of the same', that is the bureaucratic fine-tuning of regulation and internal human resource management, the shift of competences between levels of governments, or the cutback or expansion of civil service posts, and the adjustments of pay scales and fringe benefits according to fiscal requirements. What we have not seen, however, is a massive approach of 'de-privileging' the civil service (Hood 1995) as has been the case in many Anglo-Saxon countries. To the contrary, the most significant reform activity involving the German civil service (i.e. the process of administrative transformation in the wake of German unification) was driven by the desire to restore the traditional notion of the civil service. By way of contrast, reform elements borrowed from private management or market/ efficiency-driven movements (such as the reform wave of the new public management) have made inroads only to a moderate degree.

A number of individual reform programmes merit specific mention because their consequences have significantly shaped current civil service practices. First, most fundamentally, the reform of education and training (at first pertaining only to civil servants, it also set standards for public employees) during the 1970s introduced a broader element of academisation to the level of middle management in the civil service. Today's 'universities of applied sciences' date back to this reform measure, which also laid the foundation for later reform towards bachelor degree programmes for mid-level civil servants. Second, the massive quantitative changes to the public sector workforce since the mid-1990s cannot be underestimated. They also stand out when compared to other countries. Drastic cutback measures hardly qualify as 'reform' in a pro-active and qualitative sense. However, the downsizing of the total number of public administrators has been remarkable and has left its mark on the overall resources and structure of public employment. A third strand of reform, intimately linked to the size of the public sector, refers to the out-migration of public personnel to hived-off corporations. In fact, most of the managerial reform package has touched the civil service indirectly by way of formal privatisation (particularly at the federal level with regard to the national railroads or postal and telecommunications services, and a significant share of utility companies and service providers at the local government level). As a result, the rules governing the administrators who remained in public employment have largely stayed intact.

It is a matter of public debate whether this record of accomplishment sufficiently prepares the civil service as an institution to deal adequately with current and future challenges. As for demographic changes, the civil service will have to prove its attractiveness as an employer to new cohorts of talent. Not only are these talent pools drying up—just when they are needed most—but it is also quite likely that a young generation of potential applicants will bring new expectations of their desired work environment—an environment that may clash with the traditional practices of the civil service. Demographic (and cultural) changes, however, also question the extent to which the civil service mirrors the community it is supposed to serve. It flows from this that questions of inclusiveness and equitable representation of groups—in line with the aim of gender parity—are more likely to play a more prominent role in the future.

6 Lessons Learned and Concluding Thoughts

Moulded in traditional forms of Weberian bureaucratic staff organisations, the German civil service represents a classical continental European administrative system. It stands out from this category of employment systems, however, because it is relatively small in size and highly decentralised in terms of its structural layout. Its guiding principles have remained largely intact—despite the series of radical regime changes in German history—over the course of more than a century. In particular, the established public employment system has proven relatively impervious to external pressure from market/efficiency-driven reform measures in the wake of the new public management movement.

This legalist, merit-based career system of government employment comes with a series of advantages. Civil service members tend to be well trained for the functions they have to perform. In addition, training programmes and qualifications are also tailored to the specific needs of the public sector. Given the high level of strongly entrenched professional standards (underpinned by legal controls), the civil service system is geared to produce procedural fairness and low levels of corruption or cronyism and nepotism. However, the civil service also suffers from rigidity and inefficiencies that tend to stifle motivation and breed frustration among civil service members and clients of public services alike. In addition, its barriers to entry and exit work against intersectoral mobility and limit the access of public employers to sources of future knowledge and innovative ideas.

Despite its bureaucratic heritage, the German civil service shows a remarkable measure of decentralisation and adaptability. It appears to be flexible enough to accommodate different choices by sub-national governments or functional requirements by specific government agencies or local authorities. It has also proven adaptable to social and political changes. What is more, the institutional setting of the civil service as a whole is well embedded in the political environment and its system of organised interest representation. With this in mind, we seem to be on relatively safe ground in suggesting that the existing balance of political and organisational interests will keep the established employment system on a relatively stable path for future developments.

Notes

1. In 2017, the Federal Armed Forces accounted for 165,200 FTEs, which brings the total public employment (including soldiers) to 4,179,200 FTEs.
2. In fact, this legacy dates back to 1794 in Prussia or 1804 in Bavaria, when those (and other) German states formed modern executive branches of government.
3. The following description focuses on the federal level; for more details see Federal Ministry of the Interior (2014, 82–101).
4. As a (mostly symbolic) nod to making contributions, a 1999 federal law stipulates that civil servants' pay rises should be 0.2 percentage points below the pay rise for public employees. The savings are used to build up a pension fund to augment future pension payments from the annual budget (starting 2032).
5. Between 1981 and 2005, the percentage of party members among the top three ranks in ministerial departments has ranged consistently between 50 and 60 per cent.

References

DBB. (2019). Zahlen, Daten, Fakten 2019. Retrieved August 14, 2019, from https://www.dbb.de/fileadmin/pdfs/2019/zdf_2019.pdf

Demmke, C., & Moilanen, T. (2010). *Civil Services in the EU of 27*. Frankfurt: Lang.

Destatis. (2018). Finanzen und Steuern. Personal des öffentlichen Dienstes. Fachserie 14 Reihe 6. Wiesbaden: Statistisches Bundesamt.

Dyson, K. (1977). *Party, State, and Bureaucracy in Western Germany*. Beverly Hills, CA: Sage.

Federal Ministry of the Interior. (2014). *The Federal Public Service. An Attractive and Modern Employer*. Berlin: BMI. Retrieved August 6, 2019, from https://www.bmi.bund.de/SharedDocs/downloads/EN/publikationen/2014/federal-public-service.html

Hood, C. (1995). Deprivileging the UK Civil Service in the 1980s: Dream or Reality? In J. Pierre (Ed.), *Bureaucracy in the Modern State* (pp. 92–113). Cheltenham: Edward Elgar.

Kuhlmann, S., & Wollmann, H. (2019). *Introduction to Comparative Public Administration*. Cheltenham: Edward Elgar.

OECD. (2019). *Government at a Glance—Highlights*. Paris: OECD Publishing.

Reichard, C., & Schröter, E. (2018). Education and Training in Public Administration/Management in Europe. In E. Ongaro & S. van Thiel (Eds.), *The Palgrave Handbook of Public Administration and Management in Europe* (pp. 41–60). Houndmills-New York: Palgrave Macmillan.

Schröter, E. (2004). The Politicization of the German Civil Service: A Three-Dimensional Portrait of the Ministerial Bureaucracy. In B. G. Peters & J. Pierre (Eds.), *Politicization of the Civil Service in Comparative Perspective* (pp. 55–80). London, New York: Routledge.

Van der Meer, F., Steen, T., & Wille, A. (2015). Civil Service Systems in Western Europe: A comparative analysis. In F. Van der Meer, J. Raadschelders, & T. Toonen (Eds.), *Comparative Civil Service Systems in the 21st Century* (pp. 38–56). Houndmills-New York: Palgrave Macmillan.

Open Access This chapter is licensed under the terms of the Creative Commons Attribution 4.0 International License (http://creativecommons.org/licenses/by/4.0/), which permits use, sharing, adaptation, distribution and reproduction in any medium or format, as long as you give appropriate credit to the original author(s) and the source, provide a link to the Creative Commons licence and indicate if changes were made.

The images or other third party material in this chapter are included in the chapter's Creative Commons licence, unless indicated otherwise in a credit line to the material. If material is not included in the chapter's Creative Commons licence and your intended use is not permitted by statutory regulation or exceeds the permitted use, you will need to obtain permission directly from the copyright holder.

CHAPTER 14

Public Finance

Gisela Färber

1 Introduction

Public budgets are often called 'government programmes in numbers'. They represent the financial side of government activities. They cover the salaries of civil servants, interest payments on public debt and a broad variety of transfer payments to enterprises and private households as well as among governments. On the revenue side, we find taxes and fees and received grants. A specific perspective comes up on the public sector, not as a homogeneous entity, but as a multilevel system with different levels of governments and a variety of financial transactions among them.

The chapter gives an overview of public finance in Germany. It provides information on the volume and structure of expenditure and revenue, the latter with special focus on the tax system, the system of multilevel tax distribution among the levels of government and finally on public debt. The chapter refers also to the legal framework for public budgeting and accounting standards, which differ to a certain degree among the levels of government or—in the case of local budgets—among the *Länder* (federal states).

G. Färber (✉)
German Research Institute for Public Administration, Speyer, Germany
e-mail: faerber@foev-speyer.de

© The Author(s) 2021
S. Kuhlmann et al. (eds.), *Public Administration in Germany*,
Governance and Public Management,
https://doi.org/10.1007/978-3-030-53697-8_14

225

2 Regulation of Public Budgets and Budgeting

In Germany, the Federation has established the law of principles of budgeting which sets out the requirements for the regulation of public budgets for all levels of government. In addition, the federal budget code regulates all the details for federal ministries and agencies, as the budget codes of the *Länder* set out very similar detailed regulations for ministries, administrations and agencies.

2.1 Principles of Budgeting, Structures and Classifications

The law on budgetary principles was passed in 1969 in order to establish a framework for the common rules for federal, state and local budgets. This legislation aimed at establishing standardised legal procedures and structures as well as a common basis for the public sector financial statistics. The law is based on traditional principles of budgeting, of which the most important are: principle of annuality, principle of coverage in total, principle of gross coverage, principle of unity, principle of totality, principle of balancing the budget, principle of exactness, principle of efficiency and economy, principle of public information and principle of budgetary trueness and clarity.

Budget acts are rather short and must include the total amount of estimated revenue and expenditure as well as the maximum permissible borrowing amount. They include as attachment the budgetary plan, which consists of surveys of the appropriations of all ministries and the administrations and agencies in their responsibility (overall plan), revenue and expenditure according to economic categories (grouping survey), revenue and spending purposes (the so-called functional plan), a budgetary profile combining institutional and economic categories, and finally a directory list of all personnel positions to be approved.

The Federation and the majority of the states present their budgets in the traditional 'institutional structure' and still apply the cash-based accounting system. Only Bremen, Hamburg and Hesse have changed to an accrual budgetary system. Local governments have all changed compulsorily to accrual budgeting but follow a common institutional structure, although they are free to decide on their organisational structure and show a broad variety. The idea of programme budgets, which are not based on the institutional structure but on political goals and programmes, has not been successful; this information is shown, if included in the budget, in addition to the traditional items.

2.2 The Budget Cycle

A budget cycle, the period starting with the preparations leading to drafting and coordinating the budget plan through to parliamentary approval, execution, the rendering of accounts, financial control and the discharge of the government by parliament, takes about three years.

The starting point is usually the tax estimation in November, which the representatives of all 17 ministries of finance, the Ministry of Economic Affairs, the *Deutsche Bundesbank* (Federal Central Bank) as well as academics and experts from the six big research institutes undertake twice a year. On this quantitative basis, the ministries of finance determine the baselines for the new budget which will come into force more than one year after the year being budgeted for. The financial framework includes total revenue expected, the amount of expenditure to be funded, standards for inflation rates and civil service salary increases. The ministries then ask their units to deliver their 'financial needs'. The budget plan and other documents of the budget bill traditionally receive cabinet approval in the last meeting of the cabinet before the summer break. The budget bill is then submitted to the legislative bodies, the German Bundestag and the Bundesrat. From September, the German Bundestag adopts the budget bill after three readings.

On 1 January, the implementation of the budget starts. The Ministry of Finance decrees details. Particularly in the event that revenue falls behind scheduled expectations, the Minister of Finance can order a spending freeze or other specific measures to reduce expenditure. The budgetary year closes by 31 December. The institutions can only carry forward remaining spending allowances into next year's budget with a special executive permit of transfer. The Ministry of Finance renders the accounts by the end of February, which are then transferred to the Court of Audit. Usually in October, the Court of Audit delivers its annual report to parliament where the Audit Committee, a sub-committee of the Budget Committee at the federal level, examines the report. The report of the Audit Committee provides the information for granting discharge to the government.

2.3 Recent Budgetary Reforms

After timid experiences with Planning-Programming-Budgeting Systems in the 1970s, Germany continued with conservative budgeting and financial management procedures until the early 1990s, when a recession after the boom created by German reunification restricted the tax revenue of all levels of government. Local governments were the first to reform their budgetary planning and financial management procedures, following the ideas of the Tilburg model of new public management (cf. Chap. 22). Federal and state governments do not apply performance budgets.

Gender budgeting is even less widespread in Germany than performance budgeting. Here the budgetary impacts are planned and documented according to their effects on men and women (Färber, Christine). However, it is still difficult to get majorities for these types of budgets in Germany. A little more popular are the so-called citizens' budgets, which involve the citizens themselves, that is the local voters, in the budgetary decision-making process. The participation of voters in budgetary issues mainly takes place in situations where a sharp fiscal consolidation needs to be implemented. The citizens then create ideas for expenditure cut-backs and increases of revenue. Neither measure is very popular, therefore the organised inclusion of 'normal citizens' in making these difficult political decisions promises a better acceptance. However, it is unclear whether local politicians favour participatory budgeting procedures not only in periods of fiscal stress, but also when tax revenue is growing.

3 Basic Regulation for the 'Fiscal Constitution' in the Basic Law

The Basic Law regulates the fundamental rules for public sector finances in its tenth chapter. In addition, the provisions of Article 28 (2) of the Basic Law guarantee the local governments financial autonomy and, to a certain degree, tax autonomy, by granting them the right of self-administration to manage all their own affairs.

The rules of the financial constitution are based on the specific 'division of labour' between the Federation and the *Länder* in the so-called administrative federalism. The Federation passes the legislation in the majority of policy fields while the states execute federal laws as their own responsibility. The *Länder* very often delegate the execution of federal and their own laws to their municipalities, each with a slightly differing degree of decentralisation. Therefore, the Federation has the smallest administrative body, while state and local governments cover the big personnel expenditures for administration.

The budgets of all jurisdictions are independent of each other. All jurisdictions set up their proper budgets and pass them to their parliaments and local councils for legislative approval. Only local governments need legal approval from their state administrations, which is a formal approval for all municipalities delivering balanced budgets.

Article 104a (1) of the Basic Law provides that the Federation and the states cover the costs for their respective public tasks. The obligation of cost covering follows the right of execution, not the right of legislation. This means that the upper level establishing new or additional regulations does not cover the costs of its administration. Only certain laws regulating specific social transfers contain the rule that transfer payments are shared on a 50:50 basis (e.g. housing subsidies) between the federal level and the states. The respective problems of cost covering by the decentralised levels result from European legislation. Since 2005, however, Article 104a (4) of the Basic Law has prescribed that federal laws, which foresee transfer payments, allowances in kind and other obligations in favour of third parties, and which are executed by the states as their own tasks, need the approval of the *Bundesrat*.

The *Länder* have, in principle, the same right to further decentralise the administration of federal laws and their own regulations to their counties and municipalities. For several years now, a so-called principle of connectivity has been established in all state constitutions prescribing that in the case that the *Länder* decentralise additional administrative tasks to their communities, they must cover the costs. The respective detailed regulations vary from state to state, particularly with regard to the procedures on how to measure the costs of administration and how the transfer payments are to be shaped (i.e. specific-purpose grants, general grants or inclusion in the local fiscal equalisation scheme). Municipalities have won several proceedings before state constitutional courts with regard to cost covering for decentralised tasks; many more are expected in the future. Recent reforms include the provisions under Article 104b–d of the Basic Law regulating vertical specific purpose grants for investment expenditure in order to stabilise economic development and foster economic growth as well as equivalent living conditions across Germany, other specified investment purposes for state and local governments and for affordable housing policies.

The tenth chapter of the Basic Law sets out the basic rules for tax assignment in the following articles: legislation in Article 105; revenue competences in Article 106; vertical and horizontal fiscal equalisation in

Article 107; and tax administration in Article 108. Additionally, Article 109 regulates the limits of public debt and includes a specific rule to avoid budget emergencies in Article 109a. As the previously mentioned articles cover the Federation and the states, the articles following Article 110 only concern federal finance. Articles 110 to 113 set out the ground rules for federal budgeting, courts of audit (Article 114) and, more specifically, for federal public debt (Article 115).

4 PUBLIC EXPENDITURE

The volume and structure of public expenditure provides a good insight into the different tasks of the levels of government. Public sector expenditure and revenue include not only the three levels of government but also the social insurances (pensions, healthcare, long-term care, unemployment and occupational accidents), which underlie a specific governance of self-administration and for which the Federation only has the right and duty of legal control, but not supervisory control. However, they are responsible for the large budgets of transfer payments and cover about 40 per cent of the total public sector budget. They dominate public expenditure in two areas: material expenses, which are mainly the expenditures on the healthcare insurance for medical services, medications and other materials; and the pension scheme for rehabilitation services and transfer payments to the private sector, including mainly payments for pensions from the general pension scheme and unemployment allowances from the unemployment insurance. The third biggest expenditure item of social insurances comprises transfer payments within the public sector, which mainly cover payments among the social insurances, such as the contributions for pensions, healthcare and long-term care insurances for pensioners and the unemployed, including contributions from both employers and employees, which, on the other side, are deducted from the payments transfers of pensioners and the unemployed. The expenditure on personnel is the lowest for all levels of government (Table 14.1).

The respective governments of the three levels show very specific structures of expenditure too. The federal budget is dominated by transfer payments to other public sector institutions and to the private sector. The first mainly cover transfer payments to the social insurances (to the general pension scheme and unemployment insurance, the latter for expenditure in favour of the long-term unemployed); to the states for general vertical grants in the context of intergovernmental fiscal equalisation (Federal

14 PUBLIC FINANCE 231

Table 14.1 Public expenditure at government level and social insurances in 2018

(billion euros)	Federal govt	Land govts	Local govts	Social ins	Total govt
Personnel expenses	51,943	151,143	69,090	21,515	293,691
Material expenses	38,775	52,760	59,193	257,936	408,665
Interest payments	23,859	13,293	3009	81	40,242
Current transfer payments[a]	254,800	173,597	150,024	618,907	1,224,854
To other public sector budgets	193,253	133,707	69,570	257,542	654,072
To the private sector	61,547	39,890	80,454	361,365	570,782
Real investment expenditure	12,156	13,230	30,103	711	56,200
Capital transfer payments	29,002	26,730	2949	1	58,681
To other public sector budgets	10,954	16,960	1655	11	29,579
To the private sector	18,048	9770	1294	-10	29,102
./. payments from same level	-28,869	-44,284	-59,094	-255,181	-679,246
Total expenditure	385,998	398,805	260,128	647,874	1,428,512
% of total expenditure					
Personnel expenses	13.5	37.9	26.6	3.3	20.6
Material expenses	10.0	13.2	22.8	39.8	28.6
Interest payments	6.2	3.3	1.2	0.0	2.8
Current transfer payments[a]	66.0	43.5	57.7	95.5	85.7
To other public sector budgets	50.1	33.5	26.7	39.8	45.8
To the private sector	15.9	10.0	30.9	55.8	40.0
Real investment expenditure	3.1	3.3	11.6	0.1	3.9
Capital transfer payments	7.5	6.7	1.1	0.0	4.1
To other public sector budgets	2.8	4.3	0.6	0.0	2.1
To the private sector	4.7	2.4	0.5	0.0	2.0
./. payments from same level	-7.5	-11.1	-22.7	-39.4	-47.5
Total expenditure	100.0	100.0	100.0	100.0	100.0

Source: Federal Statistical Office (2018); author's own calculations

Differences of the sums result from rounding

[a]Some figures include double counting; therefore, the total figures could be lower or higher than the figures reported/percentages shown

Supplementary Grants); for a broad range and growing number of specific purpose grants according to Article 104b–d of the Basic Law; and for the refugees administration of the *Länder* and their communities. Current transfer payments to the private sector include the federal share of social transfer payments for housing allowances, parents' allowances, students'

232   G. FÄRBER

allowances, minimum pensions for people of old age and unable to work. The Federation shows the lowest spending on personnel because it does not execute its own regulations. However, personnel expenditure has been increasing above average in recent years largely due to the Federation employing increasingly more staff in the federal police services and buying equipment for its ministries and federal agencies—and sometimes probably just spending federal tax revenue growth.

The states are the 'big employers' in the public sector. This is not only because of their responsibility for the execution of federal law—which they share with their municipalities—but also because of their own tasks in the field of education (schools and universities), police, courts of law and prisons as well as tax administration, where they spend most on salaries and other salary-related costs, including pensions for civil servants. The second biggest budget item consists of current transfer payments within the public sector. These mainly cover the local fiscal equalisation scheme through which the states share their tax revenue with their local communities (see below). Current transfer payments mostly represent the states' share in the above-mentioned federal social transfer programmes.

Last but not least, local governments cover the smallest share in expenditure with 'only' €270 billion. The budgetary statistics, however, do not show the true volume of local expenditure because local communities, especially the larger ones, provide a huge variety of expensive local services—local public transportation, water provision and sewage, garbage collection, and even local construction activities—via government-owned, 'formally privatised' local enterprises. Public sector financial statistics do not include these expenditures and only account for transfer payments to them or profits paid by them. Therefore, the financial data of local governments presented underestimate the financial volume of local service production, and the public sector revenue only includes the activities of the proper 'administration' and services 'within the budgets'. Approximately €70 billion is for personnel expenditure, which has been steadily growing in recent years. This is particularly the result of increasing the number of kindergartens in line with federal regulations to guarantee early childhood care for all children from the age of three.

An even heavier burden is the increasing expenditure on social transfer payments—€800 billion in 2018—since local governments are still responsible for all remaining areas of the guaranteed minimum income system, which covers a certain proportion of the accommodation costs for long-term unemployed job-seekers, full support for people with disabilities who are not privately covered as well as for poor people in long-term care institutions who cannot cover the costs themselves. The transfer payments within the public sector are mainly payments among local governments. Among them dominate the apportionments which counties in particular and other local government associations levy on their member municipalities in order to cover their expenditure.

Finally, the specific role of local governments for real investment expenditure should be mentioned. The local communities are still the biggest investors in public infrastructure, although here other expenditure not shown in the documented investment expenditure is hidden in the accounts of the locally owned enterprises. However, the financial crisis in local budgets of the late 1990s and 2000s led to sharp cuts in investment expenditure. In particular, the poor communities in regions of strong economic structural change were not able to maintain their stock of public infrastructure.

5 PUBLIC SECTOR REVENUE

Public sector revenue is more than taxes, although these dominate the receipts. Therefore, the next chapter outlines the various revenue streams and shows the differences among the levels of government before the German tax system is presented. Finally, the distribution of tax sources and tax revenue among the jurisdictions informs about the effective tax sharing system in Germany.

5.1   Revenue in General

Taxes and compulsory contributions to social insurances amounted to €1.3 trillion in 2018. The revenue share was 60 per cent for taxes and 40 per cent for contributions to social insurances. The second important revenue source of social insurances are transfer payments, of which €255 million are transfers paid by other social insurances for the above-mentioned contributions of pensioners and the unemployed. The remaining €120 million come from the federal budget, mainly from the Ministry of Labour and Social Affairs (BMAS) in favour of the general pension fund. These latter transfer payments are designated to cover the costs not funded by earlier contributions, which are calculated in a general way. The only explicit contributions to the pension fund cover compensations for

234   G. FÄRBER

child education, that is three years of average contributions for each child born after 1998 (Table 14.2).

The federal and state governments cover their expenditure from tax revenue amounting to €351 billion (88 per cent) and €299 billion (71 per cent), respectively. Local governments, however, generate only 38 per cent of their revenue from taxes. The latter, by contrast, receive 56 per cent of their income from current transfer payments from other public budgets, and 22 per cent from the state. The majority of these transfer payments represent vertical fiscal equalisation and, in the case of the *Länder*, some horizontal redistribution. These explicitly aim to cover the structural lack of own tax revenue of the lower levels of government and include horizontal distributional effects. Payments from the same level of local government do not include horizontal equalisation payments; they

Table 14.2 Public revenue at government level and social insurances in 2018

(billion euros)	Federal govt	Land govts	Local govts	Social ins	Total govt
Tax revenue/social contributions	351,158	298,509	101,213	534,130	1,313,535
Current transfer revenue[a]	35,528	105,506	162,012	375,247	677,294
From public budgets	28,898	93,641	152,316	372,815	64,767
From private sector	6629	11,865	9696	2431	29,624
Other current revenue	31,241	37,507	47,439	4642	82,130
Sale of real assets	3175	1859	5266	147	10,447
Capital transfer revenue	3588	15,879	11,300	11	30,779
./. payments from same level	-25,611	-38,074	-56,989	-255,170	-648,917
Total revenue	398,441	419,030	269,906	659,027	1,482,112
% of total revenue					
Tax revenue	88.1	71.2	37.5	8.1	88.6
Current transfer revenue[a]	8.9	25.2	60.0	56.9	45.7
From public budgets	7.3	22.3	56.4	56.6	4.4
From private sector	1.7	2.8	3.6	0.4	2.0
Other current revenue	7.8	9.0	17.6	0.7	5.5
Sale of real assets	0.8	0.4	2.0	0.0	0.7
Capital transfer revenue	0.9	3.8	4.2	0.0	2.1
Total revenue	100.0	100.0	100.0	100.0	100.0

Source: Federal Statistical Office (2018); author's own calculations

Differences of the sums result from rounding

[a]Some figures include double counting; therefore, the total figures could be lower or higher than the figures reported/percentages shown

are mainly the apportionments in favour of county governments and other types of associations of local government. Capital transfer revenue partly follows the same goals, but is bound to cover investment expenditure and often requires a co-finance share from the recipient budgets (matched grants).

Other current revenue, which accounts for the third most important source of public revenue, is dominated by user fees and profits from government-owned enterprises. The amount of fees is bigger in local budgets because local governments provide specific public goods for their citizens and the local economy to which the exclusion principle can be applied and, therefore, the principle of equivalence. However, the fees covered in the financial statistics meanwhile only document the smaller share of local user fees because the 'big fee budgets' for water provision, sewage, waste collection, local public transportation, etc., have been privatised, although their fees remain as revenue regulated by (public) administrative law but never 'touch' a public budget.

5.2   Tax Revenue

Tax revenue, which in Germany has to follow the 'ability to pay principle', is almost completely under the legislation of the Federation. The Federation has the 'exclusive legislative competence' with respect to taxes, of which the revenue belongs to the federal budget. With respect to all others taxes, of which the revenue in part or in whole funds *Land* and local budgets, the Federation has the so-called concurrent legislative competence and requires the approval of the *Bundesrat*.

Seventy-three per cent of total tax revenue depends on two or three types of taxes, each levied in the form of several special forms of collection:

- the personal income tax consists of the wage tax on the income of employees, the assessed income tax on the profits of sole traders and partnerships as well as the self-employed, an interest income tax and a capital gains tax, which amounted to €299 billion in 2018 (38.5 per cent of total tax revenue);
- the corporate income tax for enterprises established as corporate entities (€33.4 billion or 4.3 per cent of total tax revenue); and
- the turnover tax in the form of a value-added tax for domestic sales (€175 billion, 22.6 per cent) and as a turnover tax on imports (€59 billion or 7.6 per cent of total tax revenue) (Fig. 14.1).

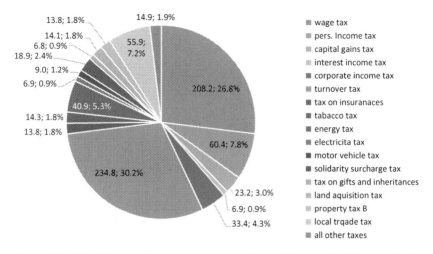

Fig. 14.1 The German tax system. Source: Federal Statistical Office, author's own calculations and for the references: Statistisches Bundesamt (Federal Statistical Office): Fachserie 14.4 - 2018, Wiesbaden 2018

The tax revenue is shared among the three levels of government. The Federation levies in addition a special surcharge tax of 5.5 per cent of income taxes intended to fund the costs of German unification.

Furthermore, the German tax system consists of a variety of excise taxes on tobacco, petrol, energy and electricity, coffee, spirits and beer (but not wine!), a motor vehicle tax and an insurance tax; the latter is 19 per cent on insurance premiums and 'replaces' the turnover tax because insurances are not subject to value-added tax. These taxes—except the beer tax—are revenues in the federal budget.

The states are entitled to receive the revenue from taxes on gifts and inheritances, land acquisition, gambling, lotteries and casinos, which are classed as taxes of smaller yield. The land acquisition tax is the only state tax for which the *Länder* have the right to decide autonomously on the tax rate. A wealth tax, which was levied until 1995 when the Federal Constitutional Court ruled the tax as unconstitutional, still exists but cannot be charged.

Local governments receive the revenue from the local property tax and the local trade/business tax. Both taxes belong to the old so-called real taxes, which are levied on the gross added value. Property tax is assessed on the gross added value of real assets (A for agricultural assets, B for all others) and the local trade tax on local business tax profits. The taxes on the amount of wages paid by an enterprise and the value of invested capital were abolished in 1979 and 1998. The tax bases and tax rates are established by federal law; local governments, however, have the right to decide on a local multiplier. A recent property tax reform gives the states regulatory power to determine the tax base; the changes, however, will only become effective in 2026.

The smallest German taxes are the so-called local consumption and expenditure taxes. These are basically regulated by the states, but local governments decide whether they want to levy them and on the tax rates. Among the local consumption and expenditure taxes are the dog tax and the entertainment tax—in the past on cinema and other local event tickets, today on peep shows and gambling saloons—local beverage tax, and second home tax. The local governments have, in principle, the right to invent local taxes as long as they are not levied on tax bases which are already taxed by the Federation and the states. In 1998, for example, the Federal Constitutional Court ruled a local package tax on single-use plates, cups and cans in Hesse to be unconstitutional for these reasons.[1]

The levels of government usually administer the taxes from which they receive the revenue. Exceptions arise regarding the vertically shared taxes. Here, the Federal Tax Office administers the capital gains tax and the VAT on imports, while the taxation offices of the states accept the tax declarations of the taxpayers, receive the tax payments, organise tax audits in enterprises for the domestic (and meanwhile the European) turnover tax and the income taxes. Tax administration is administered 'on behalf of the Federation', which means that the Federation establishes special regulations for personnel keys, administrative procedures and the application of the respective tax laws and decrees. On behalf of the Federation, the states also administer the social insurance tax and the solidarity surcharge tax.

5.3 Intergovernmental Financial Relations: Multilevel Tax Sharing Assignment

All 'smaller' taxes are revenues of the respective jurisdictions according to the territorial location of its source. This is, in general, the location of the transaction or the residence of the owner of the income or fortune. Some taxes need a specific definition, for example the tax liability on gifts and

238 G. FÄRBER

Table 14.3 Distribution of tax revenue between the federal, *Länder* and local governments

Revenue in 2018 (billion euros)	Tax	Federation	Länder	Local governments
268.6	Wage and assessed income tax	42.5%	42.5%	15%
33.4	Corporate income tax, capital gains tax	50%	50%	
6.9	Interest income tax	44%	44%	12%
234.8	Turnover tax up to 2019	4.45% + 5.05% 50.5%[b]	49.5%[b]	2.2%[a]
	Turnover tax from 2020	52.809% -€6.7 bn. (2020) -€6.9 bn. from 2021	45.195% +€4.3 bn. (2020) €4.5 bn. from 2021	1.996% +€2.4 bn. from 2020

[a] +€2.76 bn. in 2018; €3.4 bn. in 2019

[b] ./. €6.5 bn. in favour of the *Länder* in 2018; €7.4 bn. in 2019

inheritances is allocated to the residence of the donor or the heir, although many recipients live in another jurisdiction or abroad.

The three big taxes—personal, corporate income and turnover tax— are, however, vertically shared taxes according to specific keys, as seen in Table 14.3.

While the distribution keys are fixed for the income taxes, the turnover tax is, in principle, flexible. According to Article 105 (2) of the Basic Law, in the case of diverging expenditure-revenue relations of the Federation on the one hand, and the states and their local governments on the other, the key must be changed by federal law, which requires the consent of the *Bundesrat*. The vertical shares of the turnover tax have been changed several times in recent years, mostly in favour of the *Länder* (Färber 2015). In 1998, the increase in the turnover tax rate of 1 per cent was specifically transferred to the pension scheme. Since 1998, local governments have participated in the revenue with a share of 2.2 per cent. Smaller adjustments have been made by lump-sum deductions or extra payments. From 2020, the keys will change to simpler shares after the reform of the intergovernmental financial relations. De facto, the turnover tax revenue will again slightly change in favour of the *Länder*—this was a condition for

Table 14.4 Tax revenue of the different government levels and the EU before and after distribution in 2018 (billion euro)

Before distribution			After distribution		
Shared taxes	566.9	73.0%			
Federal taxes	108.6	14.0%	Federal tax revenue	322.4	41.5%
Land taxes	23.9	3.1%	*Land* tax revenue	314.1	40.5%
Local taxes	71.8	9.2%	Local tax revenue	111.4	14.3%
Customs (EU)	5.1	0.7%	EU revenue	28.6	3.7%
Total	776.3	100.0%		776.4	100.0%

Source: Federal Statistical Office (2018); author's own calculations

their approving the reform. Table 14.4 presents the revenue before and after distribution among the levels of government, including the revenue of the EU, which is administered by the Member States and then transferred to Brussels.

Horizontally, tax revenue is assigned according to the territoriality principle, which for the income taxes are the residence and the place of production principles. The wage tax of taxpayers who live in a place other than their workplace is transferred to their place of residence. The income tax and the corporate income tax liability of enterprises with several production sites is apportioned to the respective jurisdictions according to a key combining the added value and the number of employees.

From 2020 onwards, the state share of the turnover tax is distributed according to the number of inhabitants, including deductions and additional payments for those *Länder* whose revenue falls below the average per capita fiscal capacity.[2] The local fiscal capacity is included in the formula at 75 per cent. The remaining below average fiscal capacities after distribution of the state share of VAT revenue and local fiscal capacities of less than 80 per cent of the average is supplemented by specific funding from Federal Supplementary Grants (FSG) (Federal Ministry of Finance 2018).

The German multilevel tax sharing system finally contains the obligation of the states—according to Article 106 (6) of the Basic Law—to share their tax revenue from the above-mentioned joint taxes (including FSG) with their local communities. As the degree of decentralisation differs among the *Länder* and, therefore, also the financial needs of local governments, the percentage rates of state tax revenue vary from 12.75 per cent in Bavaria to 23 per cent in North Rhine-Westphalia. Most *Länder* also share the revenue of their proper tax sources often using diverging transfer rates. The majority of this income is then assigned to 13 different local fiscal equalisation schemes, which include indicators for financial needs and fiscal capacity. All financial needs indicators are based on the number of local inhabitants and in most states are supplemented by other indicators, such as the number of pupils or costs per pupil, social expenditure burdens, number of employees, length of streets. These local fiscal equalisation transfer payments explicitly aim to close the fiscal gap and provide a more equal financial balance among the municipalities and counties.

6   Public Debt

Public debt was for many years an important source for funding public expenditure. A reform of the constitutional borrowing limits in 2009, however, changed the long tradition of an ever-increasing volume of debt. Since 2011, the ratio of public debt to GDP has been decreasing, since 2013 the absolute amount too (see Fig. 14.2). The Federation holds the largest share of public debt; state and local government cover less than a third of total debt. Here again, it should be mentioned that the debt of

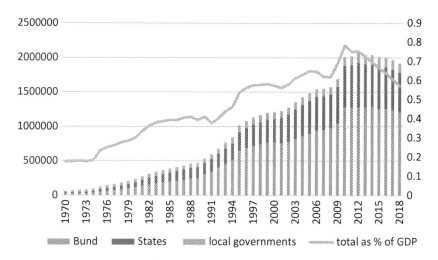

Fig. 14.2 Volume of loans and securities at the different levels of government 1970–2018. Source: Federal Statistical Office, author's own calculations and for references: Statistisches Bundesamt (Federal Statistical Office): Fachserie 14.5 - 2018, Wiesbaden 2018

privatised state and local government-owned enterprises is not included in the official statistics. However, a decline in the absolute level of public debt at all levels of government (on average) has not been experienced since the 1960s.

In addition to loans and securities, there are other types of public debt. The amounts are detailed in Table 14.5. While debt from other public sector institutions or levels of government, liabilities from deliveries of goods and services, and transactions similar to credits are of minor importance, and guarantees are only very rarely called, the cash credits of local governments have become a real political issue. Cash credits are short-term borrowings, usually used to cover a temporary budgetary deficit. In some states (Saarland, Rhineland-Palatinate, North Rhine-Westphalia, Hesse and Saxony-Anhalt) these deficits became 'chronic' during the 2000s and many municipalities have not been able to reduce or erase them. In recent years, the respective state governments have established programmes to help solve the problems, but have not been able to make sufficient transfer payments to clear the debt over a shorter term due to the underlying continuing problems of high social expenditure and the fundamental underfunding of local budgets in these communities. As a result, the Federation is currently having discussions about offering a means of financial support to achieve a quicker solution.

After the regulations to limit the public debt of the Federation and the *Länder* to budgeted (i.e. planned) investment expenditure—a rule following the principle of intertemporal equivalence—in 2009, the Federation and states decided on the requirement in future of an (almost) balanced budget. Since 2016, the Federation has only had permission to borrow up to 0.35 per cent of gross domestic product (GDP). As from 2020, the states are required to balance their budgets. Exceptions only arise for recessions and natural catastrophes (see Korioth 2016). Debt amassed in economically difficult periods and as a consequence of natural disasters is booked into a special account and must be redeemed over a shorter term.

In 2011, in response to the Euro debt crisis, particularly in the South European countries, a new debt regulation was introduced for the Member States of the European Union. The so-called fiscal pact followed the same concept as the German 'debt brake' and restrained public borrowing to 0.5 per cent for 'normal' economic development. Germany 'reserves' 0.15 per cent of GDP as fiscal space for local borrowing, which in the past was sufficient.

Table 14.5   Public debt tax revenue of the different levels of government and the EU before and after distribution as at end of 2018

31 December 2018 (1000 euros)	Public debt from the private sector	of which		Debt from the public sector	Liabilities from deliveries of goods and services	Transactions similar to credits	Guarantees
		securities and loans	cash credits				
Federation	1,213,217	1,192,266	20,951	12,138	4635	26	474,497
Länder	570,525	562,216	8309	43,628	2457	629	60,822
Local governments	132,768	97,068	35,700	13,653	5587	1019	27,398
Total	1,916,638	1,851,677	64,960	81,871	45,023	1814	562,735

Source: Federal Statistical Office (2018); author's own calculations

Against this background, the debt limits for local governments have remained unchanged. The local debt limits are covered by the state constitutions and the local government laws of the 13 territorial states. Local budgets require the approval of their *Länder*, which is part of the supervision of local authorities; it stops at either special state administrations or the counties (in the past, the lowest level of state administration). In general, local governments are allowed to finance investment expenditure by borrowing, but only if there are no other financial means (e.g. tax revenue, fees, charges and transfer payments). Since the introduction of accrual accounting and profit and loss budgets, the requirement is to have a balanced budget. This means that local authorities have to cover interest and depreciation of investments from regular revenue. According to the requirements of accounting standards, the rule of balancing the profit and loss budget includes—theoretically—all other forms of open and hidden debt too (cash credits and hidden obligations of future payments).

The broad agreement on the new 'debt brake' across the majority of the political parties did not last for long, although good economic growth created additional revenue, some of which an increasing number of governments used to redeem old debt. Taxes increased more than GDP growth because there was no majority in the Bundestag and in the Bundesrat to approve reducing tax revenue to the former ratio. The states, in particular, argued that they needed the revenue to shoulder the financial burden of increasing education and early childhood education at the local level. The Federation and *Länder* also increased the number of personnel in their police forces. The problem of below average investment expenditure in public infrastructure, which emerged during the economically difficult years of the late 1990s and 2000s, remained unsolved. In contrast to this, the particularly poorer states and local communities achieved their budgetary consolidation but only by cutting back even more on investment expenditure.

As a result, a new discussion on the reliability of the so-called black zero policy has started. A part of the discussion deals with the question of whether governments should stabilise economic development by additional borrowing, even though the incoming tax revenue is still sufficient to cover all planned expenditure. More important are the questions on how to fund the necessary investment expenditure which—after cut backs in the past—require enormous financial efforts to meet both the considerable backlog demand for costs as well as accommodate the demand for public infrastructure modernisation. In the event that investment expenditure at all levels of government exceeds 0.5 per cent of GDP in economically 'normal' times, a borrowing fund would not only be unconstitutional, but would also violate European law. Therefore, might then the consequence be that bigger investment projects are shifted to times of recession? Why should governments intentionally violate the principle of intertemporal equivalence, the so-called golden rule of funding investments, and accept instead that they are (over)burdening generations of taxpayers? Despite all the successes of breaking the long-term continuous growth of public debt because of the actual constitutional and European debt limits, politicians should no longer ignore that the actual rule does not meet the requirements of sustainability. This will probably result in a new reform in the not-too-distant future.

7   Local Finance

The local right of self-government includes financial affairs (Werner 2006). Municipalities, counties and other types of associations of local governments, therefore, need substantial autonomy with regard to deciding on their budgets, including local tax rates on their 'own' tax sources. The revenue from joint taxes, which the states are obliged to share with them according to Article 106 (7) of the Basic Law, should suffice to fund not only the expenditure for transferred tasks, but also a considerable amount of spending for the tasks of local self-government. Article 106 (6) of the Basic Law grants the right not only to the revenue from the local property and the local business tax, but also to decide on the local multiplier of these taxes. Local governments, therefore, have substantial autonomy on both sides of their budgets, although the scope of their financial decisions is restricted by the dominance of transferred tasks and the corresponding expenditure.

About 20 years ago, almost every territorial state introduced the so-called principle of connectivity into their state constitutions. The idea was that when transferring new tasks to local governments, the states would also include the necessary financial means for execution. However, reality shows that there is regional regulatory divergence with regard to (Schmidt 2016):

- the tasks specified by the principle; no *Land* has incorporated European and federal regulations into the compensation catalogue;
- the strictness of the application and duty of compensation; and
- the instruments and calculation methods of compensation.

Meanwhile, there are doubts about whether the practised principle of connectivity has helped to protect local governments against additional financial burdens, or whether it has even created new distortions by establishing a broad range of new specific grants in addition to local fiscal equalisation and disturbances to the efficiency mechanism of the annual local budget decisions. The principle is actually rumoured to prevent an efficient assignment of tasks between state and local governments as states avoid regulations in order not to create new obligations to make compensation payments.

All local fiscal equalisation schemes have two main goals: to top up local revenue due to 'chronically' deficient vertical tax assignments and to close horizontal gaps of fiscal capacities regarding local needs. As the decentralisation of tasks as well as local tax capacities differ from *Land* to *Land* (see Table 14.6), the volume of local fiscal equalisation needs to vary too.

Table 14.6 Per capita expenditure of state and local governments and aggregated state-local governments 2018

Per capita expenditure (in euro)	State and local gov. aggr.	State gov.	Local gov.	Share of local gov. of aggregated %	Local tax revenue
Baden-Württemberg	6495.3	4771.6	3595.8	55.4	1489.4
Bavaria	6953.9	4746.4	3285.4	47.2	1537.7
Hesse	7294.5	4841.2	3583.8	49.1	1602.0
Lower Saxony	5976.5	4121.9	3136.0	52.5	1181.0
North Rhine-Westphalia	6807.9	4374.3	3799.6	55.8	1406.5
Rhineland-Palatinate	5873.2	4362.0	2982.1	50.8	1183.0
Saarland	6016.4	4409.9	2564.6	42.6	1091.3
Schleswig-Holstein	7374.8	5574.6	3149.6	42.7	908.9
Brandenburg	6552.9	4988.6	3238.6	49.4	811.7
Mecklenburg-Vorpommern	6132.4	4728.6	3017.9	49.2	876.7
Saxony	6040.4	4485.2	3150.1	52.2	819.6
Saxony-Anhalt	6717.9	5126.1	3033.0	45.1	1169.8
Thuringia	5919.8	4674.2	2666.6	45.0	842.4
Territorial *Länder*[a]	6611.7	4615.0	3389.4	51.3	1318.8

Source: Federal Statistical Office (2018); author's own calculations

[a]Territorial states span a wider area and include a level of independent local governments while the three city-states Berlin, Hamburg and Bremen administer local tasks by dependent districts

246   G. FÄRBER

Table 14.7   Changes in the local shares of the compulsory tax sharing revenue of the *Länder* 2000–2019 (percentage of state tax revenue)

Land	BW	Bav	He	LS	NW	RP	Saar	SH	BB	MV	Sax
2000	23.0	11.54	22.9	17.59	23.0	20.25	20.00	19.00	26.1	27.36	26.365
2011	23.0	12.20	23.0	15.50	23.0	21.0	20.555	17.74	20.0	23.81	22.09
2019	23.0	12.75	–	15.50	23.0	21.0	20.573	17.83	21.0	26.09	22.135

Source: Fiscal equalisation laws of the *Länder*

Most states—except Thuringia, Saxony-Anhalt and Hesse, which estimate a minimum financial equipment for their communities—just apply a certain percentage to their tax revenue. The resulting sum is the basis for local fiscal equalisation. All states then start by using a rather large share of the fiscal equalisation sum for specific purpose grants, which amounted to 42.7 per cent of total fiscal equalisation grants in 2013 (Deutscher Städtetag 2013) and should actually not be much lower (Table 14.7).

The remaining amount is then distributed as unconditional so-called key grants. Key grants show—in different combinations and quantities among the states—three basic forms:

- often a part of the key sum is given as lump-sum grants—diverging for the types of local authorities—in order to cover the costs of compulsory local tasks;
- some *Länder* (e.g. Baden-Württemberg and Rhineland-Palatinate) secure a minimum fiscal capacity per inhabitant for municipalities by top-up grants to a certain percentage of the average fiscal capacity;
- all fiscal equalisation schemes contain key grants covering a certain share of the gap between financial needs and fiscal capacity for each local government.

The measurement of financial 'needs' is based on the size of the population (main approach) and other factors representing important cost factors (secondary approach). In most states, the number of citizens is evaluated by a factor increasing with the size of the municipality. The variety of indicators for the secondary approach is broad and ranges from the number of pupils or standardised school costs per pupil, number of long-time unemployed, number of employees, number of students and 'central locations' from regional planning categories, to the size of the military personnel, mining communities, spas, etc. Each community then has an indicator for abstract financial needs without any particular monetary dimension.

Fiscal capacity is accounted as the real revenue from the local shares of personal income tax and turnover tax plus standardised revenue from local property and local business tax, which is weighted by a uniform multiplier in order to avoid inefficient local tax policies. Fees and charges as well as minor local taxes are not included in the fiscal capacity.

The rate of equalisation varies between 50 per cent and 90 per cent from state to state. The 'neutral' indicators of financial needs are multiplied by a 'basic grant', which is calculated to absorb exactly the whole key sum. These local authorities receive key grants, of which the monetised financial needs indicator exceeds the fiscal capacity. If the fiscal capacity exceeds the financial needs, no key grants are available.

Although German local governments have experienced a long period of economic growth as well as growing tax and fiscal equalisation revenue, communities in certain states suffer from persistently high amounts of cash credits. In particular, the cities and counties in regions undergoing massive structural economic change 'accumulated' cash credits during the periods of recession in the late 1990s and 2000s until the financial crisis of 2008–2010 and have not been able to reduce them in the amount or as quickly as required. All states concerned have established programmes for local debt relief using transfer payments for interest payments and redemptions or—more recently in Brandenburg and Hesse—assumptions of local debt (Stolzenberg 2018). The Federal Minister of Finance has now offered to help all remaining over-indebted municipalities (particularly in North Rhine-Westphalia, Rhineland-Palatinate and Saarland) by means from the federal budget, which then needs to be matched by state financial resources. The process of intergovernmental decision-making in this important issue is ongoing.

8   Lessons Learned

Germany experienced increases in public expenditure until the late 1970s and later again to cover the immense costs of German reunification in the 1990s and 2000s, periods when economic growth had slowed down because of the recession and the economic and financial crisis and rising social insurance contributions. The tax ratio to GDP has remained fairly

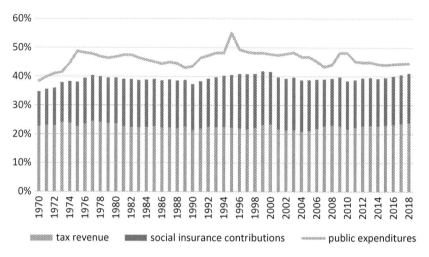

Fig. 14.3 Tax revenue, social contributions and public expenditure in relation to GDP 1970–2018. Source: Federal Statistical Office, author's own calculations and for references: Statistisches Bundesamt (Federal Statistical Office): Fachserie 14.2 - 2018, Wiesbaden 2018

stable across the economic cycles. Growth in expenditure has been slower than that of GDP in recent years, obviously as a result of the consolidation efforts to achieve the balanced budgets of the debt brake from 2020. Since 2012, the sustainable growth of GDP has helped to balance public budgets (Fig. 14.3).

However, tax revenue and social insurance contributions have grown faster than GDP since 2013 and 2017. New programmes for climate change, expensive payments for additional pensions for childcare ('mother pensions' for children born before 1992), early retirement and most recently for low income contributors, higher transfers for long-term care cases, increasing staff for police, schools and early childhood education, will enforce the recent trend of increasing rates of public spending as well as tax revenue and social insurance contributions to GDP. The gap of infrastructure investment expenditure and additional needs for the policies of climate change and new mobility concepts will set further pressure on growing public budgets (Bardt et al. 2019). Further reforms will be necessary to find legal and constitutional financial solutions. Germany faces—like many other industrialised countries—probably a turn-around of the fiscal doctrine.

NOTES

1. See BVerfG, Urteil des Zweiten Senats vom 07. Mai 1998–2 BvR 1991/95-, Rn. (1–114), http://www.bverfg.de/e/rs19980507_2bvr199195.html.
2. Until 2019, the equalisation scheme included a VAT-pre-equalisation formula and horizontal transfer payments from the rich to the poor *Länder*.

REFERENCES

Bardt, H., Dullien, S., Hüther, M., & Rietzler, K. (2019). Für eine solide Finanzpolitik: Investitionen ermöglichen! *IMK Report Nr. 152*. Düsseldorf.

Deutscher Städtetag (Ed.). (2013). *Local Finance Report 2013*. Köln: Deutscher Städtetag.

Färber, G. (2015). Fiscal Equalization in Germany—Facts, Conflicts and Perspectives. In G. Pola (Ed.), *Principles and Practices of Fiscal Autonomy. Experiences, Debate and Prospects* (pp. 113–134). Farnham: Ashgate.

Federal Ministry of Finance. (2018). Financial Relations between the Federation and Länder on the Basis of Constitutional Financial Provisions. Berlin. Retrieved from https://www.bundesfinanzministerium.de/Content/EN/Standardartikel/Press_Room/Publications/Brochures/2019-03-12-financial-realations-federation-2018-pdf.pdf?__blob=publicationFile&v=5. Download 6.1.2020.

Korioth, S. (2016). A Path to Balanced Budgets of Bund and Länder? The New Shape of the 'Debt Brake' and the 'Stability Council'. *Regional and Federal Studies, 26*(5), 687–705.

Schmidt, T. I. (2016). *Finanzierungspflichten und Konnexitätsprinzip*. Baden-Baden: Nomos.

Statistisches Bundesamt (Federwal Statistical Office). (2018). Fachserie 14.2, 2018, Wiesbaden 2018.

Stolzenberg, P. (2018). *Kommunale Haushaltskonsolidierung durch Konditionalität: Ein Vergleich der Konsolidierungsprogramme der Bundesländer und ihrer Implementation in kreisfreien Städten*. Baden-Baden: Nomos.

Werner, J. (2006). Local Government Organization and Finance: Germany. In A. Shah (Ed.), *Local Governance in Industrial Countries*. Washington: World Bank.

Open Access This chapter is licensed under the terms of the Creative Commons Attribution 4.0 International License (http://creativecommons.org/licenses/by/4.0/), which permits use, sharing, adaptation, distribution and reproduction in any medium or format, as long as you give appropriate credit to the original author(s) and the source, provide a link to the Creative Commons licence and indicate if changes were made.

The images or other third party material in this chapter are included in the chapter's Creative Commons licence, unless indicated otherwise in a credit line to the material. If material is not included in the chapter's Creative Commons licence and your intended use is not permitted by statutory regulation or exceeds the permitted use, you will need to obtain permission directly from the copyright holder.

PART III

Redrawing Structures, Boundaries and Service Delivery

CHAPTER 15

Transformation of Public Administration in East Germany Following Unification

Hellmut Wollmann

1 Transformation of Public Administration in East Germany Following Unification

In analysing the institutional transformation of post-socialist countries, East Germany has been interpreted to be a 'special' case (Wiesenthal 1995: 50). This is because in East Germany the collapse of the communist regime and the transformation of the existing system coincided with the process and dynamics of German unification and the GDR's integration into the 'old' Federal Republic. Hence, East Germany's transformation was, from the outset, propelled by a triad of exogenous factors, namely:

- 'institution transfer' (Lehmbruch 2000: 14) by extending the constitutional, legal and institutional order of the 'old' Federal Republic to East Germany;
- 'personnel transfer' as tens of thousands of West German officials and experts moved temporarily or permanently to East Germany to get involved in the transformation process; and

---

H. Wollmann (✉)
Humboldt University of Berlin, Berlin, Germany
e-mail: hellmut.wollmann@rz.hu-berlin.de

© The Author(s) 2021
S. Kuhlmann et al. (eds.), *Public Administration in Germany*,
Governance and Public Management,
https://doi.org/10.1007/978-3-030-53697-8_15

253

254 H. WOLLMANN

- 'financial transfers' from West German public budgets and social security funds to East Germany.

1.1 Institution Transfer

The institution transfer took off and gained momentum as the politico-administrative structure of the 'old' Federal Republic's 'ready-made state' (Rose and Haerpfer 1997) was extended to East Germany. This secular institutional shift set in as early as spring 1990 when on 17 May 1990 (for the first time) the democratically elected parliament (*Volkskammer*) of the (then still existing) GDR passed a new Municipal Charter that hinged on democratic local self-government. Subsequently, in July 1990, the parliament decided to re-establish the five regional States (*Länder*), which the communist regime had abolished in the early 1950s.

The most spectacular institution transfer occurred when, on the basis of the Unification Treaty signed on 31 August 1990 by the governments of the two German states, the GDR was integrated into the 'old' Federal Republic (and into the European Union) by way of 'accession' at midnight on 3 October 1990. In that unprecedented historic 'second', the constitutional and legal order of the 'old' Federal Republic was extended to East Germany, while, at the same moment, the GDR ceased to exist as a separate state and its legal world vanished.

Hence, key constitutional parameters were pre-decided during the preparation of the German unification ('exogenously' orientated towards West German requirements). In contrast to Germany, the other ex-communist CEE countries had to settle basic constitutional and institutional issues ('nation building', intergovernmental setting and accession to the EU) in conflicts and compromises between political parties and actors in the respective national arena ('endogenously').

1.2 Personnel Transfer and 'Elite Import' from West to East

The institutional transfer was accompanied and bolstered by a massive personnel transfer and 'elite import' from west to east as thousands of West German officials and specialists moved to East Germany, either temporarily or permanently, to assist the organisational and personnel transformation of *Land* and local administration. In June 1990, that is prior to unification, the ministers of the interior of the West German *Länder* decided to provide 'administrative aide' to the upcoming East German

Länder (see Goetz 1993: 451). In a similar vein, twinning partnerships were arranged between West German and East German municipalities and counties (Wollmann 1996b: 60ff.). By 1993, some 15,000 West German officials rendered 'administrative aide' in *Land* administration and about 4000 in local authorities by counselling, training and assisting their East German counterparts (Goetz 1993: 452). Moreover, a significant number of West German officials and experts moved and stayed permanently in East Germany to take up administrative top or meso-level positions. This 'elite import' aimed at filling the 'political and administrative elite vacuum' (Derlien 1993), which resulted from the resignation or removal ('purging') of most of the leading political and administrative functionaries of the communist regime. Thus, from the outset, 'administrative aide' and 'elite import' from West to East proved crucial in advancing the transformation of East Germany's administration, which again differed profoundly from the other ex-communist countries.

1.3 Financial Transfer

Finally, another key factor was the huge financial transfer from West to East. Since the early 1990s, this figure has amounted to some US$75 billion annually. This enormous flow of resources largely supported and promoted East Germany's transformation, which again has had no parallels in other ex-communist CEE countries.

However, the overall assessment that East Germany's politico-administrative transformation was predominantly driven by exogenous factors needs to be qualified on a number of scores.

First, there was no single West German model that could have been transferred to the East. Instead, the Federal Republic's political and administrative system is at all levels, and in most sectors, characterised by a considerable degree of institutional differentiation and variability so that the repertoire of institutional solutions on which East Germany's institution building could draw was, to begin with, diverse and varied (see Chaps. 8 and 9). Moreover, the West German officials and experts, who came temporarily or permanently to East Germany, carried with them in their conceptual and mental 'luggage' the diverse institutional and organisational solutions typical of their 'native' *Land* or local authority (see Goetz 1993: 452; Derlien 1993: 329; Schimanke 2001: 181).

Second, the newly elected East German *Land* parliaments and local government councils as the relevant political decision-making bodies were occupied entirely by East Germans (Wollmann 1996a, b: 77) who were politically poised and ready to take the pertinent political and institutional matters into their own hands. Therefore, notwithstanding the significant 'exogenous' influence, East German decision-makers were ('endogenously') guided by their specific 'East German' preferences, interests and goals.

Consequently, institution building in the East German *Länder* and local authorities has unfolded in organisational forms that range from (exogenously inspired) blueprint-type institutional imitation to (endogenously driven) adaptation and self-development ('autochthonomous development', Lehmbruch 2000: 14) and (even) innovation (see Wollmann 1996a, b; Kuhlmann 2003: 307ff.). As East Germany's institutional transformation took place in a spectacular simultaneity of dismantling the GDR's state structure, remoulding existing structures and building new politico-administrative institutions, this secular process bore traces of what Joseph Schumpeter, alluding to the elementary forces of capitalism, called 'creative destruction' (*'schöpferische Zerstörung'*, Schumpeter 1942).

The following account will first address the organisational dimension of East Germany's politico-administrative transformation and subsequently its personnel side.

2   Organisational Transformation

2.1   Transformation of the GDR's State Economy: The Activities of the Treuhandanstalt, THA (Trust Agency)

Since under the communist regime and doctrine the GDR state essentially owned and operated most of the economy sector, the latter's liquidation and restructuring was from the outset a prime goal and task of East Germany's adaptation and integration into the 'old' Federal Republic's politico-economic system (see Czada 1996; Seibel 1992, 2011; Wiesenthal 1995: 58). As early as 1 March 1990, the (reform-communist) GDR government decided to set up a trust agency, *Treuhandanstalt* (THA), designed to revamp the state economy while basically still holding on to state ownership. Shortly after, on 17 June 1990, the first democratically elected GDR parliament adopted a new Trust Agency Act which marked a conspicuous shift in the THA's mandate to privatise the GDR's state economy. Finally, in August 1990, anticipating imminent unification, the

THA was turned into an agency whose centralist organisational structure appeared, somewhat ironically, tailored to the GDR's previous centralised economic regime (Seibel 2011: 110). As the THA was accountable to the federal government and acted largely independent of the new *Länder* governments, it was called 'a second East German government' (Czada 1996: 99) or even 'a most powerful second national government' (as former Chancellor Helmut Schmidt put it, quoted by Czada ibid.: 94).

Under West German leadership, initially most prominently under Detlev Rohwedder, the former CEO of Hoesch (who was murdered on 13 April 1991 by the terrorist Red Army Fraction—RAF), the THA's mission was defined (in this preferential order) to privatise, restructure or liquidate the GDR's state economy. Consequently, from the outset the THA was responsible for more than 8500 state-owned enterprises with around 4 million employees, which made the THA the world's largest industrial enterprise (Czada 1996: 93). At the same time, it also took over 2.4 million hectares of agricultural land and large-scale public housing assets.

As the federal government decided that the THA was to wind up its mandate by the end of 1994, the latter acted under great time pressure. By 1994, about half of the 6545 enterprises were (entirely or partially) 'privatised', often after restructuring them in order to make them 'fit' for privatisation, 310 were transferred to local authorities and 3718 enterprises were liquidated. In addition, the so-called small privatisation was directed at some 25,000 state-owned businesses such as shops, restaurants, hotel, pharmacies, bookshops and cinemas. In total, two-thirds of the workforce lost their jobs in the process, entailing mass unemployment.

On 1 January 1995, the THA was transformed and organisationally restructured into a new political body called the 'Federal Agency for Special Tasks related to Unification' and into several smaller administrative units (see Czada 1996: 114).

The THA and its activities have evoked more discussions and controversies than any other field and sector of the GDR's transformation.

In assessing the role and impact of the THA in the economic transformation, a number of opposing views have been put forward (for a recent overview see Goschler and Böick 2017). On the one hand, some argue that given the unprecedented challenges posed by the collapse of the GDR's state economy, the THA has achieved, by and large, respectable results. On the other hand, the high unemployment and de-industrialisation that resulted from the activities of the THA and the selling off of GDR

258 H. WOLLMANN

assets to West German and foreign investors has provoked harsh criticism, including scathing critique of East Germany having been 'colonised' (Dümcke and Vilmar 1996).

2.2   Transformation of the GDR's State and Administration

The GDR's state was typical of the (post-Stalinist) 'socialist' state model based on the dual structure of the intertwined state and communist party apparatus which, by 1990, was made up of around 1000 administrative units with about 2.1 million functionaries and employees. This 'dual' structure and its strict hierarchical control comprised all tiers (central, meso and local) of public administration and, under the doctrine of so-called democratic centralism, ruled out any degree of autonomy at lower levels (Goetz 1993: 448). Fourteen meso-level administrative districts (*Bezirke*) were installed which, modelled on the (regional) '*oblasti*' in the Soviet Union, served as the regional backbone of centralist party and state rule. In formally retaining the traditional two-tier local government structure, the (191) counties (*Kreise*) and (27) 'county-free' cities were turned into (centrally directed and controlled) local-level state units, while the some 7000 ('within county') municipalities played a minimal administrative role.

Following German unification, the historic task of restructuring the defunct GDR state consisted of the triple challenge of either liquidating part of the 'inherited' administrative structures, retaining and remoulding them into a new organisational architecture, or creating new ones.

2.2.1   Central Government Level

Under the distribution formula established in the Unification Treaty about 200 of the 1000 administrative units of the defunct GDR state fell to the Federation, in particular most of the GDR's central administration (ministries and central agencies primarily based in Berlin) (Goetz 1993: 451). If not 'liquidated', institutional and personnel segments came under federal responsibility. Moreover, in some administrative areas, new federal institutions were created in the East German *Länder*, especially regional and local offices of the Federal Labour Market Administration (Wollmann 1996b: 65ff.).

2.2.2 Länder *Level*

The five new East German *Länder* (Mecklenburg-Western Pomerania, Brandenburg, Saxony-Anhalt, Saxony and Thuringia) came into existence on the date of the election of the new *Länder* parliaments on October 14, 1990.

Under the Unification Treaty, about 800 out of 1000 administrative units—that is the lion's share of the GDR's state administration (with some 1.6 million employees)—fell under the responsibility of the five new *Länder* (see Goetz 1993: 451ff.; Wollmann 1996b: 80ff.; König 1997: 226ff.). So, each *Land* government, hardly formed in October 1990, was confronted with the challenge of setting up its own ministerial offices and staff from scratch and creating a new architecture for its entire administration. Thus, *Land* ministries, the Prime Minister's Office, other central-level non-ministerial offices as well as the *Land* Court of Audit, had to be created *ab ovo* in each *Land* (Goetz 1993: 452). With regard to the lower levels of their administration, the new *Land* governments were faced with the decision of whether to liquidate the administrative units 'inherited' from the GDR state or retain and fit them into a new organisational architecture. In pursuit of this task, 'often the ruins of the former administrative structure with its personnel and material equipment became a quarry for the new administrative units' (Ruckriegel 1993; see Wollmann 1996b: 86).

From the outset, the question of whether the GDR's meso-level administrative districts (*Bezirke*) should be dissolved or retained and transformed into meso-level administrative districts in line with those traditionally (albeit increasingly contested) in place in most West German *Länder*, where they are primarily in charge of coordination and supervisory functions (see Chap. 8), took centre stage. The controversy surrounding this issue was fuelled by widespread recollections of the ominous role the districts had played under the communist regime as the regional strongholds of its centralist party and state rule. The decision of the parliaments in the *Länder* of Mecklenburg-Western Pomerania and Brandenburg to abolish the meso level—thus choosing a two-tiered architecture of *Land* administration made up of the central and the local government levels—was also largely due to this fact. By contrast, it was decided to retain the GDR's meso level in the *Länder* of Saxony and of Saxony-Anhalt and turn it into meso administrative districts (*Regierungsbezirke*) in line with their respective West German partner *Land* (see Kuhlmann and Wollmann 2019: 94).

2.2.3 Local Level

The (191) counties (*Kreise*) and (about 7500) municipalities (*Städte, Gemeinden*) were the only political and administrative structures that institutionally survived the disappearance of the GDR state. Tellingly, from early 1990 when the GDR central government was increasingly sliding into agony, until early 1991 when the new *Länder* governments became operational, it was almost solely the local authorities that bore the brunt of the secular political, institutional and socio-economic system change. In the same vein, from the beginning they were confronted with the task of fundamentally remoulding the organisational and personnel structure left behind by the GDR's centralist state.

Manifesting the radical departure from the communist regime's unitary and centralist state model, the democratically elected GDR parliament adopted a new Municipal Charter on 13 March 1990, thus essentially restoring the concept of local self-government (Kuhlmann and Wollmann 2019: 96ff.; see Chap. 9). In accordance with the 'dual task' model entrenched in the German tradition, local authorities are in charge of carrying out 'genuine' local self-government tasks that basically follow from the traditional general competence clause, on the one hand, and 'delegated' tasks transferred to them by the state, on the other (see Kuhlmann and Wollmann 2019: 161ff.).

Internal Organisation

In restructuring their administrations, the East German local authorities drew heavily on organisational designs and the practical experience of the 'administrative aides', their West German counterparts and advisers. A crucial role in this was played by the Communal Joint Office for Administrative Management (KGSt), a local government-funded non-profit consultancy organisation, which has long since acquired a high reputation and considerable influence in the field of administrative reorganisation. It should be noted that since the early 1990s, KGSt has abandoned its previous advocacy of the 'Weberian' administrative model and shifted to propagate a New Public Management (NPM)-inspired 'managerialist' New Steering Model (NSM) (see Kuhlmann and Wollmann 2019: 284 seq.). After 1990, however, when it came to the administrative restructuring of the East German local authorities, KGSt conspicuously recommended doing this on the basis of the (traditional) 'Weberian' legal rule-bound hierarchical model. Consequentially, in contrast to their West

German counterparts, the East German local authorities initially exhibited considerable restraint (Wollmann 1996a: 156; Kuhlmann et al. 2008: 856). Furthermore, under the Municipal Asset Act of 6 July 1990 and the Unification Treaty of 31 August 1990, a myriad of (social, cultural, health, etc.) organisations, which until then had operated under the responsibility of the GDR state and its state economy, were transferred ('communalised') to the local authorities. As a result, the number of local government employees virtually 'exploded' (and, for instance, in county-free cities skyrocketed within weeks from 5000 to 50,000). For the range of tasks the local authorities had to perform in order to reduce their 'overstaffed' personnel, see below.

In institutional terms, especially in facing this 'avalanche' of institutions and personnel, the local authorities chose to either organisationally integrate them into their 'core' administration or 'outsource' them in their 'corporatised' form as organisationally and legally separate municipal organisations or companies (usually as limited companies or stock companies; see Chap. 17).

Territorial Reforms and Functional Reforms
Immediately after the formation of the new *Länder* in October 1990, their governments and parliaments turned to territorially redraw (upscale) the counties whose size (averaging 80,000 inhabitants) was considered likely to seriously impair their administrative capacity (see Wollmann 2010; Kuhlmann and Wollmann 2019: 203ff.; also Chap. 16). Moreover, territorial county reforms aimed at preparing the ground for follow-up 'functional reforms', that is transferring (decentralising or deconcentrating) further administrative functions from *Land* administration to local authorities (see Kuhlmann and Wollmann 2019, 175; Chap. 16).

3   Employment Sector

In the GDR's 'cadre administration' (König 1992: 153ff.), following the Soviet Union's model, the executive and administrative leadership positions were occupied by a 'nomenklaturist elite', the members of which were directly appointed by and subjected to the communist party. By the same token, in the recruitment and staffing of personnel, the loyalty and obedience to the party was given priority over professional qualification (Goetz 1993), which fostered what was pointedly called 'politicised incompetence' (Derlien 1993: 324). The GDR's state sector had some

262   H. WOLLMANN

1100 administrative units with a total of around 2.1 million functionaries and employees. In addition, the ubiquitous state security service, commonly known as the 'Stasi', comprised approximately 85,000 official and 180,000 'unofficial' collaborators (Derlien 1993: 325).

3.1   'Elite Change' and 'Purging'

The radical transformation of the GDR's employment sector (see also Chap. 13) took place in two ways.

First, a policy was pursued of ridding ('purging') the personnel who had been involved in the communist regime and particularly in its ominous state security service (the Stasi) and to a degree deemed politically unacceptable. According to the Unification Treaty of 31 August 1990, public employees could be dismissed for 'having collaborated' (in official or unofficial capacity) with the Stasi or for having 'violated principles of humanity or rule of law' (Goetz 1993: 460; Derlien 1993: 326). The (federal) Stasi Records Agency (informally dubbed 'Gauck Agency' after its first director Gauck, who was later elected president of Germany from 2012 to 2017) was established when the Stasi Records Act came into force in December 1991 with the mandate, upon request by federal or *Länder* authorities, to scrutinise public employees and identify those possibly falling under the 'purging' verdict. By mid-1995, the 'Gauck Agency' was requested to scrutinise some 1.3 million public employees, about 10 per cent of whom were identified as 'purging'-relevant and about 1 per cent (i.e. approximately 1300 in total) were finally dismissed (see Derlien 1997: 277).[1] While the final number of 'sanctioned' cases appears relatively small, the institutionalised scrutiny process proved to be a sword of Damocles hanging over the entire process of personnel transformation.

Second, an almost complete elite change in the administrative ranks took place as the holders of higher positions of the communist regime were almost completely ousted and replaced by 'elite import' from the West or by the recruitment and appointment of East German personnel.

At the *Länder* level, the build-up of the new *Land* ministries and central-level agencies was marked by a sizeable 'elite import' (Derlien 1993: 328) from West German partner *Länder* as a significant number of executive and administrative leadership positions in *Land* administration were occupied by West German 'transferees'. For instance, initially three out of five East German prime ministers, all state secretaries, four out of five justice ministers, the majority of the ministers of economics and finance as well as up to three-quarters of the department heads and section heads in *Land* ministries were West Germans (Derlien 1993: 328; Wollmann 1996b: 79ff.). However, administrative top positions were also taken over by East Germans, albeit as a rule in less important ministries and often in lower echelons. This applied to administrative 'newcomers' who had no previous experience in public administration proper, but came from (meanwhile 'liquidated') economic enterprises or scientific institutions. This also held true for East German administrative 'old-timers' who were previously employed in technically oriented administrative segments, particularly in district- or central-level administration, and resumed new positions in qualification equivalent to ministries or agencies (e.g. environment, health) (Schimanke 2001: 180).

At the local government level, too, on the heels of the (voluntary or forced) exodus of the Communist party appointed ('nomenklaturist') position holders, a new generation of local leaders emerged. Most of them were administrative 'newcomers' with no previous experience in municipal administration and often had a professional and occupational background in engineering or natural science, many coming from management and technical functions held in (meanwhile dissolved) state economy companies.[2] Some were administrative 'old-timers' previously employed in local administration and often with a technical background. Interestingly, contrary to the *Länder* level, only a few West Germans have assumed leading positions in local administration. The fact that the East German 'new local administrative elite'—whether newcomers or old-timers—have predominantly an educational and occupational background in engineering or other technical trades makes for an intriguing difference between them and their West German counterparts, among whom a legal or quasi-legal background prevails (Wollmann 2002: 170).[3]

It is worth noting that the 'elite import' (from West to East) and the scrutiny ('purging') procedure are salient features of East Germany's transformation, which sets it apart from other ex-communist CEE countries[4] and is another aspect of its 'special case' profile.

3.2   Reduction in Personnel

As previously mentioned, after 1990 the newly formed five *Länder* and the local authorities were confronted with the challenge of reducing an 'oversized' workforce 'inherited' from the defunct GDR state. Thus, as of 30 June 1991, the number of employees of the new *Länder* totalled some

264   H. WOLLMANN

634,000, which amounted to a ratio of 39 per 1000 inhabitants compared to 29.50 in the West German *Länder* (Wollmann 1996b: 98). Between 1991 and 1999, they cut their personnel numbers by 16.24 per cent to about 30 employees per 1000 inhabitants and thereby narrowed the gap between them and their West German counterparts (see Jann 2001: 114, table 1).

As a result of the myriad of institutions and personnel that were transferred ('communalised') after 1990 to the local authorities, their workforce doubled (per capita) compared to their West German counterparts (Wollmann 2002: 168, table 5). Since the early 1990s, the number of East German local government employees has been drastically reduced and, by the end of the 1990s, had almost halved from some 660,000 in 1990 to about 340,000 in 1999 (see ibid. table, Jann 2001: 114, table), which in terms of personnel size per capita came close to their West German counterparts.

3.3 Vocational Training and Qualification of Administrative Personnel

Applying the complex legal system transferred 'from West to East', and coping with the multiple administrative tasks following unification, posed unprecedented challenges to the East German administrative personnel.

In order to prepare and train the administrative staff to master these difficulties, a huge campaign of vocational training was launched. Funded by the federal government and the West German *Länder*, crash courses were organised and offered to thousands of *Land* and local government employees (see Wollmann 1996b: 130). However, amid the operational turmoil and urgency, there was often hardly any time available to regularly attend the vocational training courses. Consequently, learning-by-doing and on-the-job-training came to prevail.

There are strong indications that East German administrative personnel, by and large, have learned remarkably fast to cope with the new legal world and task load. For instance, a study on the implementation of federal building law constituting a particularly complicated piece of legislation plausibly demonstrated that after an initial period, during which the legal provisions appeared in part to have been 'ignored' by local practitioners, the practice and standards in their implementation and application soon came to largely match those in the West German local authorities (see Wollmann 2002: 171; Kuhlmann 2003, 2004).

A major lever and driver for this fast pace of adaptation and qualification plausibly lay in the 'disciplining'—if not 'compelling'—effect which the newly established administrative courts exerted on the administrative personnel and their performance. The administrative courts played a crucial role in ensuring that the administrative practice was guided by the rule of law (*Rechtsstaat*; see Chap. 12), thus sealing the secular break from the previous regime in which public administration essentially acted under the sway of the Communist Party and which bordered on 'legal nihilism'. It is, moreover, noteworthy that the newly created administrative courts and their judges, most of whom were West German 'transferees' (see Wollmann 1996b: 100ff.), assumed an advisory and 'pedagogic' function in the interaction and exchange with their 'clients' (see Kuhlmann 2003: 202ff.).

Additionally, in dealing with the turbulence and intricacies of the transformation process, the East German administrative personnel also exhibited a disposition to seek 'pragmatic' and *ad hoc* solutions. This pragmatism arguably reflects the collective experience which the East Germans at large were prone to have under the communist regime when, vis-à-vis the endemic bottlenecks, supply gaps and malfunctions of the socialist system and economy, they learned to improvise and 'find ways out', which has, in hindsight, been pointedly called a 'chaos competence' (Marz 1992 quoted in Wollmann 1996b; 144; see also Schimanke 2001: 180ff.; Kuhlmann 2003, 2004).

4   Concluding Remarks

In conclusion, a somewhat ambivalent summary should be proposed.

On the one hand, East Germany's transformation in *Land* and local administration has proceeded remarkably fast and, after some ten years, has attained an institutional format and a performance profile that come, by and large, close to their West German counterparts (see Jann 2001: 105). The essential reason for this 'fast track' transformation of East Germany's politico-administrative plausibly lies in the fact that it was embedded in the process of German unification and driven by East Germany's integration into the 'old' Federal Republic. Thus, basic institutional decisions (e.g. relating to the introduction of the *Länder*, local self-government, rule of law/*Rechtsstaat*-guided public administration and also the inclusion in the European Union) were pre-determined and 'foregone conclusions' by the GDR's spectacular accession to the 'old' Federal Republic at midnight on 3 October 1990. By contrast, in other ex-communist CEE countries, the basic decisions on the transformation of their politico-administration (nation-building, intergovernmental architecture, accession to the EU, etc.) were often the result of protracted political conflicts and compromises (see Wollmann 2020).

On the other hand, the 'fast track' transformation of East Germany has had noticeably negative consequences. As it was strongly driven from the outset by 'exogenous' factors and actors, in particular by the triad of institution, personnel and financial transfers, East Germany's transformation came to be perceived and criticised as 'externally determined' and even as 'colonisation' (Dümcke and Vilmar 1996). Particularly the *Treuhandanstalt* that had the time-limited triple mandate to restructure, liquidate or 'privatise' the GDR's state economy has been reproached for having inflicted lasting political 'traumata' on East Germans in the wake of persisting de-industrialisation and unemployment.

5   Lessons Learned

Before finally addressing the question of whether or what lessons can be drawn from the 'East German case' by countries that find themselves in political and socio-economic transition or transformation, a note of caution is needed. The singularity of conditions under which East Germany's transformation took place should be kept in mind in order to forestall 'hasty' conclusions. Keeping this caveat in mind, the following suggestions can arguably be put forward:

- The basic decisions on the organisational (central, meso and local level) architecture should be made as early as possible in the transformation or transition process in order to relieve the decision-making process from these basic organisational issues and proceed to tackling and resolving other urgent problems of the ongoing development.
- The building of a competent, effective, efficient and trustworthy public administration should be given prime importance as being an indispensable (*sine qua non*) condition for coping with these urgent problems.
- For this purpose, the introduction and consolidation of a rule of law-bound ('Weberian'), politically independent and non-partisan public administration is absolutely essential as well.
- By the same token, of utmost importance is the establishment of independent administrative courts with qualified administrative

judges as guardians of judicial review of the public administration activities and their compliance with the rule of law (*Rechtsstaat*).

- The recruitment and employment of professionally qualified and politically non-partisan public personnel who are immune to corruption is equally of crucial importance. In order to ensure high professional (and ethical) standards of future public personnel, appropriate educational and vocational training facilities and programmes need to be put in place.

NOTES

1. For more data and references see Wollmann (1996b: 97).
2. For detailed data see Wollmann (1996b: 124, table 9).
3. For detailed data see Wollmann (1996b: 125, table 10).
4. With the exception of post-communist Czechoslovakia where, for the limited duration of three years, a comparable 'purging' procedure (called lustration) was put in place.

REFERENCES

Czada, R. (1996). The Treuhandanstalt and the Transition from Socialism to Capitalism. In A. Benz & K. H. Goetz (Eds.), *The New German Public Sector. Reform, Adaptation and Stability* (pp. 93–117). Aldershot: Dartmouth Press.

Derlien, H. U. (1993). German Unification and Bureaucratic Transformation. *International Political Science Review, 14*(4), 319–334.

Derlien, H. U. (1997). Elitenzirkulation zwischen Implosion und Integration. Rekrutierung und Zusammensetzung ostdeutscher Funktionseliten 1989–1994. In H. Wollmann, et al. (Eds.), *Transformation der politisch-administrativen Strukturen in Ostdeutschland* (pp. 329–416). Opladen: Leske + Budrich.

Dümcke, W., & Vilmar, F. (Eds.). (1996). *Kolonisierung der DDR*. Agenda Verlag.

Goetz, K. H. (1993). Rebuilding Public Administration in the New German Länder: Transfer and Differentiation. *West European Politics, 16*, 447–469.

Goschler, C., & Böick, M. (2017). *Wahrnehmung und Bewertung der Arbeit der Treuhandanstalt*. Bochum. Retrieved from https://www.bmwi.de/Redaktion/DE/Publikationen/Studien/wahrnehmung-bewertung-der-arbeit-der-treuhandanstalt-lang.pdf?__blob=publicationFile&v=24. Download 26.5.2019.

Jann, W. (2001). Leistungsfähigkeit der Landesverwaltung. In H.-U. Derlien (Ed.), *Zehn Jahre Verwaltungsaufbau Ost – eine Evaluation* (pp. 103–120). Baden-Baden: Nomos.

König, K. (1992). The Transformation of a 'Real-Socialist' Administrative System into a Conventional Western European System. *International Review of Administrative Sciences, 58*, 147–161.

König, K. (1997). Aufbau der Landesverwaltung nach Leitbildern. In H. Wollmann, et al. (Eds.) (1997), *Transformation der politisch-administrativen Strukturen in Ostdeutschland* (pp. 223–259). Opladen: Leske + Budrich.

Kuhlmann, S. (2003). Rechtsstaatliches Verwaltungshandeln in Ostdeutschland, Springer VS.

Kuhlmann, S. (2004). Evaluating the Transformation Process in East Germany: Institutional Performance of Local Administration. In J. C. Garcia-Zamor (Ed.), *Bureaucratic, Societal and Ethical Transformation of the Former East Germany* (pp. 24–65). Dallas: University Press of America.

Kuhlmann, S., Bogumil, J., & Grohs, S. (2008). Evaluating Administrative Modernization in German Local Governments. Success or Failure of the New Steering Model. *Public Administration Review, 68*(5), 851–863.

Kuhlmann, S., & Wollmann, H. (2019). *Introduction to Comparative Public Administration. Administrative Systems and Reforms in Europe* (2nd ed.). Cheltenham: Edward Elgar.

Lehmbruch, G. (2000). Institutional Change in the East German Transformation Process: The Role of the State in the Reorganization of Property Rights and the Limits of Institutional Transfer. *German Politics and Society, 37*, 13–47.

Rose, C. R., & Haerpfer, C. W. (1997). The Impact of a Ready-Made State: East Germans in Comparative Perspective. *German Politics, 6*(1), 100–121.

Ruckriegel, W. (1993). Neubau der Verwaltung in Brandenburg. In H. J. v. Oertzen, H. J. v. (Ed.), *Rechtsstaatliche Verwaltung im Aufbau* (pp. 52–59). Baden-Baden: Nomos.

Schimanke, D. (2001). Dilemmata der Personalpolitik. In H.-U. Derlien (Ed.), *Zehn Jahre Verwaltungsaufbau Ost – eine Evaluation* (pp. 179–189). Baden-Baden: Nomos.

Schumpeter, J. A. (1942). *Capitalism, Socialism and Democracy.* London: Routledge.

Seibel, W. (1992). Necessary Illusions: The Transformation of Governance Structures in the New Germany. *The Tocqueville Review, 13*(1), 178–197.

Seibel, W. (2011). The Quest for freedom and stability: Political Choices and the Economic Transformation of East Germany 1989–1991, in: Caldwell, P.C./ Shandley, R. R. (Eds.), *German Unification. Exspectations and Outcomes* (pp. 99–119). Palgrave.

Wiesenthal, H. (1995). East Germany as a Unique Case of Societal Transformation: Main Characteristics and Emergent Misconceptions. *German Politics, 4*(3), 49–745.

Wollmann, H. (1996a). The Transformation of Local Government in East Germany: Between Imposed and Innovative Institutionalization. In A. Benz &

K. H. Goetz (Eds.), *A New German Public Sector* (pp. 137–163). Aldershot: Ashgate.

Wollmann, H. (1996b). Institutionenbildung in Ostdeutschland. Neubau, Umbau und ,schöpferische Zerstörung'. In M. Kaase, et al. (Eds.), *Politisches System* (pp. 47–153). Opladen: Leske + Budrich.

Wollmann, H. (2002). Local Government and Transformation in East Germany. *German Politics, 11*(3), 153–178.

Wollmann, H. (2010). Territorial Local Level Reforms in the East German Regional States (Länder): Phases, Patterns, and Dynamics. *Local Government Studies, 36*(2), 251–270.

Wollmann, H. (2020), Institutional transformation and change after 1990 in Central East and West European countries in comparative perspective: from centralization to (re)centralisation? In *Modernization Science Newsletter, 10*(1). https://www.google.com/search?client=firefox-b-d&q=modernization+Science+Newsletter+wollmann.

Open Access This chapter is licensed under the terms of the Creative Commons Attribution 4.0 International License (http://creativecommons.org/licenses/by/4.0/), which permits use, sharing, adaptation, distribution and reproduction in any medium or format, as long as you give appropriate credit to the original author(s) and the source, provide a link to the Creative Commons licence and indicate if changes were made.

The images or other third party material in this chapter are included in the chapter's Creative Commons licence, unless indicated otherwise in a credit line to the material. If material is not included in the chapter's Creative Commons licence and your intended use is not permitted by statutory regulation or exceeds the permitted use, you will need to obtain permission directly from the copyright holder.

CHAPTER 16

Administrative Reforms in the Multilevel System: Reshuffling Tasks and Territories

Sabine Kuhlmann and Jörg Bogumil

1 Introduction

In German administrative federalism, the *Länder* take the central role as the enforcement level for federal and *Land* laws (see Chap. 8). Since the post-war period, there have been repeated attempts and initiatives to change, optimise and improve the efficiency of the traditional administrative structure, but hardly ever with decisive success (cf. Ellwein 1994). After German reunification, the East German *Länder* in particular had to adapt their administrative structures to the West German models (see Chap. 15). Since the beginning of the twenty-first century, however, all *Länder* governments have intensified their reform efforts with surprising success, measured by the extent and intensity of the changes. The reforms reached their first climax in Baden-Württemberg and Lower Saxony, and then found their way into the majority of German *Länder* in the form of

S. Kuhlmann (✉)
University of Potsdam, Potsdam, Germany
e-mail: skuhlman@uni-potsdam.de

J. Bogumil
Ruhr University Bochum, Bochum, Germany
e-mail: joerg.bogumil@rub.de

© The Author(s) 2021
S. Kuhlmann et al. (eds.), *Public Administration in Germany*,
Governance and Public Management,
https://doi.org/10.1007/978-3-030-53697-8_16

territorial and functional reforms (see Ebinger et al. 2018). One major reason for the increasing reform activity is to be found in the precarious situation of the *Länder* budgets due to escalating pension burdens, demographic developments and debt brakes (see Chap. 14). This situation opened a window of opportunity for governments to push through reforms of their apparatus. Other reasons are ideological or political in nature and are related to governments' ambitions to weaken or dissolve administrative units or levels that are regarded as difficult to control, especially after changes of government.

All *Länder* are striving to streamline, trim and (partly) concentrate their administrations, albeit with different priorities and instruments. Approaches include the merging of special-purpose authorities at the state government (*Länder*) level, the dismantling of meso-level state authorities, the decentralisation of state tasks to local governments as well as the rescaling of local governments' territorial boundaries (for a breakdown of administrative levels, see Table 16.1). In Germany, these efforts are often subsumed under the term 'administrative structural reforms' (*Verwaltungsstrukturreformen*) in a broad all-encompassing sense. Analytically, however, a distinction must be made between three types of reforms: functional reforms, structural reforms and territorial reforms, although these three types are closely interconnected. Functional reforms relate to the reassignment of tasks and responsibilities between existing administrative units and levels (centralisation/decentralisation; concentration/deconcentration). Structural reforms concern the reorganisation of the administrative structures, that is the physical dissolution, merging or creation of administrative units. Finally, territorial reforms refer to a rescaling of counties' and/or municipalities' territorial boundaries. More recently, the latter could only be observed in East Germany, whereas in West Germany territorial reforms were carried out in the 1970s (Thieme et al. 1981; Bogumil 2016; Kuhlmann and Wollmann 2019: 199ff.). The heterogeneity of structural, functional and territorial reforms across the German *Länder* has led to increasing differences in the institutional settings, task portfolios and organisational frameworks within the administrative federalism at *Länder* and local level. Accordingly, there is also a high variance regarding the outcomes and impacts of intergovernmental reforms at the subnational level, not only across *Länder* but also across policy sectors (Kuhlmann et al. 2014; for the evaluation of subnational reforms, see Kuhlmann and Wollmann 2011).

16 ADMINISTRATIVE REFORMS IN THE MULTILEVEL SYSTEM... 273

Table 16.1 Structural and functional reforms in the German *Länder* (subministerial level)

	Reforms within two-tier systems	Reforms within three-tier systems
Administrative level	Brandenburg, Mecklenburg-Western Pomerania, Lower Saxony, Saarland, Schleswig-Holstein	Bavaria, Baden-Württemberg, Hesse, NRW, Rhineland-Palatinate, Saxony, Saxony-Anhalt, Thuringia
State government level (*Land* administration)		
Upper level (higher state authorities)	Merging of higher state authorities; organisational concentration; *overall institutional trimming*	Integration of (parts of) higher state authorities into meso-level instances (administrative districts); *overall institutional trimming*
Meso level (administrative districts)	*not applicable* *(no meso-level existent)*	Integration of upper- and lower level administrative units; *overall institutional strengthening*
Lower level (lower state authorities)	Merging of lower state authorities; organisational concentration; decentralisation of tasks to local self-government level; *overall institutional trimming*	Decentralisation to local self-government level; centralisation to meso-level instances; *overall institutional trimming*
Local self-government level (counties, county-free cities, municipalities)		
Upper tier (counties and county-free cities)	Integration of tasks transferred by state government (*Länder*); partly combined with territorial upscaling; *varying degrees of institutional strengthening*	
Lower tier (municipalities)	(Limited) Integration of tasks transferred by state government (*Länder*); partly combined with territorial upscaling or increased inter-municipal cooperation; *limited institutional strengthening*	

2   Structural Reforms

The structural reforms in the German *Länder* related to a reorganisation of institutional units of the state (*Länder*) administration, specifically affecting the meso level, but also parts of the upper-and lower-level state administration. In Germany, the meso-level state administration has the traditionally assigned function to bundle and coordinate the various sector-specific administrative activities at sub-state level. The term 'meso level' refers to administrative units located between the ministerial administration at *Länder* level and the local governments. The bundling function of meso-level state authorities aims at guaranteeing the unity of the state (*Land*) and a horizontal coordination of various territorially relevant functions at sub-state level (Ellwein 1994). It is intended to limit the fragmentation and dis-connectedness of single-purpose administrative units with different or even conflicting policy responsibilities. Within the federal system of Germany, this function is however organised in very different ways. Some of the German *Länder* have three-tier systems with a territorial state administration at the meso-level (administrative district authorities), while others—mainly smaller ones—have two-tier systems in which this function is assigned to local self-government (counties). In general, the institutional variance of territorial administration at the meso level in Germany is increasing, in particular as a result of the current structural reforms in the *Länder* (cf. Kuhlmann and Bogumil 2010; see Table 16.1).

The debate surrounding meso-level instances (administrative district authorities) is first and foremost a question of whether or not a bundling and coordination authority below the ministerial level and above the local government level is required in a specific *Land*. The main points of criticism of the meso-level authorities refer to their deficits in the fulfilment of coordination and bundling functions. The reasons for these deficits may lie in the fragmentation of the administration—as is evident in the large number of single-purpose authorities—or in the internal structures of the meso-level authorities. The existence of numerous single-purpose authorities at the meso level prevents comprehensive bundling and coordination in administrative district authorities. In addition, this leads to a 'dual administration' consisting of general and specialised authorities at the meso level, such that the same tasks are performed by both a general and a specialist authority, resulting in inefficiency. If—despite the complexity in the thirteen *Länder* (excluding city-states)—an attempt is made to typify the structural reform approaches at the subnational level in Germany, two models can be distinguished: (1) reforms within or towards two-tier systems; and (2) reforms towards concentrated three-tier systems (see Table 16.1).

(1) A two-tier administration without a general meso-level instance can be found mainly in the small *Länder* (under three million inhabitants, the exception being Lower Saxony with eight million). Lower Saxony is the

only German *Land* that implemented the 'system change' in 2004 from a three-level to a two-level model (Bogumil and Kottmann 2006: 63) by way of dissolving the four administrative district authorities of Brunswick, Hanover, Lüneburg and Weser-Ems and abolishing the administrative districts. This involved an extensive deconcentration of the previously territorially and functionally bundled meso-level state administration and resulted in a significant upgrading of the sectorwise organised special-purpose *Land* administration. Accordingly, new attempts are being made in Lower Saxony and in other *Länder* with two-tier systems to reduce and merge special-purpose *Land* authorities, integrate them into the higher-level *Land* authorities or shift them to local governments.

(2) In most *Länder* (especially the larger states with the exception of Lower Saxony) a three-tier administration dominates. The lowest level constitutes the counties, the highest level the *Land* ministries and the meso-level various forms of coordinating and bundling authorities. Institutional bundling of administrative functions as part of a three-level system (ministries, meso-level and counties) is the general model found in the *Länder* of Bavaria, Hesse, North Rhine-Westphalia, Baden-Württemberg, Saxony, Saxony-Anhalt, Thuringia and Rhineland-Palatinate. Among these *Länder*, three variants of meso-level instances can be distinguished and neither their tasks nor their integration into the administrative structure are uniform nationwide: a) an administrative unit (*Landesverwaltungsamt*) which assumes coordinating and bundling functions for the whole territory of the *Land* (Saxony-Anhalt, Thuringia); b) functionally specialised directorates which, in some task areas, are responsible only for specific regions and, in other tasks, for the whole territory of the *Land* (Rhineland-Palatinate); c) the traditional form of administrative districts which are regionally oriented instances in charge of bundling and coordinating subnational public functions for specific regions within the *Land* (Hesse, Baden-Württemberg, Bavaria, Saxony[1] and North Rhine-Westphalia). In all three models, an attempt is made to achieve a far-reaching concentration of state tasks at the meso level, in particular by shifting the tasks of the lower state authorities to the meso level. Moreover, there has been a general attempt to concentrate these duties by privatising existing tasks according to political guidelines or by transferring them to the local government level and realigning some of the authorities.

Baden-Württemberg provides a prime example of this process. The multi-purpose meso-level state administration (administrative district authorities) has been substantially upgraded and functionally strengthened since 2005. In addition, numerous state tasks have been transferred to the counties (waiving territorial reforms). The core element of the reform was the complete abolition of 350 out of a total of 450 existing single-purpose state authorities, whose tasks and employees were integrated into the four multi-purpose administrative district authorities and into the thirty-five county administrations and nine county-free cities (Ebinger and Bogumil 2008). The counties received a large number of new responsibilities and emerged from the reform functionally strengthened, even though an increasing number of voices can be heard criticising the new excessive demands being placed on geographically small-scale counties with limited resources (cf. Kuhlmann 2015: 202).

3   FUNCTIONAL REFORMS: DECENTRALISATION OF STATE TASKS

Another essential feature of the reforms in the multilevel system are functional reforms related to the decentralisation of state tasks to the local governments (also called communalisation). This reform approach aims at transferring tasks typically performed by single-function/special-purpose units of the *Land* to local self-government (counties/municipalities). It amounts to a strengthening of the multi-purpose organisation at the local level (Kuhlmann 2015: 188ff.). The transfer of state tasks to local authorities can be structured in different legal ways. According to the model of 'genuine municipalisation' (see Kuhlmann and Wollmann 2019: 161ff.) or 'political decentralisation' (Kuhlmann 2015: 187), all functions that are assigned to the local governments become 'real' (genuine) local self-government tasks for which the elected local council is responsible. By contrast, under the model of 'pseudo-' (in lieu of genuine) communalisation (cf. Wollmann 2008: 259ff.) or of 'administrative decentralisation' (Kuhlmann 2015: 187), local governments receive functions that are delegated to them by the state. The responsibility for the conduct of such delegated functions lies with the local government's executive (mayor, head of county administration—*Landrat*) and not with the elected local council. The transfer of functions in the case of pseudo-communalisation or administrative decentralisation has significant consequences for the municipalities regarding both the internal relations between the local council and local executive and their external relation to the state. First, in the internal relationship, the local executive is solely responsible for the implementation of these tasks, while the elected council has, at least formally, no powers. Second, in the external relationship, the local administration is subject to a functional and administrative supervision that goes beyond the legal oversight and that also addresses the merits and adequateness of the activity concerned. By contrast, in cases of genuine communalisation (political decentralisation), the elected local council is, internally, the highest decision-making body, while externally the municipality stands only under the legal oversight of the state authorities. Although in both regards the distinction has often become blurred in local practice, it remains relevant if and when conflicts arise (cf. Wollmann 2008: 259; Kuhlmann and Wollmann 2019: 161ff.). The current functional reforms in Germany primarily correspond to the type of administrative decentralisation (pseudo-communalisation). Most often, local councils are not granted any rights of political decision-making and control regarding the new tasks transferred to them by state governments.

In Germany, the decentralisation of responsibilities is generally viewed positively on the basis of the subsidiarity principle. Indeed, a number of positive effects have been shown, but there are also some sobering empirical findings regarding the outcomes of functional reforms (see Kuhlmann et al. 2014; Kuhlmann 2010, 2015). On the one hand, there is a tendency for improved horizontal coordination capacities at the subnational level in Germany, especially after political decentralisation, but less in the case of administrative decentralisation. This seems to prove a general theory in administrative sciences according to which the integration of tasks within multifunctional, politically accountable local governments can help to improve territorial coordination within a given administrative jurisdiction. The reforms also demonstrate that the effectiveness of task fulfilment tends to be positively influenced by political decentralisation.

On the other hand, the euphoric expectations placed upon decentralisation strategies in general cannot be justified by the German experience. Decentralisation often entails considerable additional costs and burdens which sometimes overload local governments. In none of the *Länder* have state governments shown much inclination to sufficiently address the budgetary problems of local governments by reimbursing costs. Such circumstances frequently increase the risk of default on their performance obligations, implementation failures or inconsistent applications of law. Furthermore, empirical evidence shows that any type of task transfer to lower levels of government exacerbates existing performance disparities or creates new ones. Thus, irrespective of whether a genuine or a pseudo-communalisation is pursued, task transfer furthers the interlocal variation and makes the equity of service delivery shrink. It should be emphasised, however, that reform effects are also shaped by other intervening factors, such as the local budgetary and staff situation, policy properties (e.g. person-related vs. technical tasks), local policy preferences and political interests in conjunction with the salience of the tasks transferred.

Against this background, it comes as no surprise that the effects of decentralisation vary greatly across individual municipalities, types of reform policy and fields of activity. Regulatory and technical tasks, such as in the environmental sector as a whole, seem rather unsuitable for decentralisation, while distributive tasks and those heavily reliant on local networking, especially in welfare policies, can benefit from the enhanced local proximity (Kuhlmann et al. 2014; Kuhlmann 2015). It is worth noting that differing or negative reform effects can be seen to result from unresolved interface problems across administrative units, limits in local governments' territorial viability and resources, and the politicisation of newly transferred tasks.

4   Territorial Reforms

There is considerable variance across *Länder* regarding the territorial structure of counties and municipalities (see Chap. 9). Of the 295 counties in Germany, 244 have at least 100,000 inhabitants and more than 100 counties have at least 200,000 inhabitants. The average is 193,000 inhabitants in Western Germany and 162,000 in Eastern Germany. With an average of 95,000 inhabitants, the administrative counties in Thuringia are the smallest in Germany, with ten counties having fewer than 100,000 inhabitants. The total number of inhabitants in Thuringia's counties is about 40 per cent below the average for the eastern German *Länder*. The same applies to the number of inhabitants in the county-free cities, which are 47 per cent below the average of the eastern *Länder* and 64 per cent below the average of the western *Länder* (see Table 16.2). Out of a total of roughly 11,000 municipalities, there is a wide variance in territorial sizes across *Länder* too. Whereas in North Rhine-Westphalia the average size of the 400 municipalities is 45,000 inhabitants, Rhineland-Palatinate has about 2300 municipalities with 1700 inhabitants on average (see Table 16.3).

Due to the constitutionally entrenched power of the *Länder* to decide their 'own' territorial reform policy that reflects the different settlement

16 ADMINISTRATIVE REFORMS IN THE MULTILEVEL SYSTEM... 279

Table 16.2 Territorial structures of counties in Germany

Land	Number	Average size (smallest county–biggest county)	
Baden-Württemberg	35	247,162 (107,866–531,013)	986 (519–1851)
Bavaria	71	125,643 (66,644–329,981)	964 (308–1972)
Brandenburg	14	147,077 (77,993–205,520)	2054 (1217–3058)
Hesse	21	219,389 (96,201–404,995)	971 (222–1848)
Mecklenburg-Western Pomerania	6	216,915 (155,265–262,412)	3812 (2117–5468)
Lower Saxony	38	179,136 (48,670–1,119,526)	1223 (535–2882)
North Rhine-Westphalia	31	338,454 (134,947–613,878)	980 (407–1960)
Rhineland-Palatinate	24	123,574 (60,765–209,785)	783 (305–1626)
Saarland	6	165,120 (88,556–325,978)	428 (249–555)
Saxony	10	274,205 (178,346–351,309)	1757 (949–2391)
Saxony-Anhalt	11	154,398 (86,312–221,043)	1806 (1414–2423)
Schleswig-Holstein	11	200,040 (126,643–301,223)	1394 (664–2186)
Thuringia	17	94,868 (57,252–135,155)	903 (433–1305)

Source: Authors' own compilation, Federal and *Länder* Statistical Offices; inhabitants and size as of 31.12.2016

structures and varying party-political constellations, the reform strategies pursued in Germany show a high amount of variance across the *Länder*. In procedural terms, the *Länder* governments carried out their respective reform concepts by inserting a so-called voluntary phase during which municipalities were given the opportunity to 'voluntarily' adjust themselves to the territorial changes proposed. If agreement on the part of the (consulted) municipalities could not be reached, the *Land* parliament decided as a last resort by way of (binding) *Land* legislation.

280   S. KUHLMANN AND J. BOGUMIL

Table 16.3   Territorial structures of municipalities in Germany

State	Number of municipalities in total (December 2017)	Number of inhabitants in 000's (December 2018)	Average number of inhabitants of municipalities
Baden-Württemberg	1101	11,070	10,054
Bavaria	2056	13,077	6360
Brandenburg	417	2512	6031
Hesse	426	6266	14,708
Mecklenburg-Western Pomerania	753	1610	2138
Lower Saxony	945	7982	8446
North Rhine-Westphalia	396	17,932	45,282
Rhineland-Palatinate	2305	4085	1772
Saarland	52	991	19,057
Saxony	422	4078	9663
Saxony-Anhalt	218	2208	10,128
Schleswig-Holstein	1110	2897	2609
Thuringia	849	2143	2524
Federal Republic of Germany	11,054	83,020	7510
West German *Länder* (excl. West Berlin)	8394	66,823	7997
East German Länder (excl. East Berlin)	2659	12,551	4720

Source: Authors' own compilation, Federal and *Länder* Statistical Offices

In some of the West German *Länder*, comprehensive territorial reforms were adopted in the 1970s (see Bogumil 2016). The most radical approaches were pursued in North Rhine-Westphalia and Hesse, which are the most heavily urbanised and densely populated *Länder* in Germany. These reforms hinged on the amalgamation of all existing municipalities to form new territorially and functionally integrated municipalities. In both these *Länder*, the number of municipalities was drastically reduced by over 80 per cent. In North Rhine-Westphalia, this resulted in the establishment of newly integrated municipalities with an average of 46,000 inhabitants (see Table 16.3). By contrast, in the majority of *Länder*, which mostly had more rural areas and were less densely populated, a softer approach was preferred, either by amalgamating only part of the municipalities (e.g. Bavaria) or providing for minimal or practically no amalgamation (for instance Rhineland-Palatinate). Furthermore, in those areas with small-sized municipalities, a new level of inter-municipal formations was introduced with the aim of supporting the former in carrying out their functions. The proportion of municipalities that are members of an inter-municipal formation varies between the *Länder*, reflecting the different impetus of amalgamation. While in Rhineland-Palatinate it is 98.2 per cent, it stands at 47.8 per cent in Bavaria. During the wave of territorial reforms that swept across the (West German) *Länder* during the 1960s and 1970s, the counties in part went through a radical territorial rescaling by way of amalgamation as well. Nationwide, their total number was cut from 4254 to 237, which led to an average population size of 600,000.

The main objectives of the territorial reforms of the 1970s were three-fold: (1) to improve local government performance; (2) enhance capacities for fulfilling supra-local objectives, while (3) taking the aspect of proximity to citizens into account (Thieme and Prillwitz 1981: 45). Greater efficiency and cost reduction measures, pursued in the more recent (partly failed) reform attempts (see Kuhlmann et al. 2018a, b), were not regarded as the main goals at the time. As a result of the 1970s reforms, local government performance is better today. Above all, their capacity to offer services has improved, as confirmed by international experience (cf. Kuhlmann et al. 2018a, b with further references). Furthermore, the reforms led to a withdrawal of locally operating administrative units from the territory to institutional concentration, specialisation and professionalisation. As a consequence, it also led to a certain loss of territorial proximity and local political identity. The specialisation and professionalisation positively impacted the quality of service delivery, as it was now possible to maintain and expand certain services. However, there was a need for an institutional counterbalance to concentration and upscaling. A number of administrative units were thus deconcentrated and localised with the aim of bundling together the locally less specialised tasks and services that had direct contact with citizens. The lessons from this reform period are an emphasis on greater proximity to citizens, downscaling of complex tasks to municipalities and upscaling more specialised functions to centralised administrative units supported by efficient ICT (cf. Thieme and Prillwitz 1981). These lessons, however, were barely taken into consideration in the more recent (partly failed) reform debates, which focussed more on reducing costs and increasing efficiency (Kuhlmann et al. 2018a, b) (Table 16.4).

Table 16.4 Territorial reforms in the West German *Länder*

Land	Number of municipalities 1968	Number of municipalities 1978	Number of municipalities 2017	Reduction (%)
Rhineland-Palatine	2905	2320	2305	21
Schleswig-Holstein	1378	1132	1110	19
Bavaria	7077	2056	2056	71
Lower Saxony	4231	1030	945	78
Baden-Württemberg	3379	1111	1101	67
Hesse	2684	426	426	84
Saarland	347	52	52	86
North Rhine-Westphalia	2277	396	396	83

Source: Authors' own compilation based on Bogumil (2016: 22), updated

Since the early 1990s, the East German *Länder* have witnessed a proliferation of territorial reforms. The need to amalgamate local governments in these *Länder* derives from the fact that after reunification the newly established municipalities were organised into small-scale units, which could not live up to the demands of the growing portfolio of tasks emerging at the local level—let alone those tasks to be transferred from state administration (see Chap. 15). After the first wave of consolidation in the mid-1990s, the already difficult situation of several public budgets intensified due to structural weaknesses and the debt cap imposed by the EU. This situation led to a second wave of territorial reforms in 2007 in Saxony, Saxony-Anhalt and Mecklenburg-Western Pomerania. This strong reform momentum has since come to a halt with the current reform attempts in the *Länder* of Brandenburg and Thuringia. While the early reforms were often carried out by reform coalitions striving for administrative sustainability and competitiveness of their region, the new deliberations alone have become the plaything of political confrontation (see also Ebinger et al. 2018).

The situation of the *Land* of Brandenburg is an exemplary case. The population will shrink by about 10 per cent by 2030 and the average age will rise further, while the population density will develop more and more asymmetrically as a function of the distance to Berlin. Consequently, maintaining infrastructure and services will become a challenge in most parts of the country. The cross-party study commission set up in preparation for the reform of the administrative structure concluded that a territorial reform at county level is indispensable. While the appraisals were similar across Eastern Germany, the set of reform ventures vary considerably concerning drivers (big or small coalition), scope (only county level or municipal—though with time offset), target figures set, actual territorial changes achieved as well as related decentralisation processes (see above).

In Saxony-Anhalt, a territorial reform was executed at both the county and the municipal level. Following the first county-level territorial reform of 1994, the *Land* Parliament introduced further changes in 2007 under the auspices of the *Christlich Demokratische Union Deutschlands* (CDU) and the *Sozialdemokratische Partei Deutschlands* (SPD). The number of counties was reduced from twenty-one to eleven with an average of 153,000 inhabitants (ranging from 86,000 to 223,000 in 2015) and covering an area between 1400 km^2 and 2400 km^2. The three county-free cities were maintained. At the municipal level, two reforms succeeded in 2004 and 2011. As a result of amalgamation, the number of municipalities decreased by more than 80 per cent, from 1300 (2003) to 218 (2015), which have an average of 11,000 inhabitants.

Similarly, Saxony implemented territorial reforms at both the municipal and the county level. After the first territorial reform at county level from 1994 to 1996 and at municipal level in 1998, the CDU and the SPD approved another reform in 2008. The remaining twenty-two counties were reduced to ten and the seven county-free cities to three. The ten counties had between 200,000 and 355,000 inhabitants in 2012. The counties cover an area between 1400 km^2 and 2400 km^2, with the exception of one covering 950 km^2. At the municipal level, the number of units decreased by voluntary amalgamation from an original 1626 in 1990 to 540 in the first territorial reform of 1998, and to 426 as of today, while the average number of inhabitants increased to 9500.

Mecklenburg-Western Pomerania introduced the first county-level territorial reform in 1994. A further reformative attempt in 2007 was thwarted by the *Land*'s constitutional court (Bogumil and Ebinger 2008). However, in 2011 the parliament finally approved a reform with the support of the CDU and the SPD. The result was a merger of twelve counties into six and six county-free cities into two. These new counties cover an area between 2100 km^2 and 5400 km^2, corresponding to the biggest county in the whole of Germany. The population varied between 156,000 and 264,000 in 2012, with an average of 217,000. Mecklenburg-Western Pomerania has not yet carried out any territorial reform at the municipal level.

The Brandenburg Parliament agreed in July 2016 on a blueprint for structural reform of the administration in 2019 in the hands of the SPD and *Die Linke* (The Left). The reform envisaged there would be a population of at least 175,000 in the counties and 150,000 in the county-free cities by 2030. A first proposal with scientific backing that put forward merging the fourteen counties to nine and four county-free cities to one (Potsdam) met with strong opposition. Against the reservations of the parliament's study commission, the Ministry of the Interior of the *Land* Brandenburg was urged into devising a watered-down solution, reducing the number of counties to eleven. However, because of persisting opposition, the county-level territorial reform was finally discarded in November 2017.

In Thuringia, following the first territorial reform at county level in 1994, the SPD, *Die Linke* and *Die Grünen* (the Greens) approved in 2016 a blueprint and an interim law for administrative, functional and territorial reform. The territorial reform envisaged that the number of municipalities would decrease from 850 to 200 and the seventeen counties to eight, with a minimum population of 130,000 at county level and 6000 at municipal level. Of the six county-free cities, only Erfurt and Jena (with more than 100,000 inhabitants) would maintain their status (Bogumil 2016). However, the reformative plans of the *Land* government met with strong resistance from the opposition and the communal arena. Furthermore, the ratification of the interim law was declared invalid on formal grounds by the Federal Constitutional Court. As a result, the government abandoned the project on 30 November 2017 (Table 16.5).

One might wonder why the more recent territorial reforms in East Germany (Thuringia and Brandenburg) have failed compared to previous reforms in Mecklenburg-Western Pomerania, Saxony, Saxony-Anhalt and West Germany (see above). Here, there are various factors to consider. First, the political constellations have changed. In both Thuringia and Brandenburg, only very narrow parliamentary majorities were in favour of these reforms, while large political coalitions had supported them in the past. Second, the measures for consultation and active citizen participation carried out by the state government in Brandenburg to enhance support for the reforms turned out to be rather dysfunctional. Instead of

16 ADMINISTRATIVE REFORMS IN THE MULTILEVEL SYSTEM... 285

Table 16.5 Territorial reforms in the East German *Länder*

Land	Number of municipalities 1990	Number of municipalities 2001/2003	Number of municipalities 2017	Reduction (%)
Mecklenburg-Western Pomerania	1117	994	753	33
Saxony-Anhalt	1349	1289	218	84
Thuringia	1699	1017	849	50
Brandenburg	1775	422	417	76
Saxony	1623	540	422	74

Source: Authors' own compilation based on Bogumil (2016: 24), updated

supporting the government's reform agenda, the local governments, mayors and heads of county councils used the direct-democratic participatory arena as a public forum for mobilising protest against the reform. Moreover, the opposition parties (the CDU; the *Freie Demokratische Partei*, (FDP); and the *Alternative für Deutschland* (AfD)) allied themselves with the mass media and thus fuelled a highly emotionalised debate impeding any attempt at objective and evidence-based discourse. Finally, the state government overemphasised increases in efficiency as a major reform goal, which, based on earlier reform experience, raised doubts about the expected reform success and sharply contrasted with the previous reforms in West Germany. These reforms were much more guided by policies that aimed at improving local governments' performance and capacities rather than increasing efficiency and reducing costs.

5   Conclusions and Lessons for Transfer

A good decade after the entry into force of the major reform projects at national level, the administrative landscape in some *Länder* has undergone fundamental changes (Kuhlmann 2009). The bundling of responsibilities, the dismantling of double administrations, communalisation and territorial reforms are steps in the right direction towards modernising and improving the performance of subnational public administration. In order for these measures to achieve their goals, however, it is vital to ensure that they are used in a prudent and task-oriented manner and not merely as a calculated political manoeuvre or to achieve savings targets. The observation of the current administrative reforms makes it clear that, when shifting responsibilities, certain factors must be taken into account (for an international overview see Schwab et al. 2017; Kuhlmann 2010). For instance, factors such as the ability of the municipalities to provide services that are seldom required but demand a high degree of specialisation, the efficiency with which tasks are performed and the uniformity of administrative execution. The particularly pronounced tension between technical and political objectives at this level due to local proximity and the democratic legitimacy of the decision-maker is also an important factor. There is also a close connection between the possibility of functional reforms and the existing territorial structures (Kuhlmann et al. 2018a, b; Ebinger et al. 2018).

In practice, the problem is that in the field of administrative structural reforms, it is not always possible to combine technical arguments, political will and enforceability. It is not surprising that this has never fully been achieved. For example, political decisions made in both the administrative structural reform in Baden-Württemberg and in Saxony could hardly be justified from a technical point of view. However, until 2011 it was possible, at least in large coalitions, to implement (necessary) territorial reforms. In the light of past experience in Thuringia and Brandenburg, there is good reason to be more sceptical here. The majorities in each case were narrow and this certainly made the reforms more difficult. Even the earlier (reform) alliances between the local government associations and the state governments, such as in Saxony, were no longer possible as it was only a question of power. How to combine the positive modernisation will of the state governments with functional and regional reforms and integrating the knowledge of the administration into the process is still an open question and also dependent on political framework conditions. An important lesson to learn from the various waves of (successful and failed) territorial reforms in Germany is that they should not be justified mainly by the argument of increasing efficiency, but of improving local governments' capacities and performance instead. The latter effects of territorial upscaling are well documented in literature and supported by empirical findings, while greater efficiency and cost savings through mergers have not generally been recorded as they largely depend on specific context conditions and local implementation processes (cf. Kuhlmann et al. 2018a; for the conceptual background see Kuhlmann and Wollmann 2011).

A major strength of the German administrative system is that it promotes territorial and functional variations, which allow for flexible models of subnational intergovernmental organisation. This variety of institutional set-up and reform approaches encourages piloting, adjustments and learning. However, different models can lead to differences in service provision, treatment of citizens and varying institutional progress of local administration. Furthermore, a balance needs to be found between 'too small' and 'too big' territorial jurisdictions. A continuous monitoring of local governments' service quality and performance seems indispensable for identifying new reform requirements in due time and for adjusting institutional settings accordingly. Many of the organisational features and reform approaches discussed here make perfect sense in the German politico-administrative context. They constitute domestic institutional responses to context-specific problems agreed upon by state and local actors. Given such particularities, any possible transfer of the German institutional solutions described in this chapter should be approached with caution, and the respective country-specific political, administrative and cultural circumstances should be taken into consideration when drawing on lessons and translating concepts.

NOTE

1. The three administrative districts were renamed *Landesdirektionen* in 2008. On 1 March 2012, these were formally merged into one regional directorate (which continues to have regional branches).

REFERENCES

Bogumil, J. (2016). *Neugliederung der Landkreise und kreisfreien Städte in Thüringen. Gutachten im Auftrag des Thüringer Ministeriums für Inneres und Kommunales*. Bochum: Ministry of Interior Thuringia.

Bogumil, J., & Ebinger, F. (2008). Machtgewinn der Kommunen? In C. Büchner, J. Franzke & M. Nierhaus (Eds.), *Verfassungsrechtliche Anforderungen an Kreisgebietsreformen* (pp. 13–23). Zum Urteil das Landesverfassungsgerichtes Mecklenburg-Vorpommern, S.

Bogumil, J., & Kottmann, S. (2006). *Verwaltungsstrukturreform in Niedersachsen. Die Abschaffung der Bezirksregierungen* (Publication Series of the Stiftung Westfalen-Initiative, vol. 11). Münster: Ibbenbürener Vereinsdruckerei.

Ebinger, F., & Bogumil, J. (2008). Grenzen der Subsidiarität. Verwaltungsreform und Kommunalisierung in den Ländern. In H. Heinelt & A. Vetter (Eds.), *Lokale Politikforschung heute* (pp. 165–196). Wiesbaden: VS Verlag für Sozialwissenschaften.

Ebinger, F., Bogumil, J., & Kuhlmann, S. (2018). Territorial Reforms in Europe: Effects on Administrative Performance and Democratic Participation. *Local Government Studies*, *45*(1), 1–23. https://doi.org/10.1080/0300393 0.2018.1530660.

Ellwein, T. (1994). *Das Dilemma der Verwaltung: Verwaltungsstruktur und Verwaltungsreform in Deutschland*. Mannheim: BS-Taschenbuchverlag.

Kuhlmann, S. (2009). Reforming Local Government in Germany: Institutional Changes and Performance Impacts. *German Politics*, *18*(2), 226–245. https://doi.org/10.1080/09644000902870842.

Kuhlmann, S. (2010). Between the State and the Market: Assessing Impacts of Local Government Reforms in Western Europe. *Lex localis—Journal of Local Self-Government*, *8*(1), 1–21. https://doi.org/10.4335/8.1.1-21(2010).

Kuhlmann, S. (2015). Administrative Reforms in the Intergovernmental Setting: Impacts on Multi-Level Governance from a Comparative Perspective. In E. Ongaro (Ed.), *Multi Level Governance: The Missing Linkages* (Series 'Critical Perspectives on International Public Sector Management', vol. 4) (pp. 183–215). https://doi.org/10.1108/S2045-794420150000004008.

Kuhlmann, S., & Bogumil, J. (2010). *Kommunale Aufgabenwahrnehmung im Wandel: Kommunalisierung, Regionalisierung und Territorialreform in Deutschland und Europa*. Wiesbaden: VS-Verlag.

Kuhlmann, S., Bogumil, J., & Grohs, S. (2014). Reforming Public Administration in Multi-level Systems: An Evaluation of Performance Changes in European Local Governments. In E. Bohne et al. (Eds.), *Public Administration and the Modern State. Assessing Trends and Impact* (pp. 205–222). Basingstoke: Palgrave Macmillan.

Kuhlmann, S., Siegel, J., & Seyfried, M. (2018a). Was bewirken Gebietsreformen? Eine Bilanz deutscher und europäischer Erfahrungen. *dms – der moderne Staat*, *11*(1), 119–142. https://doi.org/10.3224/dms.v11i1.08.

Kuhlmann, S., Siegel, J., & Seyfried, M. (2018b). *Wirkungen kommunaler Gebietsreformen: Stand der Forschung und Empfehlungen für Politik und Verwaltung*. Berlin: Nomos/Ed. Sigma.

Kuhlmann, S., & Wollmann, H. (2011). Special Issue on Evaluating Functional and Territorial Reforms in European Countries. *Local Government Studies*, *35*(5).

Kuhlmann, S., & Wollmann, H. (2019). *Introduction to Comparative Public Administration: Administrative Systems and Reforms in Europe* (2nd ed.). Cheltenham and Northampton: Edward Elgar.

Schwab, C., Bouckaert, G., & Kuhlmann, S. (Eds.). (2017). *The Future of Local Government in Europe: Lessons from Research and Practice in 31 Countries*. Berlin: Nomos/Ed. Sigma. https://doi.org/10.5771/9783845280639.

Thieme, W., & Prillwitz, G. (1981). *Durchführung und Ergebnisse der kommunalen Gebietsreform*. Baden-Baden: Nomos.

Thieme, W., Unruh, G. von, & Scheuner, U. (1981). *Die Grundlagen der kommunalen Gebietsreform*. Baden-Baden: Nomos.

Wollmann, H. (2008). *Reformen in Kommunalpolitik und -verwaltung. England, Schweden, Frankreich und Deutschland im Vergleich.* Wüstenrot Stiftung. Wiesbaden: VS Verlag für Sozialwissenschaften.

Open Access This chapter is licensed under the terms of the Creative Commons Attribution 4.0 International License (http://creativecommons.org/licenses/by/4.0/), which permits use, sharing, adaptation, distribution and reproduction in any medium or format, as long as you give appropriate credit to the original author(s) and the source, provide a link to the Creative Commons licence and indicate if changes were made.

The images or other third party material in this chapter are included in the chapter's Creative Commons licence, unless indicated otherwise in a credit line to the material. If material is not included in the chapter's Creative Commons licence and your intended use is not permitted by statutory regulation or exceeds the permitted use, you will need to obtain permission directly from the copyright holder.

CHAPTER 17

Institutional Differentiation of Public Service Provision in Germany: Corporatisation, Privatisation and Re-Municipalisation

Benjamin Friedländer, Manfred Röber, and Christina Schaefer

1 INTRODUCTION

Recent decades have seen an increasing transfer of public service[1] provision to institutions outside the core administration. This process of differentiation in the performance of public tasks has led to significant changes in the institutional landscape. The shift from the model of the 'caring welfare state' towards the model of the 'enabling and ensuring state' has fundamentally changed the understanding of the state in Germany. Public services are no longer exclusively and directly delivered

---

B. Friedländer (✉) • C. Schaefer
Helmut Schmidt University, Hamburg, Germany
e-mail: benjamin.friedlaender@hsu-hh.de; christina.schaefer@hsu-hh.de

M. Röber
University of Leipzig, Leipzig, Germany
e-mail: roeber@wifa.uni-leipzig.de

© The Author(s) 2021
S. Kuhlmann et al. (eds.), *Public Administration in Germany*,
Governance and Public Management,
https://doi.org/10.1007/978-3-030-53697-8_17

by the core administration of the state and municipalities, but also by external (not-for-profit and private) organisations.

The idea behind the model of the 'enabling and ensuring state' is the division into different levels of responsibility for service provision (guaranteeing, providing, financing and serving as a fallback provider; see: Schuppert 2005). This kind of division of responsibilities results in a complex network of public and private actors (which can be described as principal–agent relationships).

Following the arguments of the Public Choice Theory, the reasons for the institutional differentiation in Germany are, on the one hand, criticism of the inefficiency and ineffectiveness of public administration as a monopolistic service provider. On the other hand, there have been political tendencies to push the state back in favour of the private sector (in conjunction with anti-bureaucratic, market-oriented reforms for the remaining state and more 'choice' for citizens) and to divide monolithic-bureaucratic administrations into smaller decentralised units.

Within the framework of the enabling state model, the state has a wide range of institutional arrangements to choose from in order to ensure the performance of public tasks. Public services can be produced and delivered by (cf. Reichard and Röber 2019):[2]

- different departments and units of the public core administration (in-house provision);
- corporatisation, which can be understood as the institutional transfer of tasks from administrative units into companies. Corporations remain completely or partially in state or municipal ownership. A distinction can be made between the following options:
  - partly independent institution without its own legal status and with rather limited autonomy (e.g. government-operated/semi-autonomous agency/utility) (*Eigenbetrieb*),
  - public institution and foundation under public law (*Anstalt und Stiftung des öffentlichen Rechts*),
  - local administrative association as single-purpose agency which is an association of several local authorities for the joint performance of a specific public task (e.g. water supply/sewerage or local public transportation) (*Zweckverband*),
  - legally and organisationally independent institution which, although still fully or partly owned by the state or municipality, has a minimum degree of managerial autonomy as state- or municipal-owned enterprise (*formelle Privatisierung*). It usually

takes place in the private legal form of the limited liability company (*Gesellschaft mit beschränkter Haftung*) or joint-stock company (*Aktiengesellschaft*),
- hybrid institution, such as a corporation jointly owned by public and private shareholders (also called institutional public-private-partnership (PPP));
- outsourcing or contracting out (*funktionale Privatisierung*) for which the public sector withdraws partially or completely from the provision of services by transferring a task or part of it to private organisations for a fixed period of time, but still retains the responsibility for ensuring these services (e.g. awarding of concessions). A special form of outsourcing is contractual PPPs, which means the transfer of services or functions to private companies based on contracts for a limited time period. The private organisation will generally be a commercial private enterprise, but a private not-for-profit organisation can also be considered (e.g. provision of social services by welfare associations), and
- privatisation as the complete transfer of a public task to private entities (*materielle Privatisierung*) in which the state relieves itself of all responsibility and has only a minor influence on the scope of tasks in the form of regulation (full retreat of the state).[3]

After decades of privatising public services, several municipalities have terminated concession contracts which were formerly awarded to external private suppliers or have—in a very few cases—bought back utilities. Therefore, we observe a debate about the advantages of publicly provided services *vis-à-vis* privatised ones at the local level. Re-municipalisation—which is about returning previously (in most cases, functionally) privatised public supply and disposal services to local authorities—has been on the agenda of local politicians for the last ten years.

If the state or a local authority wants to make a decision about which institutional arrangement should be used to perform a public task, the criteria of strategic relevance (i.e. the importance of fulfilling a task for implementing policy objectives), the specificity of resources (i.e. the extent of the exclusivity of public resources which are necessary for the provision of services compared to an alternative use of resource) and the cost-effectiveness of task performance by comparing production costs and transaction costs (e.g. for contract initiation, coordination and monitoring) of different institutional arrangements[4] should be taken into consideration (Warm et al. 2018). Taking these fundamentals of institutional economics into account, there is—as mentioned above—a wide range of organisational options for the provision of public services, namely corporatisation, outsourcing, privatisation and re-municipalisation. These four different options will be outlined in the next section with regard to their objectives, advantages and disadvantages as well as selected empirical findings and trends in Germany.

2 Service Provision Between Corporatisation, Outsourcing, Privatisation and Re-municipalisation

2.1 Corporatisation

According to the calculations of the German Federal Statistical Office, the total number of corporations which are fully or partly owned by public authorities at federal, state and local level is round about 15,000.[5] The majority of these corporations operate at local level (approximately 90 per cent). About two-thirds of the federal workforce and about half of the municipal employees are employed in these corporations. State-owned enterprises are responsible for more than half of the public sector's investments. The debt ratio of these enterprises is often even higher than that of the core administration. Approximately one-third of these institutions are organised under public law in the form of government-operated/ semi-autonomous utilities, public institutions and foundations under public law or local administrative associations, which are under public law and owned by several local authorities. Almost two-thirds are private-law types of corporatisation mostly in the form of a limited liability company and a joint-stock company (German Federal Statistical Office 2014; German Institute for Economic Research 2017; Hesse et al. 2017; Kuhlmann and Wollmann 2019). The legal form of the limited liability company predominates because, unlike a joint-stock company, this form enables the public owner to exert more influence on corporate strategies and business plans through articles of association (*Gesellschaftsvertrag*), assembly of owners (*Gesellschafterversammlung*) and owner instruction (*Gesellschafteranweisung*).

The aim of corporatisation, that is the transformation of administrative units into companies, is to enable these newly established public enterprises to act more flexibly and independently. This should relieve the core administration of purely operational tasks and the provision of services and position it more strongly as a strategic control unit. As a corporatisation can often focus on a single task (similar to the single-purpose agencies in Great Britain), it is expected that their formation will lead to greater professionalism and stability in the fulfilment of tasks (Reichard and Röber 2019).

Corporatisation can also be a matter of relieving political entities by pulling politically controversial issues out of the 'line of fire' of everyday party politics. Especially in the creation of companies under private law, the circumvention of public services and budget law or bureaucratic procurement law is often a motive. Moreover, there is no doubt that hidden motives also play a role. On the one hand, corporatisation can be used to 'hide' loans and thereby conceal public debt ('shadow budgets'). State-owned enterprises hold nearly 38 per cent of the state's total debt. At the local level, approximately 60 per cent of all municipal debts relate to their municipal-owned enterprises (Schaefer and Friedländer 2019). On the other hand, it can be very tempting to provide distinguished party members with lucrative and well-paid posts or to use these enterprises for party-political manoeuvring (Ennser-Jedenastik 2014; Schröter and Röber 2017).

Although it is difficult to empirically prove that corporatisation has led to an increase in efficiency and flexibility, some research results suggest that such effects have been produced—but not to the extent initially assumed (e.g. Voorn et al. 2017; Lindlbauer et al. 2015; Mühlenkamp 2015). In addition, the necessarily formal communication structures between the public owner and its corporation (e.g. in the case of a limited liability company through the above-mentioned mechanism) as well as new requirements for accountability seem to have increased the transparency of decision-making processes (Schröter and Röber 2017). Moreover, in many cases, a certain cultural change from being less bureaucratic to being more entrepreneurial could be observed (Reichard and Röber 2019).

However, corporatisation can also have some negative consequences. The process of corporatisation in recent decades has resulted in a fragmented organisational landscape. Particularly in large German cities, we find highly complex corporate structures with hundreds of municipal holdings (e.g. the city of Frankfurt am Main with more than 540 municipal holdings), which are hard to control and steer solely by the traditional bureaucratic concepts of hierarchy and planning. In some cases, corporations and their managers enjoy too much autonomy, leading to increasing inconsistencies between local policy objectives and corporate purpose.

Centrifugal dynamics can give rise to serious steering and control problems for local authorities. In addition, experiences at the local level show that performance information is insufficiently used for the control of the described corporate structures, so that important prerequisites for an effective holdings management are often still missing (Friedländer 2019; Wollmann 2016; see Sect. 3). Overall, decisions on corporatisation should be carefully prepared and weighed up to see whether the benefits of enhanced autonomy are appropriate to the loss of steering and control by public authorities.

A special type of corporatisation is institutional PPPs, which are under private law and in a mixed public-private ownership (Duffield 2010). The influence of the two owners on the company's policy formally depends on the size of their capital shares. With a few exceptions, there is a huge lack of reliable statistical data available for this type of enterprise. Based on the analysis of holdings reports, it is assumed that about two-thirds of companies at the federal and state level and nearly 40 per cent of all municipal corporations are institutional PPPs (Reichard 2016 with further references). Due to their mixed ownership, institutional PPPs differ from other forms of corporatisation in certain aspects, insofar as the two owner groups have different interests, goals, core competencies and organisational cultures. These 'trade-offs' between public and private ownership require complex modes of coordination, which can lead to extensive negotiation processes. Success in coordination efforts very much depends on how well both sides are able to tolerate different cultural imprints and competencies (e.g. basic understanding of the public interest and political decision-making processes, managerial skills or competencies in inter-sectoral cooperation) and how they can harmonise these special properties with each other (Röber and Schröter 2016).

2.2 Outsourcing

The basic idea behind the outsourcing of public tasks to private actors (also referred to as contracting out or functional privatisation) is that public administration can concentrate on its politically defined core functions and be relieved of the burden of providing services that can be produced in a better quality and more cost-effectively by other—private—organisations ('principle of subsidiarity'). In the case of 'outsourcing', a service contract is concluded between the contracting authority and the private contractor. The responsibility for ensuring the service provision remains with the state (for the following, see: Röber 2018).

In Germany there is a long tradition—in contrast to unitary welfare states—of involving not-for-profit and private institutions in the provision of public services, such as in the areas of healthcare and social services (Kuhlmann and Wollmann 2019; Grohs 2014). Moreover, numerous services (e.g. supply and disposal services), internal administrative services and annexe tasks (e.g. cleaning services) have been outsourced to private companies since the 1980s.

The main motives for outsourcing public tasks and services to private actors—particularly in the light of the challenging budgetary situation of many local authorities—are similar to those of corporatisation. It is also expected that costs of public services can be reduced by enabling private actors to be more productive due to specialisation and higher levels of efficiency as well as by lower wage levels. Beyond that, ideological convictions continue to contribute to the existence of preferences for private service providers (for more details, see below on privatisation).

Although there are no systematic and comprehensive empirical studies on the consequences of outsourcing, some experiences suggest that from the citizens' point of view quality of service provision may decline (Dahlström et al. 2018). In addition, comparative studies tend to point to similar effects in the case of corporatisation (Pollitt and Talbot 2004)—including cautious assessments that outsourcing can reduce costs under certain conditions, although there is so far insufficient empirical evidence for stronger effects on government spending behaviour (Alonso et al. 2015).

However, when making estimates of cost reduction it should be noted that potential—but often rather short-term—effects must be compared with the transaction costs associated with the outsourcing process (i.e. cost of awarding, contract design, monitoring and renegotiation). Furthermore, public authorities should avoid becoming dependent on market-dominating private providers. It is advisable for the public sector to maintain a minimum of relevant 'production know-how' as this can prevent information asymmetries between the public contracting authority and the private service provider. This also creates the possibility of still being able to competently assess the services of the private supplier with regard to their price-performance ratio (cf. Röber 2018).

After a relatively strong trend of outsourcing over the past twenty years, this institutional arrangement is now being regarded with increasing scepticism. In many cases, it was not possible to meet the savings expectations, so now there is a tendency to return to more public arrangements (see below on re-municipalisation). Outsourcing of public services can, however, be a reasonable alternative to in-house provision as long as the service is suitable (e.g. in terms of low strategic relevance or low specificity), easy to describe and easy to measure. Furthermore, the contract design should ensure successful control, and the contracting authority should be in a position to constantly monitor the process of service provision. Finally, it is important that a sufficient degree of competition exists.

These requirements become even more obvious when it comes to contractual PPPs that represent a specific form of outsourcing. Contractual PPPs are contractual agreements that allow for the transfer of services or functions to private companies typically based on long-term contracts for a period of twenty to thirty years (Duffield 2010). In Germany, they are most frequently used for physical infrastructure projects in the social sector, such as schools, hospitals or sports facilities. Based on previous experiences, this form of outsourcing has become controversial. Although contractual PPPs are mostly justified with possible efficiency benefits, there are, so far, no reliable empirical findings to suggest these efficiency gains have been made. As a result, relatively few new PPP projects in building and road construction have been launched in Germany since 2012.

Contractual PPPs tend to involve high transaction costs as the often very complex and long-term contracts require extensive adjustments and renegotiations. The theoretical concept of 'incomplete contracts'—as the key to the economic understanding of contractual PPPs—implies that, due to bounded rationalities, not all actions and their consequences can be adequately regulated for the future and that the state or a local authority runs a high risk of bearing these unregulated consequences (e.g. higher costs in the operating phase because of savings or deficiencies in the construction phase). Under these circumstances, the bundling of the different phases of a PPP life cycle, that is from planning, construction, operation to recovery, can increase efficiency and is therefore recommended for such projects. Unfortunately, in most cases, this life cycle approach is not consistently followed in practice.

2.3   *Privatisation*

Looking at privatisation—as the complete transfer of public tasks and public ownership to private entities—from a historical perspective, it can be noted that since the 1970s—not only in Germany but in all OECD countries—the idea of the welfare state and its institutions has come under pressure due to obvious, but sometimes only perceived, inefficiencies of public institutions ('state failure'). The main explanations offered for state failure are the selfish behaviour of politicians, the budget-maximising behaviour of bureaucrats, the lobbying of powerful interest groups and inappropriate pricing for public services. As a consequence of the assumed state failure—and in line with changing ideologies towards the lean or minimal state—there has been overall stronger support for privatisations in society and politics. Nevertheless, as far as privatisation is concerned, from an international perspective, Germany was among the OECD countries that pursued a cautious privatisation policy. Although there have been some privatisations of assets such as the federal government's industrial holdings, privatisations have been fairly moderate (Sack 2019). The most relevant areas of privatisation are supply and disposal, postal services, telecommunications and housing. At the municipal level, about one-third of municipalities have had experience with rather modest privatisation projects—especially in the energy and waste sector. In the last two decades, however, the policy of the European Commission for further liberalisation has increased pressure considerably (Röber 2018).

Similar to outsourcing, considerations on privatisation are primarily concerned with financial objectives (cost reduction and budget relief). In addition, however, general ideological positions ('private enterprises basically make everything better and cheaper') as well as economic and regulatory motives have played a role and fostered the private sector.

The effects of privatisation are still the subject of controversial discussion, not least because empirical studies produce mixed results. These controversies relate to different assessments of cost reductions, deterioration in quality, price increases, deterioration in working conditions, the formation of oligopolies in the markets of public services, externalisation of economic, social and ecological risks as well as adverse effects on the democratic control.

In principle, privatisation as the complete transfer of public tasks and public ownership to private entities means that a task loses its 'public' character. It can only be influenced to a limited extent by the state through regulatory policies such as general legislation and regulatory supervision. For this reason, the decisions to privatise have more serious consequences than those to outsource public tasks for a limited period of time. An important prerequisite for a successful privatisation policy is therefore that the state is not pushed back and undermined in its regulatory functions, but is in a position to set rules and—if necessary—to enforce them. Against the background of current studies on privatisation, it should be noted, particularly in the context of public services, that ownership—as a regulatory parameter—has lost its importance. Much more important in terms of regulatory policy than the question of ownership—and the resulting advocacy or rejection of privatisation—is the question of how competitive structures and regulatory regimes can be created in which public and private enterprises can operate for the benefit of society and the citizens, without this leading to misallocations, loss of efficiency or abuse of power (see Sect. 3).

2.4 Re-municipalisation

More recently, we observe an increasing scepticism about privatisation projects. In the last few years, there has been growing citizen resistance to planned municipal privatisations, and some municipalities have terminated concession contracts which were formerly awarded to external private suppliers or have—in a very few cases—bought back utilities (Bönker et al. 2016).

In other words, re-municipalisation is about returning previously (in most cases, functionally) privatised public supply and disposal services to local authorities. Consequently, it is an issue related to previous privatisation decisions. Re-municipalisation is a possible result of the revaluation of choice options in the light of former experiences with privatisation programmes.

Apart from other reasons (e.g. ensuring sufficient control of service provision, achieving synergies in municipal corporate structures and socio-economic reasons, such as contributing to regional employment policies), the global financial crisis was, without doubt, a strong driver for such a reappraisal as the neoliberal dogma of private sector supremacy has been severely damaged. Furthermore, growing doubts persist about the merits of privatisation. Potential reasons for the 'municipalisation-renaissance' are obvious failures of privatisation, anxieties of citizens, stronger self-confidence of local authorities in running their services efficiently and effectively, and increasing fears that the idea of local self-government could be hollowed out if more and more services were transferred to private entities that cannot be controlled politically (Friedländer and Röber 2016; Schaefer and Theuvsen 2012).

Against the background of this political discourse, a process began in Germany about twenty years ago—especially at the municipal level—to reverse outsourcing and privatisation, at least partially. As a result of this process, an increasing importance of public enterprises can be observed. Between 2000 and 2013, the number of public funds, utilities and enterprises rose steadily by approximately 25 per cent from roundabout 12,240 to—as already mentioned—approximately 15,000 (Hesse et al. 2017).

Some evidence on re-municipalisation can mainly be observed in the energy sector. Between 2007 and 2012, more than 160 concessions were taken over by municipalities or municipal companies. A current study has identified seventy-two newly founded municipal energy utilities in the period from 2005 (Wagner and Berlo 2015). In the period from 2000 to 2011, sales revenues of municipal energy utilities rose from €51.9 billion to €114.9 billion (179 per cent). Thus, their share of nominal GDP has more than doubled (Monopoly Commission 2013).

The concerns of many local authorities that their own utilities could not withstand competition from private energy suppliers have been diminished. Municipalities that privatised large parts of their energy supply in the early 1990s are becoming increasingly aware of the lack of influence on the supply infrastructure and urban development. The dynamic of re-municipalisation was mainly fuelled by two factors: first, the development of energy from renewable resources and second, the expiry of existing electricity and gas concessions. The share of renewable energy in Germany's total heat and electricity consumption is to increase from 20 per cent in 2020 to 60 per cent by 2050—accompanied by a 50 per cent improvement in energy efficiency. This implies a tendency towards more decentralisation in power generation with better chances for municipal public utilities to enter/re-enter the energy market. Experts assume that the trend towards re-established or newly established municipal utilities will continue. However, the takeover of distribution networks will tend to decline in the coming years due to the decreasing number of expiring concessions (Libbe 2013).

The picture in waste management is quite similar. Here we observe an increase in municipal provision. The absolute revenues of public waste disposal services increased between 2001 and 2011 by about €4.6 billion (growth rate of 33.7 per cent) (Monopoly Commission 2013). Empirical findings show that in recent years some local authorities (especially smaller cities and districts) have opted for in-house provision rather than outsourcing (Opphard et al. 2010). In other municipal service areas, the emphasis on re-municipalisation is rather low. This applies, for instance, in the water and sewage industry and in the public transport sector. Most service providers in these sectors are still public and the ratio of privatised corporations is very low.

Although the sectoral re-municipalisation tendencies go beyond the individual projects, no visible general trend towards re-municipalisation can be observed in Germany. It remains unclear to what extent these developments are of a long-lasting nature, that is whether they will tend to spread further or are more likely to decline. This can be said for Germany and other European countries where different developments can also be observed in the various sectors of public services and where the diversity and differentiation of the institutional landscape is also increasing rather than decreasing (Friedländer and Röber 2016; Wollmann 2016).

3 Lessons Learned

Each of the above-mentioned institutional arrangements has important consequences for steering, governance and management requirements, which will continue to increase rather than decrease. Practitioners facing these complex issues have to deal with various actors who can differ greatly in their goals, risk preferences, logic of action, core competencies and organisational cultures. In addition, all these issues involve micropolitics that are difficult to influence but are, in many cases, crucial.

Better management in decentralised or external institutions with no corresponding capabilities in public authorities and politics will most probably widen the skills gap, which can, in turn, lead to an uncontrollable autonomy of these institutions and too little influence on public service provision. Recent research results show that it is becoming more difficult for public authorities to strike a balance between 'freedom to manage' (e.g. managerial autonomy of corporations) on the one hand, and political control (e.g. enforcement of policy objectives) on the other, through different forms of coordination as well as embedded or connected modes, including appropriate incentive and sanction mechanisms as well as quality standards, which fit exactly to a specific organisational setting (Friedländer 2019). This requires a system of integrated coordination and management, which focusses on the core administration as well as on the various forms of decentralised and external institutions or service providers.

Looking in particular at the relationship between municipalities and their corporations, municipal codes require that local authorities exert a reasonable influence on these institutions. As a result, most German municipalities have a corporate governance or holdings management system that includes all the tasks, institutions, actors and administrative units involved in enabling a municipality as an owner to take responsibility for the control of its enterprises. This system also involves the activities of supervisory bodies and representatives of the shareholders within municipal corporations as well as political committees responsible for finance and holdings (*Ausschüsse für Finanzen und Beteiligungen*) (similar regulatory mechanisms exist at federal and state level).

Some municipal charters additionally require the establishment of an administrative unit for holdings management, which can be arranged very differently within or outside the municipal administration. In most cases, this unit is either part of the finance department or organised as a separate department or located as a staff position directly with the mayor (central organisation). Some cities use a decentralised form in which holdings management is carried out by the specialised administrative departments (e.g. housing, water and energy) or a combination of both, that is a centralised/decentralised form. In a few cities, holdings management is not part of the core administration but is carried out externally by an institution which is completely in municipal ownership (Schaefer 2004).

Apart from this, the duality of supervisory board and management board applies to the majority of municipal-owned enterprises. The German corporate law subjects owners of a limited liability company of a certain size to the rules that apply to joint stock companies by introducing a dual structure of governing boards. Moreover, individual German states require local governments to establish supervisory boards—regardless of the size of the corporation—if they opt to pursue their economic activities in the form of a private-law company. Therefore, the composition of board membership, and the selection, recruitment and appointment of individual board members are highly significant matters in the management and control of public enterprises (Schröter and Röber 2017).

In summary, the institutional options for providing public services have become highly differentiated and have, of course, their own specific advantages and disadvantages. If the public sector does not opt for in-house provision, a key challenge will be exerting an appropriate level of influence over the provision of services, which normally diminishes significantly when taking the 'corporatisation' to 'privatisation' option. It is necessary to ensure that an institutional arrangement guarantees an accessible, qualitatively appropriate and financially stable fulfilment of tasks. And finally, the service must be provided efficiently.

However, valid assessments of the efficiency of the various institutional options are difficult to make as such organisational solutions often have a time horizon of between twenty and thirty years. For this reason, the costs, effects and behaviour of the various actors can only be evaluated with a considerable degree of uncertainty. Furthermore, as already mentioned, transaction costs associated with the planning, control and monitoring of a particular arrangement of service provision play a significant role in efficiency assessments. Therefore, these 'control costs' should not be ignored.

From a more fundamental position, it should be emphasised that the debate about public versus private service provision might now be a fairly outdated discussion because both options only differ from each other in terms of property. Hence, the debate is primarily focussed on ownership issues—while questions of appropriate market structures and regulation are neglected. This only leads to an exchange of more or less ideological convictions. It is most likely that ownership issues are overestimated and less relevant for the efficiency and effectiveness of service provision.

An important starting point for correcting these misconceptions would be to take a somewhat more functional perspective rather than the traditional institutional and ownership-based perspective (state-owned versus private enterprises). Following this idea, it would be useful to have serious debates about private or public service provision regarding public tasks and services, and about which institutional arrangements and organisational structures are the most suitable for performing these tasks and public services. The brief overview of opportunities and trends in the provision of public services shows that the institutional arrangements for services provision vary, each option has its own specific advantages and disadvantages and that there is no one-size-fits-all solution.

Consequently, the public sector will need to evaluate the respective strengths and weaknesses on a case-by-case basis. In essence, it is about the conscious choice and design of the institutional structure and its steering. Decisions about organisational arrangements—which are ultimately policy decisions—make it absolutely necessary to use procedures enabling practitioners to systematically analyse current framework conditions and objectives as well as consider all possible institutional options.[6]

Table 17.1 Public funds, institutions and enterprises by legal form and authority

	Federation	Federal states	Municipalities	Total
Civil Law				
Joint stock company	11	35	194	240
Limited liability company	181	842	7758	8781
Limited partnership with a limited liability company as general partner	7	111	489	607
Other (e.g. associations)	3	9	87	99
Total Civil Law	*202*	*997*	*8528*	*9727*
Public Law				
Government-operated/semi-autonomous utility	5	230	3522	3757
Local administrative associations	-	-	1102	1102
Institution under public law	9	86	265	360
Foundation under public law	1	36	4	41
Other corporations under public law	2	39	20	61
Total Public Law	*17*	*391*	*4913*	*5321*
Total	*219*	*1388*	*13,441*	*15,048*

Source: Authors' own calculations, based on German Federal Statistical Office 2014, see: Warm et al. (2018)

NOTES

1. The German term for these services is *Daseinsvorsorge* and covers technical infrastructure (traffic and transport facilities, gas, water and electricity supply, refuse collection, sewage disposal, telecommunications) as well as social infrastructure, like healthcare, hospitals, childcare, care for the elderly, educational and cultural institutions.
2. For comparability of the internationally common distinction between different agency types, see: van Thiel (2012).
3. We can also distinguish the form of privatisation as asset sale, which refers to the sale of enterprises, property assets, land and so on. This form of privatisation plays a subordinate role in this chapter.
4. Due to the effort required for coordination and monitoring, transaction costs normally increase from 'in-house provision' to the 'outsourcing-solution'.
5. For details, see Table 17.1. In some documents, the figures vary slightly due to the reference year and the methodology used for public finance and public service personnel statistics ('shell concept') (cf. Schaefer and Friedländer 2019)

6. For these decisions, the Local Governments' Joint Agency for Administrative Management—an independent consultancy agency organised by voluntary membership of German municipalities, counties, and local authorities with more than 10,000 inhabitants—recommends a five-step procedure (see: KGSt 2010a, b). This procedure, which was developed in collaboration with the author Manfred Röber, is to be understood as a checklist or analytical instrument, which can be used for case-by-case decisions about organisational arrangements.

REFERENCES

Alonso, J. M., Clifton, J., & Díaz-Fuentes, D. (2015). Did New Public Management Matter? An Empirical Analysis of the Outsourcing and Decentralisation Effects on Public Sector Size. *Public Management Review, 17*(5), 643–660.

Bönker, F., Libbe, J., & Wollmann, H. (2016). Remunicipalisation Revisited: Long-Term Trends in the Provision of Local Public Services in Germany. In H. Wollmann, I. Kopric, & G. Marcou (Eds.), *Public and Social Services in Europe* (pp. 71–85). Houndmills/New York: Palgrave Macmillan.

Dahlström, C., Nistotskaya, M., & Tyrberg, M. (2018). Outsourcing, Bureaucratic Personnel Quality and Citizen Satisfaction with Public Services. *Public Administration, 96*, 218–233.

Duffield, C. F. (2010). Different Delivery Models. In G. A. Hodge, C. Greve, & A. E. Boardman (Eds.), *International Handbook on Public–Private Partnerships* (pp. 187–215). Cheltenham: Edward Elgar Publishing.

Ennser-Jedenastik, L. (2014). Political Control and Managerial Survival in State-Owned Enterprises. *Governance, 27*(1), 135–161.

Federal Statistical Office of Germany. (2014). Jahresabschlussstatistik öffentlicher Fonds, Einrichtungen und Unternehmen. *Statistisches Bundesamt 2014, Wirtschaft und Statistik* (pp. 307–314). Wiesbaden: Self-publisher.

Friedländer, B. (2019). *Kommunale Gesamtsteuerung öffentlicher Aufgaben: Bestandsaufnahme, Bewertung und Perspektiven.* Wiesbaden: Springer VS.

Friedländer, B., & Röber, M. (2016). Rekommunalisierung öffentlicher Dienstleistungen. Entwicklungstendenzen in vier europäischen Ländern und organisationspolitische Perspektiven. *Verwaltung & Management, 22*(2), 59–67.

German Institute for Economic Research. (2017). *Statistics of Annual Accounts of Public Funds, Institutions and Enterprises: 2003–2012, Data Documentation.* No. 87. Berlin.

Grohs, S. (2014). Hybrid Organizations in Social Service Delivery in Quasimarkets. The Case of Germany. *American Behavioral Scientist, 58*(11), 1425–1445.

17 INSTITUTIONAL DIFFERENTIATION OF PUBLIC SERVICE PROVISION... 307

Hesse, M., Lenk, T., & Starke, T. (2017). *Investitionen der öffentlichen Hand. Die Rolle der öffentlichen Fonds, Einrichtungen und Unternehmen*. Gütersloh: Bertelsmann Stiftung.

KGSt. (2010a). *Gutachten Kommunale Organisationspolitik* (Vol. 1). Köln: Self-publisher.

KGSt. (2010b). *Gutachten Kommunale Organisationspolitik* (Vol. 2). Köln: Self-publisher.

Kuhlmann, S., & Wollmann, H. (2019). *Introduction to Comparative Public Administration. Administrative Systems and Reforms in Europe* (2nd ed.). Cheltenham/Northampton: Edward Elgar.

Libbe, J. (2013). Rekommunalisierung in Deutschland—eine empirische Bestandsaufnahme. In C. Matecki & T. Schulten (Eds.), *Zurück zur öffentlichen Hand? Chancen und Erfahrungen der Rekommunalisierung* (pp. 18–36). Hamburg: VSA Verlag.

Lindlbauer, I., Winter, V., & Schreyögg, J. (2015). Antecedents and Consequences of Corporatization: An Empirical Analysis of German Public Hospitals. *Journal of Public Administration Research and Theory, 26*(2), 309–326.

Monopoly Commission. (2013). *Eine Wettbewerbsordnung für die Finanzmärkte. Zwanzigstes Hauptgutachten der Monopolkommission gemäß § 44 Abs. 1 Satz 1 GWB*. Bonn: Self-publisher.

Mühlenkamp, H. (2015). From State to Market Revisited: More Empirical Evidence on the Efficiency of Public (and Privately-owned) Enterprises. *Annals of Public and Cooperative Economics, 86*(4), 535–557.

Opphard, K., Pohl, W., Utz, J., & Hölzl, C. (2010). In- und Outsourcing in der kommunalen Abfallwirtschaft. Studie über Make-or-Buy-Entscheidungen. In Heinrich-Böll-Stiftung & VKS (Eds.), *VKS Information* (Vol. 75). Berlin: Self-publisher.

Pollitt, C., & Talbot, C. (Eds.). (2004). *Unbundled Government: A Critical Analysis of the Global Trend to Agencies, Quangos and Contractualisation*. London & New York: Routledge.

Reichard, C. (2016). Gemischtwirtschaftliche Unternehmen im europäischen Vergleich. In U. Papenfuß, & C. Reichard (Eds.), *Zeitschrift für öffentliche und gemeinwirtschaftliche Unternehmen/Journal for Public and Nonprofit Services (ZögU)* (pp. 10–24), Supplement 48. Baden-Baden: Nomos.

Reichard, C., & Röber, M. (2019). Organisationspolitische Optionen für öffentliche Aufgaben—Verselbständigung, Auslagerung und Privatisierung. In C. Reichard, S. Veit, & G. Wewer (Eds.), *Handbuch zur Verwaltungsreform* (5th ed., pp. 263–274). Wiesbaden: Springer VS.

Röber, M. (2018). Outsourcing und Privatisierung. In R. Voigt (Ed.), *Handbuch Staat* (pp. 1049–1058). Wiesbaden: Springer VS.

Röber, M., & Schröter, E. (2016). Gemischtwirtschaftliche Unternehmen: Nicht öffentlich, nicht privat—eine geniale Synthese? In U. Papenfuß, & C. Reichard

(Eds.), *Zeitschrift für öffentliche und gemeinwirtschaftliche Unternehmen/ Journal for Public and Nonprofit Services (ZögU)* (pp. 25–45), Supplement 48. Baden-Baden: Nomos.

Sack, D. (2019). *Vom Staat zum Markt. Privatisierung aus politikwissenschaftlicher Perspektive.* Wiesbaden: Springer VS.

Schaefer, C. (2004). *Steuerung und Kontrolle von Investitionsprozessen. Theoretischer Ansatz und Konkretisierung für das öffentliche Beteiligungscontrolling.* Wiesbaden: Deutscher Universitäts-Verlag.

Schaefer, C., & Friedländer, B. (2019). Finanzierung im öffentlichen Sektor. In C. Reichard, S. Veit, & G. Wewer (Eds.), *Handbuch zur Verwaltungsreform* (5th ed., pp. 433–442). Wiesbaden: Springer VS.

Schaefer, C., & Theuvsen, L. (Eds.). (2012). *Renaissance öffentlicher Wirtschaft. Bestandsaufnahme—Kontexte—Perspektiven.* Baden-Baden: Nomos.

Schröter, E., & Röber, M. (2017). Public Managers in Germany: Between Patronage and Professionalism. In *Annual Conference of the International Research Society on Public Management 2017.* Budapest.

Schuppert, G. F. (Ed.). (2005). *Der Gewährleistungsstaat—Ein Leitbild auf dem Prüfstand.* Baden-Baden: Nomos.

Van Thiel, S. (2012). Comparing Agencies across Countries. In K. Verhoest, S. van Thiel, G. Bouckaert, & P. Laegreid (Eds.), *Government Agencies: Practices and Lessons from 30 Countries* (pp. 18–26). Basingstoke: Palgrave Macmillan.

Voorn, B., van Genugten, M. L., & van Thiel, S. (2017). The Efficiency and Effectiveness of Municipally Owned Corporations: A Systematic Review. *Local Government Studies, 43*(5), 820–841.

Wagner, O., & Berlo, K. (2015). The Wave of Remunicipalisation of Energy Networks and Supply in Germany—the Establishment of 72 New Municipal Power Utilities. In *ECEEE Summer Study Proceedings* (pp. 559–569).

Warm, S., Schaefer, C., & Friedländer, B. (2018). Role and Performance of Public Enterprises: A Case Study on the Strategic Relevance and Specificity of Enterprises at the German Federal Level. *Annals of Public and Cooperative Economics, 89*(3), 543–577.

Wollmann, H. (2016). Provision of Public and Social Services in European Countries: From Public Sector to Marketization and Reverse or—, What Next? In S. Kuhlmann & G. Bouckaert (Eds.), *Local Public Sector Reforms in Times of Crisis: National Trajectories and International Comparisons* (pp. 187–204). Basingstoke: Palgrave Macmillan.

Open Access This chapter is licensed under the terms of the Creative Commons Attribution 4.0 International License (http://creativecommons.org/licenses/by/4.0/), which permits use, sharing, adaptation, distribution and reproduction in any medium or format, as long as you give appropriate credit to the original author(s) and the source, provide a link to the Creative Commons licence and indicate if changes were made.

The images or other third party material in this chapter are included in the chapter's Creative Commons licence, unless indicated otherwise in a credit line to the material. If material is not included in the chapter's Creative Commons licence and your intended use is not permitted by statutory regulation or exceeds the permitted use, you will need to obtain permission directly from the copyright holder.

CHAPTER 18

Participatory Administration and Co-production

Stephan Grohs

1 Introduction

Citizens face 'their' public administration in different roles: as more or less passive 'subjects' and 'customers', as passive 'financiers' (taxpayers), as active political 'principals' and 'co-producers' of public goods. Additionally, in some of their interactions with the public sector, citizens act as individuals, in others as members (or users) of organisations such as associations, citizens' initiatives and non-profit organisations. On the one hand, the German state tradition has long been described as seeing the state as being superordinate to society and conceiving citizens primarily as subjects (*Untertanen*) (Dyson 2009). On the other hand, influenced by Catholic social ethics, Germany developed early a strong tradition of 'subsidiarity' with voluntary organisations from the 'third sector' (Evers and Laville 2004) producing public goods alongside public bodies. These voluntary organisations were united under umbrella organisations, the so-called welfare associations, which also have a strong role in the formulation and

---

S. Grohs (✉)
German Research Institute for Public Administration, Speyer, Germany
e-mail: grohs@foev-speyer.de

© The Author(s) 2021   311
S. Kuhlmann et al. (eds.), *Public Administration in Germany*,
Governance and Public Management,
https://doi.org/10.1007/978-3-030-53697-8_18

implementation of policies. This dense partnership between the voluntary sector and the state has often been labelled 'neo-corporatism' (Heinze and Strünck 2000; Zimmer 1999).

The ambiguous relationship between state and society has changed considerably in recent decades—at both the micro level of individual citizens (Bogumil and Holtkamp 2004) and the meso level of third sector organisations (Grohs 2014; Grohs et al. 2017; Zimmer and Evers 2010). Since German reunification, 'participation' has gained increased attention from policymakers. First, citizens claimed their roles as active citizens in demanding more participatory rights. With the general increase in levels of educational attainment and value shifts towards post-materialistic orientations, the expectations of citizens to participate in public affairs increased (Evers 2019). After reunification, every German state (*Länder*) introduced new forms of direct democracy and many local governments experimented with stronger participatory processes, for example in planning decisions and budgeting. Second, established 'corporatist' modes of co-production have been challenged by new forms of citizen engagement and private for-profit actors criticising the old 'oligopolies' of welfare production. Third, there are functional reasons for actively promoting co-production. Fiscal constraints, especially at the local level, and problems associated with shrinking rural areas in some parts of Germany pose additional challenges for the provision of public services. Finally, new challenges, especially the integration of refugees since 2015, have paved the way for new forms of citizen involvement in public affairs.

The new relationship between state and citizens has been categorised under different, more or less synonymous, labels: 'participatory administration', 'co-production' and 'cooperative democracy'. Whereas the latter term is more common in the German debate (Holtkamp et al. 2006), the term 'co-production' is used throughout this article, as it is more familiar to an international readership (Bovaird and Loeffler 2012; Brandsen and Pestoff 2006). 'Co-production' describes different practices of cooperation between individual or organised citizens and the public sector in developing and implementing public goods. Apart from the classic distinction of state and society, co-production means a productive interpenetration of both spheres, ideally in a symmetric and reciprocal way. Citizens are seen as active producers and not as passive recipients of public goods. Administrative actors do not react on 'disturbances' by citizens claiming their rights, but actively develop citizens' competences and opportunity structures to act for a common cause (Bovaird and Loeffler 2012).

There are several functional and political reasons for the support of the public sector for co-production. First of all, the inclusion of additional knowledge (especially from those directly affected) fosters an effective design and participation in the decision-making processes of policies. Second, the activation of additional resources (especially voluntary work and the provision of rooms or equipment) reduces (public) costs. Third, the involvement of citizens and relevant groups can enhance the acceptance of programmes and increase the compliance of target groups. Fourth, activating citizens to participate can strengthen solidarity and 'social capital'. Finally, the experience of participation can strengthen (local) democracy and enlarge the pool of candidates for classic representative democracy (Bogumil and Holtkamp 2004; Bovaird and Loeffler 2012). To structure the following assessment on the state of co-production in Germany, I will refer to four aspects of co-production according to Bovaird and Loeffler (2012):

- co-design: participation in planning and the preparation of decision-making;
- co-decision: legislation and other forms of binding decision-making;
- co-implementation: co-production of public value through cooperative implementation; and
- co-evaluation: assessment of public performance through public consultation and evaluation mechanisms (as this dimension is still underdeveloped in Germany, its own section has been omitted in the following).

In the following sections, I provide an overview of the major reform developments since the beginning of the 1990s and focus first on participatory reforms on the 'input side' of the politico-administrative system, that is the strengthening of co-design (see Sect. 2 below) and co-decision-making (see Sect. 3 below). Second, I survey developments in matters of co-implementation (see Sect. 4 below). Each chapter first sketches out the status quo ante, then addresses major reforms, which is followed by a discussion on the experiences and problems of the new 'participatory state'. The concluding paragraph resumes the arguments, discusses future challenges of participatory public administration in Germany and identifies potential for transfer (see Sect. 5 below).

2 Co-design: From Expert Knowledge to Citizens' Expertise?

Surely one of the most common forms of co-production is the participation of citizens in the design and planning of policies in binding or mostly non-binding forms. This form of participation has its roots in formal participation in planning procedures. For example, Section 3 of the German Building Code (*Baugesetzbuch*) stipulates that the public should be informed early about the aims, purposes, alternatives and impacts of planning procedures, and is given the opportunity to comment and participate in discussions. Similar regulations apply in the context of planning procedures (*Planfeststellungsverfahren;* Section 73 of the Administrative Procedures Act, VwVfG, see Chap. 8) and within the scope of environmental regulations, for example the Federal Nature Conservation Act (Grohs and Ullrich 2019). In Bavaria, the municipal code (*Gemeindeordnung*) specifies that a citizens' assembly to deliberate on all local issues is held (at least) once a year.

In addition to these mandatory forms, voluntary non-formal participation is becoming increasingly important as part of administrative governance (Bogumil and Holtkamp 2004; Kersting 2016; Vetter et al. 2016). In these arrangements, governments and political bodies not only seek support and legitimisation for their decisions but also the specific expertise of citizens in their own affairs. Today, a plethora of non-formal and voluntary forms of participation exists, especially at the local level, but also in other public institutions. They vary especially according to the level of citizens' involvement and deliberation. At one extreme, certain participatory formats are merely informational and asymmetric in nature (e.g. citizens' assemblies and other information events that have very little room for questions concerning proposals put forward by public institutions). Examples of more dialogue-oriented instruments include 'citizen forums' (e.g. round tables, citizens' conferences and workshops, etc.), 'planning cells' (a randomly selected group of people work together to develop proposals in a limited period of time—and often learn from citizens' expertise) and mediation procedures to address escalating conflicts.

These participatory events typically focus on a specific issue and are conducted during a fixed and narrowly defined time period. More general and holistic processes are seldom. As an exception, so-called citizens' budgets have become popular in many local governments (Sintomer et al. 2016). They address the cross-cutting issue of budgeting and develop proposals for the prioritising of budget items in a regular time frame. Examples of other ongoing participation processes include municipal advisory councils dealing with different issues (e.g. environment or health) and boards for specific status groups (e.g. juveniles, immigrants and senior citizens). In these councils, interested members of the public have the opportunity to provide input throughout the decision-making processes of the authorities with a long-term perspective. Some of them are obligatory and anchored in municipal law, others are voluntary.

While citizens' petitions and referendums, which are discussed in the next section, can produce binding decisions, the voluntary forms of participation are only consultative for political actors and the administration. With their expansion, the politico-administrative system hoped for a stronger input legitimacy, aiming to increase the acceptance of controversial projects. Several problems arise from the expansion of such participatory processes. On the one hand, supplementing representative democracy with elements of dialogue-oriented participatory democracy arouses the grievances of councillors and members of parliaments concerning their future role as elected representatives. On the other hand, the non-binding character of results can lead to frustration among participants if their proposals are not ratified by councils or parliaments. This can subvert the legitimacy of decision-making and damage the (local) political culture. The legitimacy of the results of these processes is especially challenged by an asymmetric mobilisation, that is the selective participation of certain citizen groups. The 'usual suspects' in all kinds of voluntary participatory formats can be divided into two groups: in one group the well-off, well-educated citizens with enough spare time (i.e. mostly elderly academics) and those directly affected by the disputed measures (i.e. the famous NIMBYs) in the other. Whereas the first group tends to reproduce social inequalities (middle-class bias), the latter dilutes the common good with private concerns. In complex matters, citizens are often overwhelmed by the problems at stake (which can be solved by administrative actors having a competent moderator).

Some instruments (e.g. planning cells) try to avoid a misrepresentation by selecting a more or less representative sample of citizens. Nevertheless, these approaches remain isolated and are comparatively expensive. Especially at the local level, administrations are meanwhile experimenting with digital solutions (e-participation, citizen panels, online fora, etc.) and new forms of participation ('gamification'; Masser and Mory 2018) to attract broader groups of citizens and to foster the participation of younger people. Even if these procedures are controversial in terms of representative democratic theory, they can improve the quality and acceptance of decisions and introduce elements of deliberation into decision-making processes, insofar as they are supported by democratic majorities. At the same time, participation binds administrative resources and, in some cases, extensive participation can impede decision-making considerably. Therefore, increased participation is not a panacea for modern democracy and the pros and cons should be weighed up in each case.

3 Co-decision-making: From Representative Democracy to a New 'Power-triangle'?

Since the 1990s, the rights of citizens to participate in binding decisions at the local and state level have been strengthened. These reforms, primarily directed towards the municipal level (Bogumil and Holtkamp 2004; Vetter et al. 2016), were based on the introduction of elements of direct democracy through the introduction of citizens' petitions and referendums, and the direct election of mayors and heads of counties. With the exception of Baden-Württemberg and Bavaria, where both features have a long tradition, both elements were introduced by all states between 1990 and 1997 at both the state and the local level. Nevertheless, state regulation for petitions and referendums differs considerably regarding the range of topics allowed and the requirements in terms of quorums (Mehr Demokratie 2018). The federal level still denies direct democratic elements (with the exception of a revision of state territory boundaries according to Article 29 of the Basic law).

A referendum can be initiated by citizens (citizens' referendum: *Bürgerbegehren*) and by the parliament or the local council (council's referendum: *Ratsreferendum*) (see Chap. 6). For a referendum initiated by citizens on factual issues to succeed, citizens have to overcome several hurdles. First, a defined number of valid signatures are necessary. This threshold varies from state to state and depends on the size of the municipality (the larger the municipality, the lower the quorum) and varies between 2% to 3% in Hamburg and 10% in Brandenburg. Saarland, one of the smaller municipalities, requires 15% of citizens to sign (Bürgerbegehrensbericht 2018: 11). Second, if a sufficient number of valid signatures are obtained, the council must then decide on the applicability of the referendum. The most important question here is whether the issue of the initiative falls within the legally defined range. Usually, issues with direct relevance to the budget are excluded. Some states like Bavaria, Berlin and Hamburg allow referendums on a wide range of issues, while others are quite restrictive (e.g. Brandenburg, Saarland and Rhineland-Palatinate) (for details see Bürgerbegehrensbericht 2018: 11). Finally, to be accepted, a referendum must reach a certain quorum of votes to be successful. Again, the quorum depends on the size of the municipalities and the height of this hurdle differs from state to state. The lowest hurdles can be found in Bavaria and Berlin (between 10 and 15%) and Hamburg (where no quorum exists at all). The highest quorums can be found, for example, in Brandenburg, Saxony and the Saarland between 25 and 30%.

This regulatory divergence is one reason for the varying use of these instruments between the states as well as between local governments. Generally speaking, the lower the thresholds, the more often referendums take place. Of the 7503 referendums held since 1956, over one-third (2910) took place in Bavaria. Looking at the shorter period from 2013 to 2017, the picture remains the same: Bavaria held the largest number of referendums per inhabitant, followed by the states of Baden-Württemberg and North Rhine-Westphalia. The lowest numbers can be found in Saarland and in the East German states (Bürgerbegehrensbericht 2018: 19). The issues have mostly concerned public facilities, traffic projects and other public building projects.

As in the case of dialogue-oriented instruments, the new entitlements of citizens to have a say have been critically evaluated by proponents of representative democracy as a weakening of the representative elements, especially of local democracy. In the case of citizens' petitions and decisions, parliaments and city councils in particular lose their representative monopoly directly (through opposing citizens' petitions) or indirectly (through the mere threat of such a procedure, often a strategy of opposition parties). However, there are few empirical indications that this instrument is used so frequently that these fears are firmly based. In this respect, the indirect effects are more important for the decision-making processes. Referendums have also been criticised for their simplistic approach to social problems, reducing complex issues to dichotomous questions that ask for a Yes/No. In addition, referendums often show a negative bias as they mostly try to hinder projects (typically large-scale infrastructure projects) or defend existing arrangements (typically to prevent closures of public facilities such as schools, swimming baths, theatres, etc.). Positive approaches and the proposal of realistic alternatives remain in a minority of issues.

4 Co-implementation: From Corporatism to Activation and Civic Pluralism?

In this section, I first discuss co-implementation regarding civic activism for public purposes (see Sect. 4.1 below) and then turn to the transformation of welfare production by civic associations (see Sect. 4.2 below).

4.1 Activating Citizens: The Promotion of Voluntary Activism

A major effort to promote participatory approaches to co-production was triggered in 1998 by the first red-green coalition at the federal level with its emphasis on the 'activating state' (Blanke and Schridde 2001). A parliamentary committee of enquiry (*Enquête-Kommission*) on civic engagement developed a broad agenda on activating citizens for the common good. For example, the number of local volunteer agencies (*Freiwilligenagenturen*), where opportunities for volunteering are conveyed to citizens, spreads. This movement could rely on a strong latent potential for civic co-production, which is monitored on a regular basis by the survey on volunteering, commissioned by the federal Ministry for Family Affairs, Senior Citizens, Women and Youth (BMFSFJ 2017). About 45% of the German population interviewed claim to volunteer in one or another area, most of them in sports, education, cultural affairs and social purposes (BMFSFJ 2017).[1] This has increased over the past few decades and varies between regions and social groups. A larger proportion of citizens are engaged in volunteering in the west of Germany than in the east (BMFSFJ 2017: 22) and in rural areas, engagement is more widespread than in urban areas (BMFSFJ 2017: 25). Those who volunteer are usually better educated and better off (BMFSFJ 2017: 16). Besides the increase in numbers, the character of voluntary engagement has also changed over the past few decades. People spend less time on voluntary activities and younger people especially tend to engage more selectively and in less formal ways than before. They are more reluctant to take leadership roles in associations and other organisations (BMFSFJ 2017: 28). There seems to be a further potential for volunteering as a considerable number of people not already involved in volunteering express themselves willing to volunteer in the future (BMFSFJ 2017: 28). Some administrations, especially local governments, try to mobilise this latent potential for volunteering with local agencies for volunteering and other low threshold kinds of volunteering opportunities.

A large part of these voluntary activities is organised by associations and other organisations. About 70% of the German population are members of at least one association, but are not always committed in an active way (e.g. the largest 'association'—the German automobile club (ADAC)—is merely a service provider, not an arena for voluntary engagement). Among these organisations, sports clubs, educational and cultural associations organise the largest part. These occupations might seem to be merely 'private' activities, nevertheless the associations play a significant role in organising public goods and forming social solidarity and social capital (Zimmer and Evers 2010). Therefore, such associations are supported financially and in terms of free access to public facilities, for example, sports facilities or rooms in schools and other public buildings by local governments. Some local governments, driven by fiscal pressures, have gone even further and transferred the operation of public facilities (e.g. youth clubs, swimming baths and other sports facilities) to associations (e.g. swimming clubs) on condition that the association looks after the facilities and guarantees access to the wider public (Bogumil and Holtkamp 2004). This development can be dangerous if citizens feel they are being exploited for buffering budget cuts by public institutions. Participation and co-production are scarce resources. Over-use and perceived inefficacy are among the perils of all efforts to strengthen the role of citizens. If people have the impression that they are purely serving as legitimisers of *ex-ante* decisions, or that the value of their participation is being largely ignored, this is as dangerous as when volunteers feel they are being taken advantage of doing the same tasks previously performed by paid professionals.

These traditional arrangements for volunteering by associations and other organisations (e.g. voluntary fire brigades) are being challenged by an increasing orientation towards private engagement and more mobile biographical patterns. Younger adults especially tend to engage in new, more flexible forms and are not being reached by traditional associations. As modern biographies include a greater proportion of job-related geographical mobility, associations are becoming more unstable and experiencing difficulty in finding people who are willing to show enduring commitment, for example to serve in management and leadership positions in the associations. In terms of public administration, such unstable patterns on the part of associations come with the problems of maintaining reliability and continuity, necessary preconditions for the transfer of ambitious tasks.

320   S. GROHS

4.2   An End of Corporatism? Pluralising Welfare Arrangements

Building on a strong tradition of local social care by church parishes, since the end of the nineteenth century a mixed system of welfare provision has developed where church parishes and local charities run hospitals, homes for handicapped people or orphans' homes. In the early twentieth century, accompanied by the expansion of the German welfare state, this arrangement expanded to include other areas such as social care, youth welfare and a dense network of counselling institutions. In the 1920s, this scheme became regulated by law, when the 'principle of subsidiarity' was anchored in social law, claiming that the public (municipal) sector is only permitted to provide these welfare services if civil society, welfare organisations and citizens' initiatives are not able to do it on their own (Grohs 2014; Heinze and Strünck 2000). From this time onwards, the duality of public responsibility (*Gewährleistungsverantwortung*, see also Chap. 17) and organised civic provision has become increasingly institutionalised. A corporatist mode of governance has emerged at the local level with a division of labour developing between local governments and non-profit organisations unified in the so-called *Wohlfahrtsverbände* (welfare associations).[2] As a consequence, the third sector as a whole is the largest employer in Germany today. Among its organisations, the welfare associations and its member organisations represent the bulk of professional occupations. In the past, these organisations were able to channel the voluntary commitment of individual citizens and at the same time develop professional structures with employed staff to guarantee stability.

At the governance level, these non-profit organisations had privileged access to both welfare provision and political decision-making bodies, for example through functional representation in local committees, such as youth welfare committees (*Jugendhilfeausschüsse*). Services were subsidised by local governments and social insurances according to the principle of cost coverage, and the cost-bearing units generally refrained from introducing standardised measures of quality control. These arrangements were stabilised by close ties between welfare associations and local politics—often along party lines—as well as between the associations and welfare administrations. Far from being mere substitutes for state activity, welfare associations combined a role of advocacy with the mobilisation of their memberships and volunteers. In addition to the functional relief of public bodies, one of the main motivations behind these arrangements was the incorporation of the specific (and diverse) value orientations of the associations and the additional resources provided by their memberships. This has often led to a 'co-evolution' of public and private bodies, but the organisations retained their distinct identities and were also able to adapt to changing economic environments (Heinze and Strünck 2000).

These established arrangements came under pressure in the 1990s. The reasons were first of all the fiscal pressures, but also the obvious governance deficits and lack of accountability measures of the organisations (Seibel 1996) as well as demands for more 'pluralism' or 'market'. Actors from the left and the liberal side of the political spectrum unanimously criticised the corporatist oligopoly of the welfare associations and its members. From the left, the heirs of the alternative movements and self-help activists claimed their share of public financial support; from the liberal side, for-profit providers advocated for equal treatment as the welfare associations (Evers 2005). One political response to these pressures has been the implementation of managerial reform measures and the introduction of quasi-market principles, which were often subsumed under the headings of 'managerialism' or 'marketisation'. These reform measures followed the international paradigm of New Public Management (Pollitt and Bouckaert 2011) and were adapted to the German discussion on the New Steering Model (Kuhlmann et al. 2008, see also Chap. 22). These strategies were not primarily targeted at the reduction of services, but rather at the more efficient and effective allocation of resources. In this context, the activation of competition had an important role, with private for-profit actors sometimes acting as competitors to the established system. The establishment of competition between providers went hand in hand with the replacement of the traditional principle of cost coverage by fixed prices as well as the abolishment of the privileges of charities. The abandonment of the old corporatist model of welfare production was incorporated into all the relevant welfare acts (Grohs 2014).

The discussions on quality and impact measurement in the field of social services have been extensive, but the comprehensive implementation of established and acknowledged standards is still a long way off. In some areas, such as care for the elderly, a series of control measures to increase transparency in the sector (quality records, care grades) have been introduced in recent years. The degree of change differs between the subfields, as can be seen if we compare services in elderly care with youth welfare. Whereas in the care sector new actors have gained considerable market shares, in the field of youth welfare established arrangements have continued (Grohs et al. 2017, see Table 18.1).

After almost thirty years of quasi-market reforms in the German welfare system, no clear-cut conclusions regarding their consequences for the character of the organisational field, its governance mechanisms or its constituent organisations can be drawn. Despite tendencies towards privatisation and marketisation in the care sector, the so-called *freigemeinnützigen* (non-profit) organisations continue to provide the majority of social services. The growing market orientation clashes with the welfare associations' traditional roles as advocates and promoters of voluntary action.

Summing up, we can identify two competing rationales regarding the co-implementation of services in Germany. On the one hand, the traditional modes of organising voluntary work in the traditional welfare organisations are being challenged (primarily by quasi-market mechanisms) and new forms of voluntary work are being promoted on the other. One recent development is the support of so-called social entrepreneurship, which will bring more innovation through 'entrepreneurial action'. A concept promising innovative approaches, 'social entrepreneurship' seeks to develop new forms for civic engagement, which acknowledge changes in participatory behaviour and communication technology (Grohs et al. 2017). The focus on single entrepreneurial organisations may,

Table 18.1 Types of provider (in %) from 1998 to 2016–17

	Private sector			Non-profit sector			Public sector		
Care	*1999*	*2005*	*2017*	*1999*	*2005*	*2017*	*1999*	*2005*	*2017*
…at nursing homes	34.9%	38.1%	42.6%	56.6%	55.1%	52.7%	8.5%	6.7%	4.7%
…at home	35.6%	43.1%	65.7%	62.5%	55.1%	32.8%	1.9%	1.8%	1.4%
Youth Welfare and Childcare	*1998*	*2006–07*	*2016*	*1998*	*2006–07*	*2016*	*1998*	*2006–07*	*2016*
Youth welfare	3.0%	2.1%	8.8%	71.6%	72.8%	68.7%	25.3%	25.2%	22.3%
Child day care centres	0.5%	1.0%	2.9%	54.7%	63.2%	64.2%	44.8%	35.8%	32.7%

Note: slight differences in reference periods due to availability of data

Sources: Statistisches Bundesamt, Einrichtungen und tätige Personen in der Jugendhilfe. Jg. 1998, 2006, 2018; Statistisches Bundesamt, Pflegestatistik, Jg. 2001, 2007, 2019

however, distract from a far more urgent issue: how to bring about more cooperation and networking to address complex problems. Civic and public organisations working in parallel need to find new ways to cooperate. This may avoid potential losses of momentum and consolidate resources with the aim of expanding the local social infrastructure. The role of public administration in the participative state is still pivotal as participation has to be managed and coordinated more than ever.

5   Lessons Learned: Rediscovering the Citizen: About Mute Euphoria, Some Frictions and Old Patterns of Participatory Administration

Recent decades have seen a rediscovery of the citizen as a partner (and resource) of public administration—on the input side as well as on the implementation side of public policies. These developments have been driven by the changing demands of citizens, fiscal constraints and the declining effectiveness of public administration to tackle 'wicked' problems. The term 'co-production' has gained momentum as a promise for a new balance between the public sector and civil society actors. This agenda is attractive for political actors as it combines a reduced public responsibility with a potential increase in legitimacy.

Nevertheless, findings from this survey on different aspects of participatory administration in Germany reveal some friction. On the input side of co-design and co-decision-making, research shows several hitches and asymmetries which have the ability of subverting the potential for increased legitimacy and effectiveness. The perceived loss of relevance of representative democracy is an important issue and one that is voiced by most members of parliaments and local councils. This is reflected in the unwillingness of politicians to contest the role of professionals and place more trust in citizens. In addition, the question of whether citizens are willing to participate more intensively is far from clear. Many referendums fail to reach the necessary quorum and many deliberative events fail to attract participants from a broader spectrum of socio-cultural backgrounds. The hope for smoother implementation by early participation is often diluted by the experience of participation processes in large-scale planning, where planning periods are substantially prolonged (see Chap. 11) without increasing the acceptance of planning results.

On the implementation side, a major concern about co-production is that it tends to dilute public accountability, blurring the boundaries between the public, private and third sectors. The problem increases with the sheer numbers of actors involved. In the 'old' world of welfare corporatism, the associations could claim a hybrid mix of professionalism, value orientation and embeddedness in societal networks. Today, secularisation and individualisation have reduced the willingness of people to volunteer in welfare associations. Additionally, the quasi-market reforms of the 1990s have transformed the organisations themselves. The separation between the spheres of service provision and normative and social integration is wider. This signifies that simple delegation chains hardly contribute to the determination of policy results. The resulting tasks of quality assurance and effectiveness, the consolidation of participation in reliable partnerships and the intervention in cases of defection and failure by civic partners remain core competencies of public administration.

In this context, German public administration needs to assume new roles of facilitator and coordinator, but sometimes also as 'realist brakeman'. As a result, the public sector has to face new challenges, such as qualifying volunteers to deal with demanding tasks (e.g. accompanying refugees, tutoring and quality assurance). Activating people with social backgrounds typically considered unsuitable for social participation is another challenging step towards more legitimate co-production.

But there are also many opportunities. Digital transformation (see Chap. 19) can cause patterns in civic participation and co-production to change. With open government and freedom of information acts, the information base of citizens has become broader. Digital participation formats can result in lower social thresholds and allow for more attractive formats (Masser and Mory 2018) as well as help organise voluntary engagements (e.g. Uber for Volunteering). On the other hand, digital offers come with the risk of low commitment and new inequalities. At a time when traditional forms of co-production in infrastructure maintenance (*Kehrwoche*) and public security (voluntary fire brigades) are struggling to motivate citizens to contribute, it is hard to imagine that digital solutions alone can step in and help.

The German experience shows that participatory reforms and co-production have to be handled with care and need to be adaptive to local circumstances and time frames. A sensible use of civic resources has the potential to increase legitimacy and improve results. However, a naïve reliance on civil society can also dilute responsibilities and increase social inequalities. Some of the defining characteristics of the German context, such as the prominence of welfare associations, are difficult to transfer to other contexts. Other findings, for example the measures adopted to soften social selectivity in participation processes aimed at mobilising citizens for voluntary work, or the importance of institutional barriers for referendums, may be easier for interested observers to adopt.

Notes

1. All data presented in this paragraph stem from the Fourth German Survey of Volunteering, a publicly financed survey based on about 28,600 telephone interviews; for methodological details, see BMFSFJ (2017: 11–13).
2. These welfare associations are the catholic *Caritas*, the protestant *Diakonisches Werk*, the Jewish *Zentralwohlfahrtsstelle der Juden in Deutschland*, the social-democratic *Arbeiterwohlfahrt*, the German Red Cross and the secular *Paritätische Wohlfahrtsverband*. They are organised federally, resembling the basic architecture of the German federal state. Together, their subsidiary organisations and institutions represent one of the largest employers in Germany with a total of almost two million employees and more than 100,000 establishments in the fields of social services and education (BAGFW 2018).

References

Blanke, B., & Schridde, H. (2001). Bürgerengagement und aktivierender Staat. In R. G. Heinze & T. Olk (Eds.), *Bürgerengagement in Deutschland* (pp. 93–140). Wiesbaden: VS.

Bogumil, J., & Holtkamp, L. (2004). The Citizens' Community under Pressure to Consolidate? *German Journal of Urban Studies, 44*(1), 103–126.

Bovaird, T., & Loeffler, E. (2012). From Engagement to Co-production: The Contribution of Users and Communities to Outcomes and Public Value. *VOLUNTAS, 23*, 1119–1138.

Brandsen, T., & Pestoff, V. (2006). Co-production, the Third Sector and the Delivery of Public Services. *Public Management Review, 8*, 493–501.

Bundesarbeitsgemeinschaft der Freien Wohlfahrtspflege (BAGFW) (2018). *Gesamtstatistik*. Berlin: BAGFW.

Dyson, K. H. F. (2009). *The State Tradition in Western Europe*. Colchester: ECPR Press.

Evers, A. (2005). Mixed Welfare Systems and Hybrid Organizations: Changes in the Governance and Provision of Social Services. *International Journal of Public Administration, 28*, 737–748.

Evers, A. (2019). Diversity and Coherence: Historical Layers of Current Civic Engagement in Germany. *VOLUNTAS, 30,* 41–53.

Evers, A., & Laville, J.-L. (Eds.). (2004). *The Third Sector in Europe.* Northampton: Edward Elgar.

Federal Ministry for Family Affairs, Senior Citizens, Women and Youth. (2017). *Volunteering in Germany. Key Findings of the Fourth German Survey on Volunteering.* Berlin: BMFSFJ.

Grohs, S. (2014). Hybrid Organizations in Social Service Delivery in Quasimarkets: The Case of Germany. *American Behavioral Scientist, 58,* 1425–1445.

Grohs, S., Schneiders, K., & Heinze, R. G. (2017). Outsiders and Intrapreneurs: The Institutional Embeddedness of Social Entrepreneurship in Germany. *VOLUNTAS, 28,* 2569–2591.

Grohs, S., & Ullrich, N. (2019). *A Guide to Environmental Administration in Germany.* Dessau: Umweltbundesamt.

Heinze, R. G., & Strünck, C. (2000). Social Service Delivery by Private and Voluntary Organisations in Germany. In H. Wollmann & E. Schröter (Eds.), *Comparing public Sector Reform in Britain and Germany* (pp. 284–303). Aldershot: Ashgate.

Holtkamp, L., Bogumil, J., & Kißler, L. (2006). *Kooperative Demokratie: Das demokratische Potenzial von Bürgerengagement.* Frankfurt am Main: Campus.

Kersting, N. (2016). Participatory Turn?: Comparing Citizens' and Politicians' Perspectives on Online and Offline Local Political Participation. *Lex localis, 14,* 251–236.

Kuhlmann, S., Bogumil, J., & Grohs, S. (2008). Evaluating Administrative Modernization in German Local Governments: Success or Failure of the 'New Steering Model'? *Public Administration Review, 68,* 851–863.

Masser, K., & Mory, L. (2018). *The Gamification of Citizens' Participation in Policymaking.* Basingstoke: Palgrave Macmillan.

Mehr Demokratie e.V. (2018). *Bürgerbegehrensbericht 2018.* Berlin: Mehr Demokratie e.V.

Pollitt, C., & Bouckaert, G. (2011). *Public Management Reform: A Comparative Analysis; New Public Management, Governance, and the Neo-Weberian State* (3rd ed.). Oxford: Oxford University Press.

Seibel, W. (1996). Successful Failure: An Alternative View on Organizational Coping. *American Behavioral Scientist, 39,* 1011–1024.

Sintomer, Y., Röcke, A., & Herzberg, C. (2016). *Participatory Budgeting in Europe: Democracy and Public Governance.* Florence: Taylor and Francis.

Vetter, A., Klimovský, D., Denters, B., & Kersting, N. (2016). Giving Citizens More Say in Local Government. In S. Kuhlmann & G. Bouckaert (Eds.), *Local Public Sector Reforms in Times of Crisis* (pp. 273–286). London: Palgrave Macmillan UK.

Zimmer, A. (1999). Corporatism Revisited. *Voluntas, 10*, 37–49.
Zimmer, A., & Evers, A. (2010). *Third Sector Organizations Facing Turbulent Environments: Sports, Culture and Social Services in Five European Countries*. Baden-Baden: Nomos.

Open Access This chapter is licensed under the terms of the Creative Commons Attribution 4.0 International License (http://creativecommons.org/licenses/by/4.0/), which permits use, sharing, adaptation, distribution and reproduction in any medium or format, as long as you give appropriate credit to the original author(s) and the source, provide a link to the Creative Commons licence and indicate if changes were made.

The images or other third party material in this chapter are included in the chapter's Creative Commons licence, unless indicated otherwise in a credit line to the material. If material is not included in the chapter's Creative Commons licence and your intended use is not permitted by statutory regulation or exceeds the permitted use, you will need to obtain permission directly from the copyright holder.

PART IV

Modernizing Processes and Enhancing Management Capacities

CHAPTER 19

Digital Transformation of the German State

Ines Mergel

'This project has received funding from the European Union's Horizon 2020 research and innovation programme under grant agreement No 770356. This publication reflects the views only of the author(s), and the Commission cannot be held responsible for any use, which may be made of the information contained therein.'

1   INTRODUCTION

The digital transformation of German public administration is an urgent matter, given that the public sector is generally lagging far behind the private sector and especially in comparison with digitalisation efforts across Europe. As one of the largest economies in the world, Germany has consistently been ranked in the low- to mid-field of digital government rankings (see, DESI 2019). In addition, recent polls have shown that the

I. Mergel (✉)
University of Konstanz, Konstanz, Germany
e-mail: ines.mergel@uni-konstanz.de

© The Author(s) 2021
S. Kuhlmann et al. (eds.), *Public Administration in Germany*,
Governance and Public Management,
https://doi.org/10.1007/978-3-030-53697-8_19

331

German public's use of existing digital services has been steadily declining during the past few years even though large-scale investments in IT spending have been made (Initiative 21 (2018/2019)).

These developments can be traced back to delays in supporting policy developments, lacking investments for necessary modernisation and the resulting backlog in IT capacity and failures to update IT legacy systems. The multilevel system of Germany's federal, state and municipal public administrations makes the decision and implementation approach even more complicated. Many activities with respect to IT governance and implementation are outsourced to external IT service providers, leaving public administrations devoid of the skills and competences necessary to innovate on their own and relying on external IT expertise for buying and implementing digital technology (Dunleavy et al. 2006).

Recently, the German government has embarked on a large-scale reform of its public service delivery mode—all 575 public services will be digitally transformed by 2022—a reform in scale and scope that no other country has yet set out to approach (Mergel 2019). This reform plan demands certain coordination tasks across the federal system, which will be discussed in this chapter.

The goal of this chapter is to outline the recent development of digital transformation of public services in Germany, provide insights into the legal framework guiding the digital transformation efforts, its organisational embeddedness and multi-organisational collaborative governance approach, the barriers and challenges imposed by the multilevel institutional context of the German government and the observable outcomes to date.

2 Current Status of Digital Transformation in Germany

Digital innovation in the public sector is slowly progressing in Germany. This is mostly due to the independence between administrative levels leading historically to relatively independent progress across administrative levels (see Chaps. 3 and 8). Most recently, Article 91c (1) of the Basic Law aimed to heal this disconnect by mandating that federal and state levels cooperate in the planning, establishment and operation of the information technology systems required to fulfil their tasks. Article 91c (2) stipulates that the federal government and the *Länder* can define the standards and security requirements necessary for communication between their information technology systems. What remains undefined and open is how the 11,000 municipalities are going to adopt the standards set by the federal and state government administrations. Based on their self-administration right established in accordance with the provisions of Article 28 (2) of the Basic Law, municipalities remain independent in their decision making so that the use of top-down developed standards, platforms and security needs to be reviewed and additional funding needs to be made available (see Chap. 9).

Even though Article 91c has initiated a functional reform at the federal and state government levels, digitalisation efforts still remain a sore topic in Germany. While the majority of German citizens are highly active on social media and shop online (ninety-three per cent), only five per cent are willing to use digital public services (InitiativeD21 2018/2019). This is a phenomenon that needs to be understood in light of the historical circumstances of Germany's political system. Especially since the Third Reich, Germans have been very reluctant to hand over data to the government in fear of becoming transparent citizens. The power distance felt between bureaucrats and citizens is increased by a general feeling that public administrations are slow, overly bureaucratic, and that access to public services is bogged down by excessive administrative burden.

It is only recently, from 2018 to 2019, that the use of digital public services has slightly increased (InitiativeD21 2018/2019). However, many online public services and administrative apps are not used by citizens because they are inaccessible or require additional hardware to access services related to the eID and a personal service account. This is a continuous trend and comes with accessibility burdens that require a high degree of administrative literacy, which many citizens do not encounter in their otherwise personal online experiences on websites such as Amazon. de (Grönlund et al. 2007).

2.1 Legal Framework for the Digital Transformation of the German State

The legal framework governing digital transformation in Germany consists of a much larger web of laws that have developed over time. The foundation was laid with Article 91c of the Basic Law which establishes that the federal government and the *Länder* may cooperate in the planning, construction and operation of the information technology systems required for the fulfilment of their tasks. This was further developed into an e-government law, which incorporates the access to electronic information, online payments through SEPA direct debit, electronic filing, publication of regulations online, open data, and the replacement of the written form by using a government email service (De-Mail) and web access through eID (electronic identification). However, many existing administrative laws are still preventing a fast and unbureaucratic transition from analogue to digital government. Examples include the paper form requirement, required (hand)written signatures on official administrative forms, or the personal and physical *handing over* of documents (instead of digital provision).

The implementation of digital government practices follows the cooperative approach outlined in Article 91c of the Basic Law, but the administrative practice shows that coordination issues remain based on the federal approach towards negative coordination and the self-governing principle of the municipalities. Solutions are developed at the federal and state level, and it is only after the solutions have been consensually agreed upon that potentially negative consequences that might impact other stakeholders are reviewed. As a result, the *Länder* are aiming to coordinate their efforts among mid-level public managers at so-called expert conferences and are bringing the results of their negotiations to the IT Planning Council, which is a committee consisting of the state-level Chief Information Officers (CIOs), the federal government CIO as well as selected representatives of interest groups.

With the help of the IT treaty, the IT Planning Council is responsible for the planning, construction, operation and advancement of the information technology infrastructure. They set IT standards, such as safety requirements for data exchange, and coordinate the collaboration across the federal and state levels. In its amendment, this collaboration was recognised for its immense complexity due to the heterogeneity of the existing structures, processes and legal requirements. To solve this complex coordination problem, a new federal public institution for IT cooperation (FITKO) was created to support the IT Planning Council in all organisational issues and provides technical support starting January 2020. The main goal is to coordinate the multilevel coordination and to set up a joint digitalisation budget to support the digital transformation of public service delivery. This will allow the IT Planning Council to focus on its political coordination role among the *Länder* CIOs and leave technical details and implementation issues to FITKO.

Currently, most public services are, however, paper-based, still require a handwritten signature and need to be applied for in person. There are few instances where forms are already available online in pdf format. These forms are most of the time not connected to a database that would automatically transfer the data to the local authority. Instead, citizens print out the forms at home, walk them into the agency, watch a public servant type in the data and then provide a handwritten signature on a printed paper form. At times, it is possible to schedule appointments online or participate in information-based polls.

With the online access law (*Online-Zugangsgesetz*—OZG), the German government has set out to make analogue public services available by transforming them into a new citizen-centric service that will be available 24/7. Service provision will be facilitated through one federal portal to which all sixteen state portals are connected. Each citizen will have his own eID and service account, so that services are accessible and data is exchangeable between agencies when necessary. Federal, state and local government levels are required to offer 575 public services online by 2022. The implementation is currently divided into two large-scale projects:

- **Digitalisation programme**: a total of 575 administrative processes and public services will be digitised. These services are located at various administrative levels. The services are divided into fourteen subject areas. One tandem, each from the federal ministry and the *Länder*, has taken the lead for a subject area. In these subject areas, public services are prepared for digitisation. After a detailed analysis, concrete digitisation plans are drawn up for each service. Particularly important services were prioritised within the thematic areas and are developed in so-called digital laboratories. Within these labs, interdisciplinary teams of experts from specialist departments, e-government experts and human-centred designers work in cross-functional teams on user-centric solutions.

- **National portal network**: the portal provides the technical linkages to the sixteen *Länder* administrative portals and their municipalities and ensures interoperability between the three administrative levels. This is intended to provide uniform access to all digital services offered by the administration. User accounts for citizens and companies are provided in the portal network for the authentication of users to access digital public services.

One important implementation challenge remains: the municipalities are not explicitly named in the law and it is up to the *Länder* to include them in their efforts. One way to consolidate the communication and coordination to the 11,000 municipalities is the inclusion of municipal interest organisations that bring in the interests of the municipalities. At this stage, it is unclear how the municipalities will be involved beyond the initial prototypes. Some *Länder* have developed their own portals and provide the digitised services to their municipalities free of charge, while others have not yet started to plan how to involve the municipalities in roll-outs or in the subsequent use of the functional prototypes already created.

Each new law is reviewed by a federal body, the National Regulatory Control Council (*Nationaler Normenkontrollrat*—NKR; see Chap. 20 for a detailed overview of the NKR). The NKR is located in the chancellor's office and serves in an advisory role. Laws are reviewed based on their potential to increase subsequent costs, evaluate their potential to lower bureaucratic burden and to simplify existing administrative processes. The online access law is explicitly designed to lower administrative burden and to increase access to public services to those who are willing to conduct them online. However, the NKR has repeatedly highlighted in its annual reports that the actual implementation is stalling, too complex, not sufficiently coordinated, and given the way in which implementation is organised, the OZG goals might not be achieved by the deadline.

In summary, the laws governing the digital transformation of the German state are listed in Table 19.1.

19 DIGITAL TRANSFORMATION OF THE GERMAN STATE   337

Table 19.1 Overview of laws governing the digital transformation of the German state

Name of the law	Date	Content	Scope of application
Act amending the Basic Law (*Grundgesetz*) (Articles 91c, 91d, 104b, 109, 109a, 115, 143d)	29 July 2009	Amendment of the Basic Law within the framework of the Conference on Federalism II with specific focus on the cooperation between federal and state government with respect to standards and security measures	Federal, states
IT State Treaty on the establishment of the IT Planning Council	1 April 2010	Establishment and regulation of the working methods of the IT Planning Council as a steering committee for general IT cooperation	Federal, states
Law on the promotion of electronic administration (e-government law)	25 July 2013	Enables the federal, state and local governments to offer simpler, more user-friendly and more efficient electronic administrative services	Federal, states, municipal
Federal IT consolidation as part of the Digital Agenda	20 May 2015	The aim is to vertically consolidate the federal government's information technology and to ensure economic viability	The federal government commissioner for information technology
Act for the Improvement of Online Access to Public Services (OZG)	14 August 2017	By 2022, the federal government, the *Länder* and the municipalities should be able to offer all administrative services in digital form	Federal, states, municipal
Coalition Treaty of the 19th legislative period	7 February 2018	Within the scope of the coalition agreement, several e-government-related projects were agreed upon	Federal, states, municipal
Law for the first IT amendment treaty	6 June 2019	Advancing the development of IT cooperation in public administrations by FITKO	Federal, states

Source: Author's own compilation

338   I. MERGEL

3   Implementation Responsibilities of Digital Transformation in Germany

The responsibilities for different aspects of IT governance are distributed not only horizontally across different federal ministries, but also vertically throughout the multilevel system across federal, state and municipal government levels.

3.1   Horizontal Distribution of Responsibilities Across Federal Ministries

At the federal level, the responsibilities are located in at least five different federal ministries or departments.

The Ministry of Transport and Digital Infrastructure (BMVI.de) is responsible for the improvement of the Long Term Evolution (LTE) and fibre-optic broadband deployment, the promotion of digital innovation technologies in the mobility sector as well as automated and networked driving. It also develops the Federal Government's Artificial Intelligence Strategy, which was drawn up under the joint leadership of the Federal Ministry of Education and Research, the Federal Ministry of Economics and Energy and the Federal Ministry of Labour and Social Affairs. Its goal is to establish Germany and Europe as a leading AI location and thus contribute to securing Germany's future competitiveness. The aim is to develop and use AI responsibly and in the public interest. AI will also be used to automate public service delivery or proactively deliver services to citizens.

The Federal Ministry of Economic Affairs and Energy (BMWI.de) is in charge of creating a legally secure future framework for digital change and a modern net policy. The design of the digital economy (e.g., Sharing Economy) includes a strategy for artificial intelligence and blockchain. The goal is to create an intelligent interconnectedness between the education, energy, health, and transport sectors.

The Federal Ministry of the Interior, Building and Community (BMI. de) is responsible for the implementation of the Act for the Improvement of Online Access to Public Services (OZG) and the coordination of the Open Government initiative. It houses the data ethics commission and the agency for innovation in cyber security. As part of the implementation of the OZG, the BMI is establishing the national portal and the portal network as a technical prerequisite for digitalisation of public services. The work is being carried out in so-called digitisation laboratories and focusses on the different life cycles of citizens. It involves steps, such as the register modernisation and also the IT consolidation at the federal level. It has served as the initiator within the framework of federal cooperation including the FITKO and IT Planning Council committees. The BMI has increased its responsibilities within the framework of e-government projects in the execution, coordination and control of the various measures initiated. Once completed, the services provided by the BMI will be accessible to all citizens of the state. BMI is also home to the recently established project team for the conception and development of a digital innovation team and e-government agency (DIT.BUND). DIT is using human-centric design and agile approaches and serves as a think-and-do tank for the federal government.

The German Chancellory has recently established its own digital service team—Digital Service 4 Germany, which evolved out of the private sector initaitive Tech4Germany and Work4Germany, a fellowship program that places technology experts in federal ministries to collabroatively work on IT projects. The digital service team is an initiative under the patronage of head of the Federal Chancellery and is considered a technology task-force, comparable to the UK's Government Digital Service or the US' Digital Service. In addition, the federal CIO has initiated a cross-agency workgroup, NExT Netzwerk—a network that focuses on connecting federal government employees to develop and implement technology practices and competencies. The Federal Administration Office (BVA) is a federal agency in the portfolio of the Federal Ministry of the Interior, Building and Community. It performs a large number of federal administrative tasks and is active for some federal ministries and their business areas (for more details, see Chap. 5). The tasks include recovery of student loans, salaries and allowances of federal employees as well as citizenship matters. It also performs a variety of central services for other federal authorities, such as the payment of emoluments and allowances, travel expense management, time recording and personnel recruitment. The BVA has established its own organisational consultancy for other ministries and authorities and has already digitised a large number of tasks and processes. The BVA currently has around 120 digitisation and IT processes in use or under development. As the central service authority with many specialist tasks and customers, the BVA has developed a Digital Agenda, 'BVA.digital 2022', where all digital measures of the BVA are bundled and controlled. It specifically focusses on the development of the digital skills and competences of federal government employees. In addition, its agenda consists of four application areas:

1. Beihilfe App/Aid app: this is an app which allows eligible persons to quickly and easily apply for the reimbursement of eligible costs.
2. BVA.digital: in addition, eleven different digitisation principles have been developed, which serve as guidelines for the digitisation of tasks, business processes and offers.
3. Digital consulting: Federal Administration Office consultants support authorities in mastering this challenge and exploiting the potential of digitisation in a targeted manner.

3.2 Vertical Distribution of Responsibilities Across Administrative Levels

With respect to the current implementation of the online access law, the federal government is responsible for setting up the federal portal by 2022 and ensuring interoperability with state-level portals. The result will be a network of portals (*Portalverbund*) that electronically offers all public services taking accessibility criteria into consideration. The federal government is also responsible for creating user accounts and identification under the negotiated security standards. They are responsible for the federal IT consolidation. The aim of this consolidation of information technology is to ensure information security against the background of increasing complexity, be able to react to innovations and ensure an efficient, economical, stable and sustainable operation. Three strands of action lay the groundwork: (1) consolidation of operations, (2) consolidation of services and (3) procurement bundling.

The *Länder* are responsible for providing their electronic services on their own state portal and connecting them to the federal portal. The services are connected to the agencies responsible for delivering them. The challenge at the state level is that some states started this process long before the online access law was established. They have already invested in their own portal network, created partnerships with other states, selected their service providers and set their own standards. This contradicts in many ways the standards set by the law and the agreed-upon shared IT components, and new interfaces will likely need to be designed to be able to allow for nationwide interoperability—and in the future European-wide interoperability.

The municipalities and their possible distribution of tasks are not explicitly mentioned in the law. The website of the IT Planning Council states: 'The municipalities are to be involved by the *Länder*'. However, only a handful of selected municipalities are involved in the digital labs to develop service prototypes and are, therefore, at the forefront of designing digital services in one specific life phase. The majority of municipalities are not involved and are dependent on the innovativeness and coordination ability of their respective states. Some states take this task very seriously and have distributed the tasks of public service design to the municipalities, while others have not yet had early discussions with their municipalities.

4 RECENT DEVELOPMENTS: CITIZEN-CENTRIC DIGITAL SERVICE DESIGN

E-government and digital transformation have become one of the core elements of the recently elected nineteenth coalition government. The coalition agreement includes the expansion of a high-speed network and the creation of a digital portal for citizens and businesses to provide easy, secure and mobile access to all administrative services. An additional €500 million will be available for the implementation of the online access law to improve online access to administrative services. The coalition has agreed to establish an e-government agency that will jointly develop standards and pilot solutions for all federal levels more quickly than before. For that purpose, one of the hallmarks of the German public service will be reviewed: the (hand)written form requirements. According to the coalition agreement, the federal government intends to strengthen the role of the federal government's IT commissioner.

A digital council consisting of German-speaking high-profile international academics and practitioners was established to advise the chancellor's office and bring in new ideas to move the digital transformation of the German public sector forward. The honorary council has met a few times, but no public announcements were made that provide insights into the guidance that the chancellor's office receives from the council. The goal for establishing the council is to receive critical external insights on the progress the German government is making with respect to digital transformation.

Some progress has been made by establishing e-filing across all levels of government. The most prominent example is the tax e-filing system.

Using plain language, e-filing through the electronic filing system for tax returns, *Elektronische Steuererklärung* (ELSTER), has been available since 2019. With My Elster (formerly ElsterOnline-Portal), the tax administration has made a portal available through which citizens can register their own account, use their electronic filing ID to submit their tax declaration forms or request tax returns and so on.

New practices of citizen-centric public service design have initially been tried out in small pockets of the overall administrative system, originating mostly from the municipal government level. Networks such as the ANDI group (agile network for digital innovation) have started working with designers to bring innovative methods, such as a design thinking or human-centred design, to their digital transformation work (see, e.g., Ansell and Torfing 2014; Bason 2016; Junginger 2016). These bottom-up efforts have subsequently spread to the federal level and are now officially established as part of the federal digital transformation efforts. Especially in the digital labs used to derive the requirement of digital public services, interdisciplinary teams of experts from across public administration collaborate with content experts to design user-centred public services. This new form of co-production is used to design services, not from the internal logic of government but from the perspective of those who need to use digital services in the future. These users can either be internal users (public servants) or external users, such as citizens and other stakeholders. The goal is to deliver services that are easier to use, have a higher success and acceptance rate and generally make the design process more democratic in nature.

What has not been addressed in either the laws or public discussions on digital transformation in Germany is the necessary build-up of digital competences in the public sector. While Germany has signed off on the European Digital Competency 2.0 framework (EU Science Hub n.d.), it has not yet started to come up with any form of comprehensive framework on how to build digital competences in order to prepare the public sector workforce for future challenges. There are initial plans to build a government digital academy serving all three levels of government and an eGovernment MOOC to bring digital competencies to civil servants. Results from expert interviews show that public managers need to be trained in developing a digital mindset. They need to understand what the role of new technologies is and build up digital fluency to switch between different types of technologies. Middle managers responsible for the implementation of digital transformation need to learn how to use new project management techniques to guide the implementation process. Public servants, and especially frontline workers, need to be able to participate in the digital transformation efforts, understand how efficiency gains are created, encourage citizens to use the tools and reduce administrative burdens during actual usage. This will help public servants to focus on more complex issues that need to be tackled in person and leave other tasks to those willing to conduct them online or use automated public service delivery. Another important stakeholder group includes the IT service providers and consultants who need to understand public service values as an achievement of the rule of law, instead of promoting the abandonment of federalism. Surprisingly, the experts uniformly highlight that citizens' digital competences are far more formed than those of public servants and do not necessarily need to be improved. Instead, public administrations need to simplify the design of public service delivery so that no additional skills need to be developed in the future and administrative burdens are reduced.

4.1 Digital Transformation of Citizen Offices

One recent advancement can be observed in the digitalisation of local one-stop shops. These are local government initiatives to advance e-government service provision bundled on one website, so that those digitally literate citizens have an opportunity to access information about the agency and its services 24/7.

According to Schwab et al. (2019), the focus is on two advancements. One can be described as the interactive process through which appointments are made with the agency, for example, to register a car or apply for a driver's licence. The other is accessing information about services offered online, including information about office hours or the general process, and to provide some of the necessary administrative forms online. These two services can be mostly observed in cities with more than 100,000 citizens.

Among the top cities in this area is Freiburg in Baden-Württemberg (see Digital.Freiburg.de) that uses idea labs to integrate citizen needs into the deliberate design of online public services. Other cities, for example the city-state Hamburg, are providing interactive options such as the chatbot 'Frag-den-Michel'. The chatbot is AI-supported and provides help to find services, locations and office hours.

However, face-to-face interactions between civil servants and citizens are still the norm. While citizens can prepare for some of these interactions

344   I. MERGEL

using the documents and forms available online, citizen interactions are of a complex nature and need to be dealt with in an analogue discursive manner, potentially including several different agencies and not just through one frontline worker.

4.2   Digital Transformation of the Federal Agency for Migration and Refugees

Another prominent success story of a digitalised agency is the Federal Agency for Migration and Refugees (BAMF). Since the migration crisis of 2015, the BAMF has increased the number of clients it serves on a regular basis from 40,000 refugees per year to around 800,000–1,000,000 refugees per year. This massive increase in scale needed to be reflected in the internal processes and distribution of responsibilities in order to effectively coordinate and trace refugees across all levels of government (Bogumil et al. 2018). The BAMF has set up an internal IT Lab that introduces new project management tools, such as Scrum to develop software together with the process owner, product owners and users. Scrum is an iterative project management practice that introduces the development of small project steps in so-called sprints. The project team is allowed to revisit previous project steps and adjusts the directions and requirements as they go along. The result is a minimal viable product that can be used to prototype the expected final product, and additional adjustments can be made when users are invited to test the prototype. The goal is to develop tools faster with fewer errors that are immediately usable for the users. The process is more democratic in nature than the standard waterfall technique that has led to large-scale IT failures in the past. The IT lab is a rather unique organisational setup, comparable to digital service teams in the UK or the US or innovation labs in Denmark. It is located in rooms with graffiti and artwork that are not usually found in a German bureaucracy, has large windows for transparency and demonstration purposes. As part of their mission, the agency's inhouse IT lab staff also provides administrative assistance to other agencies with responsibilities related to the immigration service, such as customs, border and local police, to share their knowledge and practices.

As a starting point, BAMF has used the refugee crisis to rethink its own IT management. It has developed a series of new tools in a relatively short amount of time that help to automate tasks related to refugee processing and handle the coordination efforts with other agencies, such as the municipal and state immigration office, first admissions by the states, federal agency for employment, police, customs, federal intelligence services and others. For this purpose, tools such as the migration tracker were created according to the Dublin procedure. For each refugee case, the procedure reviews which European country is responsible for accepting the refugee. The tool is used to coordinate arrivals at the initial reception facilities, register arrivals and provide proof of arrival. All immigration offices are now connected to the migration tracker and the data can be transferred to the police and especially to the courts. All documents are scanned, electronically distributed, and are made available to the connected agencies through the MARIS system, a workflow and document management system to process all asylum-related procedures. According to those responsible for the digitalisation of the BAMF processes, the digitalisation efforts themselves were not necessarily difficult. It was much more difficult to train public servants in applying new project management practices and work on cross-functional teams together with designers and software developers and help them move towards a digital mindset to establish and accept these new practices.

The BAMF is also the initiator of the NExT network which was founded in 2018 in collaboration with the federal chief information officer (CIO) (see https://www.next-netz.de/ for more information). NExT is an interdepartmental network of digital pioneers. These are experts in different federal ministries whose common goal is to significantly shape and advance the digital transformation of German public administration. The network is divided into six working groups that focus on: how digital projects can be developed; how digital skills can be increased; what new technologies public servants need to pay attention to; how organisational practices need to be adapted; what kind of cooperation is necessary and how the results can be communicated and distributed to public sector actors. This interorganisational network has the opportunity to distribute insights from different angles of the administrative system and share insights without reinventing the wheel over and over again.

5   Lessons Learned and Practical Implications

The developments and insights gained from the digital transformation experiences in Germany lend themselves to other countries—with similarly advanced bureaucracies and IT legacy systems that have been built up over many years. In countries with a comparable institutional context, where authority for policymaking and implementation is delegated to different types of actors across levels of government and jurisdictions, Germany may be a model to emulate and adapt to other local contexts. The all-encompassing reform that tackles publicly facing administrative service is a holistic approach to get up to speed in contexts in which policy and implementation of digital services have been slow to develop.

Those who are aiming to introduce a similar approach, however, can learn from the coordination mechanisms used by Germany. The focus on co-creation together with actors at all levels of government and with external stakeholders is unique in that it includes not only all levels of government but also citizens and related interest groups. However, the administrative practice shows that there is currently an over-reliance on external consultants and government-owned IT service providers. As soon as they pull out, contracts expire or projects end, there is a need to find another approach to sustain the development and implementation of digital services. The German government will need to focus on continuous service provision and scaling up to the 11,000 municipalities where most citizens access public services.

Digital transformation of the public sector is at its core a cultural change process that needs to be carefully guided with the input of public managers and cannot be driven bottom-up by frontline workers (Mergel et al. 2019). Public servants need to be included each step of the way to provide their feedback, experience the potential changes coming their way as well as guide the transformation with their technical input.

NOTES

1. https://www.govdata.de.
2. https://www.bundeshaushalt.de.

REFERENCES

Ansell, C., & Torfing, J. (Eds.). (2014). *Public Innovation Through Collaboration and Design*. Abingdon: Routledge.

Bason, C. (2016). *Design for Policy*. New York, NY: Routledge.

Bogumil, J., Burgi, M., Kuhlmann, S., Hafner, J., Heuberger, M., & Krönke, C. (2018). *Bessere Verwaltung in der Migrations- und Integrationspolitik: Handlungsempfehlungen für Verwaltungen und Gesetzgebung im föderalen System*. Baden-Baden: Nomos.

19 DIGITAL TRANSFORMATION OF THE GERMAN STATE 347

DESI. (2019). *The Digital Economy and Society Index (DESI) Ranking.* Retrieved November 2, 2019, from. https://ec.europa.eu/digital-single-market/desi.

Dunleavy, P., Margetts, H., Bastow, S., & Tinkler, J. (2006). New Public Management Is Dead—Long Live Digital-Era Governance. *Journal of Public Administration Research and Theory, 16*(3), 467–494.

EU Science Hub. (n.d.). *The Digital Competence Framework 2.0.* Retrieved from https://ec.europa.eu/jrc/en/digcomp/digital-competence-framework.

Grönlund, Å., Hatakka, M., & Ask, A. (2007). Inclusion in the E-Service Society–Investigating Administrative Literacy Requirements for Using E-Services. In *International Conference on Electronic Government* (pp. 216–227). Berlin, Heidelberg: Springer.

Initiative 21. (2018/2019). Egovernment Monitor 2018/2019.

Junginger, S. (2016). *Transforming Public Services by Design: Re-Orienting Policies, Organizations and Services Around People.* New York, NY: Routledge.

Mergel, I. (2019). Digitale Transformation als Reformvorhaben der deutschen öffentlichen Verwaltung. *dms—der moderne staat—Zeitschrift für Public Policy, Recht und Management, 12*(1), 162–171.

Mergel, I., Edelmann, N., & Haug, N. (2019). Defining Digital Transformation: Results from Expert Interviews. *Government Information Quarterly,* 1–16. https://doi.org/10.1016/j.giq.2019.06.002.

Schwab, C., Bogumil, J., Kuhlmann, S., & Gerber, S. (2019). Digitalisierung von Verwaltungsleistungen in Bürgerämtern. In T. Klenk et al. (Eds.), *Handbuch Digitalisierung in Staat und Verwaltung.* Wiesbaden: Springer.

Appendix: Open Government

Jan Porth, Friederike Bickmann, Patrick Schweizer, and Zarina Feller

App. 1. Introduction

When considering political and administrative actions over the past decades, a general trend towards more openness can be observed (Meijer et al. 2014: 103–104). Internet portals, where large quantities of administrative data are available to be used freely by the general public, are examples of this trend, which is generally supported by technological advances (von Lucke 2017: 155ff.). Alongside the different motivations for these changes, different terms are used to describe this development. However, the term *open government* is becoming increasingly common—also in Germany—to refer to actions generally increasing the openness of the political-administrative system.

According to the Organisation for Economic Co-operation and Development (OECD), open government can be defined as 'a culture of governance based on innovative and sustainable public policies and practices inspired by the principals of transparency, accountability and participation that fosters democracy and inclusive growth' (OECD 2016: 3–4).

J. Porth (✉) • F. Bickmann • P. Schweizer • Z. Feller
German Research Institute for Public Administration, Speyer, Germany
e-mail: porth@foev-speyer.de; bickmann@foev-speyer.de;
schweizer@foev-speyer.de; feller@foev-speyer.de

The principles of transparency and participation are also part of Barack Obama's Open Government Directive of 2009. Instead of accountability, he included collaboration as the third element of open government (Executive Office of the President 2009: 1). Going back to the differences in the conceptual understanding of open government, the term is used in the context of a wide variety of policy measures in practice.

The possible advantages of open government are closely related to its principles. Civil society, the economy as well as the administration itself can benefit from increased openness of policy decisions and administrative actions, which may also strengthen the relationships between these actors. In addition, the involvement of citizens and their ideas can help to make administrative processes more citizen-friendly. Disadvantages, on the other hand, may arise in terms of extensions of policy and planning processes due to the involvement of more external actors as well as the possible demotivation of participants whose ideas or proposals cannot always be taken into consideration.

Criticism of open government further points out a possible lack of democratic legitimacy (Wewer and Wewer 2019: 11). While the understanding of the types of measures which are part of open government differs, the problems of legitimacy are not apparent for most types of initiatives. This also applies, for example, to the advisory roles of external actors in political-administrative processes, which have a long tradition in many countries and do not replace the decisions taken by elected representatives.

The Open Government Partnership was founded in 2011 as an international initiative to promote open government. So far, more than seventy countries are part of the initiative. Germany joined the partnership in 2016. The member states are obliged to develop national action plans in cooperation with civil society. The action plans comprise specific commitments in areas such as open data and citizen participation (Federal Chancellery 2019; Federal Ministry of the Interior 2017).

Germany's current national action plan for the years 2019–2021, for example, includes commitments to the establishment of an e-government agency as a digital innovation team of the federal administration, the further development and promotion of the open data environment and better regulation through participation and testing. The nine commitments by the federal government are complemented by further commitments by some state governments (Federal Chancellery 2019).

While initiatives in the context of open government can be found in various policy areas and at different levels of government, the following sections will focus on three sub-fields, namely open government data (Sect. App. 2), open innovation (Sect. App. 3) and open budget (Sect. App. 4), where a comparatively large number of activities has been identified. Each section addresses the current state of affairs at the federal level in Germany from a legal and practical perspective. The insights gained and existing potentials for further open government activities are then summarised (Sect. App. 4).

App. 2. Open Government Data

Open government data is one of the most well-known sub-fields of open government focussing on the free availability of administrative data for further use (Ubaldi 2013: 6). While the publication of administrative data enhances transparency, private companies and administration itself can also benefit from the exchange and further use of data. For some types of governmental data, such as geographical data, the provision implies considerable business opportunities for the private sector.

Since 2017, section 12a of the E-government Act (EGovG) obliges direct federal authorities to provide unprocessed data, which they collect or receive in the context of the fulfilment of their tasks, via public networks. Furthermore, Germany is legally bound by the European Directive 2013/37/EU amending Directive 2003/98/EC on the re-use of public sector information (the PSI Directive) obliging the member states to make public sector information accessible and reusable. In Germany, the directive was transposed into national law through the First Amendment of the Re-Use of Information Act (IWG). In 2019 the European Directive (EU) 2019/1024 on open data and the re-use of public sector information passed which encourages member states of the EU to extend the provision of government data for further usage, especially for economic purposes. The member states shall implement the directive into national law until July 2021.

Based on an administrative arrangement of 2014 between the federal government and several federal states, the data portal GovData[1] was established in order to collectively provide data from various public authorities on the Internet. Two types of data licences, one requiring source specifications and one without any restrictions or conditions, were developed to enable the legal reuse of the data. The decision on the licence used is taken by the provider of a dataset. Today, a wide range of data relating to various policy areas is available on the platform. In addition, open government data are available on other platforms operated by federal, state and municipal governments.

App. 3. Open Innovation

According to Henry W. Chesbrough, the economist who coined the term, 'Open Innovation means that valuable ideas can come from inside or outside the company and can go to market from inside or outside the company as well' (Chesbrough 2003: 43). By enabling inclusion of the ideas of external actors, opening up the innovation processes can generate a number of advantages, for example optimised workflows, for any type of organisation. Public authorities can also benefit from this approach.

In the context of open government, open innovation is also a possible tool for strengthening the connection between administration and the general public. Government officials can add to their knowledge, especially about citizens' needs, by allowing input from outside the public sector. Citizens, on the other hand, can participate more directly in public matters and increase their influence on governmental decision-making.

In Germany, section 19 of the Regulation on the Award of Public Contracts (VgV) further allows public authorities to establish innovation partnerships with private companies with the intention of creating innovative products or services, which are not yet available on the market. However, the use of this procurement procedure has remained limited so far. Also, the civil dialogue 'Wellbeing in Germany', which was conducted between 2015 and 2016 and included discussions between federal politicians and citizens about the living conditions and quality of life in Germany (Federal Government 2020), can be considered as an activity in the context of open innovation.

App. 4. Open Budget

Open budget refers to the opening of the budget as well as the budgetary cycle of public authorities with the objective of providing information and enabling the free reuse of budgetary data. In some cases, a consultative participation of citizens and private businesses in budgetary affairs is also intended. Comparable to many other areas of open government activities, open budget fosters transparency and participation in particular. Open budget data and open contracting can be considered as sub-areas of open budget. While the former focusses on budget data for analytical and research purposes, the latter addresses the disclosure of public authority contracts with all their contractual clauses.

In Germany, the disclosure of the budgets is required by law. According to Article 110 of the Basic Law, all federal revenues and expenditures need to be included in a budget plan, which can be part of the draft of a budget law. The draft law needs to be approved by the Bundestag, while the Bundesrat can deliver its opinion. On the grounds that the Bundestag generally debates publicly (Article 42 of the Basic Law), the federal budget is publicly available. Further provisions covering the federal budget are regulated by the Federal Budget Code (BHO).

In addition to the publication as part of the federal budget law, the federal budget is interactively and freely accessible on a website[2] operated by the Federal Ministry of Finance. The website enables a detailed exploration of the budget, including graphical illustrations of the allocations of the individual budget items, year-on-year comparisons and a keyword search.

App. 5. Lessons Learned

The German government and public authorities have become more open in recent years. Changes in political convictions and priorities coupled with the commitments in the context of the participation in the Open Government Partnership have led to a broad range of initiatives generally aiming to improve transparency, accountability and participation.

However, for some types of information and data, such as legislative texts and budget plans, it is important to note that public availability has existed in Germany for many decades, even centuries. The changes in the context of open government mainly affect the types and convenience of availability. While, for example, access to printed legal gazettes and exploring content requires substantial efforts, the full-text search of legal documents readily available on the Internet can be considered as a significant relief and, therefore, progress in terms of openness.

Although the German federal government has implemented various open government initiatives, the user groups and utilisation processes of the initiatives have not been fully evaluated yet. Further efforts could focus on gaining a better understanding of the user side of open government. If necessary, measures could be taken to reach broader groups of users, for example by developing more tailored offers and more widely promoting existing activities. New measures to promote open government by emphasising its potentials could also be addressed to the administration itself. Additional steps to improve and further develop current open government initiatives, for example by expanding data visualisations and search options, could also be considered.

Further attention should also be given to the interrelations between the various initiatives as well as the sub-fields of open government. The measures related to open innovation, for example, can largely benefit from open government data. A focus on interrelations could also support the development of a more uniform understanding of open government in general.

Besides the federal government, the state governments and many local governments have also implemented measures in the area of open government in Germany in recent years. Some larger cities, for example, operate their own open data and/or open budget portals. Furthermore, the project 'model municipality open government' by the Federal Ministry of the Interior, Building and Community and the municipal umbrella organisations have supported open government initiatives in selected municipalities with the general aim of promoting open government at the sub-national level (Federal Ministry of the Interior, Building and Community 2019). Stimulating increased collaboration and the exchange of ideas between public authorities across all levels of government could be a promising approach to further exploit the potential of open government in Germany.

App. 6. References

Chesbrough, H. W. (2003). *Open Innovation. The New Imperative for Creating and Profiting from Technology*. Boston: Harvard Business School Press.

Executive Office of the President. (2009). *Open Government Directive*. Retrieved February 3, 2020, from https://obamawhitehouse.archives.gov/sites/default/files/omb/assets/memoranda_2010/m10-06.pdf.

Federal Chancellery. (2019). *Second National Action Plan (NAP) 2019–2021 in the Framework of Germany's Participation in the Open Government Partnership (OGP)*. Retrieved February 9, 2020, from https://www.opengovpartnership.org/wp-content/uploads/2019/09/Germany_Action-Plan_2019-2021_EN.pdf.

Federal Government. (2020). *Wellbeing in Germany*. Retrieved February 11, 2020, from http://www.gut-leben-in-deutschland.de/static/LB/en/.

Federal Ministry of the Interior. (2017). *First National Action Plan (NAP) 2017–2019 in the Framework of Germany's Participation in the Open Government Partnership (OGP)*. Retrieved February 9, 2020, from https://

www.opengovpartnership.org/wp-content/uploads/2017/08/Germany_NAP_2017-2019_ENG-transl.pdf.

Federal Ministry of the Interior, Building and Community. (2019). *Modellkommune Open Government, Projektbericht.* Retrieved February 9, 2020, from https://www.bmi.bund.de/SharedDocs/downloads/DE/veroeffentlichungen/themen/moderne-verwaltung/projektbericht-modellkommune-open-government.pdf?__blob=publicationFile&v=2.

von Lucke, J. (2017). Technische Innovation—Potenziale von Open Government, Offenen Daten und Intelligenten Städten. In N. Kersting (Ed.), *Urbane Innovation* (pp. 151–204). Wiesbaden: Springer.

Meijer, A., de Hoog, J., van Twist, M., van der Steen, M., & Scherpenisse, J. (2014). Understanding the Dynamics of Open Data: From Sweeping Statements to Complex Contextual Interactions. In M. Gascó-Hernández (Ed.), *Open Government. Opportunities and Challenges for Public Governance, Public Administration and Information Technology* (vol. 4, pp. 101–114). New York: Springer.

OECD. (2016). *Open Government: The Global Context and the Way Forward.* Paris: OECD Publishing.

Ubaldi, B. (2013). *Open Government Data: Towards Empirical Analysis of Open Government Data Initiatives.* OECD Working Papers on Public Governance No. 22. Retrieved February 6, 2020, from https://www.oecd-ilibrary.org/docserver/5k46bj4f03s7-en.pdf.

Wewer, G., & Wewer, T. (2019). *Open Government, Stärkung oder Schwächung der Demokratie?* Wiesbaden: Springer VS.

Open Access This chapter is licensed under the terms of the Creative Commons Attribution 4.0 International License (http://creativecommons.org/licenses/by/4.0/), which permits use, sharing, adaptation, distribution and reproduction in any medium or format, as long as you give appropriate credit to the original author(s) and the source, provide a link to the Creative Commons licence and indicate if changes were made.

The images or other third party material in this chapter are included in the chapter's Creative Commons licence, unless indicated otherwise in a credit line to the material. If material is not included in the chapter's Creative Commons licence and your intended use is not permitted by statutory regulation or exceeds the permitted use, you will need to obtain permission directly from the copyright holder.

CHAPTER 20

The Federal Ministerial Bureaucracy, the Legislative Process and Better Regulation

Sabine Kuhlmann and Sylvia Veit

1 INTRODUCTION

Since the end of the 1990s, against the backdrop of increasing international competition, growing regulatory density and demands on the output legitimacy of legislative action, there has been a debate around the concept of 'Better Regulation' in Germany and Europe. Better Regulation reforms are directed at anchoring institutional mechanisms to ensure lower costs, enhanced effectiveness and better executability of regulations as well as improving the legislative process. First, these reforms attempt to stem the growing flood of legal norms and overregulation with the objective of the state to enhance its scope of action. Second, they are meant to reduce red tape and the compliance costs of new legislation for businesses,

---

S. Kuhlmann (✉)
University of Potsdam, Potsdam, Germany
e-mail: skuhlman@uni-potsdam.de

S. Veit
University of Kassel, Kassel, Germany
e-mail: sveit@uni-kassel.de

© The Author(s) 2021   357
S. Kuhlmann et al. (eds.), *Public Administration in Germany*,
Governance and Public Management,
https://doi.org/10.1007/978-3-030-53697-8_20

citizens and public administration. Third, Better Regulation reforms are directed at increasing the effectiveness of political interventions and at systemically considering the non-intended side effects of regulations in order to revise and improve them. While the fundamental debate surrounding reducing red tape, Regulatory Impact Assessment (RIA) and evaluation is by no means new, some facets of the more recent discourse are indeed innovative. This concerns, on the one hand, the influence of the European Union (EU) on national legislation and the bureaucratic burdens caused by adopting EU law. On the other hand, new methods for RIA have been developed, such as the Standard Cost Model (SCM) for estimating bureaucratic costs. Additionally, innovative forms of RIA institutionalisation have evolved, for instance by way of establishing independent advisory bodies by law, such as the National Regulatory Control Council (*Nationaler Normenkontrollrat*—NKR) in Germany, which brings a new quality to the discourse and practice of Better Regulation. This chapter addresses these developments and specifically outlines the role and functions of the NKR in this context.

2   BETTER REGULATION AS REFORM CONCEPT

Since the second half of the 1990s, Better Regulation[1] has been established as an international reform wave focussing on the improvement of the production, design, selection and implementation of regulations. The main aim of Better Regulation reforms is to countervail the inherent deficits of regulatory regimes such as the extensive administrative burdens on businesses, a biased inclusion of societal interests or insufficient use of scientific evidence (Lodge and Wegrich 2012). Thus, governments adopt Better Regulation reforms to increase the effectiveness of their regulations and policies but also to strengthen their (democratic) legitimacy (e.g. Radaelli et al. 2013). The concept of Better Regulation is not limited to specific policy areas as it aims 'to improve policy-making and regulation by adopting standards and procedures that govern regulatory decision-making across different public policy areas' (Bunea and Ibenskas 2017: 591).[2] Hence, Better Regulation can be classified as institutional policy (Kuhlmann and Wollmann 2019; Kuhlmann and Wayenberg 2016) or meta-regulation (Radaelli and Meuwese 2009).

Better Regulation is an umbrella term for various tools and instruments to raise the quality of both the process and output of legislation. Typical elements in the 'toolbox' of Better Regulation are Regulatory Impact

Assessments (RIAs) and its sub-forms, sunset clauses (sunset regulation), consultations, *ex post* evaluations of policies/laws, approaches to regulatory simplification and tools for risk-based or smart regulation. More recently, digitalisation has influenced this reform area and triggered a debate on the use of electronic forecasting tools and algorithms in policy-making. As RIAs are not only the most widespread tool of Better Regulation but also an instrument with many facets and sub-forms, some further explanations on this instrument are necessary.

RIAs involve a systematic assessment of the impacts of legislative proposals and other policies before they are enacted. RIAs are no new 'invention' of the more recent Better Regulation debate but have a rather long history. In Germany, a list of ten questions to be answered by the lead ministry focussing on the quality and impact of legislative proposals (the so-called *Blaue Prüffragen*) was established as early as 1984 by the federal government. The practical relevance of this list, however, remained low.

Since the end of the 1990s, increased political efforts to improve policies by systematically integrating RIAs into the legislative process have been observed in many countries. Two core elements of this reform wave can be identified. Firstly, RIAs are explicitly designed as meta-regulation (Radaelli 2010). Hence, the objective is to improve governmental legislative proposals by defining additional 'rules of the game' within the core executive. Secondly, compliance with RIA requirements is regularly supported by the creation of RIA boards or (regulatory) control bodies in charge of quality assurance and control tasks (such as the NKR in Germany). These measures have increased the practical relevance of RIAs and fostered policy learning (Fritsch et al. 2017).

The growing significance of RIAs over the last two decades has been accompanied by a process of functional differentiation, in which various sub-types of RIAs—such as Bureaucracy Cost Assessment with the Standard Cost Model (SCM) or Gender Impact Assessment—have been established in different countries. In addition, different types of 'generic' RIAs exist—the most famous being the Sustainability Impact Assessment (SIA). SIAs focus on a well-balanced appraisal of social, environmental and economic impacts, and on the coupling of sustainability policy (e.g. sustainability indicators) and impact assessment (Russel and Turnpenny 2009). In recent years, ICT development has created new opportunities for analyses and triggered the development and use of electronic RIA tools. The federal government in Germany has introduced an electronic tool as part of the SIA called eNAP (see www.enap.bund.de).

The OECD has played a crucial role as an important reform promoter in the international diffusion of Better Regulation reforms (DeFrancesco 2012). In Europe, the European Commission has also established itself as a reform promoter by pushing agendas in the field of Better Regulation under different labels. The implementation of Better Regulation measures, as well as the impact of the tools promoted by reform advocates, has become a controversial topic in academic discourse. While some scholars have underlined the potential of these reform tools to improve policies (e.g. Rissi and Sager 2013), others have criticised the reforms for being mainly rhetorical and symbolic with limited impact in practice (e.g. Coglianese 2008). With regard to RIA, empirical studies point to a mainly formal adoption in many countries and considerable implementation deficits and cross-country variation (e.g. Dunlop 2012).

3 Better Regulation and the Federal Ministerial Bureaucracy

In Germany, as in most other parliamentary democracies, the coordination and formulation of new regulations and draft laws is one of the main functions of the federal ministerial bureaucracy (see Chaps. 5 and 10). Almost 90 per cent of all federal laws passed by the parliament go back to initiatives of the federal government *(Regierungsvorlagen)* (Deutscher Bundestag 2019). The remaining ten per cent are mostly initiated by one of the two chambers of federal parliament, the *Bundestag* or the *Bundesrat*. There are at least three reasons for this dominant role of the federal bureaucracy in the policymaking process. First, despite the notion of a separation of powers between the legislative and the executive branch, in practice there is no clear dividing line. The head of government (Chancellor) is elected by a majority in the legislature. Majority fractions in parliament and the government are intertwined. Therefore, in many cases, successful legislative initiatives introduced by the *Bundestag* can actually also be traced back to the executive branch and have been written by ministerial staff. For the most part, strategic considerations or time restrictions are the reason for the decision to formally initiate these laws by the majority fractions in the *Bundestag*. Secondly, MPs and parliamentary fractions in the *Bundestag* have far fewer personnel and financial resources at their disposal to develop policy solutions than the government. The government has about 19,000 civil servants working in federal ministries and the chancellery (*Bundeshaushaltsplan 2019*), and more than four times as many civil servants in federal agencies, including governmental research agencies. In addition, a huge number of advisory bodies of the federal government have been established to provide expert policy advice on different topics (see Chap. 5). Finally, the government has substantial financial resources for commissioned research. Compared to the federal government, the parliamentary resources are rather limited: altogether, the *Bundestag* has about 6000 employees, of whom 3000 belong to the *Bundestag* administration, about 1150 work for the (currently six) parliamentary fractions (Deutscher Bundestag 2019) and the remaining approximate 1850 are employed as personal staff for the current 709 MPs in the *Bundestag*. A third reason for the executive dominance in policy formulation lies in the ability to draw on its vast amount of knowledge and policy expertise, which is located in the federal ministries and especially in their basic units (divisions/*Referate*).

Due to the constitutional principle of minister responsibility *(Ministerverantwortlichkeit)*, federal ministries in Germany are characterised by a strict hierarchy and linear organisation. Each ministry is headed by a single minister. The number of ministers and their policy portfolio is defined by the federal chancellor (there are usually between 14 and 16 ministers). Despite the fact that all legislation and important policy programmes need a cabinet majority (cabinet principle) and, as stated in the federal constitution, the federal chancellor determines and is responsible for general policy guidelines (*Richtlinienkompetenz*), ministers in Germany have a relatively strong position compared to ministers in many other countries. Every minister conducts his ministry and policy domain independently (departmental principle/*Ressortprinzip*). Thus, ministers are not subordinate to the head of government and he/she cannot instruct them on how to handle specific issues within their ministries' affairs. In the development of legislative proposals within the executive branch, the strong position of single ministers leads to a dominance of 'negative coordination'. Because of the departmental principle, the lead ministry has considerable autonomy in procedural decision-making and consulting interest groups. In policymaking processes, the chancellery exerts influence on the departments by specifying deadlines for consultation. It also has responsibility for releasing departmental legislative proposals (*Referentenentwürfe*) for interdepartmental coordination and later in the processes leading up to cabinet decision. The chancellery's capacity for fostering policy integration and enforcing its own policies is however limited, and even conflict resolution usually takes place among single ministries in the process of interdepartmental coordination *(Ressortabstimmung)*, rather than hierarchically by the chancellery (see Chap. 5). If a conflict cannot be resolved in the *Ressortabstimmung*, the coalition parties try to negotiate a solution.

The formal policymaking process within the federal government from the first draft of a new regulation to the final cabinet decision is regulated by the Federal Ministries' Joint Rules of Procedure (*Gemeinsame Geschäftsordnung*—GGO). Besides some of the organisational aspects, the Joint Rules of Procedure stipulate who has to be involved in the law-making process and at what point in time. Whenever a new draft law is presented, there is an obligation to consult other federal departments, *Länder* governments, the local level and interest organisations relevant to that particular policy. The GGO also defines the necessary formal parts of each legislative proposal, notably (a) a summary cover sheet with an overview of the expected impacts in different areas (e.g. compliance costs), (b) the draft law text itself and (c) a detailed explanation of the reasons leading to the respective draft law (explanatory memorandum).

The first attempts at systematising *ex ante* evaluation of legislation in Germany at federal level date back to the 1970s (Veit 2010). However, it was not before the year 2000 that federal ministries committed themselves to conducting a comprehensive RIA by regulating RIA procedures and competencies in the GGO. It was then, according to the provisions of Section 43 (5) GGO, that the 'consequences of a law' had to be presented in the explanatory memorandum of each legislative proposal. Section 44 (1) GGO further stipulates: 'The consequences of a law are defined as the main impacts of a law: this covers its intended effects and unintended side effects'. The following paragraphs of the GGO list some specific RIA requirements—with an emphasis on cost consequences (e.g. consequences for small- and medium-sized enterprises and implementation costs).

According to the GGO, RIAs have to be conducted by the lead ministry. Since there are no evaluation units within the different federal ministries, RIAs are usually conducted by the same division that has key responsibility for developing the draft law. Before 2006, there was no oversight body within the federal executive with responsibility for evaluating RIA implementation and quality. The Federal Ministry of the Interior was assigned responsibility for supporting the other ministries in their RIA activities, for example by publishing impact assessment guidelines. The quality of RIAs, however, was expected to be discussed by the various

20 THE FEDERAL MINISTERIAL BUREAUCRACY, THE LEGISLATIVE PROCESS... 363

ministries when coordinating a draft law. Hence, policy coordination and political compromise on the one hand, and neutral analysis of proposed policy impacts based on appropriate methods on the other, were supposed to be realised simultaneously—within the same formal procedures and by the same actors (Veit 2010). To what extent this pattern of institutionalisation changed when the NKR was established in 2006 is elaborated in the following section.

4 THE NATIONAL REGULATORY CONTROL COUNCIL

The National Regulatory Control Council (*Nationaler Normenkontrollrat*—NKR), which was established on a statutory basis[3] in Germany in 2006, constitutes a new form of institutionalisation of Better Regulation in organisational, procedural and methodological terms. The NKR is an advisory and control council of ten members that assists the German federal government with Better Regulation and reducing red tape. Its core task is the assessment of all legislative initiatives of the federal government with regard to the presentation of compliance costs and other cost impacts. The aspired political goals and purposes of regulations are thereby not subject to examination according to the NKR law (NKRG). In the following, an overview of the institutionalisation of the NKR as an independent body, its missions and tasks, operating principles and the outcomes of the work of the NKR is given.

4.1 Institutionalisation of the NKR as an Independent Advisory and Supervisory Body

The NKR commenced its work in September 2006 after the 'Act on the Establishment of a National Regulatory Control Council' (NKRG) was passed in the previous month. The establishment of the NKR in Germany is to be understood in light of two developments. On the one hand, the federal government drew on the positive response received by the Dutch government's programme 'Bureaucracy Reduction and Better Regulation'. In the Netherlands, where the SCM was developed, an independent expert and advisory body (ACTAL) had already been established in 2000. On the other hand, experience with regulatory impact assessments in Germany had shown that impact assessments were difficult to implement without an assertive authority monitoring their implementation (Veit 2010). One of the main arguments for establishing the NKR was, therefore, to set up an independent advisory and supervisory body to systematically monitor and demand that departments assess bureaucracy costs in accordance with their obligations. The NKR is located in the German federal chancellery; however, the NKR is neither supervised by nor subordinate to the federal chancellery or any other authority (Section 1 (1) NKRG). The autonomy and independence of the NKR is also emphasised through its legal anchoring. Contrary to most other advisory bodies of the federal government, disbanding the NKR requires a parliamentary majority.

The NKR consists of ten (eight until 2011) members who work *ad honorem*. They are nominated by the federal chancellor and appointed by the federal president. In Section 3 (2) NKRG, the profile for members of the council should meet the following requirements: 'The members should have experience in legislative matters within state or social institutions as well as knowledge of economic matters.' The NKR is supported by a professional secretariat with currently 11 employees who are also not subject to any directives issued by the federal chancellery or any department. They are only accountable to the NKR. The secretariat offers civil servants in the departments drafting legislative proposals assistance in implementing the assessments of compliance costs in terms of methodology, while the Federal Statistical Office administers and updates the databank of the assessment exercise. The centrepiece of the formal institutionalisation of the NKR is its obligatory involvement in the inner legislative procedure in the executive. The federal ministries in Germany are obliged to involve the NKR in every regulatory initiative at an early stage. In the phase of interdepartmental coordination, the NKR, thus, has the same rights as other affected departments (Section 45 (1) GGO). The statements of the NKR on legislative proposals—although non-binding for the government—are part of the cabinet draft and are published at the time of introducing the draft to the Federal Parliament (*Bundestag)* or the Federal Council *(Bundesrat)* as an appendix to the respective legislative draft (Section 6 (1) NKRG). If there is dissent between the NKR and the government regarding specific issues, the federal government can define this dissenting opinion as the statement of the NKR. The federal government's response is then considered in the further advisory process as an appendix to the legislative draft.

4.2 Mission and Mandate

According to Section 4 (2) NKRG, the main task of the NKR is to assess legislative and regulatory drafts before their presentation to the federal cabinet with regard to compliance with the principles of a standardised assessment of bureaucracy costs and by means of the so-called Standard Cost Model (SCM).[4] Bureaucracy costs are here to be understood as costs 'incurred by natural or legal persons in fulfilling their duties to provide information. Duties to provide information are obligations deriving from an act, ordinance, bylaw or administrative regulation to procure, make available or transmit data and other information to authorities or third parties' (Section 2 (2) NKRG). Typical examples of information obligations include completing forms and providing statistics, or reporting. In order to calculate bureaucracy costs arising from these obligations, the time and cost expenditure needed to comply with the public information obligations are estimated. Based on a common methodology, the data are multiplied by a tariff, frequency of activity and the number of cases. The result gives information in monetary terms about the bureaucracy costs that entail a legal provision, a legal area or a certain occurrence (e.g. business creation). This procedure can be applied to other target groups (citizens or public administration) in a similar manner. In December 2006, shortly after the establishment of the NKR, the provisions for regulatory impact assessments of the Federal Ministries' Joint Rules of Procedure (GGO) were extended by the obligation to ensure transparency about information obligations and bureaucracy costs for companies, citizens and public administration in the draft proposal and as part of the justification for the law.

In assessing the impacts of Better Regulation policies, critics argue, however, that the bureaucracy reduction measures are not sufficiently perceptible and tangible from the perspective of businesses and citizens. These shortcomings were a crucial reason for extending the NKR mandate in 2011 to foster a more realistic and true-to-life picture of regulatory cost assessments. Initially, the measurement of information obligations for businesses had covered only a minor (and less important) part of the regulatory costs, whereas the weightier and more perceivable part of compliance costs as well as the burdens incurred by citizens and administrations had been ignored. As a result of the extended NKR mandate, the federal ministries not only have to display details of the bureaucracy costs of legislative and regulatory drafts, but also quantify the total compliance costs incurred by citizens, businesses and administration at all governmental levels (federal, *Länder* and local). 'The term compliance costs include the total measurable time expenditure and the costs incurred by citizens, business and public authorities in order to comply with federal legislation' (NKR 2018: p. 11; Section 2 (1) NKRG). In addition to the bureaucracy costs (see above), the measurement of the compliance costs thus includes all direct costs incurred by citizens, businesses and all three levels of public administration (federal, *Länder*, local levels) by a new federal regulation. Both annual recurrent and one-off burdens—or reliefs—must be presented. The presentation of compliance costs serves two purposes. First, it ensures transparency of the cost implications of a regulatory initiative. Second, it stimulates decision-makers to think about less bureaucratic alternatives and thus minimise compliance costs in general. Without disclosing the compliance costs, a legislative draft cannot proceed to the federal cabinet—it is a binding obligation of the lead ministry that cannot be circumvented.

4.3   Activities and Results of Regulatory Scrutiny[5]

Since the establishment of the NKR in September 2006, a total of 4683 regulatory initiatives have been scrutinised, of which 330 regulatory initiatives were allocated to the period from 1 July 2018 to 30 June 2019 (NKR 2019). As mentioned earlier, the amendment to the NKRG in 2011 comprised a widening of its audit mandate from 'pure bureaucracy costs' (reporting and statistical obligations) to total compliance costs (time and money expenditures that the economy, citizens and administrations at all levels incur by following federal legal provisions) of legislative proposals. Consequently, the scope of the NKR's audit activity and the amount of regulatory initiatives with relevant impacts have increased significantly. Thus, of the 330 proposals examined between July 2018 and June 2019, 127 projects (38 per cent) had a significant impact on one-off and/or annual compliance costs, whereas 203 (62 per cent) incurred only minor or no compliance costs. Compared to the old mandate, which only included the examination of bureaucracy costs, the number of regulatory initiatives with relevant impact in the context of the NKR mandate has virtually tripled. Furthermore, it should be noted that the number of regulatory initiatives with annual burdensome impacts (82 in the reporting period) is much higher than the number of burden reducing regulatory initiatives (26). This can also be explained by the fact that a substantial part of the burdensome regulations stems from the implementation of EU directives[6] and that—for numerous reasons—there is still growth in regulatory activity and a tendency in politics to initiate new legislative projects. This has been confirmed by the increase in annual compliance costs since 2011 (first year of assessment), on balance by a total of €6.6 billion, of which €4.9 billion (74 per cent of the increase) is allocated to businesses, €1.5 billion (22 per cent) to administration and €221 million (3 per cent) to citizens. Between 2018 and 2019, the annual compliance costs increased on balance by a total of approximately €831 million (15 per cent; see NKR 2019).

The percentage distribution of the calculated compliance costs among different federal departments indicates where highly regulated intensive policy fields and strong regulatory activity can be found. Here it becomes apparent that the increase in the annual compliance costs can largely be traced back to the regulatory initiatives of the Federal Ministry of Finance with €672 million. Almost half of the initiatives scrutinised by the NKR in the reporting period were attributed to three ministries (Federal Ministry of Finance: 55, Federal Ministry of Labour and Social Affairs: 47, Federal Ministry of Transport and Digital Infrastructure: 46). On balance, only three federal ministries recorded a substantial annual relief in compliance costs: the Federal Ministry of the Environment with €156 million, the Federal Ministry of Transport and Digital Infrastructure with €65 million and the Federal Ministry of Food and Agriculture with €12 million.

5 Future Outlook and Lessons for Transfer

Thanks to the *ex ante* assessments of compliance costs for each federal legislative regulatory initiative, decision-makers in government and parliament today know with greater accuracy than in the past (and with greater accuracy than in most other European countries), which legislative proposals impose costs on citizens, the economy and the administration. This increased cost transparency has many times resulted in a reduction of bureaucracy costs[7] and, following the critical NKR reviews, enabled an improvement in legislative drafts by virtue of reduced compliance costs. In addition, the (hardly quantifiable) positive influence of the NKR's audit activities on the entire legislative process has to be considered. This is especially the case when a potentially critical NKR statement is anticipated by the departments drafting the law and before the proposal can proceed to the federal cabinet. Thus, the NKR activity has contributed to a higher institutional sensitivity for the subsequent costs of legislative action today. The NKR has become a widely accepted 'watchdog' and promoter of Better Regulation within the federal legislative process, giving permanent voice to the issues of regulatory burdens and impacts, compliance costs and red tape in Germany. Additionally, it is increasingly taking advantage of its reputation to set the agenda for other fields of administrative reform, such as digital government, modernising public registries and speeding up procedures for large infrastructure projects (see Chap. 19).

A perspective on the future of Better Regulation as a reform doctrine in public administration foresees several developments. First, the federal government could/should focus more sharply on reducing bureaucratic burdens in a more perceptible and everyday life-oriented way, thereby taking a more systematic approach to measuring stakeholders' perceptions. The low perceptibility of cost reliefs is mainly due to the broader notion of compliance costs from the citizens' and businesses' perspective, which involves, inter alia, EU legislation, *Länder* and local regulations, administrative procedures, customer-business relations, technical standards and so on (IfM—Institut für Mittelstandsforschung Bonn 2019). Thus, the citizens' and businesses' regulatory reality is shaped by a multitude of provisions and rules stemming from various sources and levels, whereas the NKR focuses solely on compliance cost reductions at the federal level. Against this background, there is a trend in Germany towards extending compliance cost measurements beyond the federal level by, for example, establishing regulatory control councils at the *Länder* level. In Baden-Württemberg and Saxony, for instance, the *Länder* regulatory control councils are responsible for assessing compliance costs resulting from regulations and administrative directives enacted by the respective *Länder* governments. In general, the multilevel perspective is a major challenge for regulatory reform policies in federal countries. The separation of the legislative function (predominantly federal level) and the administrative function (predominantly *Länder*/local levels) makes compliance cost assessments particularly wicked, but all the more important and necessary to ensure better informed, more robust evidence-based policymaking in the multilevel system. However, there is still a lack of well-functioning and generally accepted procedures in Germany that would enable *Länder* and local governments to be sufficiently involved in federal compliance cost assessments. Further improvement in Better Regulation policies could be achieved by extending the so-called one-in, one-out-rule (OIOO), which was introduced to EU legislation in 2015 on the initiative of the NKR. The

20 THE FEDERAL MINISTERIAL BUREAUCRACY, THE LEGISLATIVE PROCESS... 369

OIOO rule implies that for new legislative initiatives that incur annual compliance costs to businesses ('in'), a corresponding amount of relief ('out') must be generated by the end of a legislative term at the latest—within either the draft legislation itself or elsewhere. In the 2018/2019 reporting period, the additional costs to businesses ('in') of €120 million was outweighed by a relief ('out') of €262 million, which corresponded to a net relief for businesses of €142 million. As a result, since its introduction in 2015, the OIOO balance sheet has shown an 'out' of about €2 billion net relief for businesses. Nevertheless, this positive OIOO rule does not often tally with reality as perceived by businesses. This is because since 2015 an additional annual 'in' of €435 million resulting from the implementation of European legislation has been excluded from the OIOO rule.[8] Consequently, the NKR maintains that this is precisely why European burdens and reliefs must also be covered by the application of the OIOO rule, since it is of complete irrelevance to companies whether costs are incurred as a result of European or national legislation.

Finally, following a joint decision of the federal secretaries of state in 2013, *ex post* evaluations of legislative acts (in addition to *ex ante* cost assessments) must be carried out by the departments in a more systematic and methodologically rigorous manner, thus upholding an existing binding decision of the federal secretaries of state responsible for the reduction of bureaucracy. According to this decision, *ex post* evaluations of impacts and outcomes of new regulations (e.g. regarding political goal attainment, effectiveness, acceptance by stakeholders, unintended effects, etc.) must be conducted for all legislative acts entailing a threshold of (*ex ante* measured) compliance costs of more than a €1 million per annum. So far, however, the departments have adopted this general rule in a rather reluctant and unsystematic manner, which suggests that further adjustments and a possible standardisation are required. The implementation failure of systematic *ex post* evaluations of legislative acts illustrates the extreme importance of having not only an independent quality control mechanism for the evaluative process but also an institutionalised, competent and powerful watchdog. The German example shows that Better Regulation as cross-cutting reform measures and meta-regulation needs an advocate within government administration who cannot be circumvented by the departmental policy specialists (Jann and Wegrich 2019) because of its legal foundation and procedural integration in the pre-parliamentarian legislative process. The reduction of bureaucracy costs and—with some restrictions—compliance costs has been working well since the establishment of the NKR. However, related topics such as ex post evaluation and sustainability impact assessment (which have both been obligatory in the GGO for some years now), have not been successfully implemented so far due to a lack of organisational institutionalisation and procedural integration.

In order to further promote Better Regulation as an approach to the modernisation of state and administration, it would be desirable if other countries decided to install (independent) bodies for the review of impact assessments too. This applies to members of the European Union in particular, but to other nations as well. To this end, the NKR maintains a close liaison with six other independent bodies in Europe tasked by their government or their parliament with reviewing impact assessments and together with the NKR have formed the network 'RegWatchEurope'. Besides the German NKR, the network consists of the Adviescollege Toetsing Regeldruk (ATR) from the Netherlands, the Regulatory Policy Committee (RPC) from the United Kingdom, the Swedish Regelradet (SBRC) and the Norwegian Regelradet (NBRC) as well as the Regulatory Impact Assessment Board (RIAB) from the Czech Republic and the Finnish Council of Regulatory Impact Analysis (FCRIA). The purpose of the network is to enable the exchange of experience and knowledge among its members and the representation of common interests at the EU level, specifically *vis-à-vis* the Regulatory Scrutiny Board (RSB) of the EU Commission and, in an international context, the Regulatory Policy Committee of the OECD. These multilateral, European-scale and international exchanges offer the opportunity to share different national experiences in impact assessments with representatives from other OECD member states and thus promote the model of independent regulatory scrutiny on a European scale and in the international context.

NOTES

1. In practice, Better Regulation reforms are known by different names. Common labels include smart regulation (often used by the European Commission), high-quality regulation and regulatory reform.
2. As efforts in the area of Better Regulation often include the (increasing) use of scientific evidence and expertise to improve policy decisions and regulations, the concept is closely related to another reform concept: evidence-based policymaking (EBPM). At the core of EBPM lies the idea of a 'rationalisation' of political decision-making by systematically integrating

scientific evidence and expertise in policymaking processes and by strengthening 'positive coordination' within the politico-administrative system.

3. *Gesetz zur Einsetzung eines Nationalen Normenkontrollrates vom 14.8.2006* (Act on the Establishment of a National Regulatory Control Council—NKRG).

4. The assessment of bureaucracy costs by means of the SCM was developed in the 1990s in the Netherlands. Subsequently, this instrument spread across Europe.

5. The following summary of essential fields of activity and audit results of the NKR refers to the reporting period from 1 July 2018 to 30 June 2019 (NKR 2019).

6. A considerable proportion of the legal provisions prevailing in Germany and approximately half of the compliance costs in the reporting period stem from EU law. However, up to now, only EU directives that are to be transposed into national legislation (not EU regulations) that constitutes immediately applicable law in Germany are systematically recorded by the NKR audit in which a 'transparency gap' can be detected.

7. The 'pure' bureaucracy costs, which by definition exclusively comprise information and statistical obligations for the economy, were reduced between 2006 and 2011 by 22.3 per cent NKR (2013, p. 28).

8. This exception was carved out by a joint decision of the federal administrative state secretaries in January 2016.

References

Bunea, A., & Ibenskas, R. (2017). Unveiling Patterns of Contestation Over Better Regulation Reforms in the European Union. *Public Administration, 95,* 589–604.

Coglianese, C. (2008). The Rhetoric and Reality of Regulatory Reform. *Yale Journal of Regulation, 25,* 85–95.

DeFrancesco, F. (2012). Diffusion of Regulatory Impact Analysis Among OECD and EU member states. *Comparative Political Studies, 45,* 1277–1305.

Deutscher Bundestag. (2019). Statistik der Gesetzgebung—19. *Wahlperiode, Stand, 23*(8), 2019.

Dunlop, C. A. (2012). The Many Uses of Regulatory Impact Assessment: A Meta-Analysis of EU and UK Cases. *Regulation & Governance, 6*(1), 23–45.

Fritsch, O., Kamkhaji, J. C., & Radaelli, C. M. (2017). Explaining the Content of Impact Assessment in the United Kingdom: Learning Across Time, Sector, and Departments. *Regulation and Governance, 11,* 325–342.

IfM—Institut für Mittelstandsforschung Bonn. (2019). *Bürokratiewahrnehmung von Unternehmen. IfM-Materialien Nr. 274.* Bonn.

Jann, W., & Wegrich, K. (2019). Generalists and specialists in executive politics: Why ambitious meta-policies so often fail. *Public Administration, 97*(4), 845–860.

Kuhlmann, S., & Wayenberg, E. (2016). Institutional Impact Assessment in Multi-Level-Systems: Conceptualizing Decentralization Effects from a Comparative Perspective. *International Review of Administrative Sciences, 82*(2), 233–254. https://doi.org/10.1177/0020852315583194.

Kuhlmann, S., & Wollmann, H. (2019). *Introduction to Comparative Public Administration: Administrative Systems and Reforms in Europe* (2nd ed.). Cheltenham: Elgar.

Lodge, M., & Wegrich, K. (2012). *Managing Regulation: Regulatory Analysis, Politics and Policy.* Basingstoke: Palgrave Macmillan.

NKR. (2013). *Transparency of Costs Improved, Focus on further Burden Reduction.* Annual Report 2013 of the Nationaler Normenkontrollrat, Berlin.

NKR. (2018). *Germany: Less Bureaucracy, More Digital Services, Better Regulation.* Let's get to it! Annual Report 2018 of the Nationaler Normenkontrollrat, Berlin.

NKR. (2019). *Content First, Legal Text Second. Designing Effective and Practicable Legislation.* Report of the Nationaler Normenkontrollrat, Berlin.

Radaelli, C. M. (2010). Regulating Rule-Making via Impact Assessment. *Governance, 23*(1), 89–108.

Radaelli, C. M., & Meuwese, A. (2009). Better Regulation in Europe: Between Management and Regulation. *Public Administration, 87*(3), 639–654.

Radaelli, C. M., Dunlop, C. A., & Fritsch, O. (2013). Narrating Impact Assessment in the European Union. *European Political Science, 12*, 500–521.

Rissi, C., & Sager, F. (2013). Types of Knowledge Utilization of Regulatory Impact Assessments: Evidence from Swiss Policymaking. *Regulation & Governance, 7*, 348–364.

Russel, D., & Turnpenny, J. (2009). The Politics of Sustainable Development in UK Government: What Role for Integrated Policy Appraisals? *Environment and Planning C: Government and Policy, 27*(2), 340–354.

Veit, S. (2010). *Bessere Gesetze durch Folgenabschätzung? Deutschland und Schweden im Vergleich.* Wiesbaden: VS Verlag.

Open Access This chapter is licensed under the terms of the Creative Commons Attribution 4.0 International License (http://creativecommons.org/licenses/by/4.0/), which permits use, sharing, adaptation, distribution and reproduction in any medium or format, as long as you give appropriate credit to the original author(s) and the source, provide a link to the Creative Commons licence and indicate if changes were made.

The images or other third party material in this chapter are included in the chapter's Creative Commons licence, unless indicated otherwise in a credit line to the material. If material is not included in the chapter's Creative Commons licence and your intended use is not permitted by statutory regulation or exceeds the permitted use, you will need to obtain permission directly from the copyright holder.

CHAPTER 21

Human Resource Management in German Public Administration

John Siegel and Isabella Proeller

1 Introduction

Public administration—not only in Germany—requires a sufficient number of qualified and motivated staff to produce services, provide infrastructures and implement policies efficiently, effectively, professionally and reliably. Managing the workforce is, therefore, one of the most crucial functions in public administration. In this chapter, we take a closer—but given the complexity of the topic—unavoidably selective look at human resource management (HRM) in general, and at related issues in particular, such as pay for performance and public service motivation (for general aspects regarding civil service systems and the institutional framework for HRM, see Chap. 13).

J. Siegel (✉)
Hamburg University of Applied Sciences, Hamburg, Germany
e-mail: john.siegel@haw-hamburg.de

I. Proeller
University of Potsdam, Potsdam, Germany
e-mail: proeller@uni-potsdam.de

© The Author(s) 2021
S. Kuhlmann et al. (eds.), *Public Administration in Germany*,
Governance and Public Management,
https://doi.org/10.1007/978-3-030-53697-8_21

375

Our main argument is, paradoxically, that HRM reform has not been the focus of attention despite its obvious relevance for effective policy implementation. As opposed to the general trend worldwide towards convergence between public and private HRM strategies and practices, the workforce in German public administration is still managed in rather traditional and bureaucratic ways despite major challenges, such as digital transformation, demographic changes and attractiveness issues.

2   Fundamentals of Human Resource Management in German Public Administration

A qualified and motivated resource base is key for any public sector organisation. This applies especially to German public administration with its particularly high expectations in terms of reliability, compliance and fairness that are typical of a traditional, bureaucratic, continental European administrative system.

Human resource management is quite simply concerned with making sure that for every task there are sufficient numbers of qualified and motivated people available when and where they are needed with the necessary equipment. What may sound simple is, in fact, an extremely complex task if we consider that roughly 4.6 million individuals work in German public administration. Hence, it is not a straightforward exercise to describe HRM in public administration, particularly given that it comprises different groups, such as police officers and teachers, as well as organisations at all levels of government with varying staff sizes (from 20 to more than 100,000), different professions, cultures and traditions.

Traditionally, HRM in the German public sector has been highly institutionalised in three major respects:

- The civil service and HRM are heavily regulated and thus relatively inflexible. Compliance and equality have become dominant criteria in HR processes. In addition to relevant laws and labour agreements, legal decisions made by the administrative and constitutional courts contribute to the very complex regulatory framework.
- Values associated with traditional public bureaucracy represent the dominant perceptions and criteria of HRM. The function of the civil service is to provide stability and reliability, neutrality and

professionality. Service orientation, competitiveness, mobility and flexibility, for example, play a much less important role.

- Education and training focus predominantly on the legal framework and traditional values and tend to mutually reinforce each other. Programmes in public administration and law (many key players in the public sector HRM are lawyers) overemphasise the importance of these principles, whereas managerial aspects (e.g. strategic planning, leadership, managing costs and enhancing motivation) play a rather marginal role. Lawyers as legal professionals usually have no training at all in HRM, except for learning on the job or through (selective) continuing education.

In that sense, the institutional basis in regulative, cultural-cognitive and normative terms is relatively consistent. For example, HRM is strongly influenced by the 'traditional principles of civil service' and 'selection of the best', placing emphasis on formal qualifications, aptitude and merit, as well as seniority, experience and the privileged status of civil servants. Obviously, these values and principles are not only in line with Max Weber's concept of bureaucracy, but also form the basis for regulations and decision-making in HRM. Furthermore, divergent strategies such as abolishing the traditional civil servant status or, at least, harmonising HRM practices in the public and private sectors have never been seriously considered.

Looking at the institutional basis of public sector HRM, there are also some problematic aspects to be considered. First, the significant differences between HRM in the public sector and in the private sector (both for-profit and not-for-profit organisations) are considered normal and are rarely challenged. Second, the public sector HRM community of practice is not well organised and, thus, does barely allow for a systematic and regular exchange of experience and ideas that are essential to innovation. Further, there are neither journals on public sector HRM nor any specific regular conferences that give support for knowledge exchange and networking. Third, there is little opportunity to discuss the challenges, practices, norms or changes in managing the people working in public sector organisations. Fourth, there has been surprisingly little political attention paid to HRM (apart from occasional law making and downsizing initiatives), despite its obvious relevance for effective policy implementation. Rather, it seems that political actors take a functioning HRM in public administration for granted. Fifth, this impression correlates with the lack of interest shown by the general public and the media in these issues. This has changed only slightly and recently in the wake of the occasional performance failure in service provision (e.g. in the city of Berlin) and corruption scandals (e.g. in military procurement). Sixth, HRM is highly decentralised and fragmented.

Today, HRM in German public administration, and particularly the 'maintaining' stance on reform, faces serious challenges:

- The demographic situation and changes play an increasingly important role in staff shortages and create an even greater need for change to enhance the attractiveness of public administration organisations as employers. The downsizing efforts of previous years have contributed to an imbalanced age pyramid. At a time when a large part of the staff is retiring, labour markets are becoming less and less capable of providing the much-needed workforce.
- In the situation where staff become an increasingly scarce resource, capacity is further reduced due to high levels of part-time employment and absenteeism. For example, persistently high numbers of staff on sick leave increases awareness about the quality of work, motivation and leadership.
- The shift in the social, ethical and cultural composition of German society in general, and in metropolitan areas in particular, raises the question of representative bureaucracy. Migration in recent years has reinforced this trend. The general shift in the values of society also increases pressure on public employers to be more diverse in several regards.
- The digital transformation of government also has major implications for HRM, basically for all its functions, from capacity planning, recruiting and training to knowledge management, motivating people and innovation. In this context, deficiencies in HRM become clearly visible, such as lower employer attractiveness and insufficient flexibility in hiring IT experts, or inadequate internal qualification systems to develop the necessary competencies for an e-government.
- The public sector in Germany is also under constant pressure to reduce the number of 'precarious' forms of employment, particularly the extensive use of time-limited contracts. Furthermore, the increasing shadow workforce of external consultants and service providers draws attention to alternative forms of employment that are not usually considered part of HRM.

Even though most of these challenges also apply to other governments, HRM in German public administration is facing a considerable gap between its traditionalist, 'maintaining' stance on the one hand, and problematic outcomes and increasing pressure to modernise on the other. This strategic tension will characterise the context in which HRM develops.

In recent years, the main focus of the (limited) reform activities taking place in HRM has been on flexibilisation, particularly regarding work days and work hours, opportunities to work from home, slightly increasing mobility between sectors and within the administration, access to employment and, more recently, part-time leadership. However, overall, these efforts have resulted in no substantial changes in general HRM practices—with the noticeable exception that approximately one-third of staff currently work part-time. Apart from the extraordinary job security for those with civil servant status or permanent employment contracts, flexible working hours and part-time employment significantly contribute to the attractiveness of public administration as an employer.

3 SELECTED FUNCTIONAL AND REFORM TOPICS

Given that HRM is a complex phenomenon, particularly in a federal state with local self-government, our considerations can only take a selection of functions and reform topics into account. Therefore, we will focus on:

- HR strategy and planning;
- HR marketing, selection and training; and
- leadership

and complement these descriptions with considerations on related topics that have drawn particular attention in the international academic community and in recent German HRM debates, namely

- public service motivation;
- performance-related pay; and
- diversity management.

Consequently, many other aspects that are indeed of some importance have to be neglected. Generally, we point out that the empirical basis for this chapter is very weak because only few empirical evidence or data is available. Therefore, we also have to acknowledge that some statements we make remain merely hypothetical or preliminary.

3.1 HR Strategy and Planning

Theoretically, every public sector organisation should formulate an explicit HR strategy based on the respective government's personnel and employment policies. At the very least, it should be aware of the fundamental principles and guidelines as orientation towards HR decision-making, be able to formulate responses to major challenges facing its workforce and reflect upon emergent strategies as part of the organisational learning process. This managerialist and prescriptive stance is confronted with the reality that can basically be described as the absence of sound HR strategy in German public administration.

Even though evidence is sparse, it can nevertheless be assumed that most authorities have not formulated an explicit HR strategy or systematically evaluated their implicit ones. HRM is usually carried out operationally and reactively. Substantial analysis of HR-related strategic issues and the formulation and implementation of adequate deliberate strategies are relatively uncommon. Furthermore, few organisations use explicit guidelines or goals for strategic direction.

Instead of strategy, the key instrument used in HR planning is still the 'job positions plan' as part of the budget. Normally, it defines the number of positions the organisation is allowed to fill, differentiating between pay grades and status groups (employees and civil servants). However, exactly what the necessary or appropriate number of positions is in order to fulfil the organisation's mandate is disputable and, in fact, disputed within the respective administrations and in the budgetary process, during which changes—usually incremental—must be confirmed. Whereas the Department of Finance is typically reluctant to accept calls for an increase in the number of positions, the rest of the administration generally argues for more capacity. This bargaining process happens independent of actual staff requirements, which are difficult to rationally assess. Even though the Federal Ministry of the Interior has issued a sophisticated handbook on how to calculate the required workforce capacity analytically based on tasks and workloads, this way of identifying the 'right' capacity is hardly used in practice. The handbook is perceived to be too demanding in terms of information needs and the costs of the assessment process. Projects are implemented selectively, supported by external consultants, mostly in

21 HUMAN RESOURCE MANAGEMENT IN GERMAN PUBLIC ADMINISTRATION **381**

areas where a number of people perform similar jobs, for example in the job centres or in tax administration. In other areas like education, calculations are based on general ratios (e.g. student–teacher) and often on comparisons within the particular community of practice (e.g. comparing across the states the size of police force per capita). If downsizing efforts have been undertaken for budgetary reasons, across-the-board, top-down specifications are typical and implementation predominantly depends on actual fluctuation, unsurprisingly leading to patchy results in staff capacity. Furthermore, some government functions have better lobbying support (like education or policing) than others (like general administration), which exacerbates the imbalance. In addition, decisions take a long time to implement and show effects.

However, several more or less obvious strategic issues need to be addressed in addition to the ones mentioned above. Particularly for *Länder* governments, HR expenses and liabilities (especially for pensions) are a ticking time bomb. For example, in the (relatively wealthy) city-state of Hamburg, pension liabilities alone accounted for €33 billion in the balance sheet for 2018, whereas total assets amounted to €46 billion. In the budget, more than a third of personnel expenses go to pensioners!

Since these (and other) strategic issues have consequences, regardless of whether or not an organisation is dealing with them systematically, the tendency to ignore problems until their effects become obvious (and it is often too late to respond appropriately) can be difficult to bear. Publicly debated examples of HR planning incapacity illustrate this observation well with the example of teachers, who—surprise!—mostly belong to the baby-boomer generation entering retirement age, but very little attention has been given to workforce planning in light of the capacity (and experience) drain that has been foreseeable for decades, resulting in actual service provision and performance problems across Germany.

3.2 HR Marketing, Selection and Training

HR marketing was not systematically institutionalised in German public administration until a few years ago. If there was a position to be filled, usually an internal offering would be published first, and if unsuccessful, published in the official bulletin or a newspaper, on the website or in online job markets. As long as there were ample sufficiently qualified applicants, this approach was considered to be useful—or at least 'good enough'.

However, at a time when the public sector has an increasing number of jobs to fill mainly due to demographic change, the overall labour force is potentially stagnating or even in decline, and the gap between labour supply and demand is widening, sometimes dramatically. For example, in 2017, thirty-eight per cent of Berlin's district government staff were at least 55 years old. Between 2018 and 2026 in the city-state of Hamburg, approximately thirty per cent of staff in the police, health-related occupations and firefighting will retire. Whereas this generally applies to more than a quarter of Hamburg's city government workforce, almost forty per cent of prison staff will retire. The situation looks similar in most other administrations in Germany. At the same time, the regional labour markets are basically empty as the respective target segments have full employment.

The strategy up to now has come to seem increasingly inappropriate. This is why many organisations in German public administration have recently developed marketing strategies using several instruments like social media campaigns, creating employer brands and reflecting on their competitive positioning in the relevant labour market segments. Strategies focus less on job security (being the dominant factor explaining job or career decisions for the public sector) than diversity aspects, local patriotism and, increasingly, public service motivation (see below) as arguments. However, because most public sector organisations are late movers (with a few exceptions, like the military) and invest relatively few resources in the related efforts, the overall effects are limited. Being related to someone who works in the public sector is still an important factor that influences why young people consider working there (thus, de facto discriminating against migrants, for example).

Recruiting processes have traditionally focussed on fairness and 'selection of the best', even though no *concours* system has been established (for details on general recruitment, see Chap. 13). Hiring decisions (allegedly) follow objective, legally enforceable criteria based on position (employees) or career track (civil servants). The diagnostic instruments used are similar to those used in the private sector with a certain focus on criteria that relate to logical skills, general education, and civic engagement and (written) psychological tests, job interviews and assessment centres as methods. These methods are routinely applied with a degree of formality and usually with the participation of employee representatives. Recently, the optimisation of the recruiting process has been criticised as the long period of time it takes is a competitive disadvantage.

As in other countries, recruiting practices and the reasons why people decide to work for the public sector in Germany are prone to certain biases, in part with problematic consequences. People working in public administration tend to be more security-oriented and risk-averse, and thus relatively immobile, inflexible and reluctant to change (Tepe and Prokop 2018). These tendencies are often exacerbated during the bureaucratic socialisation process by dysfunctional incentives. This raises a serious dilemma if it is assumed that governmental organisations—particularly in Germany—will become more innovative and responsive to dynamic and increasingly demanding stakeholder expectations.

3.3 Leadership

In German public administration, as in many other countries, nowadays leadership is considered a crucial factor in the successful management of public organisations. NPM-like reforms have emphasised the role of leaders, even though managerialism has not been as influential as in other contexts. However, widened managerial accountability that results from (intra-organisational) decentralisation and the role of leadership in managing organisational change has replaced the classic bureaucratic assumption that leadership is largely irrelevant if the rules and structures work properly.

It can be assumed that the authoritarian or patriarchal leadership styles are exceptions rather than the norm, whereas delegation, coordination by means of mutual consultation and sometimes autonomy characterise leadership behaviour. Leadership practices and effectiveness largely depend on the context, and there seems to be a general consensus that there is no 'one best way' of approaching leadership in public administration. Instead, it should 'fit' the circumstances, particularly the kinds of tasks, work and followers, and so on. Given the obvious relevance of leadership, it is surprising to see that there has been little empirical research on the public sector—and only a few normative and prescriptive publications.

As a noteworthy exception, Vogel (2016) scrutinised the leadership behaviour and its antecedents in three organisations in *Länder* and local governments. He found that six orientations explain leadership behaviour: task, relations, change, external, ethical and administrative processing. These dimensions of leadership behaviour are correlated and almost evenly distributed, with the notable (and hardly surprising) exception of the significantly less perceived orientation around change. Based on his findings, Vogel doubts the common assumption that leadership is a weak point in

German public administration, even though he finds room for improvement (ibid., pp. 234).

Looking at the factors explaining leadership behaviour, the study shows the influence of a 'non-calculating' motivation and particularly a distinct management orientation of leaders related to the perceived intensity and effectiveness of leadership across all six dimensions. Furthermore, the work characteristics (in terms of task complexity) of followers, as well as goal and performance orientation, have a positive influence on leadership behaviour. However, Vogel points out that the effects often vary between intended and perceived leadership (leaders' vs. followers' perspectives).

3.4 Public Service Motivation

The concept of public service motivation (PSM) has enjoyed a lot of attention in the academic debate since its emergence in the 1990s, whereas resonance (and relevance?) in terms of practice is rather limited, at least in Germany. However, empirical research on public service motivation allows for some observations that could be relevant for public HRM, particularly for comparative analysis.

PSM is a theoretical construct originally developed and later operationalised by Perry (1996) consisting of four major categories: attraction to policymaking, commitment to the public interest, compassion and self-sacrifice. PSM can be used as a set/index of dependent or independent variables in the sense that factors explaining or influencing PSM can be scrutinised as well as the impact of PSM, for example on employment choices, job satisfaction or performance. The PSM concept has also occasionally been applied to German public administration with ambiguous results.

In a recent study based on a survey among students of public administration, Keune et al. (2018) compared their findings on the PSM of (young) civil servants with previous empirical studies in the German context. Several results should be highlighted.

First, PSM only plays a minor role compared to other motivating factors. A secure job, the compatibility of work and private life, an interesting occupation and the perceived opportunity to work relatively autonomously are more important motivating factors than PSM-related explanations. Second, among the PSM categories, working for/in the public interest (in German, the quasi-mythical term *Gemeinwohl* is used for operationalisation) is the most important, followed by compassion and the wish to help others, self-sacrifice and political motivation. Third, among the PSM elements, correlations can be observed between compassion and both political motivation and working in the public interest, and there seem to be strong links between self-sacrifice/altruism and both public interest and compassion.

However, there is little reliable evidence regarding the antecedents and effects of PSM, or patterns of change, for example during a career in the public sector. Empirical studies based on a socio-economic panel (Vogel and Kroll 2016; Breitsohl and Ruhle 2016) with considerable limitations in operationalising PSM found that social and political involvement, as well as interest in politics by people working in the public sector, are positively influenced by age and that the interest in politics is negatively affected by organisational tenure. However, longitudinal observation reveals very little variation in PSM over time. Furthermore, PSM (which generally ranks low on the list of decision criteria) for some seems to explain the sector choice of members of the 'millennial' generation.

As for the impact of PSM, Gross et al. (2019) recently scrutinised the direct and indirect effects of PSM on (self-perceived) work engagement and employee performance. They found empirical support for the hypothesis that PSM positively affects work engagement and employee performance, the ambiguous links between PSM and presenteeism and absenteeism, although no support for hypotheses assuming moderating effects of PSM on the relationships between job resources and work engagement. In explaining job performance, work engagement matters most, whereas PSM plays a far lesser role—even stress is a better explanation.

Considering the German case, the relatively high attention paid to PSM by academics seems to be somewhat disproportionate. Drawing conclusions from the results is difficult, since the empirical basis is limited. Obviously, it would make sense, for example, to appeal to the public interest in the recruitment process.

3.5   *Performance-Related Pay*

The traditional incentive and remuneration system in German public administration did not comprise substantial elements of pay for performance (PRP). Nowadays, even though there are differences between the levels of government and across the sixteen *Länder*, the remuneration systems in German public administration are still relatively similar. However, in some instances, the differences in the level of remuneration have proven challenging for some authorities. For example, the city-state of Berlin has lost personnel (e.g. in the police) to the federal government due to substantial disparities in the pay scheme. Another problem in this context is that in general the salary for a particular job is the same regardless of whether a person lives and works in a metropolitan area like Hamburg or Munich, or in a rural region where the costs of living are much lower. This has prompted some big city governments to introduce extra pay, but for all members of staff. As a third exception from the rule of equal pay, extra pay for specific jobs such as IT experts has recently been introduced.

Nonetheless, the rule is still that in order to earn a higher salary one must be a seasoned employee, more experienced or promoted to a job in a higher pay grade (where 'jumps' rarely occur). One major difference in salary is due to the distinction between the two status groups of civil servants and public employees (see Chap. 13, Kuhlmann and Röber 2006). The specific and systematic particularities between the two groups lead to significant differences in public workforce pay, but none of these differences are related to job performance.

Performance-related pay (PRP) has been on the reform agenda for more than twenty years now. In 1997, civil service laws were changed to create the option of bonuses based on performance. Today, the guidelines allow for bonus eligibility limited to maximum fifteen per cent of civil servants employed in the organisation, an individual bonus not higher than seven per cent of the annual salary, and total bonus payments of an organisational entity must not exceed 0.3 per cent (!) of the overall personnel expenses.

Pay for performance elements for public employees were introduced as part of a major overhaul of the labour agreements, becoming effective ten years later in 2007. The capacity for financial incentives should—potentially—have been increased to eight per cent of the personnel expenses, but was actually set at a much lower rate (e.g. two per cent in federal and local government from 2010 onwards). However, these incentives came with strings attached: pay for performance was intended to be based on clear and 'objective' evaluation criteria, performance agreements and reviews. Furthermore, the system was to be developed, adopted and implemented by each organisation independently. Thus, while imposing a very high standard but leaving attention to details to the organisations, HR managers and employee representatives were left dealing with the practical and fundamental challenges of implementing the system. Consequently, the outcomes from PRP were mixed and partly disillusioning. In an empirical study considering the practices of local governments in the (largest) state of North Rhine-Westphalia, Schmidt et al. (2011) and Schmidt and Müller (2013) found that even though performance-related pay had been introduced in most entities, conventional evaluation was predominantly being used for review and bonuses tended to be distributed equally, but often not on the basis of actual performance. The system lacked acceptance among the employees, had almost no effect on motivation and incentivisation was limited.

Meier (2013) surveyed twenty-one German counties and cities to analyse whether the introduction of PRP in the public service caused any crowding-out effects on intrinsic motivation and PSM. The design of the performance appraisal schemes proved to be the dominant factor influencing the perception of PRP, in particular the perceived fairness and transparency of the PRP concept. The study suggests that more than ninety per cent of employees receive at least some performance pay and that the percentage of those who receive the best performance ratings is very high (further results also in Wenzel et al. 2019).

PRP has opened much discussion and led to a number of problems in the German public sector. Some of the problems stem from the differentiation between public employees and civil servants because different regulations concerning PRP apply. In 2009, PRP was practically abolished at the federal level. Since 2014, there has no longer been any obligation to apply PRP at the *Länder* level. The unions argue that PRP does not achieve its purpose and all too often creates discord and arouses envy.

3.6 Diversity Management

In recent years, diversity management has increasingly been the focus of attention, partly due to legal changes (e.g. in anti-discrimination law) and partly because of difficulties public employers face in filling vacant positions. Furthermore, many public employers have signed the German *Charta der Vielfalt* (the Diversity Charter), a cross-sectoral agreement highlighting the commitment to diversity in the workforce in terms of age, gender, sexual orientation, handicap, ethnic and cultural background. Even though public administration has long been at the forefront in the fight against discrimination, in particular ensuring the rights of women and people with disabilities, women are still underrepresented in management positions (Schimeta 2012).

Diversity management in the broader sense is an innovation to HRM in German public administration. This might explain why there is still little research on the impacts of implemented strategies or the effects of an increasingly diverse workforce.

One of the most crucial strategic changes in diversity-related aspects of HRM is what is called 'intercultural opening' or 'receptiveness'. Many public employers are increasingly promoting the cultural and ethnic diversity policy, particularly in recruiting and training. Several city governments (like Berlin, Hamburg, Munich and the Ruhr area) have committed themselves to the goal that at least twenty per cent of all junior staff recruited should have a 'migration background' or otherwise demonstrate intercultural competences; in some states, corresponding legal obligations exist. These commitments are aligned with efforts in advertising, employer branding, revisions in selection criteria and communication. Some employers, such as the city-state of Hamburg, have been relatively successful in achieving this goal. However, in most metropolitan areas, half of the younger generation grow up in migrant families and therefore these goals do not tackle underrepresentation effectively. Another key component of these strategies is to provide training in intercultural competence for staff, such as improving foreign language skills and cultural sensitivity (among clients or colleagues) and so on. Changes in HR strategies and integration policy go hand in hand.

4   Lessons Learned

This chapter covers some general and functional aspects of human resource management in German public administration. To conclude, our initial proposition that the traditionalist or 'maintaining' stance on HRM and its reform is increasingly challenged by internal weaknesses and external threats, can be complemented by pointing out a few major paradoxes and dilemmas:

First, the highly formalised institutional framework which corresponds with bureaucratic criteria such as equality, compliance, professionalism and qualification—ultimately aimed at stability, predictability and reliability—seem problematic in an increasingly dynamic environment demanding mobility, flexibility and innovation.

Second, this could be reflected in intensifying conflict between employers and employees. Recognising that demographic trends and labour market conditions strengthen their position, employees can exert pressure on their organisations, HR departments and leaders, heightening the need for HRM to respond to their expectations. If the institutional framework is not flexible enough, public sector employment will become unattractive, thereby limiting the public administration's ability to recruit qualified and motivated staff, which it needs more than ever.

Third, the digital transformation of government could prove to be a catalyst for these dilemmas and their negative consequences, potentially resulting in the dramatic growth of a shadow workforce of consultants and external service providers, undermining not only administrative capacity (and, thus, legitimacy and attractiveness) but also further weakening public administration's competitive position in the 'war for talents'.

Finally, the greatest paradox is the low priority given to personnel on the administrative reform agenda over the past decades and the factual relevance of personnel in general, and HRM in particular, in dealing with the growing pressure and inconsistent demands from key stakeholders. Deficiencies in organisational and institutional changes or why public administration is lagging behind in digital transformation can be explained to some extent by the low level of reform activity and the lack of attention (and appreciation) paid to people working in German public administration. The situation is exacerbated by the fact that omissions of HRM reform cannot be reversed quickly as changes take years if not decades for their effects to be felt.

Regardless of our rather sceptical account of HRM in German public administration, it is worth noting that there are some examples of excellence that are comparable to practices in other sectors, for example in the military, in some federal agencies (e.g. the Federal Employment Agency), states (e.g. the city-state of Hamburg) and local governments (e.g. the city of Munich and the district office of Berlin-Neukölln). These and other cases demonstrate the opportunities of professionally managing the public workforce despite the various restrictions and the traditional bureaucratic stance. HRM can be expected to be a major focus of reform in the years to come due to the challenges described in this chapter. Last but not least, one should not forget that Germany is often envied for its reliable, professional and effective public administration, which is essentially based on its qualified workforce.

REFERENCES

Breitsohl, H., & Ruhle, S. (2016). Millennials' Public Service Motivation and Sector Choice—A Panel Study of Job Entrants in Germany. *Public Administration Quarterly, 40*(3), 49–80.

Gross, H., Thaler, J., & Winter, V. (2019). Integrating Public Service Motivation in the Job-Demands-Resources Model: An Empirical Analysis to Explain Employees' Performance, Absenteeism, and Presenteeism. *International Public Management Journal, 22*(1), 176–206. https://doi.org/10.1080/1096749 4.2018.1541829.

Keune, M., Löbel, S., & Schuppan, T. (2018). Public Service Motivation und weiterer Motivationsfaktoren im deutschsprachigen Raum. *VM Verwaltung & Management, 24*(5), 226–239. https://doi.org/10.5771/0947-9856-2018-5-226.

Kuhlmann, S., & Röber, M. (2006). Civil Service in Germany, between cutback management and modernization. In V. Hoffmann-Martinot & H. Wollmann (Eds.), *State and Local Government Reforms in France and Germany. Divergence and Convergence* (pp. 89–110). Wiesbaden: VS Verlag.

Meier, A.-K. (2013, September 11–13). *Determining Factors of the Perception of Performance-Pay Systems.* An Analysis of a Survey in German local Administrations: Paper Presented at the EGPA Annual Conference, Edinburgh (UK).

Perry, J. L. (1996). Measuring Public Service Motivation: An Assessment of Construct Reliability and Validity. *Journal of Public Administration Research and Theory, 6*(1), 5–23.

Schimeta, J. (2012). *Einsam an der Spitze: Frauen in Führungspositionen im öffentlichen Sektor.* Berlin: Friedrich-Ebert-Stiftung.

Schmidt, W., & Müller, A. (2013). *Leistungsorientierte Bezahlung in den Kommunen: Befunde einer bundesweiten Untersuchung.* Berlin: Ed. Sigma.

Schmidt, W., Trittel, N., & Müller, A. (2011). Performance-Related Pay in German Public Services: The Example of Local Authorities in North Rhine-Westphalia. *Employee Relations, 33*(2), 140–158.

Tepe, M., & Prokop, C. (2018). Are Future Bureaucrats More Risk Averse? The Effect of Studying Public Administration and PSM on Risk Preferences. *Journal of Public Administration Research and Theory, 28*(2), 182–196.

Vogel, D. (2016). *Führung im öffentlichen Sektor.* Potsdam: Universitätsverlag.

Vogel, D., & Kroll, A. (2016). The Stability and Change of PSM-Related Values Across Time: Testing Theoretical Expectations Against Panel Data. *International Public Management Journal, 19*(1), 53–77. https://doi.org/1 0.1080/10967494.2015.1047544.

Wenzel, A.-K., Krause, T. A., & Vogel, D. (2019). Making Performance Pay Work: The Impact of Transparency, Participation, and Fairness on Controlling Perception and Intrinsic Motivation. *Review of Public Personnel Administration*, 39(2), 232–255. https://doi.org/10.1177/0734371X17715502.

Open Access This chapter is licensed under the terms of the Creative Commons Attribution 4.0 International License (http://creativecommons.org/licenses/by/4.0/), which permits use, sharing, adaptation, distribution and reproduction in any medium or format, as long as you give appropriate credit to the original author(s) and the source, provide a link to the Creative Commons licence and indicate if changes were made.

The images or other third party material in this chapter are included in the chapter's Creative Commons licence, unless indicated otherwise in a credit line to the material. If material is not included in the chapter's Creative Commons licence and your intended use is not permitted by statutory regulation or exceeds the permitted use, you will need to obtain permission directly from the copyright holder.

CHAPTER 22

Public Management Reforms in Germany: New Steering Model and Financial Management Reforms

Isabella Proeller and John Siegel

1 INTRODUCTION

German public administration has often been characterised as an ideal example of a bureaucratic *Rechtsstaat* (see Chap. 2), with its functioning described along the lines of legal programming and application of law, along with its strong orientation to professional and legal accountability and compliance. According to the global trend, also in Germany, the call for a stronger results orientation and managerial culture and control emerged in the early 1990s and resulted in corresponding management reforms. In the past thirty years, two reform models have dominated the reform debate and trajectories in Germany moving towards a more

---

I. Proeller (✉)
University of Potsdam, Potsdam, Germany
e-mail: proeller@uni-potsdam.de

J. Siegel
Hamburg University of Applied Sciences, Hamburg, Germany
e-mail: john.siegel@haw-hamburg.de

© The Author(s) 2021   393
S. Kuhlmann et al. (eds.), *Public Administration in Germany*,
Governance and Public Management,
https://doi.org/10.1007/978-3-030-53697-8_22

management-oriented mode of control and steering in public administration: the New Steering Model during the 1990s, and the New Municipal Financial Management—particularly after their enactment by legislation—as of the mid-2000s. This chapter presents the core elements and claims of both reform models and presents evidence on their implementation and impact in practice. Following a description of each reform model, evidence regarding the impacts on control behaviour and mechanisms in German public administration is discussed. The chapter concludes with lessons learned from the German public management reforms for the international public management reform debate.

2 THE NEW STEERING MODEL: THE ADVENT OF MANAGEMENT ORIENTATION IN GERMAN PUBLIC ADMINISTRATION

2.1 The Reform Model

The 'New Steering Model' (NSM) is the starting point and reference model for management-oriented reforms in Germany. It was developed and advocated by an influential association of local administrators and a think-tank, the Local Government's Joint Agency for Administrative Management, often only referred to and known by its German acronym KGSt, in the early 1990s as a reform model for local government. The NSM was the title of a seminal report published in 1993, which presented a general 'managerialist' concept for local government reform (KGSt 1993). Starting from there, the model was refined and expanded in the years that followed. Although the NSM has its background in the municipal area and is a relatively clearly outlined reform model, it eventually became a term (or label) for administrative modernisation and reforms in general, which included partial reforms and reforms at other levels of government.

In terms of content, the NSM basically represents the German variant of New Public Management (NPM). For almost a decade, the reform debate in Germany was dominated by the terminology and concepts of the NSM. Its core elements include typical NPM elements such as contract management, the decentralisation of responsibility for resources, performance measurement and customer orientation.

The most crucial difference for the international discussion lies in the justifications and motives for reform. Less than in other countries, the New Steering Model was driven as a reform to reduce an excessive public sector. Paired with a deeply rooted self-confidence about the general quality of its administrative apparatus, which has been mainly based on the criteria of legality and robustness, the NSM was legitimised as an alternative strategy to strengthen the capacities and competitiveness of local governments and their administrations *via-à-vis* the private sector. Contrary to examples in the US or the UK, where NPM reforms were positioned (or labelled) as a neoliberal reform agenda, the NSM was not directed towards ideas of dismantling and cutting back the state. As a consequence, the reform model of the NSM emphasised internal reforms of the administrative organisations ('modernising') over 'marketizing' or 'minimizing' (Pollitt and Bouckaert 2017) reform elements, like privatisation or contracting out.

The central reform elements to advance the internal modernisation of local public administrations included the following:

- Output orientation should be introduced by focussing the control of administration on output objectives and indicators as opposed to the traditional, bureaucratic input controls. This shift in focus was driven by the claim that local governments should become more entrepreneurial, particularly as regards service and customer orientation.
- Decentralisation: responsibility for managing resources should be devolved to line units in order to integrate responsibilities for results and resources into the same organisational unit. The introduction of lump sum budgets for product groups (relatively broad output categories) would weaken the dominant role of resource departments. At the same time, responsibility for the results of line units would be strengthened.
- Performance agreements: performance agreements or 'contracts' should be concluded as additional formal control instruments in order to include output-oriented control variables and objectives for various hierarchical levels throughout the organisation.

In the beginning, the reform focus had been on raising cost awareness and customer orientation by increasing room to manoeuvre and the autonomy of line units in exchange for greater transparency on costs and output results according to the central idea of the NPM, that is exchanging 'freedom to manage' for 'accountability for results'. In the late 1990s, reforms and debates became more extensive—or blurred—and included other aspects, such as quality management (customer surveys), human resource management concepts and instruments, and benchmarking (Reichard 2003: 353–354). As a result, the use and interpretation of the term 'NSM' also emancipated itself from the original model and 1993 report, later becoming a general umbrella term for the use and transfer of (private sector-inspired) management techniques and instruments in public administration.

2.2 Implementation and Results

The NSM has shown its greatest effects at the local government level, while the federal and *Länder* governments have been reluctant to undertake major reforms following the ideas of NSM (Reichard 2001: 551).

In the mid-2000s, about ten years after NSM swept across Germany's local level, an evaluation study on the implementation and effects of NSM on local governments was published. The quantitative results of this evaluation were based on a survey, which included cities with populations over 10,000 and counties (Kuhlmann et al. 2008). The attention that NSM brought to administrative reform sparked unprecedented reform activism in German local government during the 1990s. As the results from the evaluation study revealed, administrative reform was no longer the exclusive business of larger communities, but embraced virtually all of the communities. Since the beginning of the 1990s, 92 per cent of local governments in cities and counties with more than 10,000 inhabitants have pursued administrative reforms. However, not all of these reforms were NSM reforms and a closer look reveals the selective reform strategies of the German local governments. Even though the KGSt emphasised interdependencies among the different elements of the reform model and the importance of comprehensive reform implementation, the actual reform practices indicated a different pattern of use by local governments. NSM was mostly used as a toolbox and list of instruments rather than a holistic reform agenda. The larger 'West German' cities tended to follow the holistic approach more often than the smaller cities and those located in the former 'East German' territories. Only 16 per cent of local governments used NSM as a comprehensive reform model aiming to implement all its various elements. A large majority (66 per cent) of local governments had never aimed for a comprehensive redesign of their control mechanisms and began by simply picking out individual instruments and elements from the NSM 'toolbox' based on their perceptions of their organisation's problems (Kuhlmann and Wollmann 2019).

The results concerning the most and least adopted reform elements are displayed in Table 22.1 and are indicative of the actual reform trajectories. First, the dispersed dissemination and implementation rates of NSM elements corroborate the use of NSM as a toolbox. Focussing on the cleavage between the implementation rates of elements for the entire administration versus only partial implementation not only illustrates the selective use of individual NSM elements, but also the selective adaptation strategies in various departments and throughout the organisational parts of the administration.

Table 22.1 Implementation of NSM elements (n = 870 mayors/CEOs of counties)

NSM elements	Entirely implemented (%)	Partially implemented (%)	(Total of) entirely or partially implemented (%)
Abolishing levels of hierarchy	34.5	25.4	59.9
Decentralised management of resources	33.1	25.2	58.3
One-stop agencies	57.5	*	57.6
Customer surveys	54.7	*	54.7
New budgeting procedures	33.1	34.4	53.3
New department structures	43.6	9.3	52.9
Internal service centres	23.9	24.7	48.6
Strategic steering units	35.9	12.4	48.3
Cost and activity accounting	12.7	33.0	45.7
Reporting	22.1	20.7	42.8
Output analysis (definition of 'products')	29.0	9.9	38.9
Contracts between top management and services	24.3	*	24.3
Contracts between politics and administration	14.8	*	14.8
Quality management	13.9	*	13.9
Decentralised/operative controlling units	10.9	13.6	

*Item not available
Source: based on Kuhlmann et al. 2008, p. 854

Second, among the most widely implemented elements, two (groups of) elements appear at the top of the list. The elements in the first group show different kinds of changes in the organisational structure emerging as some of the most widely implemented measures. These include the establishment of one-stop shops designed to improve customer orientation. But more importantly, the changes also include the restructuring of line departments into larger entities to flatten hierarchies and decentralise control.

The second-most widely implemented NSM element was the introduction of a new budgeting system, in particular lump sum budgeting. However, the lump sum budgets introduced in Germany are not performance budgets as known in the UK or Switzerland, since performance data are only loosely coupled and have no systematic link to resource allocation. The evaluation study therefore concluded that its popularity as a control mechanism might have stemmed more from its potential as an expense management and savings programme (by setting expense ceilings) rather than from its incentives to improve on performance or efficiency.

Third, concerning the 'core' NSM elements, which directly targeted a new and more performance-oriented control mode, a discrepancy arises between proclaimed reform objectives and actual measures implemented. Most obviously, the idea of contract management, for example control via performance agreements, never gained much ground in practice. Contract management between politics and administration was hardly ever implemented, while performance agreements between top management and departments were used in one out of four municipalities after all.

In sum, the actual implementation patterns displayed a clear preference for customer-oriented and structural reform elements at the expense of results-oriented approaches.

Some *Länder* launched reform projects along the lines of NSM, but these were often eclectic and limited in terms of the selection and scope of instruments. The 'NSI' reforms (New Steering Instruments), which started in Baden-Württemberg in 1999, aimed at improving the efficiency and effectiveness of the administration and results orientation in planning and control. The NSI reforms focussed on a technically widely automated budget management system, but also including decentralised budget responsibility, cost and performance accounting, and greater emphasis on executive training (see Chap. 21). The project gained unwanted publicity after a report was released by the audit court concluding that the project had shown little effects thus far, but had incurred €220 million in project costs plus annual running costs, while producing only minimal efficiency gains. Another *Land* which started an ambitious reform project was the city-state of Berlin (the other two city-states, Bremen and Hamburg, also undertook NSM reforms). In Berlin, the reform had previously been enacted by an administrative reform framework law passed in 1999. The Berlin reform foresaw the introduction of decentralised budgeting, performance contracts, cost accounting, quality management, and personnel and leadership development. The reform eventually led to the introduction of a (comparative) cost accounting system, the introduction of performance agreements and decentralised budgeting for the twelve district offices (but not the Senate administration). In sum, the effects of the NSM at the *Länder* level have been significantly weaker than at the local level.

As a noteworthy example of policy-field related reforms at the *Länder* level, the use of performance-oriented control instruments in the control of universities should be mentioned. In the federal distribution of competencies, universities fall within the jurisdiction and responsibility of the *Länder*. Roughly 90 per cent of public universities in Germany have performance agreements in place with the state ministry. They receive their funding from the state based on a performance-oriented allocation mechanism, and they also apply similar mechanisms internally to allocate resources across the various departments (Heinze et al. 2011: 132). The employment schemes for most professors also foresee that part of their salary consists of a performance component. However, such elements have not altered the dominant governance culture to become more results-oriented or managerial. Therefore, many of the objectives and performance indicators used (e.g. third-party funding, numbers of exams or students, development of junior research staff; Heinze et al. 2011: 133) refer to unambitious levels of (actual) performance, are somewhat static and not systematically linked to strategic priorities. Additionally, the traditional financial and personnel control mechanisms, combined with the constitutionally enshrined autonomy of universities, faculties and academic staff with regard to the content of research and teaching, dominate and determine the control and management culture effectively.

After some delay, the NSM discourse also spilt over to the federal level. In 1997, the then conservative federal government established the 'lean state committee', which published a comprehensive list of reform proposals more or less in line with the NPM doctrine. The following social-democratic government turned the discourse to the concept of the 'activating state', emphasising the enabling and regulating role of government (Jann 2003). However, it was only in exceptional cases that all these reform proposals translated into concrete reform measures, such as the introduction of performance-related pay (see Chap. 21) and shared service centres. Apart from this, the federal government started several new initiatives to downsize administrative entities and privatise various publicly owned corporations. The most recent study on reform trajectories at the federal level confirmed the conception of the German federal government as being a highly legalistic administrative system, and showed that management-oriented tools are less frequently used than in most other European countries (Hammerschmid and Oprisor 2016: 69).

However, there are also a number of notable exceptions to this rule. The Federal Employment Agency (FEA) has come to epitomise performance-oriented control in Germany and has been undergoing a massive overhaul and reorientation of its control mechanisms since the early 2000's. With around 100,000 employees, the FEA is the largest administrative authority of the German federal government. The FEA has introduced a comprehensive performance management system that includes an indicator-based performance agreement between the Ministry and the agency, but has spawned performance agreements throughout all hierarchical levels of the agency. The agency has oriented its control and management process around a rather strict and detailed system of performance management and controlling (reporting systems to monitor the achievement of goals), and has aligned its other management processes (such as parts of the financial allocations, team performance and management appraisals and the definition of task priorities) with this as well (Vogel et al. 2014). The largest federal authority has, therefore, also undergone a massive radical shift in control culture and is characterised today as a performance-oriented and management-oriented agency. Even though it is the largest federal authority, there have been few 'spillover effects' of the FEA and, in general, the FEA's management and control culture contrasts sharply to that of the federal government.

2.3   Impacts

Regarding the overall effects on local governments, increased customer and service orientation and cost awareness of local public administrations are the visible and unambiguous results of the NSM debate. With regard to cost and efficiency improvements, results also point to the positive impact of NSM reforms. However, the extent of this impact is contested as the cost-benefit ratio of NSM reforms and the causality of NSM versus a traditional savings policy on savings remains ambiguous. The question of whether NSM has achieved a change in the culture and control mode within public administration, thus contributing to improved political-democratic accountability or strategic management capacities, is by no means uncontentious.

The overall assessment of the NSM has sparked polarised debate in Germany. On the one hand, critics have interpreted the results in relation to the self-proclaimed goals (of the NSM model and, e.g., how they were stated by the KGSt) and have come to a rather sobering conclusion. They argue that the NSM model has a conceptual flaw, namely the division of roles between politics and administration, and the corresponding contract management that becomes conceptually problematic and practically inappropriate. Furthermore, this school of thought claims that the NSM has also failed to deliver—presumably intended—the promised efficiency gains and savings. A paradigm shift from the traditional bureaucratic model to a New Public Management, however, has not taken place.

On the other hand, the proponents of the NSM argue that reforms in local government are a necessary part of an (ongoing) process of change and learning. The fact that the local management, leadership and control practices have changed during the past twenty years, and that NSM has provided a crucial impetus and conceptual framework for this transformation is not questioned, not even by critics. Its proponents also argue that any assessment of the effects must take the specific goals, strategies and context of NSM-style reform in the adopting organisations into account, with the concept being voluntary, a suggestion and an integrated toolbox. The approaches to reform have varied significantly across local governments, as have the available resources, problem perceptions and support. Therefore, heterogeneity—and more importantly—'deviation' from the model is neither surprising nor problematic, but should be expected and considered legitimate.

3   Financial Management Reforms

A second phase of administrative reforms emerged around 2003 with amendments to the regulatory framework for local financial management. A major difference between the financial management reforms and the

NSM reforms was that the former reforms were now prescribed by law and therefore no longer voluntary.

3.1 New Municipal Financial Management

The reforms in public budgeting and accounting systems for local governments are referred to as 'new municipal financial management' (NMFM). Their start ran in parallel with the NSM debates and the initial pilot projects began in 1994. In 2003, the conference held by the ministers of the interior of all the *Länder* was unanimous in its support of the decision to adapt the framework legislation for local government budgeting and financial accounting, and to push and allow for fundamental changes in the system. The first two core principles were a shift in the accounting method from cash-based to accrual-based accounting using double-entry bookkeeping and a change in the structure of the budget to output-oriented categories. Programmatically, this type of budget is referred to as a 'product budget'. The concept has given broad discretion to the *Länder* governments in deciding how they handle conceptual and implementation details. Consequently, there is no homogenous model or standard but—de facto—sixteen more or less different *Länder* models. Despite this heterogeneity, some common core features of the new municipal financial management reforms in the various *Länder* can be synthesised as follows:

- The budget consists of two components: a cash-based finance plan and an accrual-based results plan. The financial reporting includes three documents: a balance sheet to account for the change in equity during a fiscal year, the financial report and the results reporting.
- The budget includes a three- to five-year medium-term plan, which is mainly informational in character and serves as a financial forecast instead of a strategic planning tool.
- The results and financial plans are structured into subdivisions along the lines of product areas, product groups and products as the most detailed level.
- The budget is conceptualised as a lump sum budget on the level of product groups.
- The budget is performance-oriented in that it provides performance information regarding the product groups.

With these characteristics, the NMFM is mostly in line with international standards and trends.

3.2 Implementation and Results

Since the seminal decision in 2003, the governments of the thirteen territorial *Länder* have legislated on the introduction of accrual accounting and performance budgeting for local government. While nine *Länder* have prescribed by law a shift to accrual accounting, four *Länder* have given local governments the opportunity to choose whether they want to change to accruals or keep a (modified) cash-based system. However, it would not be German federalism if the various *Länder* had not each opted for different modes of implementation and different standards for accrual accounting. An overview of the status, standard and time frame of the implementation of accrual accounting in German local governments is shown in Table 22.2.

In 2017, around 7000 local governments, corresponding to about 60 per cent of all local governments, changed to accrual accounting and have at least prepared their first opening balance sheet. The different accrual reform options are not restricted to a change in accounting method, but also comprise performance budgets in the form of 'product budgets', performance objectives and indicators (some as a recommendation, some mandatory), and lump sum budgeting.

Since 2009 and based on new legislation, the federal level and the *Länder* have also had the option to use the accrual accounting method. To date, only two out of thirteen territorial *Länder*—Hesse, and more recently North Rhine-Westphalia—have opted to shift to accrual accounting in budgeting and reporting and to performance-oriented budgeting. The remaining eleven territorial *Länder* are continuing to operate on a (modified) cash-based accounting system. Regarding the three city-states, Hamburg operates on a full accrual accounting system and Bremen on a partial accrual accounting system with accrual-based reporting, but cash-based budgeting. The city-state of Berlin uses a modified cash-based accounting system.

The federal level government still uses a cash-based accounting system. A shift to accrual accounting has never been an issue. In the late 2000s, a project for a modified accounting system was launched at the federal level, which—while remaining basically cash-based—aimed at the disclosure of assets and liabilities in a simplified balance sheet. However, the project was

404   I. PROELLER AND J. SIEGEL

Table 22.2   Implementation of accrual accounting in German *Länder* and local governments

Federal state	Reform option for local governments (LGs) (year of formal reform initiation)	Total number of LGs	LGs where accrual accounting is implemented	Reform option for the Länder administration (year of formal reform initiation)
Baden-Württemberg	Accrual (2020)	1136	197	Cash
Bavaria	Choice	2127	95	Cash
Berlin	Cash	1	0	Cash
Brandenburg	Accrual (2011)	432	432	Cash
Bremen	Accrual (2010)	2	2	Accrual (2010)
Hamburg	Accrual (2006)	1	1	Accrual (2006)
Hesse	Accrual (2015)	447	447	Accrual (2009)
Lower Saxony	Accrual (2012)	1031	1031	Cash
Mecklenburg Western Pomerania	Accrual (2012)	763	763	Cash
North Rhine-Westphalia	Accrual (2009)	427	427	Accrual (2018)
Rhineland Palatinate	Accrual (2009)	2239	2239	Cash
Saarland	Accrual (2010)	58	58	Cash
Saxony	Accrual (2013)	441	441	Cash
Saxony-Anhalt	Accrual (2013)	233	233	Cash
Schleswig Holstein	Choice (2007)	1121	502	Cash
Thuringia	Choice (2007)	866	42	Cash
Total (2017)		*11,325*	*6911*	

Source: Hilgers et al. (2018: 14)

eventually turned down by the budget committee of the federal parliament, ending the debate over accounting reforms at the federal level (Reichard and Küchler-Stahn 2019: 103). To date, the German federal government has exhibited a reluctance to change to accruals. However, some innovations (top-down budgeting framework decisions, text explications about results, realignment of the structure of the budget and the introduction of spending reviews; Reichard and Küchler-Stahn 2019: 103) have been introduced to the federal budgeting process. This approach

22 PUBLIC MANAGEMENT REFORMS IN GERMANY: NEW STEERING MODEL... 405

differs from the product budgets and the performance information per product group as used by the *Länder* and local governments. However, it can euphemistically be seen as a modest move towards a more results-oriented federal budget.

3.3 Impacts

The NMFM reforms have been one of the core reform projects over the past twenty years. The mandatory NMFM reforms have combined and underpinned two reform ambitions. First, the accounting concept should be changed to accruals in order to provide more realistic and transparent financial information based on resource consumption and not only on expenditures. Second, output-oriented control of public administration should be strengthened by product budgets with performance objectives and indicators. The debate on accounting reforms and the shift from cash-based to accrual accounting started in parallel with the NSM debate in the 1990s. It was also strongly led by the KGSt, but was not initially part of the NSM agenda. The link between the NMFM and the NSM debates only arose out of the seminal 2003 framework decision of the conference held by the ministers of the interior of the *Länder*, according to which core elements of the NSM model (product budgets, performance management) were made an integral part of the NMFM reforms.

As expected, formal adoption of the new accounting method was completed within the set time frames, at least in the *Länder* where this transition was mandatory. The impact of the reforms on management and control behaviour is less visible. A recent survey study, which included the local governments of the three *Länder*, Lower Saxony, North Rhine-Westphalia and Saxony-Anhalt (Weiss and Schubert 2020), found that slightly more than half of the surveyed local governments perceive the reforms as allowing for a more realistic overview of the financial situation and consider the reforms useful. The conviction that accrual accounting provides more realistic information about the financial situation is no longer contested. Nevertheless, the cost-benefit relation of the reforms has attracted criticism and the general relevance of cost and equity-related financial information for decision-making (as opposed to its informational appeal) is still controversial in the German debate (Bogumil 2017: 25).

Regarding the use of performance information and more results-oriented management, several studies substantiate the claim that control, or deliberation over performance objectives and indicators is still of negligible relevance in the budgeting decision and control mechanisms. Performance indicators in German product budgets usually only refer to quantitative (often not transparently) selected aspects of single products within a product group. They are therefore by no means comprehensive or designed to satisfy an organisational control ambition and are purely informational in character. Accordingly, empirical studies conclude that performance information has only been partially provided and then hardly used for control and decision-making—either within the administration or for political decision-making (Weiss and Schubert 2020: 16–18; Bogumil 2017: 25–27; Burth and Hilgers 2014; Kroll and Proeller 2012). According to Weiß and Schubert (2020: 17), only 5 per cent of local governments reported the use of performance information for the management of expenses and services at the operational level, and even less for political decision-making (3 per cent). In a different study, it was found that more than 60 per cent of members of local councils claimed that they had not perceived any changes in the budgeting process except for the accounting method (Bogumil 2017: 25).

Exploring to what extent the reform ambition of strengthening the strategic orientation of political and administrative control has been accomplished, Weiss (2017) concludes that no more than fifteen to 20 per cent of local governments make use of a minimum of medium-term, objective-oriented information and analysis in their product budgets that would eventually allow them to follow a strategic management approach. Similar results were found for the 'strategicness' of political and administrative control, with 19.6 per cent of local governments reporting to make use of strategic objectives and only 7.1 per cent of local governments using these for political control (Weiss and Schubert 2020: 17). In general, results show that although some cities have defined strategic objectives setting out priorities and guidelines, there are no mechanisms in place linking these strategic objectives to resource allocation at the product (group) level. Needless to say, while strategic objectives may exist, their impact as well as their inclusion in further control mechanisms, and particularly in resource allocation, is not (yet) readily apparent. In this vein, it is also important to note that an outcome orientation in the sense of using and including outcomes as a core variable or dimension in integrated planning—such as the integrated task and financial planning in Switzerland, and now also in Austria—has never been an element of debate in Germany. However, there are also some noteworthy exceptions to this rule where local governments have initiated a deliberate process of establishing strategic processes (e.g. the city of Potsdam, the county of Potsdam-Mittelmark and the city of Mannheim; Proeller 2015) with which to pursue a strengthening of the outcome focus as a crucial dimension for strategic control (e.g. the cities of Mannheim and Cologne).

In sum, recent financial management reforms in Germany have not had any significant effect on changing the mode or culture of political or administrative management. The product budgets used in German local governments are of a largely informational character and do not include a systemic link between performance information and the financial appropriations. This also applies to the performance budgets found at the *Länder* level. Further, the logic of financial control is still focussed on expenditures and appropriations (as opposed to results or lump sums).

4   Lessons Learned

Over the past decades, German public administration has been exposed to a number of large-scale management reforms. Conceptually, the reform models have been ambitious and in line with the international trends of those years in terms of strengthening the focus of public administration on results, strategy and management orientation. Empirically, however, reform practices have focussed rather more on the technical and structural aspects of the reform models, such as the customer orientation and cost awareness elements of the NSM and the technical accounting methods of the NMFM reforms.

As a result, the reforms of the thirty years since German reunification have not altered the basic bureaucratic and legalistic characteristics of German public administration. Control and accountability mechanisms in Germany are still primarily based on inputs and due process, and there has been no substantial increase in the capacities for strategic management. We should note, however, that it is questionable to what extent a stronger results orientation and strategic alignment would actually match the problem perception of political and administrative actors in the German public sector. For one thing, an unambiguous conclusion of the reform is that its elements aimed at redefining the role and control mechanisms for the political level have had no discernible effect. Instead, there continues to be a rather self-confident stance towards the functioning and control mechanisms of the bureaucratic system in Germany. Less emphasis has been given to the development of effective mechanisms for medium-term planning, strategic management and alignment or accountability for results compared to other countries.

The German pattern of accommodating management-oriented reforms into the prevailing legalistic administrative structure and culture has been referred to as 'neo-Weberian' (Pollitt and Bouckaert 2017), even though 'neo-bureaucratic' would be the more appropriate term. It is used to refer to the modest application of selected NPM ideas without giving up the traditional public administration model. In the German case, this can be seen in the form of an opening up to external demands through improved quality and service orientation, the introduction and expansion of participatory decision-making processes, and the provision of performance information as an add-on in financial control procedures (Kuhlmann and Bogumil 2019).

German public management reform trajectories show an enormous degree of heterogeneity. Germany's federalist structure grants considerable autonomy to *Länder* as well as to local governments. Moreover—and also related to the centrifugal forces created by federalism—coherence in the transformation process has never been a goal and cannot therefore lead to overarching reform visions or coordinated strategies. As a consequence, management reforms in Germany have been used to accommodating local preferences and priorities. By the same token, this grassroots approach to reform has come at the expense of comparability, coherence and compatibility—which is an increasing challenge to the digital transformation of government (e.g. see Chap. 19).

References

Bogumil, J. (2017). 20 Jahre Neues Steuerungsmodell-Eine Bilanz. In C. Brüning & U. Schliesky (Eds.), *Kommunale Verwaltungsreform: 20 Jahre Neues Steuerungsmodell* (1st ed., pp. 13–30). Baden-Baden: Nomos.

Burth, A., & Hilgers, D. (2014). Cui Bono? Depicting the Benefits of the New Municipal Budgeting and Accounting Regime in Germany. *Journal of Business Economics, 84*, 531–570. https://doi.org/10.1007/s11573-013-0698-9.

Hammerschmid, G., & Oprisor, A. (2016). German Public Administration. Incremental Reform and a Difficult Terrain for Management Ideas and Instruments. In G. Hammerschmid, S. van de Walle, R. Andrews, & P. Bezes (Eds.), *Public Administration Reforms in Europe: The View from the Top* (pp. 63–72). Cheltenham: Edward Elgar Publishing.

22 PUBLIC MANAGEMENT REFORMS IN GERMANY: NEW STEERING MODEL... 409

Heinze, R. G., Bogumil, J., & Gerber, S. (2011). Vom Selbstverwaltungsmodell zum Managementmodell? Zur Empirie neuer Governance-Strukturen im deutschen Hochschulsystem. In J. Schmid, K. Amos, J. Schrader, & A. Thiel (Eds.), *Welten der Bildung* (pp. 121–148). Baden-Baden: Nomos.

Hilgers, D., Frintrup, M., & Christian, R. (2018). *Sind die EU-Staaten fit für EPSAS?: Die European Public Sector Accouting Standards und die Harmonisierung des öffentlichen Rechnungswesens aus Sicht europäischer Experten.* Berlin: Institut für den öffentlichen Sektor/KPMG AG Wirtschaftsprüfungsgesellschaft.

Jann, W. (2003). State, Administration and Governance in Germany: Competing Traditions and Dominant Narratives. *Public Administration, 81,* 95–118. https://doi.org/10.1111/1467-9299.00338.

KGSt. (1993). *Das neue Steuerungsmodell: Begründung, Konturen, Umsetzung.* Köln: Kommunale Gemeinschaftsstelle für Verwaltungsvereinfachung.

Kroll, A., & Proeller, I. (2012). *Steuerung mit Kennzahlen in den kreisfreien Städten: Ergebnisse einer empirischen Studie.* Gütersloh: Bertelsmann Stiftung.

Kuhlmann, S., & Bogumil, J. (2019). Neo-Weberianischer Staat. In S. Veit, C. Reichard, & G. Wewer (Eds.), *Handbuch zur Verwaltungsreform* (pp. 139–151). Cham: Springer.

Kuhlmann, S., & Wollmann, H. (2019). *Introduction to Comparative Public Administration: Administrative Systems and Reforms in Europe* (2nd ed.). Cheltenham/Northampton: Edward Elgar.

Kuhlmann, S., Bogumil, J., & Grohs, S. (2008). Evaluating Administrative Modernization in German Local Governments: Success or Failure of the "New Steering Model"? *Public Administration Review, 68,* 851–863. https://doi.org/10.1111/j.1540-6210.2008.00927.x.

Pollitt, C., & Bouckaert, G. (2017). *Public Management Reform: A Comparative Analysis-Into the Age of Austerity.* New York, NY: Oxford University Press.

Proeller, I. (2015). Cultural Change in the German City of Mannheim. In E. Ferlie & E. Ongaro (Eds.), *Strategic Management in Public Services Organizations: Concepts, Schools and Contemporary Issues* (pp. 39–42). London: Routledge.

Reichard, C. (2001). New approaches to public management. In K. König, H. Siedentopf, & König-Siedentopf (Eds.), *Public Administration in Germany* (Vol. 1, 1st ed., pp. 541–556). Baden-Baden: Nomos Verl.-Ges.

Reichard, C. (2003). Local Public Management Reforms in Germany. *Public Administration, 81,* 345–363. https://doi.org/10.1111/1467-9299.00350.

Reichard, C., & Küchler-Stahn, N. (2019). Performance Budgeting in Germany, Austria and Switzerland. In *Performance-Based Budgeting in the Public Sector* (pp. 101–124). Heidelberg: Springer.

Vogel, D., Löbel, S., Proeller, I., & Schupan, T. (2014). Einflussfaktoren von Führungsverhalten in der öffentlichen Verwaltung. *der moderne staat, 7*(3), 459–478.

Weiss, J. (2017). Trust as a Key for Strategic Management? The Relevance of Council–Administration Relations for NPM-Related Reforms in German Local Governments. *Public Management Review, 19,* 1399–1414. https://doi.org/10.1080/14719037.2016.1266023.

Weiss, J., & Schubert, D. (2020). Doppelte Reform mit geteiltem Erfolg: Zur Wirkung der DOPPIK-Reform auf Haushaltsführung und Verwaltungssteuerung in den Kommunen. *der moderne staat, 13*(1), 1–22.

Open Access This chapter is licensed under the terms of the Creative Commons Attribution 4.0 International License (http://creativecommons.org/licenses/by/4.0/), which permits use, sharing, adaptation, distribution and reproduction in any medium or format, as long as you give appropriate credit to the original author(s) and the source, provide a link to the Creative Commons licence and indicate if changes were made.

The images or other third party material in this chapter are included in the chapter's Creative Commons licence, unless indicated otherwise in a credit line to the material. If material is not included in the chapter's Creative Commons licence and your intended use is not permitted by statutory regulation or exceeds the permitted use, you will need to obtain permission directly from the copyright holder.

GLOSSARY

The glossary is based on Introduction to Comparative Public Administration: Administrative Systems and Reforms in Europe, 2nd Edition (Kuhlmann & Wollmann 2019) with further additions by the editors and with the assistance of the Language Service of the Federal Ministry of the Interior, Building and Community.

Deutsch (German)	English
Abgabenordnung	(German) Fiscal Code
Abteilung	Directorate (-General) (*ministry*) or division (*general usage*) or department (*communal*)
Allgemeine Verwaltung	General administration
Allzuständigkeit (-svermutung)	(Presumption of) general competence
Amtsfrei/amtsangehörig	Self-governing municipality/municipality belonging to a municipal association
Angestellter	Public employee
Anstalt	Institution
Äquivalenzprinzip	Principle of equivalence
Aufgabenverteilungsprinzip	Principle of task distribution/allocation
Aufsicht	Supervision (oversight)
Bauleitplanung	(Urban) land-use planning
Beamtenstatusgesetz	Act on the Status of Civil Servants
Beamter	Civil servant
(Beamteter/parlamentarischer) Staatssekretär	State Secretary with civil servant status/ Parliamentary State Secretary
Behörde	Office/Agency

(*continued*)

© The Author(s) 2021   411
S. Kuhlmann et al. (eds.), *Public Administration in Germany*,
Governance and Public Management,
https://doi.org/10.1007/978-3-030-53697-8

412 GLOSSARY

(continued)

Deutsch (German)	English
Beschluss des Staatssekretärsausschusses (für Bürokratieabbau)	Decision of the Committee of State Secretaries (for Bureaucracy Reduction)
Beurteilungsspielraum	Margin of discretion/scope for appreciation
Bezirksregierung, Regierungspräsidium	Regional government, Regional Commissioner's Office
Bezirk/Stadtbezirk	District (of a bigger city)
Bund	Federation/federal level/federal government
(Bundes-/Landes-) Mittelbehörde	Intermediate (federal/*Land*) authority
Bundes-/Landesrechnungshof	Bundesrechnungshof (Germany's Supreme Audit Institution)/*Land* Audit Office
Bundesagentur für Arbeit (BA)	Federal Employment Agency
Bundesamt für Migration und Flüchtlinge (BAMF)	Federal Office for Migration and Refugees
Bundesamt für Soziale Sicherung	Federal Social Insurance Office
Bundesbank	*Deutsche Bundesbank* (Federal Central Bank)
Bundesgerichtshof	Federal Court of Justice
Bundeskanzleramt	Federal Chancellery
Bundesländer/Bundesland	*Länder/Land* or federal state/s
Bundesministerium für Arbeit und Soziales (BMAS)	Federal Ministry for Employment and Social Affairs
Bundesrat	Bundesrat (Federal Council)
Bundesregierung	Federal Government
Bundestag	German Bundestag (Federal Diet/federal parliament)
Bundesverfassungsgericht (BVerfG)	Federal Constitutional Court
Bundesverwaltungsamt	Federal Office of Administration
Bundeszwang (Art. 37 GG)	Federal enforcement
Bürgeramt	*Bürgeramt* (municipal office rendering administrative services for the public)
Bürgerbegehren	Citizens' initiative
Bürgerentscheid	Referendum/plebiscite
BVerfGE	Decisions of the Federal Constitutional Court (published in volumes)
CDU/CSU	Christian Democratic Union (of Germany)/ Christian Social Union (in Bavaria)
Demokratieprinzip	Principle of democracy
Deutscher Landkreistag	Association of German Counties
Deutscher Städtetag	Association of German Cities
Dezernent	Head of department (municipality)
Dienstaufsicht	Administrative supervision
Doppik	Accrual accounting/double-entry book-keeping
Echte Kommunalisierung/ politische Dezentralisierung	Genuine municipalisation/political decentralisation

(*continued*)

GLOSSARY **413**

(continued)

Deutsch (German)	English
E-GovG	E-Government Act
Eigenbetrieb	Owner-operated municipal enterprise
Einfacher Dienst/	Ordinary service/basic civil service
Einheitsgemeinde	Unitary municipality
Einrichtungen	Institutions
Ermessen	Discretion
Fachaufsicht	Expert supervision (in contrast to *Rechtsaufsicht*—legal supervision)
Fachplanung	Sectoral planning
Federführendes Ministerium (Referat etc.)	Lead ministry (division etc.)
Finanzausgleich	Fiscal equalisation (scheme)
Finanzautonomie	Financial autonomy
Flächennutzungsplan	Land-use plan
Flächenstaat	Territorial state (in contrast to city state)
Funktionale Politisierung	Functional politicisation
Funktionalreform, Gebietsreform, Strukturreform	Reform of administrative functions, territorial reform/local government reorganisation, structural reform
Gebietsgrenze	Territorial boundary
Gebietskörperschaft	Territorial community (of self-government/self-administration)
Gehobener Dienst	Higher intermediate service
Gemeinde	Municipality
(Gemeinde-/Kreis) Gebietszusammenschluss/-fusion	(Municipality–district) merger/amalgamation
Gemeindeverband (z.B. Kreis)	Association of municipalities (e.g. a county)
Gemeinsame Geschäftsordnung der Bundesministerien (GGO)	Joint Rules of Procedure of the Federal Ministries
Geschäftsordnung der Bundesregierung (GOBReg)	Rules of Procedure of the Federal Government
Grundgesetz	Basic Law (federal constitution)
(Grundsatz der) Eigenverantwortlichkeit/ Selbstverwaltung	(Principle of) own responsibility/self-government
Hauptverwaltungsbeamter/ Landrat	Chief executive officer/district commissioner
Haushaltsgrundsätzgesetz – HGrG	Budgetary Principles Act
Hessische Gemeindeordnung (HGO)	Local government law of Hesse
Höherer Kommunalverband	Higher municipal association
Höherer Dienst	Higher service
Informationsfreiheitsgesetz (IFG)	Freedom of Information Act
IT Planungsrat	IT Planning Council

(*continued*)

414 GLOSSARY

(continued)

Deutsch (German)	English
juristische Person des öffentlichen Rechts	Legal person under public law/ public entity
Kabinettsprinzip	Principle of joint Cabinet decision-making
Kameralistik	Cash-based accounting
Kanzlerprinzip	Principle of Chancellor policy guidelines
Kommunaler Betrieb	Municipal undertaking
Kommunale Gemeinschaftsstelle für Verwaltungsmanagement (KGSt)	Municipal Association for Administration Management
Kommunale Selbstverwaltung	Local self-government
Kommunalverfassung	Local government constitution
Kommunalverfassungsrecht	Local government constitutional law
Kommunalverwaltung	Local government
Kommune / Gemeinde	Municipality
Konnexitätsprinzip	Principle of concomitant financing (one meaning: obligation of a state level to provide financial compensation when transferring tasks to another level).
Körperschaft	Corporate body, corporation
Kreisangehörige Stadt	County municipality (in the two-tier system) (*kreisangehörige Stadt*)
Kreisausschuss	County committee
Kreise	County
Kreisfreie Stadt	Town constituting a county in its own right
Kreisgebiet	County area/area of the county
Kreispräsident	President of the county council
Landesbetrieb	State/*Land* undertaking
Landesoberbehörde	higher *Land* authority/higher federal state authority
Landesverwaltungsamt	*Land* Administration Office/Federal State Administration Office (*Landesverwaltungsamt*: assumes coordinating and bundling functions for the whole territory of the *Land*)
Landkreis	Rural county
Landrat	County commissioner
Landratsamt	County commissioner's office
Leistungskatalog der öffentlichen Verwaltung (LeiKa)	Public administration service catalogue
Landesorganisationsgesetz (LOG)	State Organisation Act
Mittlerer Dienst	Intermediate service
Nationaler Normenkontrollrat (NKR)	National Regulatory Control Council
Neues Steuerungsmodell (NSM)	New Steering Model (German version of New Public Management)
Oberbürgermeister	Mayor

(*continued*)

GLOSSARY 415

(continued)

Deutsch (German)	English
Obere (Bundes-/Landes) Behörde	Higher federal authority; higher *Land*/state authority
Öffentlicher Dienst	Public service
Online-Zugangsgesetz (OZG)	Online Access Act
Ortsamt	Urban district office
Organisationserlass (des Bundeskanzlers, Art. 65 GG)	Federal Chancellor's organizational decree
Örtlich/ überörtlich	Local/regional
Parlamentarischer Rat (1948/49)	Parliamentary Council (West German constituent assembly in Bonn, 1948–1949)
Politikverflechtung	Policy integration (interwovenness between levels in a federal system)
Politischer Beamter	Political civil servant
Raumordnung/Raumplanung	Regional/ spatial planning; physical planning
Rechtsaufsicht	Legal supervision
Referat	Division or section
Regierungsbezirk	Administrative district (Government region)
Reichsverfassung 1871	Constitution of the German Empire 1871
Ressortprinzip	Principle of ministerial autonomy
Samtgemeinde	Collective municipality (*Samtgemeinde*)
Sonderverwaltung	Special administration
Sozialdemokratische Partei Deutschlands (SPD)	Social Democratic Party (of Germany) (SPD)
Spiegelreferat	Shadowing division ('mirror'; e.g.: a financial division shadowing a particular department and supervising its budget)
Staatskanzlei	State Chancellery
Städte- und Gemeindebund	German Association of Towns and Municipalities
Stadtkreis	Urban district
Stadtstaat	City-state
Steuer-/Fiskalautonomie	Fiscal/tax autonomy
Stiftung	Foundation
Subsidiaritätsprinzip	Principle of subsidiarity
Territorialreform (Gebietsvergrößerung)	Territorial reform/enlargement
Träger der Sozialversicherung	Social insurance agencies
Treuhandanstalt (THA)	*Treuhandanstalt* (agency responsible for privatising formerly state-owned industry in the GDR); 'Trust Agency'
Unterabteilung	Directorate or sub-division
Untere (Bundes-/Landes-) Behörde	Lower federal/*Land* authority
Verbandsgemeinde	Associated municipalities ('double-decker' municipality)
Verhältniswahl	Proportional representation/voting

(*continued*)

416 GLOSSARY

(continued)

Deutsch (German)	English
Vermittlungsausschuss	Mediation Committee (joint committee of Bundestag and Bundesrat to solve conflicts at the final stage of the process of law making in the Federation)
Vertikale Gewaltenteilung	Vertical separation of powers
Vertretungskörperschaft	Representative body
Verwaltungsgemeinschaft	Administrative partnership
Verwaltungsgericht	Administrative court
Verwaltungsgerichtsordnung (VwGO)	Code of Administrative Court Procedure
Verwaltungsstrukturreform	(Administrative) structural reform
Verwaltungsverfahren	Administrative procedure
Verwaltungsverfahrensgesetz (VwVfG)	Administrative Procedures Act
Volkskammer	*Volkskammer* (People's Chamber—GDR)
Wahlbeamter	Elected representative (high-ranking local authority official elected for a specific term of office)
Weimarer Republik (1918-1933)	Weimar Republic
zwei-/dreistufiges System; einstufiges System	Two-tier system, three-tier system; unitary system

Printed in the United States
By Bookmasters